RELIGION MATTERS

WHAT SOCIOLOGY TEACHES US ABOUT RELIGION IN OUR WORLD

Michael O. Emerson
Rice University

William A. Mirola
Marian University

Susanne C. Monahan
Montana State University

Allyn & Bacon

Boston   Columbus   Indianapolis   New York   San Francisco   Upper Saddle River
Amsterdam   Cape Town   Dubai   London   Madrid   Milan   Munich   Paris   Montreal   Toronto
Delhi   Mexico City   Sao Paulo   Sydney   Hong Kong   Seoul   Singapore   Taipei   Tokyo

Publisher: Karen Hanson
Editorial Assistant: Alyssa Levy
Executive Marketing Manager: Kelly M. May
Marketing Assistant: Gina Lavagna
Associate Project Manager: Maggie Brobeck
Production Manager: Fran Russello
Design Director: Jayne Conte
Cover Designer: Suzanne Behnke
Cover image credits: Getty Images, Inc./Peter Arnold, Inc.
Editorial Production and Composition Service: Niraj Bhatt/Aptara®, Inc.
Printer/Binder: RR Donnelley and Sons, Inc.

Library of Congress Cataloging-in-Publication Data

Emerson, Michael O.
  Religion matters: what sociology teaches us about religion in our world/Michael O. Emerson,
William A. Mirola, Susanne C. Monahan.
    p. cm.
  Includes bibliographical references.
  ISBN-13: 978-0-205-62800-1
  ISBN-10: 0-205-62800-1
1. Religion and sociology—Textbooks.
I. Mirola, William A. (William Andrew)   II. Monahan, Susanne C.   III. Title.
  BL60.E48 2011
  306.6—dc22

                                                                  2009053892

10 9 8 7 6 5 4 3 2 1—CRS—14 13 12 11 10

Allyn & Bacon
is an imprint of

www.pearsonhighered.com

ISBN-13: 978-0-205-62800-1
ISBN-10:   0-205-62800-1

BRIEF CONTENTS

Acknowledgments   ix

Table of Illustrations   x

Preface   xii

SECTION I   Getting Acquainted   1

Chapter 1   Why Religion?   1

Chapter 2   "You Believe What?"   16

Chapter 3   Downloading God, "Big Box" Churches, and the Crystal Shop around the Corner   36

SECTION II   The Shape of Religion   54

Chapter 4   Can't We All Just Get Along?   54

Chapter 5   News Flash: God's Not Dead (and Neither is the Goddess!)   67

Chapter 6   Our God Rules (Yours Doesn't)   83

SECTION III   Religion, Conflict, and the State   99

Chapter 7   Divine Rights and Casting Down the Mighty from their Thrones   99

Chapter 8   Give Us Our Due   116

SECTION IV   Religion, Identity, and Social Inequalities   134

Chapter 9   Adam, Eve, and Steve   134

Chapter 10   The (Not So Great) Color Wall of the United States   159

Chapter 11   Who Brought the Enchiladas to My Bar Mitzvah?   172

SECTION V   More Big Questions   188

Chapter 12   Godless Science, Irrational Religion?   188

Chapter 13   End of Days? Religion and the Environment   207

Chapter 14   Do We Need God to Do Good?   226

Bibliography   238

Index   252

CONTENTS

Acknowledgments ix

Table of Illustrations x

Preface xii

SECTION I Getting Acquainted 1

Chapter 1 Why Religion? 1

What is Religion Anyway? 4

Religion Provides Comfort and Quells Dissatisfaction 5

Religion Strengthens Human Community 6

Religion Assures Us of Cosmic Order 8

A Sociological Consensus: Religion is a Human Product 10

The Promise of Sociology 12

Chapter 2 "You Believe What?" 16

Comparing Religious Beliefs and Practices 17

Christianity 18

Catholicism 19

Mainline Protestantism 20

Black Protestants 22

Evangelical Protestants 23

Other Christian Denominations 24

Islam 26

Hinduism 27

Buddhism 28

Judaism 29

Understanding Contemporary Religious Ritual Practices 30

Worship Styles to Meet Every Need 31

The Role of Beliefs and Ritual Practices 35

Chapter 3 Downloading God, "Big Box" Churches, and the Crystal Shop around the Corner 36

Changing Technology, Changing Religion 38

Virtual Spiritual Community, Identity, and Authority 41

Online Faith Community   41

Virtual Religious Identity   42

Religious Authority Online   43

What's in a Megachurch?   45

Can You Have Community in a Megachurch?   47

Other New Forms and Contexts for Religious
Community   49

Concluding Thoughts   52

SECTION II The Shape of Religion   54

Chapter 4 Can't We All Just Get Along?   54

Getting Personal   57

Religion and Social Cohesion   58

Religion and Social Conflict   62

Can't We All Just Get Along?   66

**Chapter 5 News Flash: God's Not Dead
(and Neither is the Goddess!)   67**

Will the Real Secularization Theory Please Stand Up?   69

Religious Vitality in the United States and Abroad   74

Vitality as a Product of Religious Market Forces   76

Secular Yet Religiously Vital?   78

Chapter 6 Our God Rules (Yours Doesn't)   83

What is Religious Fundamentalism?   85

Modernity   86

Defining Fundamentalism   87

The "First" Fundamentalism   88

Fundamentalism Rising   89

Characteristics of Religious Fundamentalism   90

Fundamentalism and Other Aspects of
Social Life   90

Are Fundamentalist Movements Violent?   92

Holes in Conceptualizing and Understanding
Fundamentalism   94

Measuring Fundamentalism   94

Should We Study Fundamentalism or Modern Secularism?   95

European Exceptionalism?   95

Is There Such a Thing as Fundamentalism?   96

Where Do We Go From Here?   97

SECTION III Religion, Conflict, and the State   99

Chapter 7   Divine Rights and Casting Down the Mighty from their Thrones   99

Classic Observations about Religion and Social Change   101

The Lessons from Studying Social Movements   105

The Emergence of Religious Activism   105

When Activists Get Religion   110

Any Limits of Religion's Influence on Change?   112

Concluding Thoughts   114

Chapter 8   Give Us Our Due   116

Religion and Politics in the United States   117

Why Politics?   119

"Princes, Governors, and Oppressors": Varieties of Relations Between Religion and Government   121

Religion as a Tool of the State: "You Visit Them"   122

Theocracy: "They Visit You"   123

Separate Spheres: Implications of Separation of Church and State   127

The U.S. Interpretation of Religious Freedom   127

The Disestablishment Clause and the Institutional Autonomy of Religion   128

Free Exercise and the Privilege of the Majority's Religion   130

Separation of Church and State: Freedom from Religion?   131

SECTION IV Religion, Identity, and Social Inequalities   134

Chapter 9   Adam, Eve, and Steve   134

But Isn't a Woman's Place in . . . Religion?   137

Changing Gender Roles, Changing Relationships to Religion   141

Does Religion Change When Women are in Charge?   146

Sex, Sex, Sex . . . Why Does It Always Come Back to Sex?   147

"The Homosexual Agenda!"   147

Negotiating LGBT Identities within Religious Institutions   155

Challenging and Transforming Religious Ideas about Gender and Sexuality   157

Chapter 10   The (Not So Great) Color Wall of the United States   159

How Segregated are Religious Congregations?   160

So What If Religious Congregations are Segregated?   161

Can We Find a Solution?   165
Social Ties   165
Attitudes   167
Raised Status   168
Bridge Organizations and Sixth Americans   169
But Can We Create and Maintain Multiracial
Congregations?   170

**Chapter 11   Who Brought the Enchiladas to
My Bar Mitzvah?   172**
Overarching Changes for Religion   173
Religious Changes for Immigrants   174
The Story of Karen Chai Kim   174
Lessons about Immigration and Religious Change   178
Let's Conclude   186

SECTION V   More Big Questions   188

Chapter 12   Godless Science, Irrational Religion?   188
Flashpoint: The Current Debate over Evolution   190
Religious and Scientific Creation Stories   192
Religion and Evolution: What's the Big Deal?   195
Religion's Discontent with Scientific Inquiry   195
Religion's Discontent with Darwinian Evolution   197
Religion and Science, Mythos and Logos   198
Nonoverlapping Magisteria   200
Science, Technology, and Religion   200
Religious Understanding of Reproductive Technologies   201
Godless Science? Irrational Religion?   205

Chapter 13   End of Days? Religion and the Environment   207
Environmentalism and Its Discontents   208
Religious Discontents   209
Religion Finds Environmentalism . . .   209
. . . But Environmentalism is Leery of Religion   210
Do Fundamentalist Christians Care about the Environment?   212
A Worldview of "Mastery of Nature"   212
The First Wave: Acceptance and Critique of White's Argument   213
The Second Wave: Testing "The Lynn White Hypothesis"   215
Revisting White: What was His Point?   217
Other Religious Approaches to Humans in the Natural World   218

Romanticized Religion: Indigenous Religion and Clashes
with Environmentalists   222

Is Religion the Answer?   225

Chapter 14   Do We Need God to Do Good?   226

Do We Need God to Do Good?   227

Morality and Regulation   227

Morality and Community   228

What's Religion Got?   229

Does Religion Ensure That We Do Good?   231

A Note on Violence and Moral Communities   234

Moral Relativism?!   235

Concluding Thoughts   236

Bibliography   238
Index   252

ACKNOWLEDGMENTS

Religion has always played important but complicated roles in our own lives as well as in society more broadly. We wrote this book because we believe that sociology is an insightful, but underutilized, perspective for understanding religion and its powerful effects. We hope you find this book both useful and thought provoking. Indeed, if we have answered all your questions about religion and society rather than leaving you wondering about more, we will be a bit disappointed!

We are grateful to many researchers—those who came before us as well as those who are working in this field today—for their contributions to our knowledge. We thank our editors, especially for Jeff Lasser, who reached out to us about the prospect of writing this book, for being so supportive of our vision of a text that focused on religion's interplay with broader society. Ted Knight, Brian Baker, Heather Sisan, Niraj Bhatt, and Linda Clark did amazing (and efficient) work to make this volume publishable. We also thank the many others at Allyn and Bacon who worked to see this volume come to press.

We are also grateful to our departments and our institutions, Rice University, Marian College, and Montana State University, for their support of this work. A number of individuals also deserve recognition for their assistance and feedback at various stages of this project. In particular, we would like to thank Bill MacDonald, Adele Pittendrigh, Kevin O'Neill, Renee Sallese, and Meredith Gardner for reading and commenting on various chapters. Linda Woodhead and Lori Beaman were helpful in finding material and offering insights for the religion, gender, and sexuality chapters. Undergraduate students in Montana State University's "Sociology of Religion" and "Science and Religion" classes also read and commented on selected chapters.

Finally, we would like to thank you, the reader. We welcome your feedback and wish you the best on your learning adventure.

Michael O. Emerson
Rice University

William A. Mirola
Marian University

Susanne C. Monahan
Montana State University

TABLE OF ILLUSTRATIONS

BOX 1.1   Some Definitions of Religion   9

FIGURE 2.1   A Denominational Tree for Some of the World's Major Christian Denominations   18

TABLE 3.1   Typical Religious Organizations' Purposes in Using the Internet (Horsfall 2000)   39

TABLE 3.2   Denominational Affiliation of Megachurches in the United States   45

TABLE 3.3   Percent of Megachurches by Congregational Characteristics   47

TABLE 3.4   Percent of Megachurches Reporting Activities to Attract and Keep Members   48

TABLE 3.5   Percentage of Americans Who Held Alternative Spiritual Beliefs, 1990 and 2001   51

BOX 4.1   Disagreements Over Religion or Spirituality   57

BOX 4.2   Religious Conflicts   62

TABLE 5.1   The Largest Christian Communities, 2025 and 2050   75

BOX 6.1   Your Definition of Fundamentalism   85

TABLE 6.1   Nine Characteristics of Fundamentalist Groups   91

BOX 7.1   Theodicy   103

TABLE 7.1   Religious Resources That Are Available for Social Movements (Smith 1996a)   106

TABLE 7.2   Factors Influencing Religion to Become a Force in Social Change Movements   109

BOX 9.1   Now, in Case You have Forgotten   136

TABLE 9.1   Gender Distribution within Major Religious Traditions   137

TABLE 9.2   Gender differences in Importance of Religion to Life by Religious Affiliation   138

TABLE 9.3   Gender Differences in Beliefs in a Personal God by Religious Affiliation   138

TABLE 9.4   Gender Differences in Worship Service Attendance by Religious Affiliation   139

TABLE 9.5   Gender Differences in Frequency of Prayer
by Religious Affiliation   139

FIGURE 9.1   Gender and Responses to Religion and Male
Power and Privilege   143

TABLE 9.6   Differences in Attitudes about Whether Society Should
Accept or Discourage Homosexuality, by Religious
Affiliation   150

TABLE 9.7   Impact of Religious Belief and Practices on Public Opposition
to Homosexuality for Selected Groups   150

FIGURE 10.1 Racial Composition of U.S. Congregations   160

FIGURE 10.2 Percentage of Congregations that Are Racially Mixed,
by Faith Tradition   161

FIGURE 11.1 Karen Chai Kim's Family Tree   175

FIGURE 11.2 Majority and Minority Religion Status, by Location   183

FIGURE 11.3 Moral Order Map   184

BOX 12.1   Science and Scientific Inquiry   189

BOX 12.2   Intelligent Design and Science   190

BOX 12.3   What Is Empirical Evidence?   191

BOX 12.4   More on Darwinian Evolution   193

BOX 12.5   The Creation Museum on Catastrophe   199

BOX 13.1   Mastery Over Nature   212

PREFACE

THIS JUST IN: RELIGION MATTERS!

- God's a "Big Three" Fan! There they were on the front page of *The New York Times* in December 2008: three "white as white can be" gas-guzzling SUVs. But this wasn't another story about the need to switch to hybrid cars or about how the failing auto industry companies were going to go bankrupt unless Congress gave them aid. This was a story about Detroit's churches, who were taking the desperation of the Big Three car corporations to a higher power. Detroit was praying for "God's Bailout." The SUVs in the *Times* photograph were on a stage that was the altar of Greater Grace Temple, a Pentecostal congregation in Detroit. Surrounding the cars were choir members, ministers, and the congregation, all singing, dancing, and praying for divine intervention. As the newspaper article noted, Bishop Charles H. Ellis III, the congregation's pastor, finished his sermon by leading the congregation in singing Myra Summers' gospel song, "'We're Gonna Make It,' as hundreds of worshipers who work in the automotive industry—union assemblers, executives, car salesmen—gathered deep around the altar to have their foreheads anointed with consecrated oil." Their hope was to make it through the tough times and "to combat the region's woes by mixing hope with faith in God" (Bunkley 2008).

- Who could guess that a cheeseburger could cause such a ruckus? In 2006, McDonald's agreed to alter its signature logo—the golden arches—at a dozen or so kosher Mickey Ds in Israel. According to *The Guardian International,* "The restaurant chain agreed to the change under pressure from the chief rabbi of Tel Aviv, Yisrael Meir Lau, who refused to sign kosher certificates for McDonald's branches in the city and at its university. 'When I assumed my position 10 months ago and I had to sign kashrut certificates for two [McDonald's] restaurants in Tel Aviv, I refused because my conscience wouldn't let me,' he told the Israeli newspaper, *Yedioth Ahronoth.* 'I was mainly concerned that tourists or adolescents who visit one kosher branch may jump to the conclusion that all McDonald's branches in Israel are kosher.'" At these sites, the McDonald's name will appear in blue and white, the colors of the Israeli flag, with 'kosher' alongside (McGreal 2006).

- Religion drives conflict in U.S. public schools. Here's a case in point: In 2005, *Time* magazine reported that a federal court judge had ruled that public schools in Dover, Pennsylvania, could not teach intelligent design in the science classroom because "the secular purposes claimed by the [School] Board amount to a pretext for the Board's real purpose, which was to promote religion in the public school classroom." This dealt a serious legal blow to efforts by Christian conservatives to use intelligent design as a challenge to the conclusions drawn by evolutionary biology (Scully 2005).

- Religion is central to social, economic, and political tensions in Europe. For instance, in 2005, *Foreign Affairs* examined the spread of radical Islam in Europe. The source of the threat was not newly arrived immigrants from the Mideast, however. Instead, "Jihadist networks span Europe from Poland to Portugal, thanks to the spread of radical Islam among the descendants of guest workers once recruited to shore up Europe's postwar economic miracle . . . It was a Dutch Muslim of

Moroccan descent, born and socialized in Europe, who murdered the filmmaker Theo van Gogh in Amsterdam last November. A Nixon Center study of 373 mujahideen [fighters in a *jihad,* or holy war] in Western Europe and North America between 1993 and 2004 found more than twice as many Frenchmen as Saudis and more Britons than Sudanese, Yemenites, Emiratis, Lebanese, or Libyans. Fully a quarter of the jihadists it listed were western European." (Leiken 2005)

- Many Americans were appalled to learn of the Rwandan genocide that took place in 1994 as Hutu militia massacred Tutsis in that country's bloody civil war. According to an article in *The New York Times,* "Two Catholic nuns were convicted in a Belgian court last week of helping Hutu militiamen to massacre Tutsi during the 1994 killing frenzy . . . Not only did they let Hutu militiamen into their convent to hack hundreds of Tutsi women and children to death, they helped burn more than 500 people alive in a locked garage. The sisters carried the cans of gasoline and fanned the flames, witnesses said." While news reports focus on the *ethnic* aspects of the civil war, they neglected the religious dynamics involved. Reports now document that Catholic priests, nuns, and Protestant ministers were involved in atrocities. The *Times* article did note that some religious leaders tried to stop the killings. For example, "A Hutu priest, Father Celestin Hakizimana, bribed the militiamen who tried to break in. He wore his robes to intimidate the crowd. He saved more than 1,500 people." What happens in congregations of all kinds often mirrors what is going on in the communities where they are located (McKinley 2001).

RELIGION IMPLICATED

In his 2008 book *God Is Not Great,* Christopher Hitchens wrote "Religion is poison" (13). He is not alone in his disdain for religion. Others, including Sam Harris and Richard Dawkins, have made impassioned pleas for the death of religion—the end to the madness, as some say.

Nonetheless, we note that religion remains a strong force in the United States and worldwide. Political power is—to varying degrees, in different places—distributed along religious lines, and religious groups struggle to influence and control states. Religion provides comfort, meaning, and a sense of transcendent order to people around the world, as it has for the better part of human history. Religious practice and doctrine is embedded in the daily lives of people around the world, including in the United States, and much of our social world is built on practices and beliefs that are rooted in religious traditions. This, according to religion's detractors, is the problem.

As authors, we take a different stand, viewing these realities instead as a challenge to understand religion better. Because religion is embedded to varying degrees in a wide range of social, political and economic phenomena, it is worthwhile for us to seek a better understanding of religion's social implications.

Sociologist Max Weber called on social scientists to engage in what he called value-free inquiry, or the dispassionate examination of phenomena guided as much as possible by empirical observation and separated as much as possible from the researcher's personal feelings about what is being observed. It is, of course, impossible for social inquiry to be entirely value-free since all observers have biases and opinions. Nonetheless, Weber urged those who observed and explained the social world to do their best to set aside their assumptions, preconceptions, biases, and values, and to focus instead on explaining—not judging—social phenomena. We do our best to follow Weber's lead in this book.

Thus, we do not argue for or against the existence of "god," either as an empirical reality or as a perception on the part of believers. Many people believe in a transcendent order, and whether or not we see the same order, religious belief and consequences are worth understanding. We also do not dispute the "reality" of religion. Religion is, as sociologist Emile Durkheim termed it, a *social fact* that has real and observable effects: It shapes human and collective behavior. That religion is intangible—beliefs, practices, experiences, and community that we cannot touch in a physical way—does not reduce its power in human society. Nor do we try to prove or debunk particular religious systems. Plenty of other books do that. The debunkers, in particular, give the impression that if only we could show fervently religious people the logical error of their thinking they would abandon their long-held beliefs and get with the modern, rational, scientific program.

Our primary motivation in writing this book was the observation that religion is a powerful force in our social world and does not appear to be going away. Even Peter Berger (1999, 9), who once convincingly argued the theoretical case for the inevitable decline of religion in the modern world, has conceded: "The world today is massively religious, is *anything but* the secularized world that had been predicted (whether joyfully or despondently) by so many analysts of modernity." Religion thrives. And no matter how we evaluate the content and effects of religious beliefs, practices, and communities, it behooves us to *understand* a social force like religion that has so much power in our world today. The discipline of sociology offers valuable tools for doing this.

We hope this will not be an ordinary textbook. Knowledge is a collective process that develops over time. We want you to realize that you can be part of that process. To be a learned person is to move beyond simply absorbing what others say about a topic and to critically evaluate it for its usefulness and for its holes. Perhaps in so doing, you will move our knowledge further forward, becoming part of the collective process.

Let's get started.

REFERENCES

Berger, Peter. 1999. "The Desecularization of the World: A Global Overview." In *The Desecularization of the World: Resurgent Religion and World Politics,* edited by Peter Berger, 1–18. Washington, D.C.: Ethics and Policy Center.

Bunkley, Nick. 2008. "Detroit Churches Pray for 'God's Bailout.'" *The New York Times,* December 8.

Hitchens, Christopher. 2008. *God Is Not Great: How Religion Poisons Everything.* New York: Twelve.

Leiken, Robert S. 2005. "Europe's Angry Muslims." *Foreign Affairs,* July/August.

McGreal, Chris. 2006. "McDonald's Changes its Brand to Suit Kosher Appetites." *Guardian International Pages,* March 13: 25.

McKinley, Jr., James C. 2001. "Church and State: Seeking Complicity in Genocide." *The New York Times,* June 10.

Scully, Sean. 2005. "Breathtaking Inanity: How Intelligent Design Flunked its Test Case." *Time,* December 20.

C H A P T E R

1

Why Religion?

1. What is religion?
2. What functions does it serve?
3. What is the difference between religion and "god"?
4. What is sociology?
5. Why is religion interesting to sociologists?

Religion is a pervasive force around the world. As the newsflashes in the introduction suggest, religion shapes how people behave and how they think about the world and their place in it.

Before we can understand the effects of religion in our world, however, we need to understand what exactly religion is. For many Americans, the word evokes familiar images of church, worship, prayer, traditions, and pilgrimage. Religion is harder to recognize, however, when it takes less familiar forms:

- Following strict rules that govern the killing of an animal
- Carefully washing hands before a meal
- Performing a dance or a song
- Frequently repeating a particular greeting or kind words
- Following restrictions on food or drink that have nothing to do with dieting or being a picky eater

Each of these acts is infused with religious meaning, at least to some groups of people. It is easy to overlook the significance of these acts, however, if you do not know much about religious beliefs and practices outside your own faith.

Baylor University sociologists Jerry Park and Joseph Baker recently reported the results of their survey exploring how often people "consume" (buy or view) religious goods (Park and Baker, 2007). The survey asked about art and jewelry with religious themes, sacred books, religious music and educational materials, and bumper stickers and cards with religious content (e.g., "What would Jesus do?"). Park and Baker also collected data on specific books and visual media. For example, they asked people whether they had watched *The Passion of the Christ* or *Veggie Tales.* Had they read *God's Politics* by the liberal Christian Evangelical Jim Wallis, Rick Warren's *The Purpose-Driven Life,* or Dan Brown's *The Da Vinci Code*? Had they seen TV programs like *7th Heaven; This Is Your Day,* featuring Benny Hinn; or *Touched by an Angel*? Had they read any of the *Left Behind* series, a book on Dianetics, or anything by James Dobson?

Many people recognize the religious connotations of these items. But that is probably because the exemplars—the objects the researchers chose to represent religious products—represent a fairly narrow range of religions. All but two of the exemplars are associated with variants of Christianity. The exceptions include Dianetics, which comes from L. Ron Hubbard's Scientology religion, and the TV show *Touched by an Angel,* which presents a world populated by spirits in human form ("angels") who are sent by an otherwise unnamed "holy father." The religion in *Touched by an Angel* is monotheistic, but it does not mention Christianity, Jesus, or a savior. This study's findings mostly tell us about buying or viewing products that are associated with the major religious traditions of Christianity.

What about less well known religious traditions? A vast array of religious traditions exists beyond Christianity and Scientology in the United States and worldwide. Each of these traditions has its own beliefs and practices, along with associated objects that people might buy or books or other media that people might view. Wouldn't it be interesting to know about those, too?

Perhaps you do not care about the unfamiliar. As long as you follow your own beliefs and practices, you may think you do not need to understand those of others. When it comes to religion, you may just want to mind your own business. (We doubt that this describes you! If it did, why would you read this book?) But there are consequences of not seeing the religious in the unfamiliar. We offer one well-known and tragic example.

In her nonfiction book *The Spirit Catches You and You Fall Down,* author Anne Fadiman chronicles a clash of cultures between American doctors and immigrant Hmong refugees from Laos (Fadiman 1998). Doctors in Merced, California, concluded that Lia, the young daughter of a Hmong couple, had epilepsy. Over the next couple of years, the toddler had a series of traumatic grand mal seizures that caused her parents to repeatedly bring her to the local emergency room. To the doctors, Lia's treatment was obvious: a complex regimen of medications to manage epilepsy. Nonetheless, Lia's case confounded the doctors and other hospital staff. They were perplexed by crescent-shaped indentations on her skin, not knowing that the marks resulted from a healing ceremony. They were taken aback when her parents brought traditional healers to visit her. And they were grossed out by the strange foods that her parents brought to her hospital room. (Imagine what the doctors would have thought of the pig sacrifice that the family conducted in the parking lot of their apartment building!) Most of all, Lia's physicians were frustrated when her parents often seemed to ignore their medical directions.

During the years that they treated her, Lia's doctors never wondered what her parents thought was happening to her. A language barrier complicated the situation: The parents spoke no English and the doctors spoke no Hmong. But working through translators, Fadiman uncovered the parents' understanding. They explained to her that right before Lia's first grand mal seizure, her older sister slammed the door and frightened Lia's spirit away. Whereas Lia's doctors saw an organic condition typified by misplaced electrical impulses in the brain, Lia's family saw a spirit lost in a world where bodies and spirits live side by side, in constant interaction with each other. Even if the parents spoke English, or the doctors understood the Hmong language, how would members of an ethnic group driven from their isolated home in the mountains of Laos communicate about the presence of spirits to scientifically trained Western doctors? Animistic religion was so central and powerful to the lives of Lia and her family that Fadiman wrote of the Hmong people: "Medicine was religion. Religion was society. Society was medicine." But this sort of religion, so integrally tied to every sphere of life and populated by spirits both benign and malevolent, is invisible to doctors who are trained to see the world from a Western, scientific perspective. Their understanding of disease allows no room for the existence of spirits or an influence of the spirit world on a little girl.

Add to that chasm in understanding the difference in the way that Lia's parents and her doctors *evaluated* the meaning of her seizures. To the doctors, the seizures were a serious medical disorder that needed to be controlled lest Lia suffer permanent brain damage. Her parents, though frightened by the severity of her seizures, believed that their daughter had a special connection to the spiritual world, a connection that could give her an elevated status in the Hmong community. As a result, they were not always sure that they wanted to "cure" her condition.

But her doctors knew none of this. When they were informed, years later, about how Lia's parents understood her condition, the doctors were incredulous. Animism, the injection of the spiritual into objects we encounter in day-to-day life, was alien to these doctors. More importantly, it never even occurred to them to *ask* the parents what they believed about their daughter's condition, not just because of a language barrier but because the doctors took for granted their scientific explanation of events. The gap between the scientific and religious explanations became an invisible impediment to her care: It impaired trust between the doctors and the family and led to profound misunderstandings about Lia's condition, its treatment, and her prognosis. Lia's care was compromised because of a lack of cross-cultural understanding, and everyone who encountered Lia—her family, medical staff, and social workers—experienced a lot of fear, stress, and uncertainty, partly because of the severity of her illness and partly because of their lack of understanding.

Whether the Hmong beliefs reflected scientific reality or not, they exerted a real force in this situation: Religious beliefs drove how her parents responded to and understood events, despite being *unseen* by Lia's doctors. Had the doctors recognized the distinctive Hmong religion and culture, they might have approached her treatment differently and more effectively. For example, they might have worked with her family, Hmong shamans and elders, and the family's religious beliefs and traditions to develop a treatment plan. The experience of the care process for Lia, her family, and her doctors might have been transformed by better understanding.

In this instance, and in others like it, at levels of analysis from the interpersonal to the cross-national, there are practical implications of being bound by the familiar and not recognizing the pivotal role of religion in our world today. This is why we need tools to understand religion—what it is, what it does—that allow us to see beyond that which is familiar to us to appreciate a wide range of religious beliefs and their effects on ourselves and those around us.

WHAT IS RELIGION ANYWAY?

Stop for a moment. Write or type an answer to this question: What is religion? Go ahead. Take a stab at this. We'll gladly wait.

Did you find it easy to define religion? Creating a definition that stands up under scrutiny is harder than you might expect. One approach used by sociologists (scientists who study people and human social behavior) is to create criteria that they then apply to decide whether a practice or belief indeed represents a religion. For example, Melford Spiro, an American cultural anthropologist, defined religion as "an institution consisting of culturally patterned interaction with culturally postulated superhuman beings" (Spiro 1996, 98). You may be thinking, "What in the world does that mean?" It will help if we walk through an example. Let's apply Spiro's definition to the branch of Christianity known as Catholicism. First, we'll consider whether Catholicism is an institution that consists of culturally patterned interactions. In other words, are patterns of relationships, behaviors, and beliefs embodied in it? Well, Catholicism has an organizational structure that extends from Rome into local communities worldwide. It has a hierarchy of authorities (e.g., the Pope, cardinals, archbishops, priests). It has a clearly articulated theology that covers a wide range of subjects, ritual practices, and expectations for the behavior of followers. So Catholicism meets our first criterion. As for our second criterion, do those interactions involve culturally postulated superhuman beings? "God" certainly qualifies as such a being. When we can answer yes to both questions, then we are dealing with a religion according to Spiro's definition.

If we consider the case of consumerism, we may answer those questions differently. Consumerism is certainly an "institution that consists of culturally patterned interactions." It is embodied in social and cultural practices including mass production, marketing, shopping and waste disposal, and driven by beliefs about shopping being good for the economy and an enjoyable pursuit. But consumerism has no "culturally postulated superhuman beings": The "dollar as the almighty god" really is just a metaphor. So, although consumerism is a powerful social force, it falls short of being a religion by Spiro's definition.

So, it wasn't so difficult to define religion. But the minute you settle on criteria, someone is bound to come up with a compelling counterexample, forcing you to adjust your thinking. In part, this happens because we tend to generate definitions on the basis of what is familiar to us. So, if you build your definition of religion around what is most familiar to you, and you are a typical modern Westerner, you may form a definition of religion that includes a single supernatural being: a "god" such as the one found in Christianity, Judaism, and Islam. But this definition focuses too narrowly on monotheistic traditions. Our definition should include polytheistic faiths (ones with multiple gods). As you may remember from high school mythology, Greek and Roman religious belief systems were populated with a lot of gods. Some scholars have argued that the Catholic faith posits more than one "spiritual being" because it embraces a Trinitarian conception of God in which three components—the Father, the Son, and the Holy Spirit—make up the entity of God, and because Catholicism features a multitude of saints and angels.

Even if your definition of religion includes belief in god *or* gods (plural), it may unwittingly exclude other belief systems. For example, animists believe in the existence of an unseen reality (the supernatural), but not in "gods" *per se*. The Hmong people, who believe that spirits inhabit the world alongside us, are animists. And if you extend your definition of religion to encompass beliefs and practices related to the supernatural, you will still miss other belief systems commonly understood to be religious. For example, Buddhism is oriented around *practices* that are thought to lead to a richer and fuller life but it does not involve gods, spirits, or even a supernatural realm.

Spiro provided us with a *substantive definition* of religion. A substantive definition tells us what religion is and provides criteria for elements that should be included in the category of "religion." But substantive definitions are dead ends because they are rooted in particular times, places, and cultural contexts. They blind us to what may serve as religion in other times, places, and contexts.

To avoid this trap, we may take a different approach to defining religion: thinking through what religion *does* as opposed to explaining what religion *is*. Although the content of religious systems varies widely across time and place, sociologists have identified some key *functions* that religion serves. These functions are common across widely disparate systems of belief, practice, and community:

1. Religion provides comfort and quells dissatisfaction.
2. Religion strengthens human community.
3. Religion assures its followers that there is a larger cosmic order.

Religion Provides Comfort and Quells Dissatisfaction

Perhaps the most infamous *functional definition* of religion was provided by Karl Marx when he claimed that

> Religion is the general theory of that world, its encyclopedic compendium, its logic in popular form, its spiritualistic *point d'honneur* [trans.: principle], its enthusiasm, its moral sanction, its solemn complement, its universal source of consolation and justification . . . Religion is the sigh of the oppressed creature, the heart of a heartless world, just as it is the spirit of a spiritless condition. It is the opium of the people. (Marx 1843, 53–54)

Marx believed that religion arose out of oppressive conditions and supported the status quo by justifying inequality, consoling the downtrodden, and dulling the pains of daily life. To Marx, religion was fundamentally conservative in that it confirms and reinforces existing social arrangements. It justifies laws that limit people's freedoms, it validates the rule of the powerful and oppression of the weak, and it makes sense of economic inequality and other forms of social disparity. In so doing, religion also suppresses people's resistance to oppressive systems.

To serve these purposes, religion need not take any specific form, posit a god or supernatural beings, or embody particular practices. It need only justify existing conditions and soothe those who suffer. Marx's understanding of the functions of religion does not apply to all cases, of course. As we will discuss in Chapter 7, there are numerous examples in history when religious groups stood up to *challenge* existing social arrangements—unfair laws, discriminatory practices, or economic inequality—and when religion served more to drive social change than to inhibit it. Marx did not acknowledge this fairly common use of religion. Thus, his functional definition of religion—"it is the opium of the people"—is oversimplified. It nonetheless provides a useful starting point for thinking about the functions of religion: Religion provides comfort to individuals and justifications for existing social arrangements.

Religion Strengthens Human Community

The 19th-century French sociologist Emile Durkheim offers a more comprehensive explanation of the function of religion when he writes that religion is "a unified system of
beliefs and practices relative to sacred things, that is to say, things set apart and forbidden—
beliefs and practices which unite into one single moral community called a Church,
all who adhere to them" (Durkheim 1912, 44). It is a densely worded definition, but
unpacked; it contains a number of important elements of religion: belief, ritual, sacred elements, and community. It is also a strong statement that the main function of religion in
society is to strengthen human communities.

ON BELIEF AND RITUAL   Durkheim (1912) identifies two key elements of religion: belief
and ritual. According to him, beliefs are "states of opinion and consist in representations." Essentially, beliefs are what we *think*. Rituals are "determined modes of action."
They are what we *do*. Recall that substantive definitions of religion typically try to
define the content of religious beliefs; specifically, belief in a god or the supernatural
characterizes religion.

After studying a wide variety of world religions past and present, Durkheim concluded that religions share one significant common belief. He argued that

> All known religious beliefs, whether simple or complex, present one common
> characteristic: they presuppose a classification of all the things, real and ideal,
> of which men think into two classes or opposed groups, generally designated
> by two distinct terms which are translated well enough by the words profane
> and sacred (Durkheim 1912, 34).

But what is the *difference* between the sacred and the profane? The definition of sacred
varies across religious systems, so we will not find the answer in particular objects, beliefs,
persons, or practices. There are hierarchical rankings even within the categories of sacred and
profane. Some sacred objects are *more* sacred than others, for example. So saying that sacred
elements are superior in dignity and power to profane elements does not help us distinguish
them. To solve this problem, Durkheim settles on the "absolute" heterogeneity of these categories. That is, the sacred and profane are completely and totally different from each other.
Any interaction between the two must be undertaken with the greatest of care:

> The sacred thing is *par excellence* that which the profane should not touch,
> and cannot touch with impunity . . . this establishment of relations [between
> the sacred and the profane] is always a delicate operation in itself, demanding
> great precautions and a more or less complicated initiation . . . . (Durkheim
> 1912, 38)

To distinguish the sacred from the profane, Durkheim does not focus on the specific content of the categories of sacred and profane, because these vary so widely across religious
systems. Instead, he focuses on the way that the sacred and profane are *treated* in human
societies, particularly with respect to each other:

> Sacred things are those which the interdictions protect and isolate; profane
> things, those to which these interdictions are applied and which must remain
> at a distance from the first. (Durkheim 1912, 38)

Rituals are "the rules of conduct which prescribe how a man should comport himself in the presence of these sacred objects" (Durkheim 1912, 38). Because the sacred and profane are mutually exclusive and completely dissimilar categories, problems arise when the sacred and profane meet. We have trouble imagining how the two can safely mingle: What if the profane contaminates the sacred? What if the profane is transformed into the sacred? These scenarios are understood to be socially dangerous possibilities. Nonetheless, the sacred and profane do sometimes interact—for example, when humans, whose bodies may be considered profane, touch or consume sacred objects. When this happens, people generally take great care to structure their contact with rituals, specifying a set of steps that makes interaction between the sacred and the profane safe. Thus, humans may reach out to the sacred through prayer, liturgy, dance, or song.

We see rituals, undertaken as precautions, across numerous religious traditions. Once, after attending an Episcopal worship service in an outdoor chapel, one of the authors (Monahan) proposed feeding the leftover consecrated bread to the birds. She was trying to avoid having to eat it herself. The priest who had led the service was unwavering: The bread must be consumed or saved for a later worship service. It was absolutely forbidden to throw the bread on the ground or leave it for the birds. A sacred element—the consecrated bread—cannot be treated in profane ways, even for the benefit of the birds. "Ah," your author thought, "that explains why, at the end of a communion service in a Christian church, the celebrant guzzles the leftover wine up at the altar at 11 A.M. on a Sunday morning. You can't just pour it down the drain!"

Because of concerns about the profane contaminating the sacred, Judaism understands the name of God ("Yhwh") to be unpronounceable by humans, preserving its mystery and majesty; Orthodox Judaism bans menstruating women from attending temple; and Hindus abstain from eating the meat of cows, which are sacred to them.

Thus, Durkheim argues that religion is a system with two interrelated parts: (1) beliefs about how the world is divided into distinct, mutually exclusive, and wholly encompassing spheres of the sacred and the profane; and (2) practices through which sacred objects, people, ideas, and actions can safely come into contact with the profane. But that raises the question, What is the *point* of all of this?

ON COMMUNITY   As a class exercise early in a Sociology of Religion class, we sometimes ask students to come up with a list of questions for a survey that would measure the "religiosity" of individuals, that is, how strongly people hold their religious beliefs. We remind students that they should expect to survey a culturally and ethnically diverse group of people. (Think beyond Christianity!) What questions would you ask?

To get students started, we provide a list of questions that researchers have used in the past to measure aspects of religion. We tell students that they may use, adapt, or eliminate any of these questions. Very quickly, the class eliminates questions about specific religious beliefs. Being able to recite the Ten Commandments serves as evidence of religiosity only in people who are Christian or Jewish, and being able to recognize prominent quotes from the Koran does not speak to religiosity in other traditions. Praying, attending worship services, and donating money to a church are also aspects of some religions but not others.

Common ground emerges in an intriguing place, in questions that on the surface seem not to be about religious belief and practice at all: How much time do you spend with friends who share your religious beliefs, and how likely are you to marry within your faith? In fact, most students eliminate almost all other questions before arriving at these two as ways to measure religiosity. What is intriguing is that the first question does not capture how much time a person spends participating in *religious* activities with friends who share the same beliefs, just how much time in general the person spends around such friends. Yet students conclude that it is likely to be a good measure of general religiosity. Similarly, the second question does not measure a person's engagement in religious activities with his or her spouse. Instead, it captures how likely the person is to partner for life with someone else who shares the same faith.

These questions highlight the fundamentally *social* nature of religion. That is, while religion includes beliefs and practices, these elements exist to build religious community and integrate people into that community. When students lean toward measuring the strength of religious faith through questions that focus on affiliation with other members of a religious group, they implicitly understand this.

In fact, Durkheim claims that religion happens only within a community or collective setting. Those who adhere to the notion of individual spirituality might object to that limitation, claiming that their solitary practices also constitute "religion." But Durkheim is clear that a central function of religion is to create and strengthen common bonds among members of social groups and to tie members to the group as a whole. Note that he makes no claim that individual spirituality does not exist, only that it is tangential to the cohesive function of religion for the group as a whole. The "unified system of belief and practice" matters because it emerges from the social group and belongs to the group as a whole: Beliefs and rituals are communally recounted and practiced, and together they provide vital glue that holds the social group together.

Thus, the type of people with whom you regularly interact, especially voluntary interaction on nonwork time, is generally a strong indicator of your degree of religiosity. People who hold strong religious beliefs and engage in regular religious practice often associate with others who share their beliefs and practices, irrespective of the content of the religion. Likewise, marriage within the group is a robust measure of degree of religiosity because marriage typically has both civil and religious meaning and creates a presumably permanent social tie with another person. Of course, some people marry outside their religious group. Almost everyone knows someone who has done so. But the tendency toward marrying within the group is stronger among those who profess higher levels of religiosity. In sum, religious beliefs and practices unite the community and provide a powerful foundation for the rest of social life. In Chapter 5, we will explore in more detail the ways in which religion builds community and strengthens community cohesiveness.

Religion Assures us of Cosmic Order

Peter Berger, a sociologist and a Lutheran theologian, takes a broader approach to understanding the function of religion when he argues that religion is "the audacious attempt to conceive of the entire universe as humanly significant" (Berger 1967, 28). (See Box 1.1) He argues that humans are fundamentally meaning-seeking creatures: It is our very nature to impose order on our experiences and seek meaning in day-to-day events. In so doing, we reject chaos and the possibility that events are random in nature. We see much anecdotal

BOX 1.1

Some Definitions of Religion:

- *Melford Spiro (1966):* Religion is "an institution consisting of culturally patterned interaction with culturally postulated superhuman beings."
- *Karl Marx (1843):* Religion is "the opium of the people."
- *Emile Durkheim (1912):* Religion is "a unified system of beliefs and practices relative to sacred things, that is to say, things set apart and forbidden—beliefs and practices which unite into one single moral community called a Church, all who adhere to them."
- *Peter Berger (1967):* Religion is "the audacious attempt to conceive of the entire universe as humanly significant."

evidence that Berger is right about this. A child dies, and through their grief, parents vow that the child's death will "mean something": They may start a foundation, lobby for passage of a law, or speak publicly about a larger issue related to their child's death. The child's death is transformed from an isolated, random, tragic event that happens with some degree of regularity—diseases strike, drunk drivers kill, accidents happen—to an event with meaning and larger purpose, an event connected to the greater social order. Similarly, an elderly woman wins the lottery and believes that she is being repaid for a lifetime of financial struggles and generous acts. It is entirely unsatisfying to think that picking the right lottery numbers might be just dumb luck and unrelated to the moral fiber of the lucky winner to conceive that a selfish and callous person could be fortunate enough to beat the odds.

According to Berger, humans constantly seek order and meaning in daily events as a way to fight off the alternative—the admission that our lives are full of random unpredictability, which leaves us enmeshed in the terrifying and dark morass of chaos. Chaos, or the absence of order, is terrifying to humans because it suggests a potentially risky situation over which we have no control.

One common type of order is what Berger refers to as *nomos,* the imposition of order by humans on everyday events so that events seem more predictable and stable. Schedules and appointments, laws of science, social norms such as driving on the right side of the road, and stereotypes about other people all take masses of information, actions, and events and place them in a system of humanly constructed and understood order.

But the most robust order is *cosmos,* a conception of order that links human experience to a transcendental order, providing a sense that our lives are not mere aggregations of random events but instead that our experiences are connected to some larger sacred order. As people often say in both good and bad times, "It's all part of God's plan." Events that otherwise make no sense are explained through their connection to a cosmic order. When terrorists crashed a plane into a building, Jerry Falwell, a prominent religious leader, claimed that "the pagans, and the abortionists, and the feminists, and the gays and the lesbians . . . the ACLU, People For the American Way . . . created an environment which possibly has caused God to lift the veil of protection . . ." (CNN 2001). Falwell is convinced that such a tragic event *must* be connected to some larger and sacred order. It cannot be an accident, a fluke, or a mundane failure of airport security. The universe cannot be so cruel. It must *mean* something.

In the aftermath of Hurricane Katrina in 2005, people expressed a variety of attitudes toward those who stayed in New Orleans as the storm approached. Some of the harshest evaluations came from those whose criticisms suggested that *they* would have done things differently: "I would have hoofed it out of there" said one student who was not the least bit compassionate toward—and indeed seemed disgusted by—the people who remained behind. She even said, "They got what they deserved." This student was certain that those who stayed behind were basically flawed human beings, and she insisted that their suffering was not random but deserved. Berger's lens suggests that she had a different underlying thought, something along the following lines: "I cannot believe that this was just a random event that happened to random people, because that would mean that someday something like this could happen to me. There is order in this world and nothing so awful could ever happen to a deserving person like me."

To admit that a terrifying and tragic event could befall anyone at any time is to acknowledge the significant degree of randomness in our day-to-day existence. It is this sense of inherent chaos that, with the help of religion, we fight so hard to fend off. Humans resist the notion that events are random by conceiving that the events are meaningful in some larger cosmic order.

A SOCIOLOGICAL CONSENSUS: RELIGION IS A HUMAN PRODUCT

Sociologists and anthropologists agree on one essential point: Religion is a product of human beings. Across time and place, human beings create religion: They originate belief systems, they develop rituals, and they form communities of faith. Sometimes this happened so far in the past that we forget religion's origins. But religion originates in human societies.

So what is the relationship between religion and its subject (e.g., God, gods, the supernatural and so on)? Think of it this way: Religion is the human system that reflects our understandings of reality, order, and appropriate ways to engage the sacred, whereas supernatural formulations such as a god or gods are posited as existing and are understood through the lens provided by religion. Religion is not the same thing as "god." Instead, religion creates the perception of a bridge between humans and what is variously called "god," the supernatural, or the cosmic order. It is a way for human beings to understand and to reach out and connect to something larger and unknowable that they believe is out there.

Many people find this understanding of religion to be contentious because it suggests that "god" does not really exist but is instead a product of human imagination. Peter Berger responds to this concern in an endnote to his book *The Sacred Canopy,* in which he points out that the claim that religion is a human creation does not speak to the question of whether "god" or some other larger cosmic order really exists (Berger 1967). The existence of "god" or that larger cosmic order is simply not empirically verifiable. Despite copious efforts by believers and nonbelievers, it is not possible to either confirm or disprove the existence of "god." Understanding religion as a human product, Berger argues, implies nothing about the existence of some ultimate reality.

What is most important to sociologists is that the *claim* of this reality drives the creation of religious beliefs, rituals, structures, and communities. Those phenomena *are* consequential and empirically observable. While there is no empirical evidence that religious structures, beliefs, and practices are inspired by some ultimate being, force, or order, there is plenty about religion that is worth exploring and understanding. Religion is real in its consequences and effects. And, of course, it feels real—in its substance—to believers.

It is worth examining the nature of religion that makes people take it for granted, the sense that it is simply *is* and always has been. Much of any institution's power lies in its ability to make its human roots invisible. In other words, when an institution—such as religion—is understood to be timeless, enduring, or emerging from other than human sources, that institution is more likely to be taken for granted (in the sense that people will believe and trust in it), and its stability is enhanced. On the other hand, when the human origins of an institution become apparent, the institution is often weakened in the eyes of observers.

Consider, for example, Jon Krakauer's account of the origins of *The Book of Mormon,* the text that lies at the heart of the Mormon faith, which in 2008 claimed over 13 million adherents. Krakauer recounts how Joseph Smith, a farmer in upstate New York, found buried treasure using "divining." On four attempts, Smith failed to find the treasure, but on the fifth attempt he supposedly was greeted by an angel named Moroni who had been sent from God, who allowed Smith to dig up a box that contained a sacred text written on golden plates. The text was written in "reformed Egyptian," a dead language, but Moroni gave Smith magic glasses that allowed Smith to read, translate, and transcribe the plates. When Smith completed the 116-page translation, Moroni reclaimed the golden plates and the magic glasses. As the story goes, the original translation was lost, and Moroni returned to Smith with the golden plates but not the magic glasses, so Smith relied on another technique for "translating" the text:

> Day after day, utilizing a technique he had learned from [a local girl], Joseph Smith would place the magic rock in an upturned hat, bury his face in it with the stack of gold plates sitting nearby, and dictate the lines of scripture that appeared to him out of the blackness. He worked at a feverish pace . . . averaging some thirty-five hundred words a day, and by the end of June 1829 the job was finished. (Krakauer 2003, 63)

The result was *The Book of Mormon.*

Krakauer's striking account lays clear the human roots of religion—how religion is originated by human beings. Whether you believe that Joseph Smith was divinely inspired or not, the account is unsettling because it suggests that a rapidly growing worldwide religion began with the mundane, if somewhat odd, act of a man who lived less than 200 years ago. In this case, the human roots of this religion are so obvious that it is hard to see how a faith—one that is obviously compelling on the basis of recent growth in its adherents—could have been founded on it.

But is the narrative of the founding of Mormonism really any more outlandish than the founding stories of other religions—stone tablets inscribed with text handed down on a mountain, or an individual who dies and comes back to life again? Or is the founding story more transparently a human product because not enough time has yet passed to render the belief system part of the taken-for-granted cultural landscape?

In his *New York Times Magazine* article, "What Is It about Mormonism?", Noah Feldman confronts the common response to this tale of the religion's origins:

> . . . [E]ven among those who respect Mormons personally, it is still common to hear Mormonism's tenets dismissed as ridiculous. This attitude is logically indefensible insofar as Mormonism is being compared with other world religions. There is nothing inherently less plausible about God's revealing himself to an upstate New York farmer in the early years of the Republic than to

the pharaoh's changeling grandson in ancient Egypt. But what is driving the tendency to discount Joseph Smith's revelations is not that they seem less reasonable than those of Moses; it is that the book containing them is so new. When it comes to prophecy, antiquity breeds authenticity. Events in the distant past, we tend to think, occurred in sacred, mythic time. Not so revelations received during the presidencies of James Monroe or Andrew Jackson. (Feldman 2008)

Over time, the human roots of a given religion become less visible, and the religion itself becomes more taken-for-granted as timelessly and universally real, rather than being the ideas and practices of a person or group at one particular point in time. None of this changes the fact that religion is a human product. It only explains how, over time, we come to overlook that uncomfortable reality.

People have also sought to uncover the human roots of older and more established religions, a practice that often causes discomfort and dissent within religious communities. In her memoir *The Spiral Staircase,* religious historian and former Catholic nun Karen Armstrong describes her surprise upon encountering "New Testament criticism," a scholarly body of work that examines in detail how the New Testament of the Bible was constructed. New Testament critics have concluded that the Bible was written years after the death of Jesus and that there were fierce political debates among the contributors about what to include and exclude. In addition, the text underwent numerous transformations at the hands of humans: It was translated from one language to another, people made copies that were slightly different versions, and people used gradual to abrupt adaptations of certain words. New Testament critics claim that, in all, decisions made by humans over time shaped the Christianity we know today, and the Bible is only the current record of a document that has been evolving for a long time, despite the fact that some people hold it to be fixed, sacred, and constant (or even literal). Bart Ehrman, a religious historian at the University of North Carolina, popularized New Testament criticism research in his books *Misquoting Jesus* and *Lost Christianities*. His work and that of fellow New Testament critics have elicited strong negative responses, especially from fundamentalist Christians. For example, Darrell Bock and Daniel Wallace, theology professors at the Dallas Theological Seminary, wrote *Dethroning Jesus* to counter the claims of the New Testament critics: The book's promotional materials claim that it will "help readers understand that the orthodox understanding of Christ and his divinity is as trustworthy and sure as it ever was." For Karen Armstrong, however, this scholarship was eye-opening. After she spent a lifetime in the Catholic Church, "New Testament Criticism" challenged the previously unquestioned reality of her religious beliefs by highlighting their very human roots.

THE PROMISE OF SOCIOLOGY

Students often say that they are drawn to sociology because they are "interested in people" and they have heard that "sociologists study people." Probe more deeply, and you will hear that people do "stuff" that the students want to better understand: They think, act, and feel. But the typical student has yet to grasp the full meaning of the word *people,* and with it, the inherent power of sociology.

Students of sociology often start out as closet psychologists. In order to understand people better, they take the methodological approach of focusing on individuals. They naïvely assume that if they study enough individuals—their beliefs, behaviors, and feelings—they will reach a full understanding of "people" as a group, as well. The belief has an intuitive and compelling logic on the surface, one that fits well with the way that Western culture socializes us to see the world around us as made up of individual actors with free will.

But the approach demonstrates a fundamental misunderstanding of sociology's object of study and, more important, sociology's power as a tool for explanation. To many students, the term *people* is merely the plural of *person;* it is the aggregation of two or more individuals. But to social scientists, the term *people* connotes something different: Though indeed a "people" is made up of individuals, it is noteworthy because it is larger than the mere sum of its constituent parts. Sociologists do not study individuals or "people" in the adding-up-individuals sense. "People" are not merely "persons," and sociology is not, as students often assume, the study of the experiences of individual persons, viewed in isolation from their social relationships or ties. Instead, sociology focuses on the collective itself: the nation, the community, the family, the group, the organization, and so on. It ponders all the ways that people organize themselves and examines human *arrangements*.

Those arrangements include what sociologists call "structure," or stable patterns of social relationships. Groups, communities, bureaucracies, and families are examples of institutions that demonstrate social structure. The arrangements also include "culture"—the values, norms, and knowledge of a group or society. Social practices, including recurrent patterns of behavior, are also a type of human arrangement. So the practices of going to church on Sunday, attending synagogue on the Sabbath, praying five times a day, or dipping infants in holy water all have social content and meaning. At the heart of sociology is the study of "people" in this sense, as social collectives that have ties among members, connections to other groups, shared understandings, and patterned behaviors.

How, then, can we study those human arrangements? Emile Durkheim, whose ideas about the sociology of religion we have already mentioned, was one of sociology's founders. He wrote that *social facts*—patterns of thinking, feeling, and acting— exist outside of any individual but exert force over individuals in systematic—though not wholly deterministic—ways. So when we see someone express a thought or feeling, or act in a certain way, we are often observing something larger and more significant than the individual's expression. That is, we are often observing an instance of a *pattern* that exists in society.

Our day-to-day lives are structured by an infinite number of such patterns, everything from handshaking, to "flipping the bird" (in response, of course, to different stimuli!), to valuing the newest technology, to feeling grief at a funeral. Certainly, thoughts, feelings, and actions related to religion are instances of broader patterns. A Muslim woman who wears a veil is not making a personal fashion decision but instead is engaging in the religious practice of hijab. A man who professes belief in "God's plan" did not invent that belief; instead he is drawing on an existing pattern of belief that is widespread in his social community. Similarly, an observant Jewish person who washes his hands carefully before each meal did not invent the practice, nor does he engage in it in isolation from its larger social context. People's thoughts, feelings, and actions often have their origins in patterns of thinking, feeling, and acting that exist outside them. Those *external patterns* are what interest sociologists: We note them in the thoughts, feelings, and actions of individuals, but never forget that they have an existence *outside* the individual.

These patterns of thinking, feeling, and acting also exercise "an external constraint" over the individual: The patterns have coercive power to push us to think, feel, and act in particular ways. People often initially reject or resist the idea that there are coercive social facts, because we like to think of ourselves as individualists, actors with free will. But a closer examination of our daily lives reveals endless instances where we are following well-established patterns of thinking, feeling, and acting. To name but a few: driving on the right side of the road (in the United States), saying "excuse me" when you bump into someone, avoiding eye contact in an elevator, waiting in line, applying for college or jobs, tipping service providers, kneeling during prayer, feeling teary during a wedding (although that pattern is probably related to gender!), and so on.

You might respond that people *do* violate these patterns on occasion and so there are not really any constraints. Durkheim does not dispute that sometimes the patterns are violated, but he locates evidence of their coercive nature in the broader social *response* to violation, a response from those around us and, perhaps more interestingly, from within ourselves. When people violate existing patterns of thinking, feeling, or acting, those around them often respond in a negative way: a funny look, a sharp word, a rolling of the eyes, a denial of assistance or service, or a formal punishment. Those responses remind the transgressors of the existing patterns and of the benefits of conforming to them. In that sense, the patterns and the responses to violations exert a coercive influence over us: We become more likely to follow the patterns than to violate them because we wish to avoid negative sanctions. Violations also elicit responses from within the violator, such as heightened self-consciousness, a queasy or nervous feeling in the pit of the stomach, a feeling of guilt, or an overwhelming desire to simply *conform*. The patterns exist outside of us but we have also internalized them.

Consider again the Islamic practice of women wearing the veil or the orthodox Judaic practice of women covering their hair (e.g., by wearing a wig or a scarf). As we stated earlier, this behavior is not merely a personal fashion choice; it is a religious imperative. In his book *The Culture of Disbelief,* legal scholar Stephen Carter considers cases in which nonbelievers reduce religious patterns or imperatives—to perform animal sacrifice, to consume an illegal substance, to rest on a specified day—to "individual choices," suggesting that a religious person has a choice about whether or not to adhere to his or her faith (Carter 1993). Carter argues that understanding religion as a "personal choice" trivializes faith because, in the lives of believers, religion is not a choice but a powerful social fact. It comprises ways of thinking, feeling, and acting that are external to and coercive over us. It is a particularly powerful social influence because it is made up of an interconnected set of beliefs, practices, structures, and communities and is central to the way that we think about and experience our lives.

To say that religion is a social fact does not, in any way, imply that what religion purports to represent and connect us to—the supernatural or a deity—is itself an empirically observable fact. But religion, the human-created system that connects communities to the unseen, is very much a "fact" in the social sense. It is observable, it exists outside any one person, and, as we will see, it exerts a tremendous influence in our world.

SUGGESTED READING

Berger, Peter. 1967. *The Sacred Canopy: Elements of a Sociological Theory of Religion.* Garden City, NY: Doubleday.

Bock, Darrell, and Daniel B. Wallace. 2008. *Dethroning Jesus: Exposing Popular Culture's Quest to Unseat the Biblical Christ.* Nashville, TN: Thomas Nelson.

Durkheim, Emile. 1912 (1995 trans). *The Elementary Forms of Religious Life.* New York: Free Press.

Durkheim, Emile. 1895 (1982 trans). *The Rules of Sociological Method.* New York: Free Press.

Ehrman, Bart. 2007. *Misquoting Jesus.* New York: HarperOne.

Fadiman, Anne. 1997. *The Spirit Catches You and You Fall Down.* New York: Noonday.

Geertz, Clifford. 1966. "Religion as a Cultural System." In *Anthropological Approaches to the Study of Religion,* edited by M. Banton, 1–45. London: Tavistock.

Marx, Karl. 1843 (1970 trans). "From Contribution to the Critique of Hegel's *Philosophy of the Law:* Introduction." In *The Marx-Engels Reader, 2nd Edition,* edited by Robert C. Tucker, 53–65. New York: W.W. Norton.

Spiro, Melford. 1966. "Religion: Problems of Definition and Explanation." In *Anthropological Approaches to the Study of Religion,* edited by M. Banton, 85–126. London: Tavistock.

2

"You Believe What?"

A Tour of Religious Belief and Ritual Practice

1. Why are religious beliefs and ritual practices *both* important in the study of religion?
2. How do beliefs and rituals vary across religious traditions?
3. What are "worship wars" and "Sheilaism?" Are they uniquely American religious phenomena?
4. What do sociologists think about religious beliefs and practices?

Today is December 21, four days before Christmas. Many Christians are getting ready to celebrate the birth of Christ with lights, greenery, and manger scenes that include small figures of Jesus as a baby, his parents Mary and Joseph, a few shepherds, a donkey, sheep, and sometimes three kings.

This year, today is also the first day of the Jewish holiday Hanukah. Hanukah is the eight-day festival of lights that commemorates the rededication of the Jewish temple in Jerusalem in the second century B.C.E. It also commemorates the miracle in which, when only enough oil remained to light the temple lamp for one day, the oil lasted eight days, just enough time to harvest olives and make more oil.

And we're not done yet. Today is also the festival of Yule, which is a celebration of the winter solstice, the shortest day of the year. Yule is a pre-Christian festival that continues to be celebrated by members of Wicca and other pagan groups as the time when the sun is reborn, and the Goddess gives birth to the God.

So . . . raise your hand if you are wondering why people still celebrate things that happened a couple of thousand years ago. Or why some ancient winter festival still matters today. Or why these very different celebrations all fall at the same time of the year. Religious beliefs, rituals, and experiences can thrill us or revolt us. They can bring us together as a community or make people from one group want to burn outsiders at the stake. As you may already be thinking, religion is complex and not necessarily easy to understand.

If asked, a vast majority of people in North America and Europe would probably tell you that religion is what individuals believe about the sacred. Remember the old saying about the two topics never to bring up in conversation, religion, and politics? Those of us living in the West tend to see beliefs and values as highly personalized and tend to think that they should rarely, if ever, be discussed outside our own religious group. Religion is a private matter, and we risk conflicts when we start talking to other people about what we really believe, especially to people who might believe something else!

But this viewpoint is certainly not true of people who live in other parts of the world. Depending on where you live, you may feel barraged by other people's religious beliefs. Or you may know that different religious groups exist in your community but may not often hear about what they believe or do. Yet even when we are in situations where religion seems to surround us, most of us know little about the diverse range of religious beliefs and practices. That is sometimes true even within our own faith traditions. Roman Catholics know little about the big differences among Protestant Christian groups. Christians don't know much about the different branches of Judaism or Hinduism and visa versa. How much do you know about the religious beliefs and practices of your friends, classmates, or coworkers?

To understand religion in our world, you have to realize that religious beliefs, practices, and experiences are social constructs. As noted in Chapter 1, they are rooted in communities of believers and are shaped by these believers over time. So our first order of business will be to examine the broad organizational families in which believers believe, act, and experience the sacred. As you will see, some religious groups are closely related to others. Figure 2.1 illustrates the interrelationships among Christians as one example of these linkages. While it is not possible for us to exhaustively cover every religion, this chapter will give you a sense of some of the differences that you might encounter within different traditions, along with some recent data on religious beliefs, practices, and experiences among Americans. As the chapter title suggests, often we are surprised at what religious people actually believe, what they do, and what they experience. We should remember, however, that beliefs and practices differ widely even within the same religion. The sociological lens will help us understand religious diversity and the consequences of beliefs, rituals, and experiences for people, communities, and entire societies.

COMPARING RELIGIOUS BELIEFS AND PRACTICES

Of the nearly 7 billion people in the world today, about 84% belong to one of the world's major religions (http://www.adherents.com 2005). Although specific estimates vary, a third of the world's population (approximately 31.5%) claim to belong to some form of Christianity, making it the largest of the world's religions. Of course, we will see that Christianity encompasses a vast range of different denominations and groups. Islam is the second largest religion, with roughly 1.5 billion adherents, or approximately 22% of the population. Hindus represent another 13%, or 860 million people. Buddhism, traditional Chinese religion, and the world's indigenous and animist religious traditions each make up 6% of the population, or nearly 400 million people. Judaism claims 14 million people, or 0.22% of the world's population.

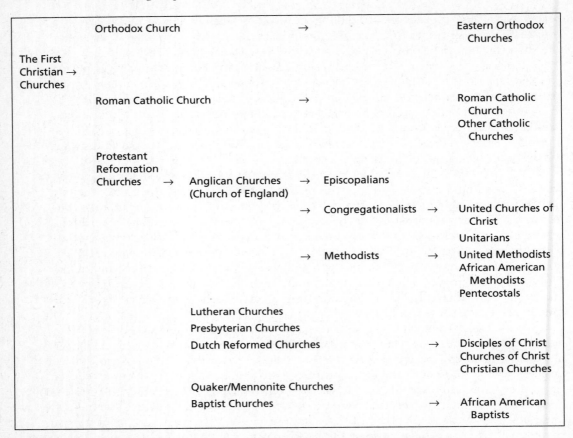

FIGURE 2.1   A denominational tree for some of the world's major christian denominations.

While these statistics may make you think that the world religions (and therefore the unique beliefs, practices, and experiences of their adherents) are concise and easily understood, these broad categories barely touch the over 10,000 different religions in the world or the 150 religions that have a million or more followers. Even Christianity can be subdivided into well over 200 denominations in the United States alone and as many as 33,830 denominations worldwide (Barrett 2001, Linder 2000, Mead and Hill 2001)! With that diversity in mind, let's explore some key beliefs, practices, and experiences that are related to these groups. Since it is the single biggest religion in the world today, we'll start with Christianity, then move on to Islam, Hinduism, and others. Hang on for the ride!

CHRISTIANITY

The core beliefs and practices of Christianity center around the life and teachings of Jesus, who is understood to be the Son of the one God and who came to earth to save humans from their sins by dying and returning to life again. Christians believe that the Bible is the word of God, and it forms the basis for their religious life and social morality, though what this means practically varies by congregation and denomination. Some Christians believe that the Bible is the literal word of God; in other words, every word is understood to be true and relevant for living today. Other Christians believe the Bible to be the "inspired" word of God, meaning that moral teachings are central to understanding one's faith and living a "good" life, though not every story or commandment is literally true or relevant for life today. There are also many Christians for whom the Bible is an important sacred text but who understand its stories and moral precepts as products of a much different historic era. As a result, the Bible may provide guidance today but no more so than other sacred texts. Most Christians believe that moral conduct in this life determines what happens to them after death. Here, too, there is much variety among denominations, but most Christians believe in an afterlife with an eventual judgment at which one must account for one's life.

Different denominations embrace and amplify different basic tenets of Christianity. We will review some differences among the main Christian denominations: the Roman Catholics, mainline Protestants, Black Protestants, Evangelicals, and other notable Christian groups.

Catholicism

If asked, Catholics would probably say that their Church goes all the way back to the days when the first Christian communities were founded by disciples of Jesus. They include congregations around the world, including Eastern European churches under the historic jurisdiction of the Bishop of Constantinople, often called Orthodox Churches, and Western European Churches under the jurisdiction of the Bishop of Rome, called Roman Catholic.

Orthodox Churches represent one of three major branches of Christianity, along with Roman Catholicism and Protestantism. There is, however, no single hierarchy that encompasses all of these churches. Instead, Orthodox denominations reflect national heritages (e.g., the Serbian Orthodox Church or the Bulgarian Orthodox Church) and the ethnic customs of their members. Most of the Orthodox Churches have formal relationships with one another, and they hold similar doctrines that are based on ancient Christian creeds. Orthodox services tend to be beautifully elaborate and ritualistic, including the movement of priests and laity. Church architecture is also often elaborate and filled with symbolic significance.

Since the 13th century, Christians in Western Europe have used "catholic" to describe churches, communities, and individuals that are loyal to the Bishop of Rome (the Pope). During most of the Middle Ages, the Roman Church dominated Western society. That domination ended with the Protestant Reformation of the 16th century, which divided European Christianity into Catholic and Protestant branches. Roman Catholicism, as a distinctive branch of Christianity, can be dated to the Council of Trent in 1545, which officially defined Roman Catholic doctrine for the first time and established the current structure of the Roman Catholic Church, which continues to be headed by the Pope.

The Roman Catholic Church is the single largest religious body in the United States and has approximately 62 million members. Three creeds form the core of all Roman Catholic belief and doctrine: the Apostles' Creed, the Nicene Creed, and the Athanasian Creed. Creeds are formal statements of belief that people say out loud. Here is the Apostles' Creed:

I believe in one God, the Father almighty, creator of heaven and earth.

I believe in Jesus Christ, his only Son, our Lord.

He was conceived by the power of the Holy Spirit and born of the Virgin Mary.

He suffered under Pontius Pilate, was crucified, died, and was buried.

He descended to the dead. On the third day he rose again.

He ascended into heaven, and is seated at the right hand of the Father.

He will come again to judge the living and the dead.

I believe in the Holy Spirit, the holy Catholic Church, the communion of saints,

the forgiveness of sins, the resurrection of the body, and the life everlasting.

As you can see in this example, creeds are statements about what Christian churches understand to be the "correct" beliefs about God, Jesus, and important doctrines. The Nicene and the Athanasian Creeds are similar to the Apostles' Creed but go into more theological detail about the nature of God, the divinity of Jesus Christ, and the relationships among God the Father, Jesus, and the Holy Spirit (the Trinity).

In addition to making these statements of belief, Roman Catholics also emphasize seven rituals or sacraments: baptism (in which babies are sprinkled with water as a sign that they are members of the community); confirmation (in which teens make a formal statement that they intend to belong to the Church); Eucharist (or Communion), which is a re-enactment of the Last Supper; reconciliation (in which individuals confess sins or bad things that they have done to a priest and receive forgiveness); matrimony (we'll assume you know that one); holy orders (in which men become priests); and anointing of the sick (with oil for healing).

Over time, seven major denominations have broken away from the Roman Catholic Church while retaining many of its beliefs, liturgical styles, and basic theology. These denominations are still classified as Catholic (though the pope may disagree!). For example, the American Catholic Church is a federation of independent churches founded in 1988 whose members are committed to basic Catholic beliefs and sacraments. They are, however, more liberal in their social and political beliefs than the Roman Catholic Church. There are also Old Catholic Churches founded by a combination of mostly Swiss, German, and Austrian Roman Catholic priests who refused to accept the dogma of papal infallibility. In the United States, Old Catholics are more conservative than Roman Catholics and have attracted conservative Roman Catholic priests who opposed some of the changes brought about in the 1960s by the Second Vatican Council (such as the elimination of Latin services). The Liberal Catholic Church was founded in 1916 as a reorganization of the Old Catholic Churches in Great Britain. It combines traditional Catholic forms of worship with freedom of individual conscience and thought. Okay, you get the idea. This diversity of traditions shows that just because someone says that he or she is Catholic doesn't mean that the person believes or worships in the same way as other Catholics. There's often more to it.

Mainline Protestantism

As we noted earlier, the Protestant Reformation broke the Roman Church's monopoly on Western Europe. A huge diversity of Protestant denominations grew out of this historical event. Mainline Protestant denominations include the United Methodist Church, the Disciples of Christ, the United Church of Christ, the Anglican or Episcopal Church, the Evangelical Lutheran Church of America, the American Baptist Church, and the Presbyterian Church,

U.S.A. Each of these denominations developed out of unique historical and regional circumstances. But despite their differences, they share much in common. Each is affiliated with the National Council of Churches in the United States, supports a moderate to liberal social agenda, and generally accommodates changes in the broader culture. We will highlight three denominations in particular to give you a sense of their differences: United Methodists, Churches of Christ, and Anglicans.

One of the largest mainline Protestant denominations, United Methodists started as a movement within the Church of England between 1738 and 1790 under the leadership of John and Charles Wesley. Methodist churches focus on simplicity of worship (unlike the more elaborate rituals of Anglicans), love of one's neighbor (especially the poor and disadvantaged), personal piety, and evangelism. Methodists believe in the Trinity and the sinfulness of humanity. They also believe that the Bible is the inerrant (without error) word of God and that humans need to be converted and to repent, need justification by faith, sanctification, and holiness, and can expect future rewards or punishments in heaven or hell. There are two formal rituals in United Methodist churches: baptism and the Lord's Supper (communion).

In America, United Methodists represent the core of what formerly was called the Methodist Episcopal Church. Historically, this denomination drew members from among small business owners, the middle class, and the skilled working class. Although they are more liberal in their social attitudes than other types of Methodists, United Methodists share most of the same doctrines and worship styles that other Methodists follow.

Sometimes referred to as Churches of Christ, Christian churches trace their roots to the early 1800s when a small group of Presbyterians and Methodists set out to restore what they saw as the structure and doctrine of first-century Christians. Followers believed that the Word of God was sufficient to form the basis for worship without the addition of any creeds or other human interpretations. This represents a significant break with Anglicans and United Methodists, since worship in both traditions includes reciting creeds and formal rituals like the Eucharist (the Lord's Supper or communion). Mainline Protestant denominations in the United States include two Christian churches, or Churches of Christ: the Disciples of Christ and the United Church of Christ (UCC). Like other mainline Protestant groups , Disciples and UCC churches hold liberal theological and social attitudes. Disciples of Christ churches are marked by informality, openness, individualism, and diversity. Membership is granted to anyone who professes to believe in Jesus Christ and who has been baptized by being dunked completely in water, in small pools or tanks of water often built right in the church itself. Some of the core beliefs are that Christ is the only head of the church, that the Bible is the basis for faith and practice, that Christian character is the measure of church membership, that individual members are free to interpret the Bible as they see fit , that "Christian" is an appropriate name for all followers of Christ, and that Christian unity is the goal of all believers. These churches are organized as democracies in which local congregations determine their own policies regarding programs and budgets, as well as the extent of their engagement with social issues such as war, racism, and gay rights.

Anglicans grew out of the Church of England, which severed its alliance with the Pope during the reign of Henry VIII in the 1500s. Britain was an empire that dominated the globe until the first half of the 20th century and exported its religious tradition to every one of its colonies. These branches were reconstituted into national churches after each colony gained independence. The Anglican Communion links these national bodies around the world. The largest Anglican Churches are in Uganda and Nigeria. In the United States, the Church of England became the Protestant Episcopal Church. An American version of the *Book of Common Prayer* is at the center of Anglican worship and belief. Anglicans, like Roman Catholics, use the Apostles' Creed and the Nicene Creed as the basis for their beliefs. For them, as for other mainline Protestants, baptism and Holy Eucharist are central to the ritual life of the church. Worship styles vary from "high church" traditions, which have more elaborate ritual and ceremony, to "low church" traditions, which have less ceremony. Anglicans in the American mainline Protestant tradition vary considerably in their social and theological attitudes, from very conservative to very liberal, though as a group American and Canadian Anglicans are more liberal than those elsewhere in the world.

Although the preceding short discussion doesn't do justice to these groups, we hope that you're beginning to see that within Christian denominations there are points of strong unity (like belief in Jesus Christ) and points of hot disagreement (such as the elaborateness of rituals or how much the Bible and tradition should determine the way that churches operate today).

Black Protestants

The Reverend Martin Luther King, Jr., observed that Sunday mornings were the most segregated hours of the week. We will explore this idea further in Chapter 11. For now, we focus on Black Protestantism as an independent category of denominations linked by theology and race. The core of Black Protestantism is a set of historic African American religious bodies founded in the days of slavery: the African Methodist Episcopal Church (AME), the African Methodist Episcopal Church of Zion (AMEZ), and the Christian Methodist Episcopal Church (CME). Also central, but more internally diverse, are Black Baptist churches, including those associated with the National Baptist Convention, U.S.A., and the National Baptist Convention of America. Numerous Churches of God in Christ and Pentecostal churches also fall into this category. At first glance, you might think that these denominations represent too much theological diversity to be all grouped together. Yet the common experience of racial inequities that has shaped African American people makes these denominations more similar to one another in their social and religious attitudes than they are to white mainline or evangelical denominations.

Several Black Protestant denominations broke away from largely white denominations, often in protest against segregation and discrimination. Black Methodists broke away from their white Methodist counterparts in the 18th century. Although they share doctrine and liturgical traditions with United Methodists, almost all members of this church today are African Americans. For example, the AME Church, one of the largest Methodist denominations, was founded in 1787 as a protest against racial discrimination and segregation. The AMEZ Church was founded as an independent Methodist denomination in 1769 by members of New York City's John Street Church in protest against racial segregation in the Methodist Episcopal Church. The Colored Methodist Episcopal Church was created in 1870 out of the General Conference of the Methodist Episcopal Church, South. The name was changed to the Christian Methodist Episcopal Church in 1956. Its doctrines remain parallel to its parent church.

Beliefs vary widely among African-American Christians. For example, members of the Church of God and Saints in Christ focus on the Old Testament doctrines. In the late

19th century, Williams Saunders Crowdy, a son of former slaves, had a vision calling him to form a church whose aim was to live according to a literal understanding of the Old Testament law. Sometimes called Christian Israelites, members of this church have no connection to historic Judaism but celebrate Jewish holy and feast days as prescribed by the Bible. They also believe in the Seven Keys of doctrine: repentance, baptism, consumption of unleavened bread and water in the Lord's Supper, foot washing (the ritual washing of members' feet as Jesus did at the Last Supper, commanding them to do the same to each other as the symbol of being a servant to all), obedience to the Bible (especially the Ten Commandments), the holy kiss (following Saint Paul's encouragement to "greet one another with a holy kiss"—Romans 16:16), and the Lord's Prayer. Today this denomination has 40,000 members in 200 congregations.

Evangelical Protestants

Evangelical denominations include the Assemblies of God, Holiness Churches, Missouri Synod Lutheran Churches, Churches of the Nazarene, Southern Baptists, Jehovah's Witnesses, Full Gospel, Apostolic Churches, Churches of God, and many more. Many of these churches have their roots in religious revivals of the late 19th and early 20th centuries. Historically, these denominations have resisted what they perceive to be the more liberal theology and social agendas of mainline Protestant churches. Most Evangelical groups see their standards of moral behavior as absolute, applicable to all people, and unchanging. A belief in an imminent end of the world and the return of Christ also are common among Evangelicals. Additionally, these churches emphasize the importance of having a "born-again" conversion experience. Not all churches in this category share all of these beliefs or emphasize them equally. For analytical purposes, sociologists divide the broad category of Evangelical Christians into three subgroups: Fundamentalists, Pentecostals, and Evangelicals. It is important to understand that while these groups share a common theological approach in that they hold literal views of the Bible, they vary in what this view implies for their religious practices or experiences.

Christian fundamentalism, for example, emerged as a counterforce to secularizing trends, including modernity, science, and academic scholarship. It was founded by Dwight L. Moody in the 19th century. Fundamentalist Christians establish firm boundaries between themselves and the broader culture. In some traditions, women do not cut their hair, based on St. Paul's New Testament recommendation. Others forbid members from going to the movies, wearing make-up, or listening to rock music. One example of a Christian fundamentalist church, the Apostolic Faith Church, was founded in Portland, Oregon, in 1907 by Reverend Florence L. Crawford to restore the doctrines and style of life taught by Christ and early church apostles. Christian fundamentalist churches teach the doctrines of biblical inerrancy and stress justification by faith, entire sanctification, and the baptism of the Holy Spirit as on the Day of Pentecost. Membership requires being born again and believing in the doctrines of the group. Dancing, movies, smoking, drinking, using cosmetics, gambling, and participating in other forms of popular entertainment often are banned, as is marriage to people who are not members of these churches. Christian fundamentalism is one type of relationship between religion and broader culture, a relationship that we will explore in more depth in Chapter 6.

Pentecostal groups emerged in the early 20th century out of the larger Holiness movement in American Christianity. *Pentecostal* refers to the first Pentecost, the 50 days after Christ's resurrection, when the Holy Spirit was said to have come upon the early Christians, allowing them to speak unfamiliar languages. Pentecostalism's founders preached that the Gifts of the Spirits (e.g., speaking in tongues, healing the sick, and prophecy) were available to modern Christians. Exhibiting these gifts is evidence of being "filled with the Spirit," an important aspect or even requirement of salvation and inclusion in the church community. Most Pentecostal denominations are theologically and socially conservative. They emphasize belief in the Trinity (with special emphasis on the role of the Holy Spirit), the literal and infallible interpretation of the Bible, belief in Jesus Christ as a necessary condition for salvation, the personal return of Jesus to earth, and the responsibility of believers to spread the teachings of Christ around the world. Two sacraments are commonly practiced: adult baptism (by full immersion in water) and the Lord's Supper (communion). In some Pentecostal Churches, faith healing (in which prayers and other rituals are believed to heal illnesses) is also practiced and is considered a sacrament. The Church of God in Cleveland, Tennessee, founded in 1886, is one of America's oldest Pentecostal churches. Many Pentecostal congregations separate themselves from the broader culture, though that is changing.

As a group, Evangelicals increasingly engage the outside culture in everything from their use of media to their musical styles to their dress. They include Southern Baptists and the Christian Church, also called Churches of God. The name Southern Baptist reflects the divide among Baptists that resulted from slavery and the Civil War. Although they are Biblical literalists, Southern Baptists have historically believed in the autonomy of the individual believer when it comes to reading and interpreting the Bible. Sermons are central features of their services, as is time for individuals to repent for their sins, "receive Jesus," or rededicate themselves to God. While some Southern Baptists use traditional hymns, others are increasingly adopting contemporary musical styles, performed with "praise bands," groups of musicians that include drums, guitars, keyboards, and percussion. A relatively new Evangelical denomination, the Vineyard Churches International, grew out of the Vineyard movement in California in the 1970s. It adopted charismatic traditions in the 1980s, organized as a body in 1983, and is now headquartered in Texas. Like the Southern Baptists and other evangelicals, Vineyard Churches embrace evangelical and charismatic or Pentecostal theology, including belief in the infallibility of the Bible, human sin, salvation, and the open expressions of spiritual gifts such as speaking in tongues and divine healing. In contrast with old-school evangelicals, however, they make effective use of Christian rock music and informal worship styles.

Other Christian Denominations

Though they are clearly branches of Christianity, many denominations do not fit neatly into these broad categories. Consider Christian Scientists, Jehovah's Witnesses, the Latter-day Saints (Mormons), Unitarian Universalists, and Pietist denominations such as the Society of Friends (Quakers). You may wonder: "What do any of these groups have in common with each other?" The answer is, "Not much, except that they are all Christians!" These denominations do not share any of the core characteristics associated with Evangelical churches and, unlike mainline Protestants, they do not belong to the National Council of Churches.

Mary Baker Eddy founded the Christian Science Church in 1879 with the goal of recovering the primitive Christianity of the early church and its lost practice of healing.

Members seek spiritual truth through participation in Christian healing and by reading church publications and Eddy's own writings.

Founded in the 1870s, Jehovah's Witnesses believe in one almighty God, Jehovah, and believe that Jesus Christ was the first of God's creations. They believe that Christ's sacrificial death opened the chance for humans to have eternal life and that following the destruction of wickedness, Christ and the righteous will rule the earth in a global paradise. During the 1930s and 1940s, Jehovah's Witnesses fought many court battles over freedoms of speech, press, assembly, and worship. There are now almost 6 million Jehovah's Witnesses worldwide.

Joseph Smith organized the Church of Jesus Christ of Latter-day Saints, also known as the Mormon Church, in 1830. Members believe that Smith was divinely directed to restore the gospel to the earth. They recognize both the Bible and the Book of Mormon as scripture. Although Mormons resemble some conservative Protestant denominations, they differ by holding the key beliefs that both God the Father and Jesus have bodies of flesh and bone; that people will be punished for their own sins and not for original sin; and that all humans, dead or alive, can be saved. Mormons practice baptism by immersion, lay hands on people to help them receive the Holy Ghost, and participate in the Lord's Supper. They believe in the gift of speaking in tongues and in visions, prophecy, and healing. Although there are other types of Mormons that have broken away over the years, the Latter-day Saints headquarters in Salt Lake City represents the majority of Mormons worldwide.

Pietist denominations have their roots in a 17th-century German revival movement to continue Martin Luther's reformation. They focus on the moral and spiritual life of believers. Pietism's lead theologian, Jakob Philip Spencer, encouraged pastors to build a "religion of the heart" by having small groups of Christians meet for study, prayer, and mutual encouragement. Pietism influenced the development of the early Methodist movement in England and spurred the First Great Awakening in 1740s America. Three main branches of Pietism continue today in the Brethren, Friends, and Mennonite Churches.

Brethren view the church as a community of brothers and sisters who come together to build their own inner spiritual life, to pray, and to study Scripture. They rely on the Holy Spirit to work inside each believer to bind that person to the community. They strive to live simple lives and initially tried to put even the most minute details of early Christian life into practice, including dressing in very plain clothes and refusing to take oaths or engage in lawsuits. The Society of Friends, founded in England by George Fox in the 1650s, affirms that every person possesses an Inner Light of spiritual endowment placed there by God. As a result, they reject the authority of clergy, liturgy, and sacraments; they are exceptionally service minded; and they are outspoken in support of universal equality. Though they value the Bible, they believe that truth is unfolding and continuing. Founded in Central Europe in the 1520s, Mennonites were radical Protestants who rejected both Luther's and Calvin's reformation movements in favor of modeling their lives on Christ's Sermon on the Mount. They emphasize spiritual community and separation from secular society. You may know Mennonites, as well as Friends and Brethren, for their role in antiwar protests and their refusal to join the armed forces.

In 1961, Unitarian and Universalist churches in the United States and Canada merged to create Unitarian Universalism. This group believes in one God but is distinguished from almost all other Christian traditions by not believing that Jesus was divine or that he was the unique son of God in human form. The group values flexibility, freedom of conscience, and local autonomy. They believe that all people will be saved regardless of whether they believe in God.

As you can see, Christians hold very diverse beliefs and practices. Our overview only begins to tell the story. Like all religions, Christianity reflects the broader culture. Christianity, thus, looks very different in Africa than it does in South Asia or Central America, and it demonstrates differences that go beyond language. In many places, Christianity has evolved to include older local beliefs and rituals in ways that would be unrecognizable to Christians from other parts of the world. For example, as described by Philip Jenkins in *The Next Christendom,* many new Christian groups in Africa have retained traditional African religious practices such as animal sacrifice and ancestor worship. The incorporation of traditional practices is not limited to African Christianity. Jenkins (2002, 121) also quotes Taiwanese Catholic Bishop Chen Shih-kwang: "We do mass, then we venerate the ancestors." This isn't what most North American Christians would think of as "typical" Christianity! As we will see later, understanding how new religious beliefs and practices are shaped is key to understanding the role of religion in the contemporary world. But are these same forces shaping the beliefs and practices of other religions around the world? You bet! Let's turn our attention to the other largest religious groups in our world.

ISLAM

Islam is the world's second-largest religion. Prior to the events of September 11, 2001, and the ongoing conflicts in the Middle East—especially in Iraq and Iran—most non-Muslims in North American and Europe knew little about Islam. There are five key beliefs and five pillars of ritual behavior in Islam. Muslims believe that there is one God; that there are angels; that there have been many prophets in addition to Mohammed but only one message; that there will be a final judgment; and, finally, that it is possible to know God and God's will in this life (Mead and Hill 2001). Required rituals include the *Shahada,* stating that there is no God but Allah and that Mohammed is his prophet; *Salat,* praying five times a day while facing Mecca; *Zakat,* giving alms; *Siyam,* observing the one-month Feast of Ramadan, which includes daily fasting; and *Hajj,* making a pilgrimage to Mecca at least once in one's lifetime. The Qu'ran is the Muslim scripture and, like the Christian Bible, contains the direct revelation of God (Allah), providing Muslims with moral direction for their beliefs and daily life. In addition, religious laws and observances, codified in *Sharia,* shape daily life. *Imams,* who are heads of local mosques, interpret *Sharia* law and the teachings of the Qu'ran to the faithful.

As in the case of other religions, the form of Islam dictates specific beliefs and practices. There are four major forms: Shi'ism, Sunnism, Sufism, and the Nation of Islam.

The divide between Shi'a and Sunni Muslims goes back to the death of the Prophet Mohammed. One group of his followers (Sunni Muslims) believed that Mohammed wanted a close friend and companion, Abu Bakar, to be his successor because the Prophet appointed him to lead prayers at his bedside just before he died. Another group (Shi'a Muslims) thought that the Prophet wanted his son-in-law Ali to be his successor because on his way back from Hajj, he took Ali's hand and told those around him that if they wished to follow the Prophet, they should also follow Ali. Over the centuries, these two branches of Islam have sometimes conflicted.

Sufism is less a separate branch of Islam than a theological and worship tradition within Islam. Sufism teaches that God is everywhere and in everything. Sufism generally puts less emphasis on living according to strict laws and more on the subjective feeling of God's love. Sufis aim to experience divine joy all the time and use dancing as a means to help induce religious experience in worship.

The Nation of Islam is a uniquely North American expression of Muslim religion, rooted in African American communities, that was founded by Marcus Garvey and other leaders of the African Pride Movement in the early 20th century. For African Americans, the Nation of Islam provides a religious tradition that is closer to their African roots and less laden with the ideological baggage that ties Christianity to the history of slavery and segregation. While some within the Nation of Islam, including Louis Farrakan's followers, believe in Black nationalism, Warith Deen Mohammed took over the organization in 1975 and has brought it closer to traditional Islamic belief and practice. American domestic and foreign policies since 9/11 have made it vital that we understand Muslim beliefs and practices. More than ever before, the United States is now directly engaged with a variety of Islamic nations and groups. Some have developed intense hatred of the United States and its military. Others try to overcome stereotypes that equate all Muslim believers with suicide bombers in Iraq and Afghanistan. Once again, we see how religious beliefs can differ radically across traditions and groups, even within the same religion.

HINDUISM

Hindu belief and practice originated in India around 1500 B.C.E. There is no single hierarchy or leader to define legitimate or appropriate beliefs and rituals. As a result, Hinduism adapts to local contexts and is a diverse faith tradition that closely reflects the region and traditions of the communities that practice it. Although Christians often assume that Hindus worship many gods and goddesses, they are actually all forms of one God, called Brahman, the original spirit and creative force of the universe. God is reflected in as many as 33 million forms and incarnations, each of which is best understood as reflecting a particular attribute of God (Kurtz 1995, 30). Behind them all is a divine unity.

Hindus see the One reflected in a trinity of Gods: Brahma, the creator of the universe; Vishnu, its maintainer; and Shiva, the destroyer who brings new life. Most Hindus worship Vishnu or Shiva though in recent years other deities like Devi, the Mother Goddess, who is sometimes linked with Parvati, the wife of Shiva, have become popular. The worship of Krishna, either as a personification of Vishnu or as the supreme being in his own right, is also widespread among Hindus worldwide. Each manifestation of God has highly specialized functions and powers. Faithful Hindus venerate the gods and goddesses who can meet their present needs. So, for example, Ganesha, an elephant-headed god, helps believers to overcome obstacles and aids people in times of trouble. Lakshmi, the consort of Vishnu, brings wealth and purity.

Hindu sacred texts include the Vedas, but their role is different from that of the Bible for Christians or the Qur'an for Muslims. Although the Vedas provide a guide for worship and rituals and include both hymns to sing and the philosophical teaching of Hinduism, most ordinary Hindus do not follow the Vedas in their worship. Instead, the narrative poem *Bhagavad Gita* is increasingly viewed as scripture by contemporary Hindus. The *Bhagavad Gita* teaches that there are three means to salvation for all: pursuing knowledge, doing work appropriate to your caste, and showing devotion to God (BBC 2004).

Dharma is a core Hindu belief that captures the idea of duty and moral righteousness in behavior. It covers "the pursuit of all legitimate worldly ends," whether they are financial, political, social, or even sexual (Madan 2006, 18). Dharma is the goal of moral living. For Hindus, responsibilities in life depend on who one is, most importantly the social caste or varna into which one is born. The *Bhagavad Gita* reduces karma to each caste's assigned duties. Brahmans have a duty to study and teach, Kshatriyas to rule and protect, and Vaishyas to pursue trades, earn and lend money, and engage in farming and agriculture. The lowest varna, Shudras, have a duty to serve the other castes. Duties are strictly divided: Appropriate or required actions for one caste are forbidden to others, and those who deviate from their duties are believed to suffer.

Karma are the actions that one takes to achieve dharma. Karma includes the idea that all of our actions have consequences for our future reincarnations in the cycles of birth, death, and rebirth (samsara). That cycle eventually ends when one's soul is freed from this cycle (moksha) to join with the spirit of the universe. Right actions result in rewards, and wrong actions in punishments, if not in this life then in the next.

Hinduism is less a collective practice than an individual one and is based more in domestic than public life. Madan (2006) notes that the head of the family conveys Hindu religious values through life cycle rituals, ritual feeding of ancestors, domestic worship of related gods and goddesses, and pilgrimages. Hindu individuals chant the names of their favorite gods and goddesses; offer them food, incense, and flowers; and perform other acts of devotion, such as pilgrimages to a deity's shrine.

BUDDHISM

Buddhism originated after the sixth century B.C.E. It emerged from followers of Siddhartha Gautama, the Buddha or Enlightened One, and his teachings. After many years of living a life of wealth and privilege, protected from pain and suffering, Siddhartha set out to discover the realities of material existence. He began by rejecting his past life of wealth to follow a monastic path of self-denial. Eventually, he also rejected this lifestyle and adopted the Middle Path, living a life of neither wealth nor poverty. He devoted himself to meditation and one day achieved a state of enlightenment while sitting under the Bodhi tree (i.e., the "tree of awakening"). Over time, two main traditions arose within Buddhism: Theravada and Mahayana. Other forms emerged as Buddhism spread to different Asian countries including Tibet, China, Japan, and Korea.

Theravada Buddhism is an elite form of Buddhism that is linked to the specialized life and religious devotions of monks who live together in communities called *sanghas*. In this tradition, there is no worship of a deity. Spiritual beings exist, but they are of limited significance. What matters most is meditation on the Buddha's teaching and making one's own way toward enlightenment without the help of gods or goddesses. Like other forms of Buddhism, Theravada Buddhism emphasizes the illusory character of the material world. Detachment through meditation is required to achieve enlightenment. So strong is the mandate to be detached from the material world that monks may not even touch money. They rely entirely on outside support and patronage for their food, drink, and clothing and for the upkeep of their monasteries.

Mahayana Buddhism embodies a more complex understanding of the relationship between the spiritual and material worlds. As it spread, Mahayana Buddhism was more open to local traditions and customs, and it has developed into more of a lay-oriented tradition than a monastic one. Anyone, not just monks, can achieve enlightenment and liberation from suffering (BBC 2002). Worship of local gods and goddesses characterizes this tradition, and ritual practices include burning incense, offering food and flowers, and chanting.

Both branches of Buddhism embrace four Noble Truths and an eightfold path to enlightenment. These tenets make up the Dharma, or teaching, that all Buddhists must follow. Ideas that are central to the four Truths include the beliefs that life is suffering (Dukkha), that desire or craving is the source of all suffering (Trsna), that detachment from desire is possible (Nirvana), and that the Eightfold Path is the way to achieve enlightenment. The Eightfold Path requires those seeking enlightenment to live with Right Knowledge, Right Aspirations, Right Speech, Right Behavior, Right Livelihood, Right Effort, Right Mindfulness, and Right Absorption. Adherents will escape the endless cycle of birth, death, and rebirth if they faithfully try to live according to these principles. Like Hindus, Buddhists believe that all of our actions have consequences (karma) that shape, positively or negatively, the conditions we will experience in our future lives.

Buddhist ritual is as varied as the locales to which it has spread. Venerating the Buddha, not as God but as the example of one who has achieved enlightenment, is central to worship practices. Buddhists can worship at home, as it is not essential to go to a temple to worship with others. At home, Buddhists often set aside a room or a part of a room as a shrine that includes a statue of Buddha, candles, and an incense burner. Worship in Mahayana tradition takes the form of devotion to Buddha and to Bodhisattvas, enlightened beings who have delayed entering paradise so that they may help others attain enlightenment. It is common in this tradition to see worshippers seated on the floor facing an image of Buddha and chanting. As in the case of all religions, there are also special festivals during which members practice unique forms of worship and devotion. One such Buddhist festival is Wesak, celebrated on the full moon in May. It celebrates the Buddha's birthday and, for some Buddhists, marks both his birth and death. As a part of this festival, statues of the Buddha are ceremonially washed as a symbolic reminder for worshippers to purify their minds from greed, hatred, and ignorance (BBC 2002).

JUDAISM

Although Jews represent less than one percent of the world's religious adherents, Judaism is among the world's oldest religions. Judaism gave birth to Christianity, but it takes a very different approach in its beliefs and practices. Apart from a belief in the oneness of God, there is no unifying creed among Jews. Instead, Judaism emphasizes the observance of rituals and ethical practices. Contemporary Judaism is based on the Torah, but generally does not follow all the ritual practices, including animal sacrifice, that it mandates. Over time, as it became more difficult to observe the Torah's commandments for daily living, Jews placed more emphasis on the unfolding interpretations of these commandments, taking into account how the times and circumstances had changed from the situations that early Jews faced. Around 600 C.E., the Talmud was codified, providing a basis for how to interpret the Torah. The Talmud includes a list of 613 commandments that Jews must follow in daily life and a process for making sense of faithful religious practice in a constantly changing contemporary world (Mead and Hill 2001).

There are two general types of Jewish rituals: seasonal liturgies that follow a lunar calendar and individual liturgies that correspond to key moments in the lives of individuals. The Jewish liturgical year begins in September with the High Holy Days of *Rosh Hashanah* and *Yom Kippur. Rosh Hashanah,* the Jewish New Year, is celebrated with great joy. For the 10 days that follow it, however, Jews reflect on their lives, repent of their sins and shortcomings, and try to make restitution for wrongs that they have done in preparation for *Yom Kippur,* the Day of Atonement. Other feasts follow, commemorating key moments in Jewish history. *Succoth* reminds Jews of the 40 years that the Israelites wandered in the desert following their release from slavery in Egypt. *Hanukah* celebrates the restoration and purification of the Temple in Jerusalem during the revolt of the Jews against the Greeks. *Passover* recalls the period of slavery itself and the manner by which God freed the Jews from Egyptian bondage. *Shabuoth* commemorates the occasion when Moses received the Torah. Rituals related to the lives of individuals and families are observed weekly in Sabbath observances and more occasionally in rites of passage, such as the circumcision of male babies on the eighth day after birth and Bar Mitzvah and Bat Mitzvah ceremonies to initiate young men and women into adulthood.

The beliefs and rituals of Jews vary depending on the branch of Judaism. Hasidic and Orthodox Jews are the most conservative: Both groups take a literal reading of the Torah and Talmud, believing that their teachings are absolute and not open to reinterpretation. Conservative Judaism follows the rules of the Torah and Talmud but allows for reinterpretation of ancient Jewish teaching in light of contemporary experience. Reform Judaism holds that the rules in the Torah related to social justice and peace are more important than the observance of rituals and dietary laws. Reconstructionist Judaism is the newest branch of Judaism. Reconstructionists hold to the importance of Jewish heritage while seeking new ways to experience the sacred in the modern world. Like the denominational differences within Christianity, different organizational branches of Judaism follow different beliefs about what is authentic or true.

We have just taken an abbreviated tour of the world's religions. We have neglected important traditions, including Baha'i, traditional Chinese religions rooted in Confucianism, Shintoism, Sihkism, Jainism, Contemporary Paganism, Wicca, and thousands of indigenous religious traditions including those of Native Americans, African tribes, and many others. Nonetheless, an important lesson emerges: Religious beliefs are reflected in practices, and vice versa, and beliefs and practices often motivate our actions both within and outside our faith communities.

UNDERSTANDING CONTEMPORARY RELIGIOUS RITUAL PRACTICES

Religious beliefs are never the whole story of any faith tradition. For most of the world's religious people, religion is less a matter of what you *believe* intellectually and more what you *do*—your everyday behaviors and ritual practices—and also what you *experience*—the subjective feelings, emotions, and states of being that result from these behaviors. So, for example, if we try to determine what makes a "good" or "faithful" Jew, we would observe that a person's commitment is understood through his or her faithful participation in Sabbath services, celebration of Seder meals during Passover, observation of other holy days like Rosh Hashanah and Yom Kippur, hospitable and charitable behavior toward neighbors, and study of the Torah. What a Jew *believes* about the theology underlying any or all of these ritual acts is secondary to doing them.

As we have observed again and again, religious beliefs are tied to and embodied in what believers actually *do,* the rituals that they perform as part of their devotion. We have already discussed some rituals and observances across the world's religions. Rituals have fascinated sociologists because they are the visible manifestations of a religious tradition. It is not always possible to clearly observe changes in beliefs. However, since rituals always involve individual or collective action, we can observe how they evolve and adapt to new circumstances or contexts. By analyzing what people do and how they do it, we come to see how religious rituals strengthen and reaffirm group beliefs and unite the group that participates in them. Even when rituals are performed by an individual in the privacy of that person's own home, they tie the believer to the Sacred and by extension to all those others who share in the same beliefs. We can also observe how the changing needs of members can alter how these rituals are performed, either in their content or their styles.

Rituals vary by tradition. Ritual processions, sacraments, lighting candles, burning incense, and eating certain kinds of food in particular ways are common elements in many religious traditions. Sometimes rituals focus more on *how* things are done than on *what* is done. Spontaneous expressions can be a ritual act, as can shouting. Even prayers can be ritually formulaic. Growing up in an evangelical church, one of the authors (Mirola) learned to disparage the idea of reciting prayers out of a book as many congregations do. Church members were taught to pray spontaneously, using whatever words they wished, so he would pray: "Lord, I just want to thank you . . . I just praise you . . . I just want to ask . . ." Notice anything? The words "I just . . . " are commonly used. It may sound funny, but listen closely to prayers offered in many of today's nondenominational and evangelical churches, be they large megachurches or small congregations of born-again Christians. You will hear this prayer structure coming from those who are most committed to spontaneity. Looking back, it is clear how ritualized such prayers were, no matter what the motivation was behind them. In examining the variety of religious rituals, it is imperative to look past the grand ceremonies that take place in congregations to see all the small and new forms that ritual behavior might take. Furthermore, we must keep in mind that it is never the content of an action that makes a ritual religious; rather, it is the meaning that people attach to doing something in a particular way.

Worship Styles to Meet Every Need

Religious groups around the world take diverse approaches to worship. Roman Catholic and Orthodox Christians have maintained their commitment to historic liturgies that emphasize formal rituals and sacred mysteries. Many Protestant Christians embrace relative simplicity in worship and focus on preaching rather than on formal rituals like Holy Communion. One might recognize a mainline Protestant congregation in North America by its staid formality and intellectualism and an evangelical one by its unabashed emotional joy and congregational participation. Even in Jewish traditions, different forms of worship characterize Hasidic, Orthodox, Conservative, Reform, and Reconstructionist congregations. Orthodox Jews use only Hebrew in rituals, while Reform Jews use both English and Hebrew. Also, Orthodox men worship separately from women and children, separated by a screen. Among Reform Jews and Reconstructionists, men, women, and children all sit together. Over time, the defining features of worship are transformed in response to changing culture in some groups while other groups maintain older forms of ritual practices.

To transform or maintain tradition can be a source of intense conflict for some religious groups. In some cases, primarily in industrial countries, religious groups have entered into what we might euphemistically call *worship wars*. These disputes over the forms and content of rituals and religious services pit traditionalists against modernists.

Traditionalists prefer the music, styles, and structure of their historic religious traditions, whereas modernists argue that worship styles ought to keep up with the times and follow trends in the larger society. When you think about it, there have always been disagreements over worship styles. During the English Reformation in the mid-1500s, many Christians wanted to hold on to Christian traditions that were common at this time, such as elaborate processions and rituals, beautiful images of saints, the use of candles, and the use of Latin as the main language for services. Extreme Protestant reformers didn't want anything to do with such theatrical nonsense. They wanted services to be simple and to be based only on elements found in the Bible, which was now printed in English. They destroyed images, melted candles, and ripped up the ritual robes. In between these extremes were people who wanted to keep some traditions but also were happy to embrace some change. Needless to say, those worship wars resulted in people on all sides being imprisoned or burned at the stake. And note that the fights weren't really over the big belief questions, like those dealing with God or salvation. People fought over keeping or getting rid of candles. Now all this may seem silly to you. But, the forms that worship takes dictate the ways that people encounter the sacred. To suggest changing these forms is to challenge the sacred itself.

As we'll see in the next chapter, change in worship continues to occur, but so do the worship wars. Let's look at some ways in which contemporary groups have tried to redefine what authentic and relevant worship looks like.

Christian churches are maintaining and even rediscovering traditions in a wide variety of ways. Many mainline Protestant congregations are reviving historic rituals and liturgies. In doing so, these churches have begun to look and sound increasingly similar to one another, whether they are Presbyterians, Methodists, or Lutherans. For instance, these denominations have adopted a common *lectionary,* or set of Biblical readings used during services. Believers practice the ritual of Holy Communion or Eucharist during Sunday morning services more frequently than in the past. And, most interesting of all, these churches have added other ritual activities throughout the church year that once were used only in Roman Catholic or Orthodox religious practices. The return of rituals such as saying prayers at the Stations of the Cross and consciously observing Ash Wednesday, Lent (the 40 days of abstinence before Easter), and Advent (the four weeks before Christmas) point to a renewed interest in historic Christian ritual and liturgy among many mainline congregations.

Monastic traditions also are being rediscovered by mainline Protestants across the nation. Musically, religious chant has become popular again. During the 1990s, the Benedictine monks of Santo Domingo de Silos reached the top of the pop music charts with their CD *Chant,* and a nonreligious music group, Enigma, uses chant and synthesized music to create a popular sound that is heard in dance clubs from New York to L.A. Musical ensembles specializing in medieval church music, like Chanticleer and Anonymous 4, are very popular recording artists among mainline Protestant and Roman Catholic audiences alike.

Taizé services have been gaining in popularity as well. Taizé is an ecumenical community of around a hundred brothers from different Christian traditions located in a small village in eastern France. Tens of thousands of people, mainly between the ages of 17 and 30, come each year to spend time at the community, reflecting on their faith. Using prayer and music from the Taizé community, Catholic and Protestant congregations around the country have begun to add Taizé services of singing and silent meditation to their traditional worship services.

Labyrinth walking is another medieval tradition that has garnered interest among Christians. In 1991, Dr. Lauren Artress, canon for special ministries at Grace Cathedral (Episcopal) in San Francisco, created a model of the 13th-century labyrinth in Chartres Cathedral in France. Within the Christian mystical tradition, walking the labyrinth is a form of meditation. As you walk the labyrinth, you empty your mind while you meditate and pray. Labyrinth walking empowers people to find and do the things to which they feel called or drawn.

In other churches, modern elements predominate. Contemporary worship styles have proliferated in many Christian congregations and local congregations have developed a variety of alternative services. In the next chapter, we will explore some of these in depth. Some congregations offer services at times other than Sunday mornings to better fit the flow of life and work of would-be participants. Music is a prime target for stylistic makeovers. Some congregations have moved away from traditional hymns and adopted songs with more upbeat sounds that invite worshipers to sing, clap, and even dance. Words to songs are projected on a wall or screen and many congregations have a full band, complete with drums, guitars, and keyboards to play along. Preaching has also gotten a makeover. Ministers walk around more and use a more conversational style when they talk to their congregations. Many of these trends have been around since the 1960s. What is new is their adoption for the express purpose of attracting new members, especially young ones.

Prominent Protestant congregations in Indianapolis, Indiana—two mainline Protestant and one Evangelical—illustrate these trends. Radio advertisements for "Second at Six" invite people who are suspicious of traditional church services to explore their spirituality in an informal context at Second Presbyterian Church. Having services on Sunday evening is a way for the church to attract college students and young adults who are prone to sleeping in or working on Sunday mornings. Meanwhile, Meridian Heights Presbyterian Church hosts two services on Sunday morning, one with traditional worship styles and one with contemporary music called Alive Time. Advertisements for these services show a mother and father who are formally dressed, while their kids wear hip clothes and sunglasses. The message is clear: Meridian Heights offers something for everyone. Trader's Point Christian Church has a separate ministry for young adults called Common Ground, which began in 1995 and is held in a former Baptist Church building far from the main church. The services held for Common Ground participants regularly draw more than 300 college-aged and twenty-something people. There is little overlap with members who attend the regular Trader's Point Sunday services. At Common Ground services, the lights are dim, the music is loud, and the preaching is minimal. In this congregation, the minister is more like a storyteller than a traditional preacher.

Just as congregations vary in their rituals, so do individuals. Take, for example, the now famous phenomenon of Sheilaism that was uncovered by Robert Bellah (1985, 221) and his colleagues in their classic study *Habits of the Heart*. Sheila Larson was a nurse whom Bellah interviewed as a part of his study of community life in America. Here are her words:

"I believe in God. I'm not a religious fanatic. I can't remember the last time I went to church. My faith has carried me a long way. It's Sheilaism. Just my own little voice . . . It's just try to love yourself and be gentle with yourself. You know, I guess, take care of each other. I think He would want us to take care of each other."

Bellah and his colleagues noted that Sheila had summed up the totality of her religious belief and practice in a few simple sentences. Sheila's example is often used to illustrate how individualized religion has become, to the point that each believer practices private rituals that make sense to him or her, with no need for a religious community. Many believers would not see Sheilaism as a legitimate expression of religion, much less Christianity. But it points to social forces that give rise to new ways of experiencing one's religion.

Are these trends—worship wars, Sheilaism—meaningful outside contemporary North American Christianity? In recent years, some people have worried that traditional ritual is in permanent decline. Some think that formal ritual is dying not only in North America and Europe but also in the developing world as globalization moves other societies forward. But ritual is an essential part of religion, a way to express belief and build community. Its forms may change over time, but change is not the same as the ritual dying. For example, many new Christian groups in the developing world practice unique mixes of indigenous religious rituals and mainstream Christian rituals, with 21st-century styles and even content. Let's look at two examples from Africa and the Philippines.

> In 2000, the Roman Catholic archbishop of Bloemfontein, South Africa, not only suggested that Christians might be permitted to honor their ancestors through blood libations, but that ritual sacrifice of sheep or cows might be incorporated into the Mass. . . . Critics reacted with horror, as much because the suggestion violated animal rights as on grounds of heresy . . . In keeping with the concept of consecration, the Congolese church uses a profession rite in which a drop of the candidate's blood is placed on the altar cloth. Such practices make great sense in African terms, and it would be easy to justify the practice with an arsenal of biblical texts. (Jenkins 2002, 131)

> El Shaddai was founded in 1984 by Brother Mike Velarde, who looks and behaves like a U.S. mega-star televangelist. The group's meetings, hundreds of thousands strong, look like nothing so much as a 1960s rock festival . . . El Shaddai followers raise their passports to be blessed at services, to ensure they will get the visas they need to work overseas. Many open umbrellas and turn them upside down as a symbolic way of catching the rich material blessings they expect to receive from on high. (Jenkins 2002, 67)

As you think about these examples, do you see them as backward-looking, superstitious religious practices? Or are they innovative ways for contemporary religious believers to be in touch with the sacred in ways that link their pasts to the present and, sometimes, to the future?

And what about ritual innovation in non-Christian contexts? Most of the world's religious people practice rituals that have been handed down for centuries or even millennia. Even these religions, however, have adapted their rituals to the new contexts in which they found themselves.

For example, when Buddhism reached Japan, a 13th-century monk named Nichiren Daishonin sought to reform Buddhist practice by focusing on the Lotus Sutra as the supreme, authoritative Scripture. Nichiren encouraged followers to read this Sutra daily, but he emphasized that they should interpret it in light of the present-day situation. He believed that classical Buddhist teaching no longer led to enlightenment but was responsible for all that was wrong in the world. While Nichiren Buddhists chant and study like other Buddhists, they also keep a small scroll, or Gohonzon, a replica of the original scroll of Nichiren, on a home altar that they face during their daily chanting.

Likewise, Hinduism has adapted its forms of worship and devotion to the local regions where it spread. And in Islam, Sunni Muslims pray five times a day, while Shi'a Muslims can combine their prayers and pray only three times a day.

As religious beliefs and ritual practices move across the world and encounter different cultural contexts and the constraints of living in new times and places, we can expect them to evolve just as they have done since the first humans expressed their reliance on the natural world through religious rituals for hunting, planting, childbirth, death, and sickness.

THE ROLE OF BELIEFS AND RITUAL PRACTICES

Part of our job as sociologists is to describe the broad roles that religious beliefs and practices play in shaping the dynamics of the groups that claim them and the dynamics of the communities and societies in which they are embedded. The concept of group is key; as students of religion, you can't fully understand the diversity of religious beliefs, practices, and experiences through the study of individuals. As Durkheim argued a century ago, religion is a social product created by the group that has consequences for the world, good as well as bad. As we will discuss further in Chapter 4, religion is an important means for maintaining social stability in societies around the world, but it can also be the basis for conflict and change. Because beliefs and practices are dynamic, we can't predict how they will continue to be transformed in the face of the forces of globalization, another discussion that we will return to later in the book.

Remember too that the meaning of beliefs and ritual practices is flexible and can be fought over by different groups of believers. What makes sense to one group is dismissed as superstition by another. As we will see in the next chapter, authentic beliefs and ritual practices are changing all the time. We need to expect these changes and be ready to investigate the effects of change on religious groups themselves and their communities. There's always something new to discover.

SUGGESTED READING

Bellah, Robert, Richard Madsen, William M. Sullivan, Ann Swidler, and Steven M. Tipton. 1985. *Habits of the Heart: Individualism and Commitment in American Life*. New York: Harper and Row, Publishers.

Jenkins, Philip. 2002. *The Next Christendom: The Coming of Global Christianity*. New York: Oxford University Press.

Juergensmeyer, Mark (ed.). 2006. *The Oxford Handbook of Global Religions*. New York: Oxford University Press.

Mead, Frank S. and Samuel S. Hill. 2001. *Handbook of Denominations in the United States, 11th Edition*. Nashville, TN: Abingdon Press.

Roof, Wade Clark Roof. 1999. *Spiritual Marketplace: Baby Boomers and the Remaking of American Religion*. Princeton NJ: Princeton University Press.

3

Downloading God, "Big Box" Churches, and the Crystal Shop around the Corner

Religious Adaptation in the High-Tech, Digital Age

1. How have the Internet and other forms of communication technology shaped religious beliefs, practices, and organizations?

2. Is it possible to build a virtual spiritual community that serves all social functions of religion?

3. How do megachurches balance their size and scale while simultaneously building intimacy and community among their members?

4. Are New Age shops, organic food stores, Christian bookstores, and wellness centers just places of business, or are they new forms and contexts for religious identities and communities?

The digital age of the 21st century has initiated fundamental changes to the world in which we live. Like the printing press, the telephone, and television before them, computers, the Internet, iPods, and cell phones have all transformed the ways in which we communicate, meet prospective love interests, read books and newspapers, and yes, even experience the sacred. A person of faith from almost any faith tradition, past or present, can search the Internet and find not only websites that house extensive information on beliefs and practices, but also entire sites for experiencing religious rituals and community with the click of a mouse. More advanced sites allow a worshipper to actually participate in a ritual via webcams and interactive technology. New religions also appear regularly on-line, attracting seekers and the curious public to explore and experience the sacred in new ways, from the sublime and traditional to the novel, odd, and even dangerous.

Religion in our world is changing in other ways as well. The phenomenon of suburban megachurches across the United States put small community churches on the defensive. Megachurches offer vast auditorium seating, state-of-the-art light and sound equipment, and contemporary music, dance, and theatrical performances that seem at times more like Broadway than church. Willow Creek Community Church, outside Chicago, for example, attracts thousands of people to its weekly services. The style of the services and the themes addressed in the preaching are contemporary. Addressing the needs and the tastes of today's churchgoers while simultaneously maintaining a classically evangelical message of faith in Jesus Christ are at the top of these churches' priority lists. They are very unlike the "little country church" on the edge of town of nostalgic memory. In many ways, these "big box" churches represent both a break with tradition and also a conscious attempt on the part of religion to adapt to a new generation of churchgoers.

New Age shops, organic food stores, Christian and non-Christian bookstores, and spas and wellness centers in big and small towns across the country provide yet another way for individuals to touch the sacred, or at least to buy things that will help them do so. Even in a Midwestern city like Indianapolis, a weekly free newspaper called *Branches* that is available all over town provides information on upcoming events for all things spiritual, including events representing a diverse range of Eastern religious traditions. Between the New Age notices for drumming circles, yoga classes, and psychic fairs, there are articles regarding health and wellness, eating right, and organic foods, and ads for massages and spas. Furthermore, in the checkout lines of stores like Whole Foods, a national grocery store chain that offers a variety of organic as well as conventional foods, one finds, not *News of the World* or the *National Enquirer,* but magazines focused on Eastern religious traditions, back-to-nature lifestyles, and food and healthy living. Somehow, new forms of spirituality and even old forms of religious practice are being bought and sold along with a gallon of milk and a loaf of whole-grain bread.

What is fascinating to us as students of religion is how at various points in recent history all of these new expressions and contexts for religious beliefs, practices, and experiences have been both hailed as the inevitable future of all religion and condemned as threats to the traditional practice of religion. We will take a middle approach in our examination of these new contexts for religion and the sacred here. Online religion, megachurches, and alternative forms of spirituality are adaptations by religious groups to our changing world, and each has an impact on what religion looks like and how it operates. As we will explore in this chapter, the ability to download God, to get convenience and low prices at a big-box church, or even to stop by the local Christian bookstore for a new book on keeping a Christian family strong all demonstrate that religion in our world is changing into forms that are far removed from the traditional forms that we expect to find.

These new forms also raise some complicated questions that haven't yet received clear answers either from those within religious communities or from those of us who study them. For instance, online rituals are devoid of a "real-time" community. They do not require the full participation of a believer in the same way that a church service might. The online worshipper can multitask while worshipping. She or he might play solitaire, balance a checkbook, and, of course, take care of laundry, prepare meals, and even take phone calls without ever interrupting the ritual itself. Is this, then, the same ritual experience as the original form? What does community mean when there are 10,000 people attending a particular church service? Can big-box churches fulfill the traditional functions of religion as well as smaller congregational settings can? Whether they can or cannot, the new forms of Christianity do add to the religious vitality of communities and pressure other congregations to become more intentional about who they are and what the sacred means to them.

And what about the pagan shops, the grocery stores, and the spa treatments? Are they local means for individuals to pursue their spiritual journeys, or are they businesses, pure and simple, turning spirituality into a commodity and selling it to those who can afford to buy it? Of course, we will only just begin to explore these questions in this chapter. Yet, in our examination of these new contexts for religious beliefs, practices, and experiences, we must keep in mind that religion has always adapted itself to changing conditions. Let us turn our attention first to online religion and see how this adaptation has affected the global religious landscape.

CHANGING TECHNOLOGY, CHANGING RELIGION

Technology has had a hand in shaping Christianity since the Protestant Reformation, which was fueled by the invention of moveable type and the printing press. These developments allowed people to print Bibles, religious tracts, and other religious materials cheaply and in enough quantities that they became accessible to ordinary people. Prior to this time, of course, religious texts were painstakingly reproduced by hand and beautifully illuminated by skilled monks and nuns. Such works were accessible only to the clergy and the literate upper classes, who had both the time and the financial resources to use them.

For an ordinary person in medieval Europe, religion was visual and physical: something to be witnessed and experienced through the ceremonies of the Mass, by taking part in processions, by noticing the smell of incense that wafted through church buildings, and by participating in countless other rituals that were part of pre-Reformation Christianity. Religious leaders were the only people who had access and authority to read and interpret the Latin texts of the Bible for their congregations.

Enter the printing press: soon, religious texts that were printed in the common language of the people, instead of Latin, were widely available. Not only did access to these texts change as a result of technological innovations, but so did the form and structure of Christianity (O'Leary 1996). The most obvious shift came because nonclergy could read religious texts for themselves, since the texts were available and written in the common language. More significantly, however, was the fact that ordinary people could now *interpret* for themselves the meaning of the words of the Bible. The old forms of religious authority were undermined by this technology, and new forms of Protestant Christianity emerged that were focused, not on the visual and physical aspects of rituals and beliefs, but on the printed words. Christianity was irreversibly transformed as a consequence.

It is necessary to engage in this brief look back in time in order to clarify the point that the impact of technological change on religion is not new. Furthermore, looking at the role of technology among Protestant reformers also makes it clear that technology sets in motion forces that are not always foreseen by those who use the technology to achieve religious ends. Initially, Protestant reformers probably saw the printing of religious texts as a way to replace the outdated system of church control over theology and Biblical teaching with a more appropriate system that allowed all people to have access to these texts, but the result was something akin to pandemonium. Groups battled over the true meaning of texts and split apart over different interpretations, then split again on yet another set of issues. Much to the dismay of religious leaders, control of religion by official leaders gave way to a more democratic and individualistic approach, all thanks to technology making the texts available to everyone.

We hope that you can already begin to see the parallels between this period in history and our own time, in which technological changes whip around us daily. When television made possible the new reality of an "electronic church," mainline Christian leaders expressed concern that religious broadcasting would reduce the numbers of people going to church and the amount of money that people gave to local congregations (Stacey and Shupe 1982, p. 291). Their fears were never fully realized, however, because most religious television broadcasting was dominated by evangelical pastors such as Jerry Falwell and talk show hosts like Pat Robertson, whose at-home audiences were already members of evangelical and fundamentalist congregations that were sympathetic to the messages they heard on TV. In Stacey and Shupe's (1982) study of those who watched religious programming on TV, church attendance was highly correlated with viewing of that programming. This evidence suggests that those who watch religious television are still participating in local congregations. In short, the "electronic church" is a supplement to traditional church, not a replacement for it.

Around the world today, the rise of online religion is causing controversies, not only among Christian groups, but among other world religions as well. If you Google any of the world's contemporary religions, you will be amazed not only at the number of informational sites that you will discover—what Hadden and Cowan (2000) call "religion online"—but also at the number of sites that are designed for the practitioners of these traditions, which Hadden and Cowan distinguish as "online religion." There are extensive sites that explain the religious beliefs and practices of the world's religions, discuss sacred texts, muse on the implications of religious beliefs for social and political issues, and serve as soapboxes for religious individuals and groups that seek to challenge the validity of other religions. Online religion has become a way for an ever greater number of religious groups to be socially visible, and most religious groups and congregations increasingly feel the pressure to maintain their own websites to communicate with their own members and to advertise services and events.

Sara Horsfall (2000) summarizes the basic uses of the Internet by religious groups. (See Table 3.1.)

TABLE 3.1 Typical Religious Organizations' Purposes in Using the Internet (Horsfall 2000)

1. **External Communication**
   - Evangelical outreach
   - Publicity/Public relations
   - Directories/Contact information
   - Legitimation

2. **Information Sharing**
   - Publication of religious texts and materials
   - Study aids: Bible searches/text searches/concordances
   - Genealogical information
   - Sales of religious items

3. **Internal Communication**
   - Directories/Contact information
   - Official communication of doctrine/policy/directives
   - Discussion among members
   - Published testimonies
   - Sharing resources/Web links
   - Education
   - Daily inspiration
   - Prayer requests

As you can see, different religious groups use the Internet for a variety of purposes, some oriented toward others outside the religious group or congregation and some focused on its members. The Internet is perceived to be a prime way to communicate the religious mission of the group and to invite curious visitors to learn more. In this sense, much of the use of the Internet by religious groups involves outreach and evangelism. Many mainstream religious congregations feel that the Internet is the key way that new members can be recruited, if by no other means than providing dates and times for services and events that will bring these individuals to the congregation itself. Studies of new religious movements that use the Internet, however, suggest that a very small number of people actually join a religious group through Internet interaction alone (Mayer 2000).

More and more, religious groups are using the Internet as a means for individuals to actually participate in rituals, attend services, and interact with other believers. It is important to remember that much of that online religion interaction remains fairly limited in scope. Congregations might have live broadcasts of services that viewers can watch much like they would watch a service on television. Other churches are becoming more creative. At St. Ann's Catholic Church (http://www.themass.org) in Scranton, Pennsylvania, for example, viewers can witness the daily mass online, though, obviously, without the ability to actually receive the blessed bread and wine. Other Catholic websites offer users the opportunity to light candles on behalf of special needs and to pray the rosary. On Anglican websites, the daily offices of morning and evening prayer are available. One site, simply listed as the Mission of St. Clare (http://www.missionstclare.com), actually provides music so that the viewer can sing the service music in "karaoke" style. The Greek Orthodox Archdiocese of America also offers live broadcasts of divine services in New York, New Jersey, Connecticut, Michigan, and California.

Islam also has an online presence. It is possible to say daily prayers on some Muslim sites and it is possible to take a virtual Hajj. Bunt (2000, 146) notes that, of the 71 mosques in Singapore in 2000, a third of them had basic homepages that gave visitors the opportunity to pay the obligatory *zagat* tax, to use a matchmaking service, and to find local sources for Hallal foods.

Judaism, too, has its virtual identity on sites such as www.ritualwell.org, which provides information on a full range of Jewish rituals, with resources to assist the viewer in creating his or her own rituals. Temple Israel of Greater Miami broadcasts its services live in audio and video formats.

Many other religious groups, some representing seemingly long vanished religious traditions, are slowly joining the online revolution and broadcasting their services. Ancient Egyptian worship is one such religious tradition. It was revived in Chicago in 1988 by Tamara Siuda, recognized by the state of Illinois in 1993, and recognized by the federal government in 1999 (Krogh and Pillifant 2004). This group maintained two websites, one that presents information about beliefs and practices in ancient Egyptian religion with a virtual shrine and another that includes classes for would-be members and a password-protected portion for full members that granted access to online biweekly worship services.

More technologically savvy religious groups can take a further step toward virtual religious services. Second Life (http://www.secondlife.com) allows users to create avatar for themselves—alternative, animated, online selves. Users can then join virtual services and be present virtually in the online worship space. The avatar can participate physically in the service, standing, kneeling, clapping, or sitting as required. Other users who are also there can see one another's avatars and can communicate with one another before and after the services. Regardless of your religious preferences, computer programs, including QuickTime and YouTube, make it possible for anyone with access to the Internet, anywhere in the world, to be a part of an online community.

VIRTUAL SPIRITUAL COMMUNITY, IDENTITY, AND AUTHORITY

For sociologists, online religion raises many important questions. Is a virtual community the same thing, in terms of its dynamics and influences on people, as a real community that is based on face-to-face interaction? What does it mean for individuals to have authentic religious identities in a technological context where having multiple personalities is commonplace? And most importantly for religious leaders, how does a religious group ensure that religious belief and practice remain orthodox when anyone can go online and circulate his or her own spin on what constitutes true beliefs and practices? Sociologists have only just begun to explore the impact of this new technological format for religion, so we are far from having any definitive answers to these questions (Dawson 2000, Hadden and Cowan 2000). However, let's briefly explore the issues that are emerging as we consider the impact of cyberspace on religious community, identity, and authority.

Online Faith Community

As we have already mentioned, the introduction of televised church services caused many in the religious community to fear, among other things, that this new technology would pull people out of church communities and contribute to growing social isolation. Decades later, such fears have proven to be incorrect. The same fears have re-emerged about religious services on the Internet, fueled by the added possibility that, unlike television, the Internet allows those who use it to develop online relationships and a sense of community. From what we know of those who participate in online religion, the Internet can foster new forms of relationships as well as reinvent what "community" looks like for religious believers. If these forms of interaction are not identical to older ones, proponents of online religion ask "so what?" and point to the many positive ways that online religion encourages community building.

What online religious communities provide most clearly is access to an inexhaustible supply of active, dormant, and extinct religions. Whether one is in search of community in a Jewish synagogue or pagan coven, the Internet allows one to join with others who share a set of beliefs and practices to worship, build relationships, and interact by being online at the same time. For those who follow ancient or marginalized faith traditions, joining together online is a way to build social bonds among otherwise isolated individuals. What is truly remarkable about the community-building potential of online religion is that it can be truly global in scope, because, regardless of where you are in the world, you can join in the practice of your religion or spiritual tradition with others (Dawson 2000). Finally, online religion allows a person to be a part of more than one community at a time, something that is not always possible in real time. Spiritual "seekers" can join in chat room relationships and participate in online rituals with others from the safety of their own homes. Chats can continue at all times of the day or night; there are no limits to how much interaction takes place, unlike to the situation in real-time religious communities, where relationships and interactions are structured around particular times and days of the week. In the virtual practice of religion, a person can more easily explore diverse spiritual communities and experiences simultaneously.

But sociologists and religious practitioners alike highlight several key drawbacks that balance these potentially positive aspects of online religious relationships and community. Of course, the first and foremost challenge to online religion is that, regardless of how many people we chat with online, we remain alone while we do it (Turkle 1995). These just isn't enough research yet to say whether the known social benefits of relationships, such as group integration, social support during times of crisis, and the many mental and physical health benefits, emerge from virtual relationships. Also, online relationships tend to be built around singular interests, in this case, religious beliefs and practices. In a real-time faith community, there are occasions for community participation in leisure-time activities, social outreach work, neighborhood projects, or political engagement, all of which reveal the multidimensional character of each person and of the others with whom he or she is relating.

Building relationships and community is an inherently messy business. All kinds of strain and conflicts are possible as individuals from different backgrounds confront one another. When a person is online, there are usually no visible indicators of that person's race, gender, class, or sexual orientation. These aspects of our selves and the obstacles that they can pose to building communities are inescapable in our real-time relationships (Schroeder, Heather, and Lee 1998). Virtual communities—despite the many ways that they can facilitate interaction—cannot replicate these kinds of challenges, so the interactions that proceed in them may not be as genuine. This is not to say that a virtual religious community can't plan an event for people to get together in real time, but does it then cease to be only a virtual community? Likewise, while some religious rituals can be performed at home or online, many important religious rituals—baptisms, the Catholic mass, Seders, pilgrimages to Mecca—cannot be performed alone. Finally, there is the challenge posed by the fact that not everyone in the world has online access. For those of us living in a technologically advanced nation and society, it is easy to assume that everyone has access to computers and knows how to navigate the Internet or even download software to view online broadcasts. While the Internet seems to widen the scope of who can access online religion or participate in it, only those with up-to-date computer technology and high-speed Internet access can reasonably do so (Dawson 2000, Turkle 1995). Clearly, we need to learn a lot before we can accept or dismiss any of these claims about online religious communities.

Virtual Religious Identity

One of the powerful implications of virtual identity formation is the way in which the technology allows us to create personal "profiles" that reflect as much or as little of ourselves as we wish to reveal online. The Internet allows us to be quite narrow as an online self if we so desire. Furthermore, we can create as many different identities as we wish, each with its own unique aspects. June, an 11-year-old who used her mom's Internet account to play online, sums up this idea when she says to an interviewer: "I don't play so many different people online—only three" (Turkle 1995, 256). Once again, the Internet frees users to present themselves as religious believers and practitioners in many different ways. As noted in the preceding mention of religious seekers—those who explore what it means to belong to many different religious and spiritual communities—the Internet allows people to express their multiple spiritual interests and desires in ways that would be difficult in real time. By crafting several online personalities, one can fully participate in Ancient Egyptian religious rituals, be a "technopagan," and join an evangelical praise service, overcoming the inherent problems of age, gender, ethnicity, or other characteristics that might hinder participation in any or all of these religious contexts.

This kind of freedom, however, can have its downside. First, the ability to create multiple virtual religious identities raises the question of which one, if any, is the authentic religious identity. At no point does Internet technology require us to create a whole, multifaceted identity. Rather, it revels in—and almost mandates—the fragmentation of our identities. Although many postmodernist scholars would not see this as a problem, most religious groups would. Virtual religious identities can skew our experience in several ways. If we wish to display only a partial identity during participation in an online religious ritual or as part of a community—for example, if a woman wants to participate in a male-only religious ritual—we can do so. We can even become fully integrated into a virtual religious community. But this experience generates what Turkle (1995, 236) calls the "Disneyland Effect," in which the simulated experience becomes taken for granted as the real experience. As we noted before, much of these thoughts are speculative. The impact of Internet technology on the construction of an individual's spiritual identity requires more research and perhaps requires us to challenge our own assumptions about what a religious identity ought to look like and how it ought to develop.

Religious Authority Online

A third set of issues that online religion raises has to do with the nature of religious authority. As Brenda Brasher (2004, x), observes, with regard to access to the Internet and the information available online, "Those who possess the means and skill to access it will have so much information at their disposal that they can challenge the expertise of professionals, and flaunt the jurisdictions of recognized [religious] authorities." If there has been a common theme in how people view the Internet, it is the observation that it promotes a democratic leveling of people, groups, and ideas.

New religious movements like Heaven's Gate (which remains an active site online, despite the tragic mass suicide of its members in 1997) and movements that were thought to be long extinct, such as worship of the ancient Sumerian goddess Inanna (http://inanna. virtualave.net/inannashrine.html), both find a place online, as does the Vatican (http:// www.vatican.va), Muslims (http://www.islamonline.net, an extensive site), and many other more familiar religious groups. When we consider this online religious diversity, it is important for us to remember that there is no privileged access for some religious groups over others, nor is there a means for ensuring that only certain approaches or ideas within a religious group are expressed online. So, while the Vatican may maintain a site to promote official, orthodox teachings of the Roman Catholic Church, many other Catholic sites exist that reinterpret or challenge those teachings or reject them outright. In turn, Vatican officials can counter the information that is on these sites, but they cannot control the existence of the information. This is what we mean by "democratic leveling." For some, this inherent capacity to circulate divergent religious ideas and to challenge official ones is the great strength of online religion. For religious leaders, however, the Internet poses a substantial challenge to their authority.

Yet, despite the many ways that the Internet has freed users to explore differing religious beliefs and practices that are independent of existing religious authorities, religious leaders, rather than fleeing from the Internet, have come to use this technology to reinforce their own authority. Consequently, the Vatican's website isn't simply one among many, but rather, as the authoritative voice of the Catholic Church, it is likely to be the first (and possibly only) place that anyone seeking Catholic teachings about any theological, social, or political subject might go. By controlling the information on their own websites, religious leaders can use the Internet to circulate the precise messages they wish to convey to the world.

But the problems posed by online religion are about more than access to information about religious teachings. Online technology also poses a challenge to the ability of religious groups to control or limit access to religious rituals. Some religions do not wish to allow anyone to have full access to all the rites that are central to religious practice. They allow only people who have been initiated into full membership in the faith community to participate. These groups may structure their websites in a way that maintains their own hierarchical authority.

For example, people who wish to join the group of ancient Egyptian worshipers that is based in Chicago must go through an extensive online initiation course to become full members. The application requires the consent of a person's family member or guardian for individuals who are under 18, who are married, or who have a caregiver (Krogh and Pillifant 2004). Only those who successfully complete this process receive the password that allows them to join the live broadcasts of the Egyptian rituals. So, as this example shows, while users have free access to some websites, technology also exists to limit access,—another way to preserve religious authority.

In sum, we argue that the spread of new forms of high technology will force more and more religious groups to adopt some level of online presence. They may not all use this technology for the same purposes or to the same extent, but they will feel the pressure to create room for their understanding of the sacred online. Moreover, cyberspace is equally open to disseminating information on traditional beliefs and practices and on new beliefs and practices, so traditional orthodox belief and practice is not inevitably doomed by the new technology. Yet it is equally important to note that the Internet is not a blank canvas that has no impact on the religious traditions it presents. The structure of the technology itself puts constraints on how core ideas and messages are communicated, which by definition changes the content of those ideas and messages. Brasher (2004, xii) argues,

> "As they have attempted to make themselves at home in the social space of the Internet, religious organizations have had to define themselves in a menu-driven, protocol-determined space where images reign. Overt multiplicity, messy answers, and explicit contradictions work against web site aesthetics. Engaging with the Internet can propel religious organizations toward reductionism, minimizing diversity, complexity, and the unknowns that add spice and texture to a traditional heritage. Official religious web sites tend to present the tradition as a harmonic, unified singularity, and suppress dissent. Alternative opinions need not apply."

Once the "Disneyland Effect" kicks in, religious organizations may feel pressure to conform their real-time rituals and community gatherings to approximate the experience that participants find online. Bunt (2000) found that Islamic sites have to look "appropriate" in terms of the graphics that they display and the links that connect viewers to high-profile sites. Anthropologists have also found this effect in religions that formerly required people's physical presence and participation at gathering places but that are now taking advantage of the legitimacy and authenticity bestowed by adopting "televisual styles" that resonate with the tastes of the local population. As one study of Candomble, an Afro–Brazilian spirit-possession religious tradition, noted: "One's mother, neighbors, and colleagues from work will definitely be more impressed when a celebration marking an important moment in one's religious life 'almost looks like TV'" (Van de Port 2006, 457). And so, as in the early days of television, "People soon wanted the production quality and professionalism of radio and television to be exhibited in *local* worship events. Rather than participants in a faith community, people started to think of themselves as an audience and began acting like observers at worship" (Brasher 2004, 16).

WHAT'S IN A MEGACHURCH?

In addition to finding the sacred online, some Christians are embracing another new context for Christian belief and practice at "big box" churches, also known as megachurches. This label, hinting at similarities to places like Costco and Wal-Mart, reflects the sheer size and scope of the congregations in these religious ministries. In their 2007 study of U.S. megachurches, Thumma and Travis (2007, 1) report that there are approximately 1250 Protestant churches that have weekly attendance of over 2000 people.

This finding itself tells us two important facts about the phenomenon of these types of congregations. First, the label megachurch is almost exclusively limited to Protestant congregations. Most of these congregations could be categorized broadly as evangelical Protestant, though there are Black Protestant and mainline Protestant megachurches as well. (See Table 3.2.)

Second, a megachurch has a minimum of 2000 attendees on any given Sunday morning, with an average attendance of 3585 people, as of 2005 (Thumma and Travis

TABLE 3.2   Denominational Affiliation of Megachurches in the United States

Affiliation	Percentage
Nondenominational	34.0%
Southern Baptist	16.0
Baptist (Unspecified)	10.0
Assemblies of God	6.0
United Methodist	5.0
Calvary Chapel	4.4
Christian	4.2
Four Square Gospel	1.2
United Church of Christ	1.0
ELCA Lutheran	1.0
Vineyard	1.0
Other denominations (each <1.0%)	16.2%

Source: Thumma and Travis (2007, 27).

2007, 8). It is important to know these distinguishing features because many Roman Catholic congregations may count thousands of members belonging to their geographical parish, though they do not typically attend in such high numbers on a weekly basis.

The work of Scott Thumma and his colleagues examining these churches (2005, 2007) is the most extensive research to date on the subject. It helps us understand these types of congregations and how they are shaping and being shaped by the American religious landscape. (See also Ellingson 2007.) Because so much of what most of us think we know about these churches comes from media sources that focus only on the vast size of the congregations or the views of the most politically vocal pastors from these churches, our ideas are incomplete at best or totally inaccurate at worst. Let's look at some of the basic data that Thumma and Travis (2007) provide on these congregations.

Megachurches are found all over the United States, though they tend to cluster in some unsurprising regions, notably in the South and Middle West. About half of all these churches are in a region that extends from Maryland south to Florida, west to Texas, north to Oklahoma and Missouri, and back east to Kentucky and West Virginia. The three states on the west coast contain another 19% of all megachurches. New England has the smallest percentage, only 1%, of the nation's megachurches. Thumma and Travis (2007, 10) report that half of megachurches are in newer suburbs established within the last decade or two, a quarter of megachurches are in older suburbs, and the remaining quarter are in urban areas. Although these churches attract thousands on any given week, very few attract such huge numbers all at once. More commonly, megachurches have several services that are often radically different in style or emphasis, to accommodate those who attend.

Megachurches are perhaps best known for their diversity in contemporary worship forms and styles (Thumma, Travis, and Bird 2005, 22). Most of these congregations use praise bands as their music source, with 94% using drums, 93% using electric guitars or bass guitars, and 84% using pianos "always" or at least "often" during their services. Ninety-five percent of these congregations use visual projection equipment as well. Yet there are a few megachurches that use more traditional forms of worship, including hymns, structured readings from the Bible, communion rituals, and recitations of creeds. What makes megachurches unique is their willingness to experiment with innovative worship styles and change what they do as needed. Moreover, because many of these churches have multiple services, it is possible for one megachurch to include a quieter and more formal traditional service, a rock-and-roll–style service, and many other variations, each targeting the different tastes and aesthetics of a subset of the congregation. Regardless of which type of service they attend, most people characterized their church as filled with a sense of God's presence (53%), inspirational (52%), joyful (50%), and exciting (43%) (Thumma and Travis 2007, 151).

Contrary to our cultural stereotypes of the type of people who attend megachurches, Thumma, Travis, and Bird (2005, 25) found that people from a wide range of social backgrounds attend services at these churches. (See Table 3.3.)

Though most adults in megachurches are white, Thumma and Travis (2007, 28) report that between 10% and 12% attract a predominately African-American congregation, while 2% are predominately Asian and another 2% are mostly Hispanic adults. While they don't provide data, Thumma and Travis (2007) note that megachurches attract adults from a wide range of income levels and occupations. In approximately 65% of these churches, 41% of adults are college graduates. In 45% of megachurches, more than 41% of the adults are under the age of 35, and in only 9% are there as many people over the age of 60 as there

TABLE 3.3 **Percent of Megachurches by Congregational Characteristics**

	% of Regularly Attending Adults			
	<40%	41–60%	61–80%	81–100%
College graduates	36%	38%	20%	7%
Age 35 or younger	53	35	11	1
Age 60 or older	91	8	0	1
New to congregation	56	27	12	4
Have children at home	39	45	15	2

Source: Thumma, Travis, and Bird (2005, 23).

are under age 35. Most adults are new to these congregations, having joined in the last five years. In 65% of churches, more than 41% of households have children under the age of 18. The people who attend these churches, then, are young, relatively well educated, parents, and new to the church. They clearly are not on the margins of American society.

CAN YOU HAVE COMMUNITY IN A MEGACHURCH?

Let us consider the meaning of *community* in the new religious context of a megachurch. Whereas online religion presents the challenge of being in community while sitting at home alone, belonging to a church with several thousand members raises the question of how all those people ever have the chance to interact in such a way that they feel tied together as a spiritual community. In fact, megachurches do an excellent job of creating a sense of community, according to surveys of the people who attend their services. In their initial report, Thumma, Travis, and Bird (2005, 7) found that 72% of individuals who attended megachurches agreed that their church was "like a close-knit family." Other familiar aspects of community life abound as well; people who attend report having close friends at church, knowing as many or more people at their megachurch as they did when they attended churches with smaller congregations, and feeling cared about (Thumma and Travis 2007, 46). The question remains: How exactly do these churches make this happen?

One of the central ways that megachurches help develop this sense of family and community is to use small groups. Forming small groups has been a dominant way to build relationships, facilitate spiritual growth, and develop outreach activities in American congregations over the last few decades (Wuthnow 1994). Megachurches have taken this structure and run with it. Sometimes these small groups are designed to incorporate newcomers into the church by having them join an informal group to discuss the previous week's service and message. Other groups are designed to further members' spiritual development through prayer and Bible study. Still other groups cover a wide range of church-related activities and secular pursuits. Whatever their focus, megachurch pastors create these extensive networks of small groups to "make the big church small" (Thomas and Jardine 1994, 277).

The feeling of community is also maintained in megachurches through a variety of other means. First, these churches rely on families and friends to invite new people to attend a service at the church. These informal ties also help newcomers feel comfortable in the otherwise overwhelming context of the services. In addition, in some of these congregations, as Thumma and Travis (2007) note, the ushers intentionally keep track of the individuals who sit in particular sections of the church week after week. While this practice may seem a bit like taking attendance, it also ensures that individuals who visit the church feel looked after and cared about. Being recognized by an usher can be extremely refreshing to people who, in the process of church shopping, often felt invisible; they believe that someone in the congregation cared enough to make them feel like they belonged.

In addition to attentive ushers, megachurches use an extensive staff of paid and unpaid people to make sure that the services and programs of the church are successfully conducted (Thumma, Travis, and Bird 2005). Megachurches typically have an average of 20 full-time, paid leaders and 9 part-time leaders. In addition to leaders, these churches have, on average, 22 full-time and 15 part-time administrative staff. Volunteers are also crucial to the operation of these churches. Thumma, Travis, and Bird (2005, 10) found that, again on average, these churches have 284 volunteers who work five hours a week or more. Working or volunteering are additional opportunities for building community among those who attend megachurches. Newcomers are quickly connected to the congregation through small groups, volunteer opportunities, new member classes, or, in some cases, assignment to a formal "mentor." (See Table 3.4.)

By intentionally attracting visitors to their churches and keeping them as members of the congregation, not only do megachurches continue to experience amazing growth, but they also provide people with new forms of spiritual community. It is important to keep in mind, however, that megachurches cannot sustain themselves purely by their size and the entertainment value they offer to their audiences week by week. Their size alone is intimidating and potentially alienating. Building community in these churches requires them to incorporate many old-fashioned patterns for interaction—handshakes, meal-sharing, intimate relationships in small groups, and opportunities to work shoulder-to-shoulder on outreach projects. That they seem to have been successful is a testament to the continued importance of sustained personal interaction to maximize feelings of belonging and social support.

To sum up, just as Internet technology is shaping what the practice of religion looks like, megachurches, too, are having a profound impact on the American religious landscape. Megachurches are not the end of traditional Christianity as we know it, but they certainly are affecting what a Christian congregation looks like and how it worships. Megachurches continue to attract the attention of young, suburban professionals because they provide them with practical ways to develop their faith and to experience the sacred. In doing so,

TABLE 3.4	Percent of Megachurches Reporting Activities to Attract and Keep Members	
Invitation to participate in a fellowship or other small group		88%
Orientation classes for new members		78
Invitation to volunteer for service in congregation or community		69
Designated people to extend hospitality, invitations for meals		58
Followup visits by clergy, lay leaders, or members		52
Other activities		22
No planned procedures or activities		3%

Source: Thumma, Travis, and Bird (2005, 13).

megachurches make use of multimedia and contemporary music in ways that clearly resonate with the wider cultural shifts in American society. Formality, tradition, liturgy, and denominational heritage have become increasingly foreign to new generations of Americans.

But megachurches do not just create one more niche in the religious landscape for those who enjoy their evangelical and nondenominational cultural forms. Congregations of many types and traditions are feeling the cultural pressure that the megachurch phenomenon creates. In a 2007 study of the impact of megachurch styles and aesthetics on a set of Lutheran churches in southern California, Stephen Ellingson argues quite forcefully that there is a sense of crisis among traditional congregations that has its roots in the success of megachurches. The argument begins with the premise that people neither understand nor own the denominational traditions of their churches. Consequently, membership decline, especially among mainline Protestants, is facilitated by the churches' reluctance to change and update their worship styles to attract new and younger potential members. If congregations want to thrive in the 21st century, they should adopt contemporary worship, an emphasis on emotion and experience, and above all, minimize formality and tradition. In a word, they should become as much like megachurches as possible. What is remarkable about the churches in Ellingson's study is that more often than not, church leaders made changes to worship and programs as a result of receiving these messages secondhand, in materials circulated and presented by "experts," not as a result of any direct and consistent reflection on either the internal dynamics of the congregations themselves or on the dynamics of the churches' own communities.

What we see happening with megachurches then is twofold. On one hand, megachurches represent yet another adaptation of religion to the cultural changes that are occurring in the rest of American society. They intentionally seek to reach a specific audience with their largely evangelical and nondenominational forms of the Christian message. As such, megachurches have been incredibly successful in developing new methods for carrying out the basic function of religion to build community. On the other hand, megachurches introduce new pressures onto other types of congregations that push them to adopt similar forms of organization and worship, while simultaneously—and often unwittingly—causing these churches to change their traditions and theology as well. In short, megachurches are "colonizing" mainline Protestantism (Ellingson 2007, 178). For congregations that follow the megachurch models, there is no way to go back to older forms of tradition and the order of earlier times. Megachurches clearly meet the spiritual needs of many contemporary American Christians. They also force all others to become more aware of how they live out their respective traditions in a postmodern, consumer-driven, tradition-averse world.

OTHER NEW FORMS AND CONTEXTS FOR RELIGIOUS COMMUNITY

Religious beliefs and practices in the 21st century continue to be a blend of tradition and innovation. Although many believers use technology to experience the sacred—either online or through megachurch multimedia events—others see these forms of religious enterprise as alienating, cold, and lacking humanity. In the contemporary world, growing numbers of people seem to be on quests for experiences of the sacred and now more than ever are likely to describe themselves as "spiritual but not religious." British sociologists have characterized this state of affairs as a "believing, not belonging" culture (Davie 1994). Today, there is a burgeoning market for books, consumer goods, and services designed to help us on our spiritual quest. What are sometimes classed as New Age shops sell crystals, incense, and other tools for touching the divine in ourselves and in nature. Christian bookstores, too, offer devotional books, candles, angel statues, and DVDs to aid one's personal spiritual growth. And there has been a veritable explosion of wellness centers offering yoga classes, massages, and aromatherapies (for people and sometimes for pets, too). While these kinds of shops are not new, their expansion into a multibillion-dollar industry that transcends religious and denominational boundaries *is* new (Roof 1999). Moreover, the recent increase in demand for renewable energy and organic food is also tapping into a concern for nature that borders on the spiritual and, occasionally, on the formally religious. Of interest here is the degree to which these shops and centers are providing people with alternative ways to pursue their individual spiritual journeys, paths that do not require people to associate with an organization, have a religious identity, or formally believe in God in order for them to engage the sacred.

For the purposes of this discussion, we are limiting our focus to beliefs and practices that we will term *alternative spiritualities,* meaning that they do not represent traditional religious beliefs and practices that one might find in a congregational setting. We choose not to call them New Age beliefs and practices because that oversimplifies them. Alternative spirituality encompasses two broad categories of beliefs and practices (Glendinning and Bruce 2006, Sointu and Woodhead 2008). The first category centers on the collective sets of beliefs and practices that revolve around divination. These include belief in and use of horoscopes and astrology, tarot cards, psychic readings, channeling (a practice in which a "channeler" either speaks with spirits and relays their messages to others or has his or her body taken over by a spirit, who then speaks directly through the channeler), and other practices. The second category addresses the wide range of beliefs and practices regarding personal health and wellness. These include, but are not limited to, holistic and alternative medicines and therapies, massage, yoga, diets, and aromatherapies.

The relatively meager research that has been done on these types of beliefs and practices finds that alternative spiritualities are about consumer choice *par excellence.* Individuals assemble their own sets of beliefs and practices that they find personally meaningful and instrumental. Consequently, alternative spiritualities function as religious supermarkets, where individuals borrow at will from any and all spiritual traditions from the past and present (Houtman and Aupers 2007, 306). Alternative spiritualities commonly draw on selected beliefs and rituals from Eastern religions like Hinduism and Buddhism and indigenous religious traditions of Native Americans (Jenkins 2004, Mears and Ellison 2000, Roof 1999). They provide a highly individualistic means of encountering the sacred by maintaining a core emphasis on the central aspects of identity and community: healthy and authentic relationships, especially with one's own body. Wade Clark Roof (1998) notes that in many of these new forms of spirituality, community and relationship building includes the fostering of human relationships with not just other people but all of nature.

Houtman and Aupers (2007, 307) argue that at the center of all alternative spiritualities is the "belief that in the deepest layers of the self the 'divine spark' is still smoldering, waiting to be stirred up, and succeed the socialized self." Humans are socialized to live inauthentic lives, structured by the impersonal and dysfunctional institutions that dominate contemporary society. The Internet could be seen as a contributor to this socialization because it allows us to live through our fragmented, online selves instead of being a whole person all the time. Alternative spiritualities often also represent a rejection both of traditional forms of religion (especially Christianity) and Western scientific rationality.

Individuals who embrace these alternative spiritual practices are on quests to find their whole authentic selves again. And while an individually focused quest seems to contradict the very basis for community, a common thread links these practices: the belief that developing an authentic self happens in relationships with others, not apart from them (Houtman and Aupers 2007, Sointu and Woodhead 2008).

But who follows these kinds of alternative spiritual practices? This is a difficult question to answer because to date, most sociological studies of alternative spiritually have relied on qualitative, narrative, and life history data to describe what it means to be a part of this group. Also, because there is no single set of unifying beliefs and practices that links everyone in this group, most statistical data simply reflect a wide range of questions that cover the basic areas of divination and wellbeing. For example, in 2001, the Gallup Poll released a report on Americans' beliefs in things related to the paranormal. Individuals were asked whether they believed in channeling, the power of the human mind to heal the body, communication with the dead, astrology, ESP, telepathy, and reincarnation. Table 3.5 reports the percentage of Americans who responded positively about these things in 2001, compared with the percentage in a similar study conducted in 1990.

Overall, belief in these phenomena has increased, especially among people who are under 30 years old, female, and highly educated (Gallup Poll 2001). In their study of individuals who tend to buy New Age materials, which used a sample of 1014 residents of Texas, Mears and Ellison (2000, 300) found that 28% believed that it is possible to communicate with the dead, 31% believed in reincarnation, and 43% believed that they could heal themselves by restoring balance between their bodies and the forces of nature. When they expanded their survey questions to include core beliefs about the self, Mears and Ellison found that 66% of their respondents believed that all spiritual truth comes from within each person and 78% believed that people are in charge of their own lives and that they can be whatever they want to be.

Another study used data from the 2001 Scottish Social Attitudes Survey, which collected information about the full range of alternative spirituality practices engaged in by participants, rather than just the beliefs they held (Glendinning and Bruce 2006, 404). Of the individuals sampled, 19% used horoscopes with some regularity, and 8% tried fortune telling, tarot, or astrology, with 5% and 6% in each group, respectively, finding these practices to be important in their lives. The survey also found that 21% of the Scottish sample

TABLE 3.5 Percentage of Americans Who Held Alternative Spiritual Beliefs, 1990 and 2001

	1990	2001
Power of human mind to heal the body	46%	54%
Communication with someone who has died	18	28
Astrology	25	28
Reincarnation	21	25
Channeling	11	15
ESP	49	50
Mental telepathy	36	36

Source: Gallup Poll (2001).

used alternative medicines and therapies and 11% used yoga or meditation regularly. In this case, 20% of individuals who used alternative medicine and therapies found them helpful, and 9% of those who used yoga or meditation said they were important in their lives. Glendinning and Bruce (2006) observed that women, people under 55 years old, and people with high levels of education were most likely to engage in practices related to personal well-being, although it was uneducated women who were most likely to use divination. (See also Sointu and Woodhead 2008.)

Despite the wide range in context for these studies, alternative spirituality, as represented in various beliefs and practices related to divination and well-being, is a small but growing segment of the spiritual landscape. Yet there is no easy way to pull together these kinds of beliefs in a single creed for alternative spirituality, making it even more difficult to generalize anything about individuals who follow it. An additional challenge is the fact that many people who use aromatherapies, massage, meditation, or even astrology do *not* see a spiritual dimension to these activities. For example, a participant in a Native American sweat lodge ceremony may participate not to connect with anything spiritual but only to clear his or her mind and body of stress, as one might in a steam room in a gym. Often, the "suppliers," the people who conduct the ceremonies, read the tarot cards, give the massages, or mix the herbal remedies see a spiritual dimension in these activities, but that doesn't mean that the consumers who utilize or pay for them share these beliefs.

Many people in the mainstream religious realm see alternative spiritualities, at best, as techniques to hoodwink people who are seeking for a spiritually easy way out. Robert Wuthnow (1998), in addressing this rush to individualized forms of spirituality, argues that the spiritual realm works for people in the contemporary world because it remains on the margins of daily life and demands little of us; it doesn't require us to do anything uncomfortable, which by definition is likely to be inauthentic. But there must be more to these practices than an easy way out of the obligations of more traditional religious belief and practice. The development of an authentic inner life by using practices that focus on the body and mind—as well as building healthier relationships with others and with nature—clearly resonates with a generation of people who are confronting the damaged and dysfunctional links between themselves and others and between themselves and the natural world. Roof (1999) suggests that even congregations within the mainstream of the American religious landscape have moved to incorporate the ethic if not the actual practice of personal wellness techniques and recovery therapies. For example, some congregations offer sessions on "centering prayer" that focus on personal development, while others offer 12-step groups in the format of Alcoholics Anonymous. In addition, many groups are created within congregations to help young people, old people, men, women, gays, business people, members, and nonmembers fit the traditions of that religious practice to their own personal and professional needs and life experiences. Alternative spiritualities may represent an adaptation to new social and cultural dynamics that is separate from mainstream religion, but collectively they are also contributing to the changing dynamics within the beliefs and practices of religious groups.

CONCLUDING THOUGHTS

In this chapter we have seen the new ways that religion and religious organizations are adapting to technological and cultural shifts in our society. As with all such shifts, these changes may be frightening for some and may be considered long overdue by others.

Nevertheless, we must appreciate how the forces of social change and cultural adaptation, regardless of their sources, are neither completely benign nor entirely threatening to traditional religious belief and practice. It is clear that change can be disruptive. It calls into question long-standing beliefs and ways of doing things. Change creates confusion and frustration among those who don't believe that it is good. Change also can result in conflict, hostility, and the possibility of denominational or congregational break-up. People whose religious traditions are being picked over and used out of their original context—like many Native Americans—may disagree over who has the authority to determine when, how, and by whom religious beliefs and practices may be used.

At the same time, however, the kinds of changes we have discussed here can force religious groups to reflect on how best to make their traditions relevant to the world and people of today. As we saw in our discussion of online religion, the Internet can resurrect long-dead religious beliefs and practices as well as forming and disseminating new ones. The development of new forms of religious organization—such as megachurches—puts pressure on all other religious groups to re-evaluate and modify their practices. Religion in our world constantly evolves and adapts, even though from our own individual perspective our own traditions may appear to have always remained the same. It is essential for us to keep an open, but critical, mind about the long-term impacts of these religious adaptations in order to fully understand the causes, content, and consequences of all forms of religious change.

SUGGESTED READING

Brasher, Brenda E. 2004. *Give Me That Online Religion*. New Brunswick, NJ: Rutgers University Press.

Davie, Grace. 1994. *Religion in Britain Since 1945: Believing Without Belonging*. Oxford: Blackwell Publishers.

Ellingson, Stephen. 2007. *The Megachurch and the Mainline: Remaking Religious Tradition in the Twenty-First Century*. Chicago: University of Chicago Press.

Hadden, Jeffrey K. and Douglas E. Cowan (ed). 2000. *Religion on the Internet: Research Prospects and Promises*. Volume 8 in the Religion and Social Order Series. New York: JAI-Elsevier Science, Inc.

O'Leary, Stephen D. 1996. "Cyberspace as Sacred Space: Communicating Religion on Computer Networks." *Journal of the American Academy of Religion* 64: 781–808.

Sointu, Eeva and Linda Woodhead. 2008. "Spirituality, Gender, and Expressive Selfhood." *Journal for the Scientific Study of Religion* 47 (2): 259–276.

Thumma, Scott and Dave Travis. 2007. *Beyond Megachurch Myths*. San Francisco: Josey-Bass Publishers.

4

Can't We All Just Get Along?

Cohesion and Conflict in Religion

1. How does religion help create social cohesion?
2. How is cohesion related to conflict?
3. What are the functions of conflict for cohesion?
4. Why do people of different faiths sometimes get along, and sometimes not?

Sicily. If you have heard of it, it's most likely in conjunction with La Cosa Nostra, more commonly known as the Mafia. But of course, Sicily is much more. An island state of Italy that is situated at the mainland's southern tip, Sicily is in many ways a world unto its own.

Almost all of its approximately 5.5 million citizens are Catholic, and Catholicism is steeped into the culture and daily life of Sicilians. It has dominated life on this island for nearly 1000 years. Religion is of vital importance here. This does not mean that everyone regularly attends Mass. Not everyone does. But Catholicism does permeate almost every aspect of society, including day-to-day activities, art and architecture, the way that people relate to one another, town celebrations, and pronouncements by heads of state. Nearly every town, no matter how small, has at least one Catholic church, and usually the town is organized around its main or original church. Holidays are more appropriately labeled Holy Days, as they typically center on celebrations of patron saints or other religious festivities. As one observer of Sicilian culture wrote, "Almost all public places are adorned with crucifixes upon their walls, and most Sicilian homes contain pictures of saints, statues, and other relics. Each town and city has its own patron saint, and the feast days are marked by gaudy processions through the streets with marching bands and displays of fireworks" (Wikipedia 2008).

The Catholic religion in Sicily serves important social cohesion functions. Part of being Sicilian is being Catholic. It shapes Sicilians' life experiences, gives them meaning and purpose, influences family life, provides the contours of the yearly calendar, and provides norms, values, and key rituals that help solidify people's sense of belonging in their communities and in the company of a higher power.

But what about those Mafiosi who are supposed to have such influence on the island? (One of the authors was told by a Sicilian professor who specializes in studying the Mafia that as of 2010, over 80% of the businesses in Sicily pay "protection" money to the Mafia.) Are they Catholic?

In name, almost always. But in practice? Well, it is true that they often attend Mass, respect religious traditions, and contribute money to support religious festivals and churches. They show respect for priests, and part of their code is never to disturb or kill a priest, for they view themselves as men of honor and consider things related to God to be of a higher order than even the Mafia. To some extent, religion and culture have merged in Sicily, and some of the ideas of the Mafia are part of the practice of Sicilian Catholicism.

And what do the people of Sicily who are not part of the Mafia (the large majority of Sicilians) think of the Mafia? Many Sicilians either tolerate or outwardly support Mafia members—often out of fear, sometimes out of respect for the order and other advantages that they bring. When questioned by outsiders, Sicilians frequently deny that any such organization exists.

But Father Giuseppe Puglisi (pronounced "Pool-yee-zee") was different. Though he was a native of Sicily, he did not respect the Mafia. In fact, he thought they were decidedly anti-Christian. Like most Sicilians, he was born to working-class parents and grew up working class. He entered seminary at the young age of sixteen and then served in a country Sicilian parish that was affected by a bloody vendetta.

He had seen the violence and fear that the Mafia wrought upon Sicilians. He had also noticed how they infiltrated so many aspects of Sicilian life, including, in his view, the very understanding and practices of Catholicism. Although the Mafia members were baptized in the Catholic Church and were practicing members in good standing, in Father Puglisi's eyes they were decidedly pagan, a holdover from pre-Christian times.

Father Puglisi felt that it was his Christian duty to God and his flock to resist the Mafia. The Mafia fenced stolen goods, sold drugs, engaged in extensive extortion, controlled the construction and other industries, and heavily influenced politics. (Just two years before this chapter was written, the governor of Sicily was indicted for himself being a Mafioso.) But even worse, according to Father Puglisi, the Mafia eroded civic and social life in Sicily and compromised the authentic practice of Catholicism. After centuries of experience with the Mafia, Sicilians had become cynical about political effectiveness and trustworthiness and had come to misunderstand aspects of their faith. In fact, they had become apathetic. Those who tried to change things only suffered at the hands of the Mafia's "men of honor."

When Father Puglisi was assigned as the parish priest in one of the poor sections of Sicily's largest city, Palermo, he decided that enough was enough, and he worked to effect change. He was outspoken about the evils of the Mafia. He taught his parishioners to resist their ways and to overcome apathy. He focused mostly on the children, wanting them to have a new and better Sicily. He taught them to take hold of their faith and use it to resist the Mafia by refusing to collaborate with them, buy their fenced goods, admire them, take or sell their drugs, or participate in traditional religious celebrations that were largely paid for by the local Mafia members. He encouraged them to see the Mafia for who they really were and to engage in alternative, more authentic Catholic practices, such as the Stations of the Cross. Father Puglisi refused the money and gifts that the Mafia offered him—even those from members of his own parish. He decried their practices from the pulpit, and he worked tirelessly to support the people of his parish in resisting the Mafia.

For these reasons, Father Puglisi was revered, loved, and respected by many people. He was brave, bold, and fully Sicilian, in the best sense. He was a role model. On his 56th birthday he spent the day, not sleeping, eating treats, or opening presents, but rather doing his daily round of pastoral duties—visiting families in his parish, conducting two weddings, and hosting a conference with parents who were having their babies baptized. That evening, he returned home and stepped out of his car, only to be confronted by a man with a gun equipped with a silencer.

When Father Puglisi saw the man, he simply said, "I was expecting you." The man then violated the code of honor, put the gun to Father Puglisi's head, and shot the beloved priest to death.

Four years later the killer was arrested. He was a low-level Mafioso and a practicing Catholic who had been baptized in the parish where Father Puglisi ministered. The man had been ordered to "take out" the priest by Mafia bosses, who were also practicing Catholics baptized in the local parishes.

During this time, there had been a particularly violent period of Mafia activity that included the murders of high-ranking officials, deadly bomb explosions, blown-up bridges, and bloodstained streets. But the murder of a priest caused a huge outcry. Massive crowds followed his funeral procession. The Pope came to Sicily and spoke about Father Puglisi, calling him a witness to true Christianity. Later, Father Puglisi was recognized as a martyr for the faith. And Sicilians united themselves even more around their Catholic faith, a faith now increasingly defined as one that was different from the one practiced by the Mafia members. (The story of Father Puglisi was taken largely from Cunningham, 2002).

We tell the story to introduce the topics of this chapter—social cohesion and social conflict, and their intimately related nature. Sicily, like many places, is a land of contrasts. It is more thoroughly infused by one religion than are most modern societies, and Catholicism produces a strong social cohesion among Sicilians. It serves to bring people together and infuse their lives with order and meaning at the individual and family level, at the parish level, at the community level, and at the nation level.

But in a somewhat unique way, this religious conformity and resulting social cohesion is threatened by the continued presence of fellow Catholics—the Mafia—who have defined an alternative way of understanding and practicing Catholicism. Some people might consider them to be misguided, offenders of the faith, or even heretics. Conversely, the Mafia would view the behavior of more traditional Catholics as acceptable, so long as they did not interfere with Mafia activities. When they do interfere, they then are misguided, offenders, or heretics.

Thus, in the midst of centuries-old social cohesion exists centuries-old internal religious conflict. Non-Mafia members respond to the conflict by calling the Mafia Christian heretics, attempting to excommunicate them, and uniting around the faith and especially around religious leaders. Mafia members respond by attempting to buy favors, trying to compromise and change the faith, and using terror and murder. These differing responses heighten social cohesion on both sides. Conflict has the effect of actually strengthening the boundaries and group identity of conflicting parties.

Such is the way of social and religious life. Cohesion and conflict, as Meredith McGuire (1997) notes, are two sides of the same coin. They need and feed on each other.

Some people use the fact that religion can lead to conflict as evidence that religions are false. This conclusion is premised on the assumption that conflict is negative. But it need not be. For example, in the case of Father Puglisi and the Mafia, he could have chosen peace (give in to the Mafia's version of the faith) over justice, but he viewed justice—and the subsequent need for conflict—as a higher religious goal than the avoidance of conflict. This chapter will explore these ideas further.

GETTING PERSONAL

Have you ever had disagreements or even arguments over religion or spirituality with others, perhaps with family members, friends, or even people you don't know well? If so, what have the disagreements been about? Stop and think about these disagreements for a moment and then summarize them in the accompanying box that follows. If you have never had any disagreements over religion or spirituality, you can write "none."

BOX 4.1

Disagreements over Religion or Spirituality

_____

_____

_____

_____

_____

_____

If you have had disagreements over religion or spirituality, do you see any themes to those disagreements? If you have never had disagreements over religion, why do you think you have not, and why do you think others do have such disagreements?

Our interactions with other people are characterized by agreement and disagreement, cohesion and conflict. Sometimes you get along with your best friend, and sometimes you don't, perhaps occasionally to the degree that you stop talking to each other for a while, or even stop being best friends. One of the issues on which you might disagree with friends is religion. In the contemporary United States, we mostly _don't_ talk about religion in public. Certain topics are considered to be too volatile to be discussed in polite company—religion, politics, race, and the like. But among close friends, such social taboos can be loosened, and you may, one late night in the dorm, get into a discussion of religious views. You might be surprised to learn the "crazy stuff" that other people believe. Perhaps your discussion will turn more into heated debate, with some people questioning and others defending certain religious views. Or perhaps you'll mostly agree with one another and instead talk about the "crazy views" of others who are not in the room.

In subsequent sections, we explore why people sometimes have disagreements over religion, while at other times they seem perfectly able to coexist. As part of this discussion, we consider whether religious conflict is only about religion.

RELIGION AND SOCIAL COHESION

In many societies, including that of the United States, religion is considered to be a private affair, a set of convictions that an individual holds or rejects by choice. But one of the first sociologists, Emile Durkheim, demonstrated that, to a great extent, religion is a social affair. He analyzed what he considered to be the most primitive of religions—totemism—and then broadened his theory to apply to all religions. Durkheim concluded that whatever else religion is, it is *the worship of the group.* By this phrase, he meant that religion contributes to the cohesion of the group and expresses its unity through shared norms and values, rituals enacting these norms and values, and consequences for heresy (such as ex-communication or even death). Rituals incorporate members into the group by reminding them of the meaning and obligations of being part of the group.

Thus, according to Durkheim, religion is symbolically and literally the worship of the group, because people experience the group to be a power above and beyond the individual. Religious beliefs are collective representations, that is, group-held beliefs expressing something vital about the group itself and reaffirming the group's shared meanings and core beliefs. Participation in religious worship can dissolve boundaries between people and unify them if only for a brief time during which their entire focus is beyond themselves, on a unified object of devotion.

It is vital for you to grasp what Durkheim is saying here, so we will consider an extended example. Think of your favorite musical group of all time (perhaps it is Outkast, Los Lonely Boys, Coldplay, or . . .). We will use U2, but in the discussion that follows you should substitute your favorite.

You love to listen to the music of U2. As you often say, it's less satisfying to listen to other music since you discovered U2, because, although other music is good, U2 is so superior that they are almost otherworldly; their music is beyond the capabilities of mere mortals. (We exaggerate, of course, but this is what we often do with friends to make a point!) For years, you have listened to their CDs. You have memorized the words to dozens of their songs. You are struck by how deep their songs are, by how much meaning they pack into a four-minute song. You are enamored of the passion in Bono's voice, and mesmerized by the Edge's magic on the guitar.

Then you hear news that is almost too good to be true. U2 is going to do a 10-city U.S. tour, and one of those cities is yours. You call your close friends, who are your close friends in part because they also love U2, and you tell them the news. After shouts of joy, you all agree that no matter what it takes, you are going to the concert. Tickets go on sale in three days, and you use the time until then to plot your strategy for getting the money that you will need and for getting online to order the tickets as soon as they are available. At 12:01 A.M. on Thursday night, with your friends by your side, you are online requesting four tickets (one each for you and your three friends). You are successful, and though the tickets cost you $200 apiece, you have no doubt that it will be more than worth it. You got great seats, and it is going to be a grand experience to see U2 live!

The two-month wait for the big day is the longest two months in the history of humanity. (OK, so we exaggerate a bit again.) Days go by slowly, weeks drag on. But you are driven by the anticipation of the big night. You and your friends make plans for how you will get to the arena, what time you will leave, who is driving, and what you will wear.

Finally the big day arrives. You don't sleep much the night before because you are too excited. The hours of the big day go by in a blur. You go to class, but your professor sounds like one of the adults in a Charlie Brown TV special. You can't wait to get back home and get dressed for the big show. And finally that time comes. You rush home, planning out exactly what you will do to be ready by 4 P.M., when your friends are due to arrive.

And arrive they do. In fact, since they are as excited as you, they actually are all at your place by 3:50 P.M. You all are smiling broadly, feeling a bit jumpy, and raring to go. You pack into the car, and head off to the restaurant. The food is good, the company even better. You laugh together, talking about what you will do if Bono happens to call you up on stage.

You are all glad when you have finished eating and can finally head to the arena. You have to pay $20 to park, but you don't even care. This is THE CONCERT, and mere money is not going to get in the way of your enjoyment. After parking, you walk the five blocks to the arena. Clearly, about ten thousand other fans wanted to get there early as well, because the parking lots are already overflowing, and you share the walk to the arena with the many thousands of other people going to the same place.

The presence of all of these other U2 fans only increases your excitement. All the fans with their U2 shirts and banners, some even sporting Bono glasses, really get you pumped. Into the arena you all flow, and wow, you see it, the stage where U2 will be tonight, after the warm-up band. Oh warm-up bands, why do they bother, you came to see U2!

The wait for the show to start is excruciating. You are so excited that you are beside yourself. The arena is loaded with the anticipation of the 18,000 people who are packed into it. Finally, a local radio DJ comes out on stage and says "Hello [your city name here]!" The arena erupts, for all of you know that this signifies the start of the show. After the DJ makes some introductory comments, he announces the warm-up band and they are greeted with ear-splitting applause. They play seven songs. They are good, real good. You enjoy their music, but to be honest, you can't wait until they are done. Bring on U2!

The warm-up band finishes. You are told that there will be a 20-minute intermission, and the house lights come up. Ugh, so close yet so far. You wait, and wait, and wait. Finally, the house lights flicker. A cheer rises up. Then the house lights go down; it is completely dark. The cheers grow louder, deeper, as if from the people's souls. From the darkness, a light show begins on stage, pulsating like your heart.

And then, after all the waiting, all the anticipation, and all the planning, there before your eyes appear the members of U2. They rise up in unison from under the stage, the Edge playing an opening riff to a familiar song on his amazing guitar, the other three waving at you, yes, you could swear, they are waving at you. The arena is beyond loud. Thunder is shaking the place. You are screaming as loud as you can but you cannot even hear yourself. You don't care, this is unbelievable.

As the first song begins, the moment and all the anticipation catch up with you. You feel short of breath and weak in the knees, almost as if you are going to faint. Fortunately you do not, and the music is in full force. There they are in front of you, so close you can almost touch them. Bono is singing now in that passionate voice. That voice and that music, it is driving right down to your core. You have never quite felt this way before. The experience is almost mystical. After the first two songs, Bono finally talks, greeting all of you, telling you that they all intend to have an amazing time together. This is not just a concert, he says. We are here to change the world, and you are the world changers. Yes, yes, yes.

The concert is like a dream. You are so focused on the band, on the music, on the message, and on the sea of humanity all celebrating together. Bono later gives an impassioned talk about overcoming poverty. He says that you are part of the generation that will solve one of the world's greatest problems; he asks everyone who has a cell phone to hold it up, illuminated. Knowing that this moment was coming, all 18,000 people are ready. In unison, they wave their lighted cell phones, swaying gently together, back and forth. Bono is up on stage doing the same. Then U2 begins to sing one of their all-time classics, while all the people in the audience continue to sway with lighted cell phones held high. This moment is so amazing, your heart feels too big. Life's problems, at least for this moment in time, don't matter. You feel alive, wholly and completely. You feel an attachment to the other people in the arena that you cannot explain. This night is one that you will never forget.

What happened to you at this concert is what Durkheim says happens in religious worship. Even though at a concert you are with thousands of people you don't know, during that time you can feel as one, your individuality melted away as you surrender to the power of the group, all eyes and hearts fixed on the same object of devotion. If such social cohesion can happen at a concert, imagine the power that a religion can generate when it brings together people who may indeed know one another, when there are clear objects of devotion, when people gather to acknowledge and celebrate what they believe and who they are. The next time the Pope or the Dalai Lama takes a trip, watch the massive crowds, the throngs of humanity pressing to get a glimpse of him. It will make the U2 concert seem like mere child's play.

A few years ago we interviewed several hundred Americans about their religious faith. We sat in their homes and asked them many questions, including, toward the end of the interview, "What if you were to just give up your faith, just chuck it and live without it?" People were dismayed by the question. They either could not imagine such a thing, or if they could, they thought it would make them despondent. One woman literally started crying at the thought. Why, we asked them, is the idea of living without faith so hard to imagine? The answer was that, to these people, their faiths were not just something they believed or did. Rather, religion was who they were (both their individual and social identity), it gave them purpose and meaning, and it united them with fellow believers. To "just chuck their faith" was like throwing away their lives.

So we see the power of religion for social cohesion. But this view assumes that, as in Sicily, nearly everyone in a community is of the same faith. In reality, large modern societies are highly diverse and include all types of religions and spiritualities, as well as believers, agnostics, and atheists. Take the United States, for example. Sure, there are lots of Christians, though they are divided among Roman Catholics, members of the Greek Orthodox church, and Protestants. But there are also followers of all the other world faiths. What is more, so many alternative spiritualist faiths—Rastafarianism, EST, the use of crystals—exist in the country that it is difficult even for scholars who are studying such phenomena full time to keep up. And about 1 in 10 Americans claims to be agnostic or atheist or simply not to care about religion.

How can a nation be united amidst such diversity? Enter what scholars call Civil Religion. If you have never heard the term before, you might think that it means "polite religion." You are not that far off: Although the term *civil* refers to the public sphere of a nation, the religion that is developed for that level must be polite, as we will see.

Scholars define Civil Religion as "any set of beliefs and rituals, related to the past, present, and/or future of a people ('nation'), which are understood in some transcendental fashion" (Hammond 1976, 171). Civil Religion, like any religion, stirs a sense of awe and sentiment within its followers. All presidents refer to a generic God. (We don't know to what God they are referring specifically, but it is to a being or force spelled with a capital letter.) This God is thought to have special concern for the United States and is repeatedly asked to bless the nation. It is expected that God will want to do this, for the nation is thought to embody all that this God desires for humans: democracy, individual freedom and liberty, and the pursuit of happiness and economic gain.

Civil Religion in the United States has its objects of devotion, such as the flag (never let it touch the ground, never fly it upside down, put it at half-mast when tragedy strikes, fold it with military care if you are taking it down), the national anthem (put your hand on your heart, remove your hat, and focus on the flag while singing it), and the Constitution (revere this document as the Holy Book of Civil Religion, the final arbiter of Right and Wrong). It has its ordained theologians or religious scholars who decipher what the Holy Book is meant to say: judges, especially the Supreme Court. (They are almost supreme beings—the most learned among us of the Civil Religion; they are appointed for life, wear religious-like robes, are rarely seen except when they are hearing cases, and sit at the Civil Religion's version of the judgment seat.) The ultimate leader of Civil Religion is the elected president, who is charged with bringing us together under the power of this religion. The ultimate leader is both a prophet—challenging people to dream bigger and be better—and a priest—supporting people in times of trouble, encouraging them that God is on their side and will impart blessings as long as they stay true to the Civil Religion.

To see Civil Religion as it is enacted by its ultimate leader, the president, read the words of Barack Obama excerpted from his November 4, 2008, presidential election acceptance speech:

"[W]e have never been just a collection of individuals or a collection of Red States and Blue States, we are—and always will be—the United States of America. It's the answer that led [people] . . . to put their hands on the arc of history and bend it once more toward the hope of a better day. . . . [You proved that] a government of the people, by the people and for the people has not perished from this Earth. . . . [Yet] even as we celebrate tonight, we know the challenges that tomorrow will bring are the greatest of our lifetime. . . . The road ahead will be long. Our climb will be steep. We may not get there in one year or even one term, but America, I have never been more hopeful than I am tonight that we will get there. I promise you—we as a people will get there. . . . [We need] a new spirit of service, a new spirit of sacrifice. So let us summon a new spirit of patriotism, of service, of responsibility where each of us resolves to pitch in and work harder and look after not only ourselves, but each other . . . In this country, we rise or fall as one nation, as one people. . . . the true strength of our nation comes from . . . the enduring power of our ideals—democracy, liberty, opportunity and unyielding hope. . . . Our union can be perfected. . . . This is our chance to answer that call. This is our moment. . . . [We] reaffirm that fundamental truth—that out of many, we are one. . . . [We] respond with that timeless creed that sums up the spirit of a people: Yes We Can. . . . God bless you, and may God bless the United States of America." (Barack Obama. November 4, 2008. Presidential Election Acceptance Speech. Chicago, IL.)

Notice that in his acceptance speech, President-elect Obama, like all presidents before him, speaks in lofty terms and frequently refers to ideals. He especially emphasizes that, although we are diverse, we are one people, united under the principles in which we all believe (the Civil Religion values). Empowered by our unity, we share a can-do spirit. Yes, we will face tough times (the prophetic voice), but we will emerge victorious because we are unified and we stand for what is good, true, and right (the priestly voice). And may America's God bless us, God's people and God's nation, as we go forth toward Nirvana ("Our union can be perfected").

Thus, religion serves a powerful social cohesion function. When almost everyone belongs to the same religion, as in Sicily, religion is a social glue that is infused in the totality of life. When there is religious diversity within a nation, the nation often creates a new religion that we have called Civil Religion to broadly incorporate all persons, regardless of their faith tradition.

If we think of religion—even Civil Religion—as a cultural resource that we selectively use and appropriate, then we see how it can also lead to conflict with others who have a different interpretation of the same faith, a different faith, or no faith at all. Just as important, the more socially cohesive a religious group is, the more vigorously that group will defend its beliefs, practices, and ways of life against threats. Religious conflict, then, can arise out of religious cohesion. We now turn to the topic of this conflict.

RELIGION AND SOCIAL CONFLICT

In his book *Religion and Social Conflict,* Robert Lee (1964, 3) opens with a now-classic statement: "The society without conflict is a dead society. Hence the most peaceful place in the world, in terms of the absence of conflict, is a graveyard."

Outside a graveyard, humans have conflict, including religious conflict. It is our task as sociologists to better understand where, when, and why conflict occurs, and we seek to do that briefly in this section. But before we do, take a moment to identify three religious conflicts that you know of (not the personal disagreements you identified early in the chapter, but religious conflicts involving groups of people). If you cannot think of any off the top of your head, search the Internet, using keywords such as "religious conflict." Write three conflicts in the accompanying box.

BOX 4.2
Religious Conflicts

   1.

   2.

   3.

To help us understand these conflicts, let's draw on a core tool of sociologists, the the sociological imagination (Mills 1959). The sociological imagination distinguishes between personal troubles (my friend and I had a disagreement over religion) and social problems (people from religious group A and religious group B often kill each other). Personal troubles involve a few isolated individuals and probably can be explained simply by the personalities of the people involved, but when whole groups clash, looking at the characteristics of individuals will not explain the conflict.

The sociological imagination understands that all individuals are embedded within groups, which are embedded in larger societies, which are themselves embedded in a specific time in history. The Hatfields and McCoys feuded not just because of what was occurring between them at the time, but because it had been their long history to do so. Part of the identity of each of these clans was to dislike the other. If either group stopped the feud, it would have risked a complete loss of identity.

As you review the three religious conflicts that you identified, can you use the sociological imagination to explain why the conflicts occur? That is, explain the conflicts without resorting to explanations involving the characteristics of individuals. What do you come up with?

Let us first classify the types of religious conflict and then examine why each may occur:

1. Conflict between religious groups (between, say, Buddhists and Zoroastrians)
2. Conflict within a religious group (Catholicism in Sicily, for example)
3. Conflict between a religious group and the larger society. (Mormons once believed that it is permissible for a man to marry more than one woman, but the larger society did not.)
4. Conflict between religious group and a nonreligious group or sector. (Fundamentalist Christians object to the teaching of evolution in public schools, while public schools attempt to avoid religious particularism)

If you examine the three specific religious conflicts that you wrote down, they should fit into at least one of the preceding four categories. (If they don't, you have come up with a new category of conflict!)

To consider why religious conflict occurs, let's first think about why conflict in general occurs. On the surface, it seems simple: People and groups conflict because they disagree. Fair enough. But why do they disagree? Because they don't see eye to eye, you might say, or because they have different perspectives, or because one group is trampling on another group. OK, we grant you that. But we really aren't getting very far here. It is sort of like telling someone you are from Cokato, Minnesota. "Where is that?" the person will ask, to which you reply, "Six miles east of Dassel." "Where is Dassel?" to which you reply, "Six miles west of Cokato." All true, but not that helpful.

Let's go back to our original explanation for conflict: "People and groups disagree." But we know for sure that not all disagreements lead to conflict. We may disagree with another person's religion, or with all religion, but that does not mean that we necessarily engage in conflict with those who follow other religions. Religious conflict, then, can be better defined as *groups or individuals acting against resistors, in an attempt either to preserve or to change religious beliefs, rituals, or ways of being.* (See, for example, Marty 1964 and Weber 1947.) Notice that according to this definition, action is required, and that "it takes at least two to tango." If the other group simply gives in, there is no conflict. Also, one set of actors is seeking a goal that is in opposition to the goal of another set of actors, and they care enough to engage in conflict.

There are two additional aspects of religious conflict. The first aspect, noted earlier, is that the social cohesion of religion on one side of the coin implies social conflict on the other side of the coin. Connected to, and elaborating on, this "two-sides-of-the-same-coin" concept is that conflict has several functions for social and religious life. At least as far back as the early 1900s, scholars have noted that conflict can have positive aspects. But it was Lewis Coser's 1956 book, *The Functions of Social Conflict*, that developed this idea fully. According to his work—and subsequently supported by hundreds of studies—conflict between groups serves several positive functions:

1. ***Clarifies boundaries.*** A Hindu fully understands what it means to be Hindu only by knowing what a Hindu is not (the boundaries). This understanding is best achieved through conflict with non-Hindus, because it forces Hindus to clearly define who is in the group and who is not.

2. ***Solidifies identity.*** Conflict helps to firm and deepen group identity. If groups are going to be challenged or to challenge another group, they will continue to do so only insofar as they understand who they are in relation to other groups. Thus, if Hindus are conflicting with Sikhs, not only are the boundaries between the two religious groups sharpened, but both groups come to see their individual and group identities as being intimately tied, respectively, to being Hindu and being Sikh.

3. ***Increases social cohesion.*** We have come full circle, or in keeping with our metaphor, we have turned the coin again. Cohesion fuels conflict, and conflict fuels cohesion. You may fight with your sibling and berate each other mercilessly, but let some outsider attack your sibling, and bam: You rise to your sibling's defense. External conflict increases internal cohesion.

4. ***Strengthens ideological solidarity and participation.*** This is a fancy way of saying that conflict with outside groups also means that the members of a religious group come to think more alike. External conflict leads them to gain a greater clarity about what they believe and value, and again, these values become clear markers of being a member of the group. Another important benefit of conflict for a group is that it increases participation as people rise to the defense of their group.

5. ***Augments resource mobilization.*** Groups in conflict can do more than groups that are not in conflict. They get more donations of money or goods, members devote more time to the group, and members are more willing to sacrifice for the good of the group and to overcome the enemy.

In terms of social cohesion within religious groups, then, it is in a group's best interest to conflict with outside groups, though that is not nice to say in polite company. Accordingly, it is unfortunate, but asking people to love the whole world and all that is in it just doesn't work very well for building group strength. Of course, it could work if the world was engaged in conflict with aliens from another planet or some other type of outsider group.

Perhaps these benefits of conflict are why if we wish to maintain social cohesion and group strength, we can never be without conflict of some sort. As Emile Durkheim wrote in a famous example, imagine an isolated monastery full of completely devoted monks who are solidly committed to their faith, each following the hundreds of rules set forth by the abbot, each fully devoted to their object of worship. What seems to outsiders like the slightest deviation—hair a half-inch too long, praying for 3 hours and 58 minutes instead of the expected 4 hours, wearing a garment that is light brown instead of medium brown—would be met with great moral outrage and considered to be a clear violation of the group's way of life. And if some monks decided not to correct their moral violation, but instead began to claim that it is OK to wear light-brown garments, internal conflict would result. If it continued long enough with no clear resolution (neither side gives in nor is able to impose its will on the other group), the groups would split into two monasteries. In short, if there is no conflict from without, conflict from within will arise. (Think of those Catholics in Sicily who tolerate the Mafia version of the religion and those who oppose them.)

Internal religious conflict can arise over any number of issues: acceptable musical styles, traditional versus modern worship, clergy/laity battles, male versus female rights and behaviors, generational differences, the number of parking spaces that are available, whether men must grow beards to worship properly, or how short women's skirts may be. The list goes on, but you get the point.

If conflict has so many positive functions and is almost inevitable, why don't we see even more religious conflict, especially violent religious conflict? Here are a few reasons. First, as Robert Wuthnow (2005) finds in his book on the challenges of religious diversity, people actually know very little about religions other than their own. They know that religion X is different from their own religion Y, but they don't really know much detail beyond that. Insofar as they do not know details, they do not feel threatened, and their religious understandings are not challenged. To put it bluntly, often there is no religious conflict because people don't much care what others are doing or believing. They are busy enough dealing with the conflicts within their own group.

Religious conflict *does* happen when one religious group's way of life impinges upon by another group, be it religious or not. But full-scale violence is usually avoided because there are typically other avenues for dealing with the conflict and because the continued existence of the conflict actually benefits the group. (See the five positive functions of conflict listed previously.)

Sociologically, there is another reason that extreme levels of conflict between religious groups are limited. In most societies, social diversity is a reality. People occupy multiple roles, move in several spheres (religious, work, neighborhood, school, etc.), and maintain social relationships across several groups. Suppose that a religious group is in conflict with public schools, claiming that the schools teach secular humanism and are anti-God. A number of public-school teachers are probably members of the religious group. It will be hard for these members to engage in an extreme level of conflict both with their employer and their peers. They will seek to moderate the conflict.

Hence, the more groups are cross-cut with the same members, typically the less likely it is that severe conflict will occur (Blau and Schwartz 1984, McGuire 1997). The biggest trouble—conflict that results in bloodshed—tends to occur when there are concentrations of roles. When members of religious group A all tend to be lower class, to share the same ethnicity, and to live on the west side, while members of religious group B tend to be upper class, to share a different ethnicity than members of religious group A, and to live on the east side of town, there may be tremendous religious conflicts. In fact, any sort of conflict between groups can be at the same time a religious conflict, a class conflict, an ethnic conflict, and a regional conflict. Because religion may be a sacred marker that accentuates and stands for all the divisions between groups (Hanf 1994, 202) many conflicts labeled as religious conflicts may not really be about religion.

To learn more about such occurrences, research the Internet and read about the conflict that existed among Bosnians, Croats, and Serbs (or the conflicts in Rwanda or the Sudan). The ostensibly religious conflict among the Bosnians, Croats, and Serbs led to the deaths of thousands, the slaughter of families, and the disruption of life for many years. But were differences in religion really the basis of the conflict? You might also investigate the hundreds-of-years-long conflict between Protestants and Catholics in Northern Ireland. The conflict is much more than a religious conflict.

CAN'T WE ALL JUST GET ALONG?

Can't we all just get along? No, we cannot, and yes, we can. The irony is that both statements are true. Religious groups need social cohesion to survive and thrive, but strongly cohesive groups often conflict with other groups. And the conflict actually has positive effects for the internal cohesion of the group.

Civil Religion is the attempt on the part of diverse nations to create a religion that overarches the particular views of the religious *and* the nonreligious people in the country. Such a religion is necessary, it seems, to take individuals beyond mere loyalty to the specific groups to which they belong and to create cohesion and commitment to the nation. But the Civil Religion that strengthens internal national unity becomes, at the same time, a basis for conflict with other nations. Whether we talk about it explicitly or not, America's Civil Religion distinguishes the United States, setting us up as different from other nations in our relationship to a sacred order. Our Civil Religion establishes group boundaries and feeds conflicts with those viewed as outsiders, including other nations.

Some religious groups, admirably, attempt to be nonexclusive and open to all, lowering their boundaries, regardless of their religious beliefs. This doesn't work so well, because it makes it difficult to have clear boundaries, clear identities, and strong membership commitment, unless, of course, the group is in conflict with other groups, such as religious groups, which think that the first group's approach is heresy or not religion at all. In such a case, being "open and accepting" becomes an identity, boundaries are drawn to delineate the group from the intolerant groups, and membership commitment rises in defense of their views.

But when the boundaries are drawn, this open and accepting group is no longer open and accepting of all people, just other people who share its views. Such is the irony of social and religious life. In later chapters we will use some of this knowledge to understand fundamentalist movements and even religious violence. It will become clearer how the tension between religious cohesion and religious conflict plays out: Yes, we can all get along, and no, we cannot.

SUGGESTED READING

Coser, Lewis. A. 1956. *The Functions of Social Conflict.* Glencoe, IL: The Free Press.
Durkheim, Emile. [1915] 1965. *Elementary Forms of Religious Life.* Translated by J. W. Swain. New York: Free Press.

Wuthnow, Robert. 2005. *America and the Challenges of Religious Diversity.* Princeton, NJ: Princeton University Press.

CHAPTER

5

News Flash: God's Not Dead (and Neither is the Goddess!)

1. Have contemporary societies become more secular over time?
2. What does religious vitality mean? What does a religiously vital society look like?
3. Is it possible for individuals to be more religious while their societies become less so?

Once upon a time, many say, society was *religious*. Now, unfortunately, some would say, it is *secular*. Once religion informed and shaped all parts of our lives—education, family life, work, politics, and health care were all infused with religious meaning. Now, the story goes, religion is confined to Sunday morning and we largely forget our religion the rest of the week. Purported evidence of this decline abounds. More people used to attend religious services regularly. More people used to believe in and practice their particular religion's teaching every day. And, most importantly, religious organizations and leaders enjoyed a high level of respect and authority within communities. In short, the past, it is assumed, was a "Golden Age of Faith."

And now, just look around and see what is happening. In many sectors, attendance at religious services is declining. Individuals feel less bound by a particular religion's strictures. Instead they assemble their own mix of beliefs and practices to suit themselves and their lifestyles, like "Sheila," whom we introduced in Chapter 2 (from Bellah et al. 1985). Others flat-out reject all religion and sometimes proudly announce their atheism at family gatherings or social events. Religious leaders are increasingly viewed with suspicion and ridicule because, while they require their members to obey their teachings and give money to support their enterprises, they themselves are found guilty of abuse and immoral conduct. Perhaps worst of all is the attitude, shared by many, that religious groups and their leaders are out of touch with contemporary life. For the religiously inclined, the sense that the world is changing and leaving religion behind causes great concern: Will religion lose all of its social significance and eventually disappear?

Sociologists, too, wonder about the future of religion. For years, they have observed a shift away from what once seemed like a more religiously dominated world. For example, public education once explicitly taught a Protestant morality, but now religion instruction has been removed from schools. Hospitals, once run as religious charities, are increasingly run as for-profit organizations with no religious ties whatsoever. And, as you may have noticed, many people get testy when religion comes up in political debates, as if it had no place in our government.

To account for the changing role of religion in society, and especially for its apparent decline in importance, sociologists developed *secularization theory*. Secularization theory links the decline of religion with the rise of some other important qualities of modern societies, especially rationality, bureaucratization, and impersonality. These qualities are by-products of some big social changes, including the development and expansion of a capitalist economic structure, the rise of a political system run by bureaucrats, and the dominance of a cultural view of the world that is based in scientific rationality. The consequences for religion have been significant. Sociologist Max Weber has argued that the modern world has been "disenchanted": The magic and the mystery once present in everyday life have vanished, replaced by a cold-hearted rationality that emphasizes efficiency and calculability. Religion, once the glue that held people's worlds together and a force that exerted authority over almost all aspects of people's lives, fell by the wayside. Or so the story goes.

But think again! Over the last two decades, sociologists of religion have also observed amazing changes in the religious sphere and in the vitality of it. They point out that despite the fact that the United States is among the most economically, technologically, and militarily advanced nations on earth, it also has among the highest reported levels of belief in God. Pretty clearly, the forces of capitalism, bureaucratization, and science did not pass us by, but somehow religion survives. Some denominations are seeing more success than others, however. While more liberal denominations have noted declines in membership, conservative Christian churches are seeing surges in attendance. As we already observed in Chapter 1, the market for religious products is huge and shows no signs of slowing down; it's a multibillion-dollar-a-year industry producing books, films, clothing, jewelry, diets, holistic healing techniques, and many, many other goods and services, all consumed by a public that is seemingly ravenous for all things religious and spiritual.

Worldwide religion remains a strong force despite the spread of technological advances and economic development. In the Southern Hemisphere, Christianity and Islam together continue to attract millions of followers, even as those societies undergo dramatic economic change. Moreover, around the world, the rise of fundamentalism attracts millions of people to strict and decidedly antimodern religious beliefs and practices. Recall, for example, the suicide bombings and terrorist attacks around the world that are committed by religiously motivated extremists of many faiths. Is religion on the decline? Hardly—indeed, it's quite the reverse.

The question of whether contemporary societies have become more secular is thus a controversial one. Its answer depends on how we define *secularization* and how we see it working. But its flip side—strong religious vitality—cannot be overlooked either. It's a conundrum if you think, as some sociologists do, that religious vitality is the *opposite* of secularization. Here we argue, in line with other sociologists, that, in many of their forms, secularization and religious vitality are related, not in opposing, but in complementary ways. Finally, toward the end of this chapter we will bring both sides of these debates together and examine the paradox of living in an increasingly secular, yet religiously vital and vibrant world.

WILL THE *REAL* SECULARIZATION THEORY PLEASE STAND UP?

Secularization theory has been a central way of thinking about what has happened and is still happening to religion in our world ever since Max Weber first posited the emergence of the industrial society. Modernity was spurred on by the development of a capitalist economy that was founded on making as much money as possible, as well as the expansion of state structures that were based on legal and impersonal regulations and relationships. Together, these twin institutions, capitalism and the bureaucratic state, played key roles in making society less clearly "religious." Weber and others after him argued that religion would be increasingly marginalized as society became more dominated by scientific thinking and discovery. This theory resulted from a cost–benefit mentality rooted in capitalism and the modern state, which controlled all other social institutions (the economy, health care, education, media, and even family) through a complex bureaucratic structure of regulations intended to ensure the efficient operation of society as a whole. In short, religion was no longer the institution controlling education, health care, or much else outside of the religious sphere. Religious explanations for sickness, a variety of natural phenomena, and even the origins of the universe gave way to scientific theories that were based on scientific evidence collected through research. After stripping away these religious explanations and meanings from everyday life, we are left with a world that is rational, impersonal, and bureaucratic, lacking the "enchantments" and mysteries of life in the premodern world. The bottom line is that Weber and other social theorists simply assumed that religion and modernity were antithetical; logically, then, as the forces of modernization increase, religion's power and influence must decrease.

Since Weber's time, other social scientists took for granted that religion was in decline. Some went so far as to suggest that it would disappear completely. Peter Berger put the matter quite succinctly: "As there is a secularization of society and culture, so is there a secularization of consciousness. Put simply, this means that the modern West has produced an increasing number of individuals who look upon the world and their own lives without the benefit of religious interpretations." (1967, 107–108) In other words, fewer and fewer of us think about our lives, friends, food, work, and other aspects of our existence as needing—much less *having*—religious significance. So there's a vicious circle here. Religions lose their influence in society, causing fewer people to think and act religiously, which in turn further undermines religion's influence, until it basically disappears (Stark 1999, Tschannen 1991).

Then again, maybe the experts were all a little premature in predicting religion's disappearance. Over the last two decades, in the face of conservative religious resurgences worldwide, as well as the continuation of traditional religious beliefs and practices and the explosion of "holistic and alternative spiritualities," sociologists of religion have rejected this version of secularization. Nevertheless, an ongoing debate has raged about whether, given a rejection of secularization as the "death of religion," secularization theory as a whole has outlived its relevance as a way to understand religion today.

On one side of the debate loom the challengers: Jeffrey Hadden, Rodney Stark, Roger Finke, William Bainbridge, and even secularization's former advocate, Peter Berger, among others. All these experts contend that religion is alive and well and will continue to be so, given the extensive data that show continued commitment to beliefs in God, adherence to the Bible, the practice of prayer, and so on. Stark (1999) hoped to put the final nail in the intellectual coffin of secularization with the declaration that it should "Rest In Peace" and that it is high time we, as students of religion, get over it and move on.

On the other side of the debate are those who continue to want to rescue secularization theory from its detractors: Karel Dobbelaere, Mark Chaves, Peter Beyer, David Yamane, Frank Lechner, and a host of others who do research on secularization and religious vitality with data from North America and Western and Eastern Europe. Unlike earlier theorists, they don't believe that religion will go away completely. Instead, they focus on the declining power of religion at a societal level. They share an understanding of secularization as fundamentally a *descriptive* term that characterizes the forces at work shaping entire societies, rather than a predictive one that hypothesizes some inevitable future for the religious beliefs and behaviors of individuals.

Dobbelaere (1999) builds his argument on an understanding that in modern society institutions are differentiated according to the functions they serve for society as a whole. This idea has been long connected to the work of Emile Durkheim, about whom you read in Chapter 1. As modern societies develop, their institutions become ever more specialized and develop their own unique cultures, with their own norms, values, language, and mechanisms for operating (Luhman 1989). Societies' institutions become more independent from one another while simultaneously remaining integrated through the operations, regulations, and policies of the bureaucratic state.

What does all of this have to do with religion? Dobbelaere argues that this process is precisely the way that secularization takes place. Secularization, according to Dobbelaere (1999, 232), is "a process by which the overarching and transcendent religious system of old is being reduced in a modern functionally differentiated society to a subsystem alongside other subsystems, losing in this process its overarching claims over the other subsystems." In other words, society develops a separate "religious" arena. As its own subsystem within society, religion freely develops its own unique forms of organizations, values, and ways of doing things. This is just another way to say that it develops its own *culture* and *subcultures*. But the cultural forms of religion are distinct from those of the economy, the state, science, law, and other institutions. Consequently, what may hold true and make sense in the religious sphere in terms of values, norms, and language does not necessarily hold true or make sense in the economic realm, in science, in education, or in medicine.

For instance, many religions value charity and encourage their followers to give selflessly of their resources. Yet if you, as a CEO, walked into a meeting of shareholders of a transnational corporation and suggested increasing the wages and benefits of employees worldwide because your religious faith requires economic justice for workers, or if you announced that you planned to accept a smaller profit margin for the company for the same reason, we may safely assume that you would be laughed out of the room and quickly become unemployed as a result.

The impact of this secularization process on religion is tremendous. Once religion has been separated into its own sphere of influence, separate from the state, which now governs and represents many different social groups, then religious rules—even the ones that at one time were widely accepted as universal—can no longer be used to regulate behavior for an entire society. So, for example, while one person's religious tradition may forbid the use of birth control, the drinking of alcohol, or the eating of pork, such regulations can be applicable only *within* the religious group; prohibitions against these behaviors cannot be made into law if the larger society includes many people who view such behaviors as acceptable. Even in contemporary Middle Eastern societies where civil law is based on Muslim religious law, only selective religious laws are enforced by the governments. Highly religious Muslim states—despite the prohibition on these behaviors in Islam—tend to leave economic behavior (like accumulating profit, earning money from interest, and allowing wealth to concentrate in the hands of a few) relatively unregulated, but may highly regulate gender roles and sexual behavior. Why does this happen? It's because these nations are all dependent for their economic well-being on continued participation in the capitalist world economy, an economy that is based on the accumulation of profit, the earning of interest, and the concentration of wealth, all of which stem from decidedly secular motives.

Chaves (1994) and Yamane (1997) simplify Dobbelaere's ideas by arguing that secularization is best understood in terms of the declining scope of religious authority, shrinking to cover only matters of faith rather than also covering economics, education, politics, or health care. Chaves and others perform a threefold test for the decline of religious authority, measuring its decline at the societal, organizational, and individual levels. (See also Dobbelaere 1999.)

At the *societal* level, secularization refers to a general decline in religious authority over other social institutions. As noted previously, this trend reflects the idea of religion becoming one institution among many and no longer maintaining any priority over other institutions in its values, norms, or directives for how best to create the "good" society. Think about what this means for religion in practical terms. In the spring of 2008, Pope Benedict XVI, the head of the Roman Catholic Church, set out new doctrines that expanded the scope of what the Church considered to be mortal sins, meaning that they were serious violations of the Ten Commandments and other central Biblical teachings. Among the new sins added to the list of mortal sins were ruining the environment, carrying out morally debatable scientific experiments, allowing genetic manipulations that alter DNA or compromise embryos, and perpetrating injustices that cause poverty or the excessive accumulation of wealth in the hands of a few. These are now official doctrines of the Church, violations of which are supposedly punished by consignment to hell. Yet despite this new exposition of religious authority over the economy and the scientific world, the practical consequences of the doctrines are nonexistent for anyone who is not Catholic. The Pope no longer has real authority to regulate the operations of capitalism or the scientific community. He can speak and make pronouncements, but whether individual business people or scientists pay attention is completely up to them.

Think about marriage for a minute. Most of us think of a classic marriage ceremony as a religious event, because it is held in a church or synagogue and presided over by clergy. However, in Christian terms, such a ceremony is more properly called "matrimony," and some denominations consider it to be a sacrament. Marriage, however, is a civil event-based on legal definitions. It occurs, not when vows are made in church or blessings are pronounced, but when the legal document is signed in the presence of witnesses. This is why every minister in the United States, regardless of religion, at the end of the ceremony says "In the name of the state of . . ., I now pronounce you husband and wife." Notice that it is not the religious authority of the minister that creates the marriage, but the intention of the two people involved and their legal act according to the laws of the particular state. In many European nations, all couples get married in a registry office and then some go on to have a separate religious ceremony to bless the union at another time. Is this societal-level secularization? Most definitely, it is. Not only does the example of *matrimony* versus *marriage* illustrate a real differentiation between the powers of religion and those of the government, but it also illustrates that it is the state, which has the greater authority. Any couple married by the state is legally married; however, a couple that participates only in a religious ceremony without fulfilling state requirements would not be considered legally married.

At the *organizational* level, secularization occurs at the level of religious organizations themselves (Chaves 1994, Dobbelaere 1999, Luckmann 1967). In this sense, secularization refers to internal changes occurring within religious groups that change how they look and how they operate, changes that make them look and act more like other organizations. Schools, churches, social service agencies, and hospitals all look and act like businesses. Their internal structures and cultures begin to resemble one another. Karl Marx made this argument years ago, of course, when he argued that this homogenization was due to the spread of capitalism, which eventually forces all other institutions into a dependent relationship with it, even so far as to impart its language, norms, and values to them.

But what does this mean in religious terms and how is it related to secularization? The increasing diversity of modern society creates religious markets in which religious groups compete for members. Such competition means that the groups need to appeal to religious consumers, who now have many different options to meet their spiritual needs, much in the same way that competing businesses all want to attract your attention and dollars by appealing to your needs and wants. This pressure leads to a change in religious groups' messages, which suggests that each group's members are "customers" who must be pleased and placated rather than expected to obey the authority of the minister or the religious tradition itself. As we saw when we discussed the phenomenon of megachurches, these internal changes mean that attending religious services begins to have a lot in common with activities like going to the mall, enjoying a grande latte at a Starbucks, or attending a rock concert.

Further evidence of internal secularization lies in the fact that religious leadership is increasingly left to lay people rather than clergy. A democratization of religious authority has emerged in Roman Catholic congregations, driven in part by the decreasing numbers of clergy. This is occurring in some mainline Protestant and Evangelical congregations too. Ministers now ask people to call them Bob or Jane, instead of Reverend or Pastor or Father, as a way to make people feel more comfortable by assuring them that religious leaders are "just people," like them. Likewise, buzz words from the business world become more common among religious groups that try to find "best practices," to "assess outcomes" of programs and ministries, and to exercise "due diligence" in hiring and appointing new leaders. Outside programs and charities are expected to provide accountability by reporting back to congregations that support them. Any new project requires conversations with "stakeholders." And so it goes. The language and culture of the business world, including concepts such as return on investments, investor confidence, outcomes assessment, and customer/client satisfaction, become the cultural forms of religious organizations, even those, which were founded on the principles of giving without expecting anything in return, following the golden rule, and caring selflessly for the poor, widows, and orphans.

Finally, at the *individual* level, as we begin to see from these examples, secularization can have an impact on the authority of religious leaders, doctrines, and traditions, affecting what individuals actually believe and what they do when it comes to their individual faith. This is the most problematic dimension to secularization for the sociologists who reject this theory. These scholars counter that if *society* is becoming more secular, then there must be a decline in religious belief and practice among *individuals,* an expectation that clearly flies in the face of the evidence, at least in countries like the United States, that individuals still report high levels of religious belief and practice. Yet religious belief and practice can exist quite apart, and in many different forms, from the ones that are considered "orthodox" by religious leaders and organizations. Survey data suggest that there are wide gaps between the official teachings of religious groups and the day-to-day attitudes and behaviors of their members. Think about the following examples: "My priest and church doctrine forbid me as a good Roman Catholic from using various forms of birth control, yet I still use them." Or this: "I believe in God, yet can be quite happy thinking about God in the form of Jesus, Allah, Jehovah, Krishna, or even as the Goddess on occasion, all the while happily attending my own traditional Protestant church, which rejects the idea that God is reflected in any form other than Jesus Christ." As in the past, believers today mix and match their religious symbols and images in as many ways as they wish. Linda Woodhead has argued that these shifts are especially evident in the way that women in the United States and Europe increasingly are disaffected from religious traditions that do not support them in their contemporary roles as professionals and do not help them balance their work and home lives, leaving them to move into new forms of spirituality that will help them cope with these experiences (Sointu and Woodhead 2008, Woodhead 2008). We'll revisit this situation in Chapter 9.

Even religious affiliation itself is declining as the number of unaffiliated people continues to increase. A recent report on religion in the United States noted that "unaffiliated" people—those who report not belonging to any faith group—now compose 16.1% of the population, up from 7% in the early 1990s (Pew Forum on Religion and Public Life, 2008a). In addition, the report observes that one in four people between the ages of 18 and 29 years reports not being affiliated with any religious group. (See also Hout and Fischer 2002.) Moreover, the report notes that three times as many people moved into the unaffiliated category as moved out of it. This is not to say that all of these individuals are atheists or agnostics" Three-quarters of the unaffiliated group simply reported not being affiliated with any religion in particular (Pew Forum on Religion and Public Life 2008a).

Over time, the religious marketplace has become one in which individuals, rather than clergy, official doctrine, or traditions, set the terms of beliefs and practices. Phillips (2004, 149) points to these shifts as clear consequences of secularization in spite of the development of an active and competitive religious marketplace: "Excommunications no longer incur public stigma. Defectors and apostates can't be fined, flogged, or banished. In this setting, churches only exert influence over those who freely offer their allegiance."

In any case, it is important to understand that there is a great deal of variation in the ways that secularization unfolds, if it in fact does so, in local communities, nations, and regions of the world. Even though some people take clear sides in the secularization debate, nothing about these processes is simple or straightforward. As Chaves (1994, 752) notes, "secularization occurs, or not, as the result of social and political conflicts between those social actors who would enhance or maintain religion's social significance and those who would reduce it." What is significant about Chaves' point is that, in good sociological fashion, the outcome of any social process, including that of secularization, is never fixed or inevitable. Real people, acting in concrete times and places, make real differences in how these processes play out. In this sense, even as some aspects of our world are becoming more secular, religious groups and individuals remain vital forces in it.

RELIGIOUS VITALITY IN THE UNITED STATES AND ABROAD

So far, our discussion seems to support one side of the secularization debate, leading us to agree with secularization proponents. But while structural changes in the world continue to affect religious authority, as this chapter's title suggests, neither God nor the Goddess—whether new or old, singular or multiple—is dead. Religious belief, practice, and experience remain an important presence in the lives of most of the world's population and in the world's geopolitical order. Sociologists use the concept of *religious vitality* to describe the level of religious activity in a community, nation, or region of the world. In much of the work done in this field, religious vitality and secularization are pitted as opposing sets of concepts. However, we will argue that these terms are describing sometimes related, but separate, phenomena. Now that we know something about the effects of secularization on religion, what exactly does a religiously vital society look like, what forces drive this vitality, and how does religious vitality vary around the world?

Religious vitality has been examined by researchers using a wide variety of quantitative, statistical measures. Typically, questions about people's beliefs, sense of belonging, and religious and spiritual practice, and the role of religion in the public arena, have all been used to define vitality. Let's look again at data from the Pew study of religion in the United States. This recent survey of 35,000 Americans reveals that there is an active religious market with several hundred different Christian denominations, as we discussed in Chapter 2. In this market, we see evidence of people switching their membership among religious groups over their lives. The study found that 28% of respondents had left the religious tradition in which they were raised for either another tradition or none at all. The study notes that "if change in affiliation from one type of Protestantism to another is included, roughly 44% of adults have either switched religious affiliation, moved from being unaffiliated with any religion to being affiliated with a particular faith, or dropped any connection to a specific religious tradition altogether" (Pew Forum on Religion and Public Life 2008a, 5). Yet, overall, 83.9% of Americans belonged to some religious faith tradition, out of which 78.4% belong to Christian traditions. Compare these statistics with those describing religiosity in a country like Great Britain, where church membership has dropped to 10% of the population, or France, where only 8% of the population are practicing Catholics (Bruce 2001, 197; Jenkins 2002, 95)! Jenkins (2002) argues that, in contrast to Europe, there is and will continue to be an explosion of Christian populations across nations in the Southern Hemisphere.

It is important to note that while the United States and Germany both appear in this table, much of the increase in these countries' Christian populations results from immigration from the world's Southern Hemisphere.

TABLE 5.1   The Largest Christian Communities, 2025 and 2050

Nation	Estimated Christian Population (in millions)		
	2000	**2025**	**2050**
United States	225	270	330
Brazil	164	190	195
Mexico	95	127	145
Philippines	77	116	145
Nigeria	50	83	123
Democratic Republic of Congo	34	70	121
Ethiopia	36	65	79
Russia	90?	85	80
China	50?	60	60
Germany	58	61	57

Source: Jenkins (2002, 90)

Vitality is about more than affiliation and membership, both of which can disguise the decidedly nonreligious lives of those who belong to religious groups in name only. Let's consider what people actually do and what they believe. While there are many measures of religious belief and practice that we could examine, let us for the moment consider some key questions that are often asked on surveys about religion, to measure church attendance, prayer, belief in God, and belief in an afterlife. According to the 2006 General Social Survey, approximately 70% of Americans report attending religious services at least once a month and 31% report attending services at least once a week. Ninety-two percent of Americans report belief in God or a higher power of some sort, of which 62% have no doubts at all about God's existence (Davis and Smith 2006). Sixty percent report praying at least once a day and 73% report that they believe in life after death. The 2004 American General Election Survey found that 77% of their respondents considered religion to be an important part of their life (National Election Studies 2004).

As noted previously, studies of religious vitality in Europe return much different results on these kinds of measures. For instance, Need and Evans (2001, 237) found that, among church members in Orthodox Eastern European nations, 31.8% of Romanians, 26.8% of Ukrainians, 16.3% of Bulgarians, and 11.0% of Russians attended church more than once a month. In Catholic countries of Eastern Europe, the findings were higher, but only Poland was close to the figures for the United States, with 76.6% attending services more than once a month. In other countries, 44.2% of Slovakians, 34.8% of Lithuanians, 23.8% of Hungarians, and 17.6% of Czechs reported attending church more than once a month.

Fewer studies have collected these types of survey data from nations in Africa, Asia, and Central and South America, so we don't know as much about how beliefs and practices vary there, but we do know that Christianity is vibrant in the developing world in ways that leave our ideas of vitality in the north in the dust (Jenkins 2002). Among Christians in the global South, religious vitality is manifested through the active adaptation of Christian beliefs and practices, the literal reading of the Bible, religious healing, spiritual conflict and warfare, prophecy, and social justice, all woven together with a wide variety of traditional beliefs and rituals that are indigenous to Africa, Asia, and Central and South America, including polygamy, divination, animal sacrifices, and the veneration of one's ancestors. While religion ultimately always adapts itself to new conditions and cultures, globally Christianity is vital precisely because it is creating entirely new forms of faith and practice that meet the needs of the millions of believers in the Southern Hemisphere.

Vitality as a Product of Religious Market Forces

Religious economics

Market model

But what force drives the religious vitality of a community, a nation, or even a whole region of the world? Social scientists point to various factors that help to make a location religiously vital. Recently, market-based (sometimes called "rational choice") models of religious vitality have received a lot of attention, both good and bad. In these models, religious groups are a part of a big religious market that is subject to the same basic principles as any other economic market. You may have heard about how "supply and demand" and competition drive a capitalist economy. Market models of religion assume that religious groups are in competition with each other. Each church, temple, and synagogue has a supply of "religious goods and services," and they compete with one another for "customers" (us!) who demand different things to meet their religious needs. Think about all the religious groups in your hometown. Market models of religion assume that all the congregations in your town are fighting it out to gain your business and to keep your loyalty by offering you what they think you want from your religion.

Chaves, Schraeder, and Sprindys (1994) summarize three forces that shape how religion marketplaces work:

1. The more free the religious market is from state regulation, the more services religious groups will provide and the higher the quality of these services will be.

Okay, let's explain this a bit. Many Americans think that state-controlled businesses and industries provide worse service than privately owned ones. In a religious context, this same principle means that the more independent a church is, the more it will work hard to provide you with the best religious goods possible. Why? Because this group doesn't want you to get your religious goods somewhere else, so it is motivated!

2. The more individuals are required to invest their time and energy in their sector of the religious market, the more they will feel that they have some control over it, which in turn will lead to higher levels of individual participation.

Let's unpack this one, too. How many of you have parents who assume that if you have to work and pay for your education on your own, it will be more valuable to you and you'll do your best at it? Religious markets work the same way. The higher the cost of "religious goods" in terms of time, effort, and money, the more likely the consumers will value their religion and participate in it. Low-cost, low-effort religion doesn't give people any reason to participate.

3. The more open and free the religious market is overall, the more varieties of religious belief and practice will develop to meet the needs of religious consumers.

Again, we'll borrow economic ideas and apply them to religion. Just as the free-market system is assumed to encourage people to start new businesses and find better, more efficient ways to do things, a free religious market allows new religious ideas and groups to appear to meet the needs of the religious consumers. Religious consumers choose to affiliate with particular religious groups where the benefits—spiritual or practical—outweigh the costs of belonging. Now, time and place matter here. The religious marketplace in Indianapolis is not the same as the one in Los Angeles, Des Moines, or Bridgeport, much less London, Mumbai, or Kinshasa, so there will be some variety in the groups that are competing and what each group is offering, but you get the idea.

Market models have also been used to illustrate vitality at an organizational level. Rodney Stark, Roger Finke, and other scholars are particularly well known for their works, which provide evidence that congregational vitality is rooted in the diversity, competition, and the degree of regulation in the religious market of a particular community. Although we don't have room to cover the many different pieces of data that are employed to support rational-choice models of religious vitality, one study in particular stands out. Finke and Stark (2000) studied changes in congregational growth and vitality among United Methodists in the California–Nevada Conference. Their study was not designed specifically to test the rational-choice approach, but their work illustrates how it operates at an organization level. In short, they examined how the tension between a congregation and the dominant culture shaped its overall vitality. They found that a new generation of more evangelically minded pastors in the United Methodist Church were affiliating themselves with church movements that sought to return the church to a more traditional position on a variety of theological and social issues, such as the authority of the Bible, the divinity of Christ, and the source of salvation being uniquely belief in Jesus. Simultaneously, these ministers were outspoken against inequalities that were based on gender and race, and were in favor of increasing support for the poor. Other ministers were operating in reverse, decreasing the tension between their congregations and the surrounding culture by relativizing their stances on these traditional beliefs. Finke and Stark found that, as a consequence of increasing the relative "costs" to belong, the high-tension congregations witnessed overall increases in the levels of membership, expenditures, and attendance figures, compared with those of congregations that pursued positions that were in lower tension with the dominant culture. Apparently, high-tension congregations carve out a niche in the religious market that increases their distinctiveness and appeal over their competitors.

#10

It is important to keep in mind that, like secularization theory, market model theory is not universally accepted. The majority of studies that use market models have faced many challenges to their ideas and the data that they use to try to support them (Beyer 1997, Phillips 1999). One criticism of market models is based on their focus on Christianity in Northern Hemisphere, with data taken from the United States, Canada, and Europe. Most of these studies examine competition between religious groups in principally Christian religious markets and make assumptions about forms of religious participation as individual measures of vitality that make sense only in the context of Christianity. For example, there is a strong bias in American Christianity to determine religious commitment and devotion on the basis of the beliefs that people hold. As we noted in Chapter 2, many other religions do not assess devotion or orthodoxy on the basis of what you *believe,* but rather what you *do.* It is difficult to know whether the market models make any sense at all if applied in other societies or to other religious markets that include Muslims, Hindus, Sikhs, or other religious groups. Only a 1994 study by Chaves, Schraeder, and Sprindys demonstrates that these supply-side approaches to religious vitality are applicable to religions other than Christianity. Their study examined the impact of state regulation of religion on the rate at which Muslims make their required once-in-a-lifetime pilgrimage to Mecca.

Of course, other approaches to explaining religious vitality can be found in the sociological literature. Christian Smith (1998), in his study of American Evangelicals, favors the spirit of a market model but does not embrace all of its language or implications. Smith offers a *subcultural identity* approach to religious vitality, broken down into two arguments about religious persistence and religious strength. Smith's claim about religious persistence is as follows: "Religion survives and can thrive in pluralistic, modern society by embedding itself in subcultures that offer satisfying morally-orienting collective identities, which provide adherents meaning and belonging" (118). In other words, religious groups are subcultures. Most people interact with, befriend, and marry people from religious groups that are similar to their own, as we discussed earlier. This tendency creates a group context that allows people to believe and do things that wouldn't make sense to the majority of people in society. The group continues to reassure believers that their ideas make sense, even when it seems like everything else in the world says they don't. Belief in miracles from St. Jude, belief in a six-day creation as described in the Bible, the practice of sacrificing animals as offerings to gods, the belief that crystals can heal you, the practice of washing in the Ganges River in India to remove past sin and bad karma—these are all beliefs and behaviors that a variety of the world's religions have embraced. However, unless you belong to a group that thinks these things make sense, your reaction to hearing about them probably includes disbelief, confusion, and perhaps even revulsion or ridicule. This is Smith's point. Even the most seemingly outrageous ideas and behaviors—those, which seem the least in step with life in 21st-century America—will never be in danger from the forces of secularization so long as there is a group that believes them.

As for the strength of any particular religious tradition in a religiously diverse society, Smith goes on to state that "those religious groups will be relatively stronger which better possess and employ the cultural tools needed to create both clear distinction from and significant engagement with other relevant out groups, short of becoming genuinely countercultural" (118–119). In his analysis, religious vitality is driven by the basic human need to create a sense of meaning about the world and to reinforce feelings of belonging to some group of like-minded people within a society that is made of many different groups with many different beliefs, values, and ways of acting. Because individuals actively seek to have these needs met, religious pluralism itself allows many religious groups to emerge to meet them. In the case of American Evangelicalism, the evangelical subculture reinforces a distinct religious identity that is built around evangelical theology and religious practice. What makes Smith's approach an improvement on pure market models of religious vitality is that it is not necessary to think either that religion is in decline or that it is totally alive and growing in contemporary societies like the United States. Rather than forcing us to choose one over the other, it allows us to consider that perhaps both things are happening at the same time.

SECULAR YET RELIGIOUSLY VITAL?

So the final question remains: Is it possible for people in society to be more religious while their societies overall become less so? This is the paradoxical position of religion in the 21st century. Since 2001, most North Americans and Europeans have been bombarded with the many ways that religion remains a vital and not always positive force in the world at large. For many of us, even the most devout, this comes as something of a surprise, because religion in countries like the United States, even in its most visible, seemingly public forms, remains largely a personal matter. Religion is in fact separate from the work of government, capitalism, science, health care, and other social institutions. In countries in Africa, Central and South America, Asia, and the Middle East, such a separation is inconceivable. Religion there is an active force that is involved in all aspects of social life. Then why, in so many of the debates among the scholars mentioned in this chapter, does there seem to be a desire to declare once and for all that the world is secularizing or that religion is alive and well? There seems to be little appreciation that these two alternative descriptions of what's happening to religion in our world are not mutually exclusive; rather they are parallel and complementary.

Those who study religion, especially proponents of religious vitality and religious market models, find it difficult to embrace this nuanced approach. To speak of religious authority declining and of religion differentiating into its own separate sphere of influence seems to carry with it the need to say that this is not a good thing or that religion will inevitably die or fade away. Many students of religion carry with them a set of normative assumptions about the roles religion *should* play in the social world—or that they, as persons of faith themselves, wish it to play. So, to save religion from the fate that some scholars incorrectly believe is predicted by secularization theory, they focus on how vibrant and innovative *the religious sphere* itself seems to be. They focus also on religion's engagement with secular institutions, portraying this as the final word on religion's continued vitality in this postmodern and distinctly nonsecular age (Finke 1992). We argue, however, that we must understand religion in our world in all of its complex and paradoxical reality.

So we are back where we started with the trends of secularization. From the beginning, Wilson (1982) and others have asserted that, although secularization proceeds at the societal level, it is not inevitable that most individuals will relinquish their interest in religion, their beliefs, or their religious practices. Thanks to globalization, religious markets in many North American and European contexts have become increasingly diverse, but this diversity alone does not automatically translate into religious vitality (Voas, Olson, and Crockett 2002). All the same—as we have already noted—a great deal of evidence exists for continued high levels of religious participation in the United States, as well as evidence that points to low levels of religious participation in Western and Eastern European nations. In both cases, immigration from the global South has played a significant role in maintaining high levels of religious participation (Jenkins 2002).

Yet rational-choice theorists argue that pluralism and diversity in religious markets force religious groups to actively compete for members by improving and changing their religious products to achieve greater appeal to a portion of religious consumers, as if an unregulated religious marketplace makes all religious choices available to all religious consumers. While some religious consumers might feel that they have choices about which groups to join, many other believers in the United States and abroad would disagree that they had or have much choice in their religion. Think about your own case here. What does it mean to have a religious "choice"? If you belong to a particular religion, could you really just decide that you like another one better and make the change? Probably few of us would be able to say yes to that. We grow up in particular religious traditions that are connected to our race, our ethnicity, our social class, and any number of other factors. We can't or don't easily jump ship from one religion to another, one day being a devoted Pentecostal and the next being a Buddhist. So what does having a "choice" mean here?

Another problem with the rational-choice approach is that it assumes that all religious groups are operating more or less on equal footing and simply need to make the right pitch to consumers to increase their membership. But this is not how most religious groups gain or lose members at the local level. People join or leave religious groups when the transitional costs are lowest. For instance, a Christian is more likely to switch among types of congregations and even denominations within the same religion, than to switch to a different religion altogether. Likewise, even within an open religious market, we do not find Jews, Muslims, Hindus, Buddhists, or any other types of religious shoppers switching among religious traditions.

The religious sphere's own setting of cultural limits on the range of choices that are available in the religious market is also the source of its vitality. Contemporary religion, segregated into its own sphere of influence and authority, gives rise to innovation and reflexivity in order to meet the needs of new generations of would-be believers. As we saw in Chapter 3, religious groups carefully watch changing cultural currents and modify both the messages and the media that they use to communicate to meet the stated or imagined needs of religious believers. This scenario is, of course, radically different from that of a fixed religious market in which traditions are, to a certain extent, frozen and cannot be changed. It is also a response to the "shopper," "seeker," or "questing" approaches to social life taken by individuals in the modern, differentiated social world. Today, within structured limits, we try to maximize the numbers and varieties of choices that we have available to meet our needs. Dan Olson (1993, 35) describes us "moderns" in the following way:

> "The very forces of modernization that disrupt the homogeneity of preindustrial community simultaneously give moderns greater control over the construction of their personal networks, control that can be used to rebuild networks of shared identity. The difference between contemporary subcultures and the preindustrial community lie in the greater freedom of moderns to choose which elements of their identity they will emphasize in the construction of their personal networks and the degree of their involvement in subcultures based on those identities. Moderns are freer to shape their personal networks and thus their own identity."

The implication for religion is clear. Today's believers are freer (not totally free, however) to make some choices in the religious market, to join groups that fit their needs and experience, to leave them again when their needs are not met or they experience life changes, and to assess religious groups with the full fervor of consumerism—trying to get the best spiritual bang for a buck.

Such an approach also underscores the shifting authority of religious traditions and their leaders. Although an individual may choose to worship in a particular way, to behave in proscribed ways or not, and to hold to or reject the doctrines of a faith tradition, now—unlike in times past—the individual believer is in a position to pick and choose what beliefs, behaviors, and experiences work best. The individual need not embrace the totality of the tradition or recognize the authority of religious leaders to dictate how that person's faith should shape his or her attitudes and behaviors. Evangelical women selectively interpret the pronouncements of their ministers on the roles of women in the household (Beaman 1999). Highly educated and politically liberal Protestants in the United States increasingly "believe without belonging," when faced with a growing cultural association between being religious and being conservative (Hout and Fischer 2002). And, as Roof (1999, 85) found in his survey of baby boomers, "one third of the respondents agreed that 'people have God within them, so churches aren't really necessary' . . . Even 13 percent of born-again Christians agreed!" Roof (1999, 110) goes on to say, "People now take a more active role in shaping the meaning systems by which they live and must themselves determine how to respond to this widening range of suppliers, all contending with one another in creating symbolic worlds." Couple the declining legitimacy of religious authority over the everyday lives of believers with high levels of commitment to classic forms of religious expression and many new forms of spirituality, and one sees the paradox: secular yet vital.

It is important to note that, as stated by Chaves (1994) , the decline and institutional segregation of religious authority does not occur without some resistance on the part of those who have an interest in maintaining some religious control over society. The process of secularization, therefore, may provoke political movements to restore the presence and power of religious authority. In many ways, as we consider the entry of clergy and people of faith into politics over the last three decades, we can see the rationale for such an argument. Hunter (1989), in his hotly debated, but important, book *Culture Wars*, argues that, as a result of the liberalizing forces of government, the economy, and the media, special-interest groups, religious denominations, and political parties have realigned themselves in opposition to these "secularizing" forces. Consequently, a cultural divide has emerged and has prompted the familiar battles over abortion, gay rights, education, government funding of the arts, and a host of other issues. In these conflicts, religious actors figure prominently on both sides of the divide, but as in the case of any conflict, much depends on who can gain the most resources and who has the backing of more people. As Hunter (1989, 158) observes:

> "This conflict is 'about' the uses of symbols, the uses of language, and the right to impose discrediting labels upon those who would dissent. It is ultimately a struggle over the right to define the way things are and the way things should be. It is therefore more of a struggle to determine who is stronger, which alliance has the institutional resources capable of sustaining a particular definition of reality against the wishes of those who would project an alternative view of the world."

For those whose world views and values are threatened by any perceived decline in religious authority, the only alternative is to organize and fight back against the sources of those threats in whatever form they take: societal, organizational, or individual.

Hunter's thesis has been contested since he published it, but other scholars have examined these same forces in local community contexts. Demerath and Williams (1992, 202) illustrate the push–pull relationship between the forces of secularization and those of what they call "sacralization." They suggest that secularizing forces can and do provoke sacralizing reactions in ways that may even give the sacralizing side political victories. For example, in Springfield, Massachusetts, it became clear that, although in many ways religion is no longer a driving political force in the city, it still has significant effects. Clergy and coalitions of various religious groups push for a variety of political changes in the city. Sometimes, these political engagements support liberal causes such as funding in the city for low-income neighborhoods, and sometimes they support more conservative ones like limiting abortion access in the city and shifting sex education in schools toward abstinence. However, even though these victories for the forces of sacralization certainly seem to reflect religious vitality and resurgence, Demerath and Williams describe the victories as fundamentally limited, short-term gains in the face of long-term losses of religious authority in local communities. Religious victory over individual political issues is not the same as victory in reinstating the power of religious organizations and leaders over the moral order of a community as a whole.

Of course, in recent years, we have witnessed the transformation of these local sacralizing movements into more extreme forms of global religious political activism. Branches of Christianity, Islam, and other religions form fundamentalist movements around the world. These movements arise partly in response to the secularizing forces of global capitalism, global political and military forces, and, perhaps most significantly, the introduction of American and European cultural practices that threaten traditional ways of life and values. Lechner (1991, 1114) states this directly: "No fundamentalism without (prior) secularization." As paradoxical as it sounds, religious vitality and declining religious authority go hand in hand. We will look in more detail at fundamentalism and how its various forms have unfolded around the world in the next chapter.

SUGGESTED READING

Chaves, Mark. 1994. "Secularization as Declining Religious Authority." *Social Forces* 72 (3): 749–774.

Finke, Roger and Rodney Stark. 2006. *The Churching of America, 1776–2005*. New Brunswick, NJ: Rutgers University Press.

Jenkins, Philip. 2002. *The Next Christendom: The Coming of Global Christianity*. New York: Oxford University Press.

Luckmann, Thomas. 1967. *The Invisible Religion*. New York: The MacMillan Company.

Roof, Wade Clark. 1999. *Spiritual Marketplace: Baby Boomers and the Remaking of American Religion*. Princeton: Princeton University Press.

Smith, Christian. 1998. *American Evangelicalism: Embattled and Thriving*. Chicago: University of Chicago Press.

Stark, Rodney. 1999. "Secularization, R.I.P." *Sociology of Religion* 60 (3): 249–274.

Swatos, William H., Jr., and Kevin J. Christiano. 1999. "Secularization Theory: The Course of a Concept." *Sociology of Religion* 60 (3): 209–228.

Tschannen, Oliver. 1991. "The Secularization Paradigm: A Systematization." *Journal for the Scientific Study of Religion* 30 (4): 395–415.

Woodhead, Linda. 2008. "Gendering Secularization Theory." *Social Compass* 55 (2): 189–195.

6

Our God Rules (Yours Doesn't)

Why Is There a Rising Tide of Fundamentalism Around the World?

1. What is fundamentalism?
2. Why is fundamentalism growing?
3. What do fundamentalists want?
4. What is the influence of fundamentalism in the world?
5. Should we study fundamentalism or secularism?

The headline in the February 15, 2008, Associated Press article read, "Youth Organization Wants a Return to Wholesomeness." Led by the Christian-based group Teen Mania Ministries, hundreds of teens took to the streets of the Big Apple, New York City, for an event called Recreate. Through chants, signs, and speeches, the youths and young adults called for recreating music, film, fashion, television, and other media without the explicit, aggressive language and imagery that is so common in these mediums. 2008 was a presidential election year, so they also announced eight questions to be sent to the presidential candidates, including, "What should be done to stop glamorizing the things that are destroying my friends, like drugs, alcohol, and sex?" And "How will you ensure that the freedom to practice Christianity will not be taken away?"

One of the young adults at the rally was Rebecca Bjerke, age 21. Along with two of her friends, she explained to a reporter why she came to the rally: "To make change for our generation, to just stand up and say, 'We're tired of all the filth.' . . . You know, music and songs that are constantly so negative—just making us numb to the abuse of alcohol and drugs and sex and pornography and all that kind of stuff."

Would you call Rebecca Bjerke a religious fundamentalist? How about the rally—was it a gathering of fundamentalists? Debra Sweet, national director of the organization World Can't Wait and part of a group standing across the street to protest the Recreate rally, certainly thinks it was. According to Sweet, "These are hard-core fundamentalists leading youth . . . on a moral equivalent of a crusade." Others among the World Can't Wait protest group, who conducted chants such as "Away with all gods," believe groups such as Teen Mania Ministries lead young people to eschew critical thought and to blindly follow their fundamentalist leaders.

So what is going on here? How can people of the same nation have such radically different views? And why are they taking these views to the streets, willing to invest their time in such events? This one event is but a microcosm of what is taking place across the globe, literally and figuratively being "recreated" in nation after nation, driven, it appears, by religious commitment.

Another newspaper headline and article can help us to understand this rising tide. The November 27, 2005, edition of the *Dallas Morning News* featured a section headlined, "10 Ideas on the Way Out. . . . [T]he world's leading thinkers identify ideas and institutions they believe are not likely to survive the next 35 years." What were two of the first three ideas not likely to survive? The sanctity of life and monogamy (religious hierarchy was fourth). Although secularized people might celebrate these changes, such proclamations are fundamentalist fuel. Perceived as direct attacks on their way of life and all that they hold dear, such predicted and actual changes serve as rallying points for millions of people around the world to organize and resist. And so they do.

Many scholars now write that without modernization and secularization there would be no fundamentalism. For centuries, it has been understood that the processes of modernization—such as urbanization and pluralism—lead to secularization. As original sociologist Max Weber and others after him have suggested, secularization is the demystifying of the world, during which religion is relegated to a smaller and smaller role among a decreasing number of people and organizations. Secularization proceeds until whole strata of people (say, the Western intelligentsia) and entire societies (say, those of Northern and Western Europe) operate without any apparent reference to or reliance upon religion. Religious faith becomes individualized and, for many, outdated, something like a historical artifact, part of the cultures of long-gone, superstitious peoples.

At least, this is the view and experience of those who developed the secularization thesis, namely Western academics. But as former secularization theory proponent Peter Berger (1992) now writes, secularization theory failed to anticipate something: that this demystification of the world provided within in it the seeds both for resistance to demystification and for the world's remystification. These movements, organizations, and people who resist demystification, or who remystify, have come to be called fundamentalist.

Far from disappearing, religion and religious movements appear to be resurging around the globe. According to research, there are fundamentalist movements in Africa, the Middle East, Latin America, North America, and Asia, including India. Such movements exist in multiple religions, including Judaism, Hinduism, Islam, Sikhism, neo-Confucianism, Christianity, and Buddhism. These movements have political influence. Gabriel Almond et al. (2003, 1) observe:

"Since the Iranian Revolution, purported fundamentalist movements have risen to the highest levels of power in five countries—in Iran in 1979, in the Sudan in

1993, in Turkey, Afghanistan, and India in 1996, and in India again in 1998 and 1999. There have been even more frequent penetrations by fundamentalist movements into the parliaments, assemblies, and political parties of such countries as Jordan, Israel, Egypt, Morocco, Pakistan, and the United States."

What is more, as we can see, hear, and read, fundamentalism is at times associated with violence, such as suicide bombers. Fundamentalism is in the news and is having global impacts.

In this chapter, we outline the contours of research by sociologists and others on the resurgence of conservative religion around the globe, the meaning of religious fundamentalism, its characteristics, and the implications of such movements for modern life. We review history, identify perspectives, provide a critical overview of existing research, and discuss the areas that scholars must visit to collect data if we are to move forward in understanding these world-shaping phenomena.

WHAT IS RELIGIOUS FUNDAMENTALISM?

Do you remember in Chapter 1 when we asked you to actually stop reading and write an initial definition of religion? We want you to do the same here, but rather than defining religion, define fundamentalism. Without definitions, it is hard for us to communicate and learn about topics. Write your definition in the box, and then read on to see how your definition compares with those of scholars who make their living thinking about such things.

BOX 6.1

Your Definition of Fundamentalism

_____

_____

_____

_____

_____

_____

Defining fundamentalism is not an easy task because it is such a common and loosely used term, thrown around like a baseball in the media, in political arenas, and during backyard arguments.. Sometimes the term *fundamentalist* is used to describe any group that takes religion seriously or that views religion's role in public life to be greater than the labeler wishes it to be. The term also might be used for people who are regarded as being too religiously confident or who engage in action stemming from religious conviction. Thus, not only are the Christian religious right in the United States and the global Al Qaeda Muslims called fundamentalist, but so too are teen groups rallying for cleaner song lyrics and videos, or local parent groups who want restrictions placed on Internet access in local schools. Groups that want their religion to be practiced purely are called fundamentalist, as are groups pushing for an overhaul of the national or global political system, even if they are mostly culturally connected to a religion.

So what is fundamentalism? Perhaps more so than many other concepts, fundamentalism is a contextual phenomenon: It cannot be defined without understanding the social reality that surrounds it. As we noted earlier in the chapter, many scholars think that fundamentalism cannot be understood apart from modernity nor exist outside of modernity. Thus, to provide a working definition of fundamentalism, we begin with a brief overview of modernity.

MODERNITY

The social sciences arose out of the conditions of modernity, or, at the very least, modernity animated the work of early sociologists. Marx, Weber, Durkheim, and others were interested in the social implications of a modernizing world. Increasing modernity meant not only an increasing division of labor, but also a division of life (Bruce 2000). Social life was no longer a cohesive whole, but divided into distinct spheres. One's coworkers, neighbors, and fellow worshipers could be and most often were different sets of people (a situation that, by the way, often leaves us feeling stretched in too many directions and feeling exhausted). Moreover, social life became divided into public and private realms, and people were expected—nay required—to act differently in the separate arenas.

Another core aspect of modernization is the rationalization of the world. Much of life is regulated using policies and procedures, science, administrative rules, and the like. Life must be predictable. A McDonald's hamburger must taste the same no matter where it is purchased in the world, so its production and distribution must be rationalized. Deities have little role in such a worldview. The laws of the market are devoid of religious content, and the invisible hand is not supernatural.

Along with the division of social life and rationalization came industrialization and urbanization. These processes heighten cultural pluralism. They physically brought together many people who had a variety of perspectives to serve burgeoning economies or to live in new colonies. Pluralism—both cultural and structural—is often the linchpin concept in secularization theories. Given the variety of religions, coupled with both the division of social life and the primacy given to economic pursuits, religion ends up being relegated to the private sectors of social life, divorced from formal roles in government, economics, and eventually education, medicine, and other areas. What is more, exposing people to a variety of religious and nonreligious ideologies, secularization theorists argue, *relativizes* religion, a concept that is foreign to most religions, especially those with a singular god. As Peter Berger (1967) conceived of religion, it is a sacred canopy under which the entirety of life is explained and security is generated. Modernization rips the sacred canopy, and, at best, people are left with sacred umbrellas (Smith 1998).

Modernization thus squeezes out religious influences from many spheres of society and greatly reduces religion's role in others. And modernization, following its own logic, begets more advanced forms such as postmodernization, the continued individualizing and relativizing of the world. Even science comes into question in such a world. In the postmodern era, truth can only be spelled with a capital T at the beginning of sentences, for truth is individualized and relativized. Whatever works for you is good for you, and whatever works for me is good for me. And what is *good*? We each get to define that too.

Given this vast pluralism, societies and their governments are able to claim less and less as common to all. Tolerance and acceptance rise to the top as the most widely shared values. In such societies, the ultimate offense is to suppose that individuals cannot personally define what is good for them, to presume that there is some outside moral guide that is common to all. All previously taken-for-granted social arrangements—such as monogamy—are questioned, and the values of tolerance and acceptance make it difficult for societies to reject many behaviors and perspectives. Modernity becomes an ideology that values change over continuity, quantity over quality, and commercial efficiency over traditional values (Lawrence 1989, 27). The result of these processes is to threaten religion by reducing it to nothing but individually held beliefs, a clear Durkheimian violation of the meaning and role of religion in society.

Defining Fundamentalism

So what is fundamentalism? In one of the first and most careful sociologically based theoretical works on fundamentalism, Riesebrodt (1990 [1993 trans.], 9) defines fundamentalism as "an urban movement directed primarily against dissolution of personalistic, patriarchal notions of order and social relations and their replacement by depersonalized principles." The fact that he defines it as an urban movement is most interesting, given that fundamentalists are often characterized as backwater, country folk who are out of step with the modern urban world. In the follow-up book to the five-volume *Fundamentalism Project*, Almond et al. (2003, 17) define fundamentalism as "a discernible pattern of religious militancy by which self-styled 'true believers' attempt to arrest the erosion of religious identity, fortify the borders of the religious community, and create viable alternatives to secular institutions and behaviors." Antoun (2001, 3) offers a definition of fundamentalism in the context of modernity as a religiously based cognitive and affective orientation to the world characterized by protest against change and the ideological orientation of modernism.

My, oh my, what do these definitions really mean? We will explore their meanings in more detail soon, but let's first consider what they have in common and examine some initial objections to these definitions. Each of these definitions supposes that fundamentalism has a transnational, transcultural character. That is, they suppose that fundamentalism can be defined apart from its specifically unique historical circumstances. Some critics of these definitions argue that the term *fundamentalism* only applies to theologically conservative U.S. Protestants. They make this argument because the term was first used to describe the Protestant movement (see next section), and because it is meant to apply only to a subset of people within a religious tradition. Muslims, for example, often argue that they cannot be called fundamentalist simply because they take the teaching of the Qur'an and their faith seriously. If that were the criteria, they say, then all Muslims are fundamentalist. And if this is true, the term ceases to be of use.

Serious critiques have been leveled at work that examines fundamentalism as a global phenomenon. Critics charge that such work often conflates conservative religious movements with postcolonial national religious movements. Others criticize what they view as the immensity of differences that have to be brushed aside to view, for example, U.S. Protestant fundamentalists and Hindu national fundamentalists as the same conceptually. Some scholars are willing to apply the term to conservative movements within Judaism, Christianity, and Islam, but not other religions. Riesebrodt (2000) has responded that from a sociological perspective, the fact that resurgent conservative religious movements share many features in common is highly relevant, because it suggests that such movements have risen under similar sociological conditions. For this reason, he argues, despite important differences across these movements, knowledge can advance by considering fundamentalism to be a sociological category in need of theoretical and empirical development.

How fundamentalism is defined and interpreted depends a great deal on one's perspective. From a modern, secular viewpoint, fundamentalists are reactionaries, radicals attempting to grab power and throw societies back into the dark ages of oppression, patriarchy, and intolerance. These fundamentalists are misguided, scary, and even evil. Supporters of modernization view themselves as being unlike these fundamentalists. They see modernists as good, reasoned people, lovers of freedom and human rights. Again, from their own viewpoint, because they believe that they think more clearly than fundamentalists and value empirical evidence and individual rights more highly, modernists can see that fundamentalists are wrong.

But fundamentalists and their sympathizers feel like Western versions of modernization are rushing over them in a tidal wave of change, ripping apart communities and destroying values, social ties, and meaning. To these changes, some groups say, "No." When they do so out of their religious conviction, they are called, by modernists, religious fundamentalists. Think back to the opening of this chapter, which described the youth gathering Recreate on one side of the New York City street and the "modernists" on the other side of the street protesting these misguided youths' rally.

Fundamentalists and their sympathizers see their stand against the tidal wave of change as honorable, right, life preserving, and a life calling. They are people fighting against the heavy hand of secular oppression, emptiness, anomie, destruction, and the restriction of their freedom to believe and practice as they wish. As Bruce (2000, 117) states, "Fundamentalism is the rational response of traditionally religious peoples to social, political and economic changes that downgrade and constrain the role of religion in the public world. . . . [F]undamentalists have not exaggerated the extent to which modern cultures threaten what they hold dear."

THE "FIRST" FUNDAMENTALISM

So where did we get this term, fundamentalism? The term was first used to describe a conservative strain of Protestantism that developed in the United States, roughly from 1870 to 1925. During at least a portion of this period, the United States was arguably the world's leader in modernization. As U.S. religious historian George Marsden (1980) and others discuss, this original fundamentalist movement was foremost a religious movement and took its name from a series of pamphlets called "The Fundamentals: A Testimony of the Truth," which were published from 1910 to 1915. These pamphlets outlined the fundamental, nonnegotiable aspects of the Christian faith, as agreed on by conservative religious leaders of the time. Unlike many fundamentalist movements today, U.S. Protestant fundamentalism of the early twentieth century was not so much a battle with the secular state as it was an intrareligion fight with other U.S. Protestant people and organizations. These other U.S. Protestant people and organizations were attempting to modernize their religion to be, in the progressive Protestant view, relevant for a new time. Fundamentalists of this era were militantly opposed to modernizing the Christian faith and militantly opposed to cultural changes that were endorsed by modernism. As Marsden (1980, 4) notes, "fundamentalism was a loose, diverse, and changing federation of cobelligerents united by their fierce opposition to modernist attempts to bring Christianity into line with modern thought."

In the aftermath of the 1925 Scopes Trial—a trial drawing intense national publicity that pitted traditionalists against modernists over the teaching of evolution—in which fundamentalists went from being respected members of society to a ridiculed group, fundamentalists essentially retreated into their own private world, where they stayed for many decades. While they were there, they quietly developed their own institutions that were parallel to those of modernist organizations, created strategies for influencing society, and prepared well-trained leaders. Their reemergence in the public eye in the 1970s coincided with the resurgence of conservative religious movements around the globe.

FUNDAMENTALISM RISING

In the 1970s, fundamentalism appeared to hit the world stage from out of thin air. Although there were earlier movements, such as the Jewish Gush Emunim (the Bloc of the Faithful) in 1974, the Iranian Revolution was the first unmistakable indicator of a growing phenomenon. Fundamentalism also resurged in the United States, this time as a much more politically active strain. Fundamentalist movements emerged in most of the world's religions on most of the earth's continents. Something was happening. In a 1979 article, Ethridge and Feagin noted that there was no coherent sociological definition or theoretical context for the term fundamentalism. And no wonder. The accepted wisdom among those who studied religion and society was that societies were secularizing. According to secularization theories, religion was not supposed to resurge and take a center spot on a global stage.

Nancy Ammerman was among the first sociologists to conduct an in-depth study into the lives of contemporary fundamentalists and to draw connections between fundamentalism and modernity. Her book *Bible Believers* (1987) described U.S. fundamentalists. Ammerman's work was followed by Bruce Lawrence's book *Defenders of God: The Fundamentalist Revolt Against the Modern Age* (1989), in which he argued that fundamentalism is an ideology rather than a theology and that it is formed in conflict with modernism. His study set the groundwork for the study of fundamentalism in sociology; in his view, fundamentalism is a transcultural phenomenon that is located in a developmental historical framework. He understood fundamentalism as a sociocultural category with common roots in its encounter with the modern world.

In interpreting the resurgence of religion, sociologists have largely gone in two different directions from that of Ammerman. Some have held fast to secularization theory and viewed the wave of fundamentalisms around the globe as a collective last gasp of old-time religion. In this view, modernism has swept the globe, and religions are making one final but ultimately futile attempt to preserve themselves as social players.

Another school of thought—what Warner (1993) calls the "new paradigm"—argues that modernization and secularization serve as fertile soil for religious resurgence, especially of the more fundamentalist strains. As we discussed in the last chapter, where the signs of modernization are strongest—measured as religious pluralism and urbanization, for example—so too is individual religious involvement (Finke and Stark 2005).

There are other, smaller voices contributing to understanding the global rise of fundamentalism. But as Riesebrodt (2000) outlines, all these explanations, dominant or not, are lacking in that they do not adequately answer three vital questions: (1) why these movements emerged, (2) why they emerged at this point in history (largely since the 1970s), and (3) what their future significance may be. Much work must yet be done to answer these questions.

CHARACTERISTICS OF RELIGIOUS FUNDAMENTALISM

To date, the most comprehensive study of fundamentalisms around the world has been carried out by religious historians Martin Marty and Scott Appleby. After a decade of exhaustive case study research, with contributions from dozens of scholars studying fundamentalist groups and movements across five continents and within seven world religious traditions, and after five volumes of reporting and analysis, this global study identified nine interrelated characteristics of fundamentalist groups, five ideological and four organizational. (See Table 1.)

On the basis of these characteristics, Almond and colleagues argue that Judaism, Christianity, and Islam, which have clearly defined sacred texts, dualistic worldviews, and "end times" theologies, have the most fully developed fundamentalisms across the world's religions. But there are also critiques of these fundamentalist characteristics. For example, Larry Iannaccone (1997) points out that the authors of these traits say that only 2 of the 18 religious movements they studied score high on all nine traits. In contrast, he states, religious movements that were not given any consideration by this or most other research, such as Jehovah's Witnesses, score high on every trait. Some religious movements are called fundamentalist even if they do not seem to perfectly fit the characteristics, whereas other movements that do fit the characteristics are not called fundamentalist. This finding points to weakness either in clarity or consistency of definition. Many studies of fundamentalism implicitly assume that fundamentalists can only exist within established world religions. Do you think this is a reasonable assumption? Why?

FUNDAMENTALISM AND OTHER ASPECTS OF SOCIAL LIFE

In addition to studying the rise of fundamentalism, studies are increasingly examining the relationships between fundamentalism and social life. Some studies look at the relationships between fundamentalism and race, class, gender, family, education, and age. Other studies examine innovative techniques and the particular views of fundamentalists, their moral reasoning development, and their relationship to science.

One consistent finding of these studies is that fundamentalists are strong traditionalists on matters of family and gender relations. Patriarchal families, with distinct and separate roles for males and females, are core components of fundamentalist beliefs and practices across religions and continents. Certainly this is a major clashing point with modernity and a central social arrangement that fundamentalist groups fight to maintain. Because traditional families and gender roles play a core role for fundamentalists, they are, not surprisingly, strong opponents of homosexual behavior or any official acknowledgment or sponsorship of alternative family arrangements. Such acts and arrangements are viewed as cooperating with sin and simply cannot be accepted. They also are direct challenges to the worldviews of fundamentalists. As much as any other aspect of modernity, the push to change the definition of family, gender, and acceptable sexual activity has pulled fundamentalist groups into active political involvement. Indeed, as we noted earlier, Riesebrodt (1990 [1993 trans.], 9) goes so far as to define the essence of fundamentalism as concerted resistance to the "dissolution of personalistic, patriarchal notions of order."

TABLE 6.1	**Nine Characteristics of Fundamentalist Groups**

Ideological	1. **Reactivity to the marginalization of religion:** Fundamentalism is first and foremost a defense of a religious tradition that is perceived to be eroding or under attack by modernization and secularization. Without this scenario, a movement is not properly labeled fundamentalist.
	2. **Selectivity:** Fundamentalism is selective. Rather than simply defending a religious tradition, it selects and reshapes aspects of the tradition, particularly aspects that clearly distinguish the fundamentalists from the mainstream. What is more, such movements affirm and use some aspects of modernity, such as much of modern science, modern forms of communication, and other technologies. Finally, certain consequences or processes of modernity are singled out for special attention and focused opposition (such as abortion for U.S. Christian fundamentalists).
	3. **Dualistic worldview:** Reality is clearly divided into the good and the evil, light and darkness, righteousness and unrighteousness.
	4. **Absolutism and inerrancy:** The texts of the tradition (the Qur'an or Bible, for example) "are of divine (inspired) origin and true and accurate in all particulars" (Almond et al. 2003, 96). Fundamentalist movements in religions that do not have a clear sacred text (such as Hinduism) often hold one text, or set of texts, over others.
	5. **Millenialism and messianism:** History has a miraculous and holy end. At the end of time, at the entry or return of the hoped-for one (the messiah, the hidden Imam, etc.), suffering will end, evil will be vanquished, and believers will be victorious. Judaism, Christianity, and Islam offer the most certain assurances; other traditions, although they tend to borrow from religion's "end times" certainty of these three, lack such fully elaborated assurances.
Organizational	6. **Elect, chosen membership:** Those in fundamentalist movements view themselves as called, selected out, and set apart for their mission to defend the religious tradition.
	7. **Sharp boundaries:** People are either members of the fundamentalist group or they are not. The boundaries are clearly set; there is no confusion. A person is saved, righteous, a follower of Allah, or a defender of the faith, or else that person is not.
	8. **Authoritarian organization:** Fundamentalist movements are typically organized around a charismatic leader or leaders, while others are the followers. The leader is viewed by the followers as someone who is specially chosen by the deity, someone who has near supernatural qualities or special access to the deity, and someone who is virtuous, a model for the followers, and in possession of special training and insight into the sacred texts.
	9. **Behavioral requirements:** As an extension of the dualistic worldview, behavioral requirements are both elaborate and specific. Rules about appropriate speech, dress, sexuality, drinking, eating, family formation, children, entertainment pursuits, and other behaviors are common and create sharp boundaries.

Source: Almond et al. (1995)

In an effort to better understand the rise of fundamentalism, some scholars are examining what are called contextual effects. Contextual effects consider the impact of the composition and values of the surrounding neighborhood, community, or region on the rise and makeup of fundamentalism. For instance, Moore and Vanneman (2003) have studied the effects on gender attitudes of the proportion of fundamentalists in a U.S. state. They find that greater proportions of fundamentalists in U.S. states are associated with more conservative gender attitudes of white nonfundamentalists in those states, even after controlling for individuals' own religious affiliation, beliefs, and practices. So fundamentalist movements may have an effect on the overall gender attitudes of people in their state. Or possibly it is the opposite—that more conservative gender views lead to more fundamentalists. In another study, Lizardo and Bergesen (2003) use a contextual approach that shows much promise for understanding why some fundamentalist movements are violent and some are not, an issue we explore in the next section.

ARE FUNDAMENTALIST MOVEMENTS VIOLENT?

On a global scale, religious violence seems to occur nearly every day. On the day that this section was written, 33 women and children receiving holiday toys from soldiers in the Middle East were killed by religiously motivated violence. During the time it took to write this chapter, literally hundreds of people lost their lives as a result of religiously motivated violence. Religious groups plot and kill people from other religions; they kill people in their own religion whom they view as either accepting modern, Western ways or selling out their religion; they kill people who are simply in the wrong place at the wrong time.

The groundbreaking work *Terror in the Mind of God* by Mark Juergensmeyer (2003) provides a sociologically rich perspective for understanding the links between fundamentalism and terrorism and violence. First, not all religiously based violence is carried out by fundamentalists. Sometimes, in fact, religion is used as a justification for violence by people and groups without specific religious ties. Second, not all fundamentalist groups are violent. In fact, most are not. Even though there are many fundamentalist people and groups in the United States, for example, there has been less violence here than, say, in many nations of the Middle East. And when fundamentalist-based violence has occurred in the United States, it is often the work of an individual operating alone, without the organized support of a religious group.

Still, many cases of religious violence are committed by extremist fundamentalist groups and the number of these cases is growing. But why? Juergensmeyer finds in his extensive research among Sikhs, Muslims, Jews, Christians, and the Japanese Aum Shinrikyo sect that the confrontation between religion and the secular state is increasingly framed as a cosmic war that one group or the other will win. For fundamentalists, it is a battle between the good, true, and right versus the bad, false, and wrong. The end goal is to see religion restored to its position at the center of public consciousness. The result is that politics become increasingly "religionized" (as opposed to religion becoming increasingly politicized). Religion is making its claim on public life, rejecting relegation to the private sphere. To make this claim, religious groups sometimes (or for some groups, *often*) use violence to make their position and presence known. Religious violence, Juergensmeyer argues, is theater. It dramatizes conditions and perspectives. As part of this theater, "images of martyrdom, 'satanization,' and cosmic war have been central to religious ideologies" (Juergensmeyer 2003, 219). These images and ideas have empowered people and groups to act, provided them with an identity, and given them political legitimization. "Performance violence" by religious groups is almost exclusively symbolic. It is performed to dramatize a cause and it is buttressed by absolutism and moral justification.

What is more, because the war is framed in cosmic terms with a millennial outcome (the good will triumph eventually), fundamentalists do not believe any length of time is too long to fight the battle. Some leaders of fundamentalist groups expect battles to continue for hundreds of years, and others do not even expect the war to be completed in human history. Within such views, compromise is not an option. The end result is that religion, in spiritualizing violence, has given terrorism tremendous power. The reverse is true as well. Terrorism has given religion power. Neither can be ignored in our current world.

But we are left with the question of why fundamentalism leads to or condones violence in some cases but not in others. Iannaccone (1997), among others, argues that violence should be attributed to the religious–political environment rather than to religion itself. He claims that when religion is unregulated by the government—that is, when the state allows religious diversity, does not squelch religion, and does not favor one religion over another—violence is rare and limited to isolated individuals. Violent religious groups arise in countries where the state suppresses religious freedom or favors one religion over others. "Whereas government regulation and state-sponsored religion encourage sects to fight both church and state, a truly competitive religious market encourages religious tolerance and mutual respect if only as a matter of necessity" (Iannaccone 1997, 114). Considering that religious violence and terrorism are playing an apparently increased role around the globe, we are improving our understanding of violence and religion but still have much more to learn. Perhaps you can contribute to our understanding.

Lizardo and Bergesen (2003) provide one promising approach to better understand religious violence. They look at terrorism—religious and nonreligious—contextually. They consider the important context to be a nation's location in the world and historical period. They find that during periods of hegemonic supremacy, terrorist activity is concentrated in the periphery. When terrorism occurs in core nations (in Cold War terms, the United States and its allies), it comes largely from native leftist groups. That is, attacks are concentrated internally, within the group's own nation, and tend not to be religiously motivated. During these periods, the international community considers such violence to be the purview of the specific states. But the systemic anomie resulting from a more competitive configuration of power and from hegemonic decline projects violence transnationally, from attacks in the semiperiphery to attacks on the core, on targets that are both within core nations and on core outposts. What used to be called "local problems" come to be viewed as crimes against humanity and civilization. As Russian and U.S. global power have declined, religiously motivated transnational violence from people and groups in semiperiphery nations has increased.

On the theme of context, scholars of fundamentalist movements have noted that fundamentalist strategies and approaches differ by region, religion, and type of nation–state. Although some fundamentalist Muslim groups may use acts of violence or attempted (and at times successful) coups, for instance, U.S. Protestant fundamentalists have largely followed the strategy of working within the system by influencing a political party and affecting change via the party platform, selected candidates, and elections. Violent acts perpetuated by U.S. Protestant fundamentalists, such as abortion clinic bombings, underlie political agendas but do not characterize their overall strategy of creating political and social change. This strategic difference may be in part due to their structural location in a core nation of the world.

HOLES IN CONCEPTUALIZING AND UNDERSTANDING FUNDAMENTALISM

Measuring Fundamentalism

Quantitative studies of fundamentalism often don't define or measure fundamentalism consistently or completely, so it is difficult to compare findings across studies. For comparative-historical approaches, fundamentalism is most often measured as organizations and movements that are identified as such. There is, of course, some tautological reasoning here: First, one selects fundamentalist groups and movements, and then one studies them to see what they have in common, and the result is fundamentalism.

According to Woodbury and Smith (1998), fundamentalism may be a binary variable, but it cannot be measured simply along the characteristics discussed above. Rather, one must add historical understanding to particular religious movements to know which are fundamentalist, which are not, and why. Woodbury and Smith focus on conservative U.S. Protestant Christianity to argue that there are historical, organizational, and ideological differences between fundamentalists and evangelicals, two groups that are often treated both in sociological literature and media reports as the same group.

Imagine you wanted to develop a survey to see whether you or any of your classmates are fundamentalists. What questions would you use? That is to say, how would you "operationalize" the concept of fundamentalism so that you could actually measure it? To date, quantitative operationalization of fundamentalism lacks richness of measurement, often owing to data limitations. Most often, in order to identify U.S. Christian individuals (usually Protestant) who are fundamentalist, the concept is operationalized as believing that the Bible is literally true, word for word. Other common measures are membership in a denomination determined to be fundamentalist and professing to be "born-again." Although all these measures may be indicators, they are by themselves weak indicators of fundamentalism. We must develop better multiple measures and include them on surveys, or our knowledge of fundamentalism will continue to be incomplete and perhaps even wrong. The measures we need to develop should operationalize our theoretical understanding of fundamentalism.

Self-identification is an alternative measurement strategy. It is used on its own or in conjunction with other indicators. The strategy consists of asking people whether they consider themselves to be fundamentalist. Certainly there can be problems in this measurement method. Do all people who are fundamentalist know this is the term that describes them? And do all people who are not fundamentalist know not to describe themselves that way? And do people who are fundamentalist and know it want to describe themselves with the term, or do they prefer a different one because of the negative connotations of fundamentalism?

In sum, fundamentalism can be and has been measured by denominational or group affiliation, beliefs, practices, and self-identification. Because the concept is so complex, single measures should be avoided. It's important to note that if fundamentalism is a generalizable concept, then the study of fundamentalism should explore measures that can be used across religions and regions.

Should We Study Fundamentalism or Modern Secularism?

If fundamentalism is rooted in the context of modernity, might modernity and its followers be the topics on which scholars should focus their study? Consider the words of sociologist Steve Bruce (2000, 116–17):

> "In the broad sweep of history fundamentalists are normal. There is nothing unusual in people taking religion very seriously. What we now regard as religious 'extremism' was commonplace 200 years ago in the Western world and is still commonplace in most parts of the globe. It is not the dogmatic believer who insists that the sacred texts are divinely inspired and true, who tries to model his life on the ethical requirements of those texts, and who seeks to impose these requirements on the entire society who is unusual. The liberal who supposes that his sacred texts are actually human constructions of differing moral worth, whose religion makes little difference to his life, and who is quite happy to accept that what his God requires of him is not binding on other members of his society: this is the strange and remarkable creature."

Most Western-trained academicians and journalists are carriers of modernism and secularization (Berger 1992). According to their worldview, fundamentalism is odd. But given the broad sweep of history, perhaps knowledge of religion and the state would advance more rapidly if it focused more closely on the "strange and remarkable creature" that walks without a god and on the societies that operate without religious suppositions. As Christian Smith and his colleagues have argued, secularization is not the inevitable result of some invisible hand of modernity. Rather, it is the result of careful, planned, coordinated events and confrontations over the course of decades within multiple sectors of society (Smith 2003). It may be fruitful to study such processes and the actors involved in them.

European Exceptionalism?

So what's up with Europe? It has modernized, just as the United States has. It has secularized, just as the United States has. But throughout the world, Northern and Western Europe stand alone as the only places where modernization and secularization have not given rise to a fundamentalist response. Why did Europe secularize so thoroughly, with so little religious pushback compared to other places?

Scholars who are developing or working within the sociology of religion's "new paradigm" posit that state-sponsored churches in European nations led to the demise of religion when modernization and secularization set in. Supported by the state, religious professionals were not motivated nor forced to find ways to make religion appeal to the populace. Their churches and their salaries were guaranteed. When its actors lacked an entrepreneurial drive, religion became outdated for the masses.

But this does not seem to be a wholly adequate answer. Is it true that every state-sponsored religion dies out in the wake of modernization and secularization? Do only nations that have state-sponsored religions secularize? Do all nations that have state-sponsored religion secularize? Do all nations without state-sponsored religion remain highly religious? Or if pluralism leads to secularization, as many scholars have suggested, why does pluralism seem to have such wildly varying effects on different nations?

Management and sociology professor Wayne Baker (2005) offers an explanation for why levels of modernization do not universally predict the degree of a society's secularization. Addressing the discrepancy between the recent rise of fundamentalism in the United States and its relative absence in Europe, Baker notes that a different type of cultural heritage is at work in the United States compared with the heritage in European countries. The cultural heritage of the United States is based not on common ancestry or language, but on Civil Religion. The cultural core of the United States is ideological and traditional and is therefore not as susceptible to secularization in response to modernization. Traditional values that are considered to be religious do not depend solely on the prominence of religious institutions. Baker notes that the United States has maintained its overall level of adherence to traditional values from 1981 to 2001 and remains extremely traditional as a whole compared with its modernized European counterparts. Baker's insight that traditionalism and secularization are tied to a country's cultural heritage seems to be an important one that can help generate sociological explanations of the emergence of fundamentalist movements and of European exceptionalism.

Is There Such a Thing as Fundamentalism?

Some scholars completely reject not only the term *fundamentalism*, but the entire scholarly enterprise studying fundamentalism. For example, Iannaccone (1997) argues that the reason scholars struggle to find agreement about the content, causes, and consequences of fundamentalism is that the concept, theoretically, leads us down a dead-end path.

Instead, he argues that we should study sectarianism. "Sectarian religion is high-powered religion rooted in separation from and tension with the broader society" (Iannaccone 1997, 114). The tradition of contrasting and studying strict and lenient forms of religion is old, dating back not only to the beginnings of the sociology of religion, but to Adam Smith's *Wealth of Nations* (1776 [1965]). Studying sectarianism allows researchers to build on much solid theory and empirical work, such as the social benefits of strict religions, the reasons that people join such religions, and the reasons that such religions are attractive to people at the margins of society. Moreover, rather than viewing resurgent conservative religion as rooted in conditions of recent modernity, scholars analyzing sectarianism can view such movements as a pervasive tendency that is found to a greater or lesser degree throughout history. Studying sectarianism avoids the problems of explaining why fundamentalism seems only to have appeared on a global scale since the 1970s, long after modernity had appeared on the scene in some places, and only shortly after it had appeared on the scene elsewhere. Even more importantly, working from a classical understanding of positivist science, the sectarian concept allows us to perform clear tests of hypotheses, aiding theoretical advancement.

Even if they do not accept such critiques, scholars of fundamentalism still must address these critiques and demonstrate why conceptualizing fundamentalism as something relatively new is advantageous for advancing our knowledge of religion and society.

WHERE DO WE GO FROM HERE?

Volumes of research have been published on fundamentalism in the past 25 years, far more than can be summarized in these few pages. Yet it is clear that substantially more scholarly work remains. In this chapter we have highlighted some of the vital questions that still lack answers. For all the usefulness of the concept, and for all the progress that sociologists have made in studying the worldwide resurgence of religion, there are still essential debates and questions that must be addressed.

Even as scholars continue to focus on fundamentalism, they do so in conjunction with their understanding of modernity, its processes, and its carriers. Understanding both concepts and their interrelations better will push our knowledge forward. Scholars should also take Iannaccone's (1997) challenge—that we study sectarianism rather than fundamentalism—seriously. Perhaps the view that religion experienced a general decline only to resurge since the 1970s is not the most advantageous theoretical viewpoint. Considering that the number of sectarian groups has fluctuated for a very long time, perhaps we need to redefine fundamentalism. When the field has more conceptual and theoretical coherence, it will need some standards for measuring fundamentalism. Too many different and, in our view, incomplete ways of measuring fundamentalism now pass the eyes of reviewers and end up in journals, muddling our understanding of the concept. For example, when we examine the relationship between religion and environmentalism in Chapter 13, we will encounter a number of other ways in which social scientists have measured "religious fundamentalism," each of which has the weaknesses identified here.

We think it will prove fruitful to conceptualizing, theorizing, and measuring fundamentalism for scholars to undertake more ethnographic work on fundamentalist movements, attempting to understand who joins fundamentalist movements and why, what their goals are, how they view nonfundamentalists, and how they view and interpret life events. At the same time, in keeping with our suggestion of understanding fundamentalism by studying modernism, ethnographic work asking these same questions is essential to understanding modern, secular movements.

It will also prove fruitful for sociologists to undertake more comparative studies of fundamentalism that place the movements in their proper historical context. Such work can help us understand how—if at all—fundamentalism is related to changes in globalization (increasing trade flows, greater economic integration, threat of homogenization, and loss of communal identity) and nations' locations in the world. Ultimately, scholars must seek to understand the role that resurgent religion will have in the future, including its connection to violence. Will secularized nations and peoples be a temporary phenomenon in the long religious history of the world? Will modernity eventually offer all that people seek, and will religions weaken? Will religion and secularism continue battling endlessly? Will religion continue battling religion?

These issues and queries must now be taken up with great care, precise thought, and the best research tools available. As world events suggest, ignoring these issues and questions is a luxury we can no longer afford.

SUGGESTED READING

Almond, Gabriel A., R. Scott Appleby, and Emmanuel Sivan. 2003. *Strong Religion: The Rise of Fundamentalisms Around the World.* Chicago: University of Chicago Press.

Antoun, Richard T. 2001. *Understanding Fundamentalism: Christian, Islamic, and Jewish Movements.* Walnut Creek, CA: AltaMira.

Bruce, Steve. 2000. *Fundamentalism.* Malden, MA: Blackwell.

Juergensmeyer, Mark. 2003. *Terror in the Mind of God: The Global Rise of Religious Violence, 3d ed.* Berkeley: University of California Press.

Marsden, George M. 1980. *Fundamentalism and American Culture: The Shaping of Twentieth-Century Evangelicalism 1870–1925.* New York: Oxford University Press.

Riesebrodt, M. [1990] 1993 trans. *Pious Passion: The Emergence of Modern Fundamentalism in the United States and Iran.* Translated by D. Reneau. Berkeley: University of California Press.

7

Divine Rights and Casting Down the Mighty from their Thrones

Does Religion Block or Encourage Social Change?

1. Does religion inevitably help to keep things the same?
2. Is there a link between religion and forms of social inequality?
3. Many religions believe in justice. Can religion help to bring it about?
4. What factors limit the ability of religion to bring about change?

Think back to any course you've taken in history, especially any that dealt with Europe. You may remember that before the 19th century in Europe, and somewhat later in preindustrial societies elsewhere in the world, the wielding of power by rulers in most human societies was justified by linking the ruler to the sacred forces of the universe. Chiefs, kings, nobles, and other leaders ruled because they were chosen by the gods to do so.

In Christian Europe, North Africa, and the Middle East, this approach to the intersection of religion and secular political power had its roots in the Christian New Testament. In his letter to the Romans, St. Paul states, "Let every person be subject to the governing authorities. For there is no authority except from God, and those that exist have been instituted by God. There he who resists the authorities resists what God has appointed, and those who resist will incur judgment" (Romans 13:1–2). Almost 400 years later, Saint Augustine of Hippo argues in his work *The City of God* that God has instituted the authority of civil governments, even when they seem to be acting contrary to or in an antagonist way toward the Church. It was not for another 1200 years that "divine right theory" took on a more extreme form when a French bishop, Jacques-Bénigne Bossuet, argued that kings, whether they ruled well or poorly, were accountable only to God and consequently that their actions could not be questioned or opposed. Wow! It doesn't get much clearer than that. Rulers can do what they want because God has put them in charge. They rule. We obey. For any of us to challenge government is to challenge God. We'll give you a minute to let that sink in!

While you may have learned about divine right theory before, you might not know that similar ideas exist in other religious traditions. In some Islamic traditions, for example, the ideal and only appropriate political structure is a theocracy, literally "the rule of God," which does not separate secular and religious authority at all. Allah rules through human representatives whose task is to enact laws that reflect Allah's will (Usman 1998).

Almost 2000 years ago, as the result of Chinese military conflicts that replaced the *Shang* dynasty with the *Zhou* dynasty, a new political philosophy called the *t'ien ming*, or "Mandate of Heaven," gained prominence to make legitimate the authority of the *Zhou* military victors. Like its parallels in Christian and Muslim history, the Mandate of Heaven requires those who rule to do so in ways that support the welfare of the people with justice and wisdom. As long as a ruler does this, Heaven mandates that they and their family will remain in power for generations. However, unlike the situation in Christianity or Islam, the Mandate of Heaven could be removed from a ruler's dynasty if the ruler did not take care of the people or was unjust. This is quite a difference from Christian versions of divine right theory. In China, you had to be a "good" ruler. You had to make sure your people were happy and that society worked well overall. If you didn't do this, you were in trouble. You would lose your Mandate. In such cases, the people are free to oppose and rebel against unjust rulers, and it is in fact their duty to do so. Japan's rulers also had a Mandate to rule, but their Mandate originated in the belief that the rulers were the direct descendants of the goddess of the sun (Hane 1991).

In all these examples, religious beliefs and practices helped to maintain the political and economic power structures of the societies in which they were used. One of the key observations that early social theorists made about religion as a social institution was that religion functioned specifically to support the status quo of society, in political, economic, and cultural terms. In other words, religion was always "conservative" in the sense that its operations conserved society or kept society from changing.

From a sociological perspective, religion's conservative nature has important implications when it comes to understanding how power and inequality operate in a specific society. On the macrosocietal level, religion can maintain the power of individuals or groups through beliefs like the divine right of kings or the Mandate of Heaven. On the microsocietal level, it teaches individuals to accept the structure of society as it exists, even when the structure has negative consequences for the majority of people. Anyone who questioned the power structure in any of its forms or operations throughout history could be put in prison, tortured, or even killed for challenging the divinely ordained order of things. Yet, over the last century and a half, we have witnessed religious leaders and ordinary believers using their faith as the basis for challenging the power structures of societies around the world. From the antislavery and early labor movements of the 19th century to the Civil Rights movement of the 1960s, in the anticolonial movements around the world, in the pro-life movement, and many other social movements, in all these events religious beliefs, practices, leaders, and organizations find roles in challenging the status quo. In this chapter, we will explore some of the classic theoretical statements about religion and social change that help explain why religion so often seems only to support the status quo. We will also look at insights from the study of social movements to see under what conditions religion can become a force for social change, what it brings to these kinds of social struggles, and what the consequences are of religiously motivated activism for both the religious traditions and the society in question.

CLASSIC OBSERVATIONS ABOUT RELIGION AND SOCIAL CHANGE

Because many of the early social theorists were interested in the changes that were occurring in Europe and North America due to industrialization and the changing landscapes of politics following the French and American Revolutions, their observations and thoughts about the role that religious groups and people play in society must be understood with that social context in mind. In Chapter 1, for instance, we briefly discussed Karl Marx's famous statement that "religion is the opium of the people." Of all his statements in the thousands of pages that he wrote, this is one of the most memorable, and many people either strongly oppose it or agree with it. But people rarely consider why it made sense for him to write this statement in 1843.

As a result of capitalist expansion in the 19th century, European—and later American industrialization—was restructuring the social class system. The old system of feudalism, in which the kings, queens, lords, and ladies ruled and the peasants worked, was being replaced. Industrialization brought about a new system of social classes with capitalist employers, who owned most of society's productive property, including land and the new factories, and also controlled all the profits that their businesses earned. An industrial working class labored in these new factories for starvation wages, an arrangement that some outspoken labor advocates called "wage slavery." Now you may be thinking: "Hold it. What about the middle class?" We will grant that, at this time in history there were some people—such as small shopkeepers, blacksmiths, and farmers—who were neither employers nor workers. But the large, significant middle class that you may be thinking of didn't come into existence until more than a century later.

Now let's get back to religion. Supporting the status quo of this new capitalist system with its extremes of wealth and poverty were Christian congregations of all types. Religion supported these new forms of class inequality more often through its silence than in formal statements like divine right theory. Although the negative results of industrialization, like hunger, disease, chronic unemployment, and threats of revolution were all around them, most religious leaders never said much about them. Those problems were economic issues, after all, and ministers were supposed to worry about people's souls, not their jobs. Religious leaders encouraged church members to live good Christian lives by being obedient to religious teachings and to see the dynamics of the world as part of the spiritual battle between good and evil, righteousness and sin, and God and the devil. Ministers usually observed that wealth and poverty simply expressed the social differences given to each person by God in which people receive the legitimate result of their intelligence and labor. Wealth and poverty were just part of the natural order. (The poor, after all, were always to be with us.) Ministers also implied—or directly stated—that wealthy people demonstrated more moral behavior than did the poor, who were assumed to be poor because they wasted what little money they had on alcohol and tobacco. But most of all, the significance of religious support for the capitalist system was in the manner in which it diverted the attention of the working classes and the poor away from the real-world social causes and the lived experiences of their poverty. When religious messages addressed economic inequality, they did so in a way that patted the wealthy on the back for their right living and gave the poor hope that they would go to heaven after they died, where there would be no death, hunger, mourning, or pain, provided that they endured these inevitable trials here on earth and remained obedient to their church's teachings.

This was the historical context, then, when Marx dismissed religion from playing any positive part in changing society, especially through efforts to alleviate economic or any other form of injustice. Religion diverts attention *away* from practical conflicts between the powerful and powerless, rich and poor, and bosses and workers in the realm of capitalist production and directs it *toward* a mystified struggle between good and evil on some abstract, spiritual plane. But Marx also understood that religion was something that was attractive to exploited or oppressed peoples because it provided some degree of actual comfort and solace to those whose lives were painful. By likening religion to opium, a drug that numbs and deadens pain, Marx underscores the real and material nature of the suffering and oppression that drives people to seek relief in religion. The problem, as Marx saw it, was that, instead of diagnosing the true cause of the suffering (capitalism) and encouraging those who were oppressed to fight back and end it, religion links suffering to otherworldly, and therefore false, causes (sin, the devil, God's wrath, hell), telling them to be passive and patient and wait for change in heaven.

For further evidence in support of this position, consider the many ways that religion in the 20th century, up to our own time, has supported a variety of economic, political, racial, and sexual expressions of inequality. In the days of the American Civil Rights movement, white clergy regularly preached about the Biblical basis for the system of racial segregation in the American South. Well-known ministers such as Reverend Jerry Falwell, who later went on to found the Moral Majority, and Dr. W. A. Criswell, one-time pastor of the largest Southern Baptist Congregation in the country, which was located in Dallas, preached against any attempt to integrate American society and condemned those who supported integration as working against God himself (Freeman 2007). Other ministers tried to support the basic equality of Southern Blacks as children of God while simultaneously defending segregation as a theological reality. For example, J. Harold Smith (1950, 15, 28), a southern Evangelist with his own radio program, tried to defend both the rights of African Americans *and* segregation. In preaching on the Radio Bible Hour in 1950 from Del Rio, Texas, Smith argued:

> If America turns from God's answer, and fails to keep her RACES PURE by SEGREGATION, there will be neither WHITE nor NEGRO race remaining. But SHE WILL TURN INTO A NEGROID RACE OF PEOPLE! . . . God wants the races to be BLACK, YELLOW, or WHITE, like He intended them to be. He does not delight in a mixture. We all want pure food and have PURE FOOD LAWS. We want purity in our worship and medicine. Why not have it in our RACES?

But as we noted before, religion does not always work to legitimate the status quo in such obvious and extreme ways. Most clergy in Northern Ireland, for example, rarely speak out about the sectarian violence that continues between Protestants and Catholics there; instead, they shy away from generating bad feelings and conflict among their parishioners (McAllister 1998). Silence on these issues is another way in which religion acts as an agent of social control.

Marx's critique of religion as a conservative social force was picked up by later generations of social theorists and reformers who challenged religious groups on many issues, including their support of slavery, colonialism, segregation, male domination and privilege in society, and discrimination on the basis of sexuality and gender.

Approximately 80 years after Marx, Max Weber built a more nuanced argument about religion, power, and inequality that introduced the concept of *theodicy*. For Weber, as modern society became more bureaucratic and rational, its culture increasingly raised questions about "causes and effects" and "means and ends." If I do X, then Y will result. Or, put in a different way, if I want to achieve Y, then I ought to do X. People act on the basis of the meanings that they give their actions (things they want to do or know they ought to want to do) and also act as a result of their interests in achieving certain outcomes. But life is not that simple.

Many times, we do all the right things and yet do not achieve what we expect or are told we ought to achieve as a result. Students study hard and still fail exams. Employees put

---

BOX 7.1

Theodicy:

A concept used by Max Weber to explain systems of belief that help to explain human suffering, inequalities, sickness, and other negative aspects of human life and society.

---

in long hours and sweat only to have their wages cut or to be fired. A poor nation in the developing world builds a McDonalds restaurant in their capital city to be just like countries in Europe or North America, yet the country remains poor and marginal. In each of these cases, there is a discrepancy between behavior and its results. In religious terms, this problem can be summed up as "Why do bad things happen to good people?" "Why do the good die young?" or even the words of Jesus himself when he says "My God, my God, why have you forsaken me?" What Weber (1967 [1922]) observed is that people's individual experiences of the inequalities of modern life—inequalities that are based on class, prestige, and political power—create discrepancies in what people believe. Why do the poor, who follow their mandated religious beliefs and practices devotedly, remain poor, living lives of hardship, hunger, and sickness; while the rich, who seem to violate many religious teachings, end up living lives of comfort? It just doesn't make sense.

Into the gap between what we believe should happen and what actually does happen in our experience step theodicies. Theodicies explain why these discrepancies exist at all—especially the ones that result from the widespread misfortunes of whole groups of people—and help us to resolve them in our minds. It is important to realize that, because not every social group in society experiences these negative consequences in the same way, different forms of theodicies emerge to help explain various groups' experiences. Theodicies of *suffering* are the religious beliefs that help the lower classes of society come to terms with why they are poor, powerless, or otherwise marginalized in society, and what they can do—if anything—to gain some degree of redemption. Weber observes (Gerth and Mills 1964, 275),

> One can explain suffering and injustice by referring to individual sin committed in a former life (the migration of souls), to the guilt of ancestors, which is

avenged down to the third and fourth generation, or—the most principled—to the wickedness of all creatures *per se*. As compensatory promises, one can refer to the hopes of the individual for a better life in the future in this world (transmigration of souls) or to hopes for the successors (Messianic realm), or to a better life in the hereafter (paradise).

Regardless of the specific causes and solutions that a particular poor person's religious tradition identifies, a theodicy of suffering helps explain why things are the way they are in the lives of those who are at the margins of society.

In contrast to the theodicies that are developed to explain the lives of the poor, there are theodicies for those with power that explain the gaps between these people and other groups ranking below them in society. For the elite, theodicies of *dominance* answer the difficult question of why their lives are so full of resources while others have so little: "Strata in solid possession of social honor and power usually tend to fashion their status-legend in such a way as to claim a special and intrinsic quality of their own, usually a quality of blood; their sense of dignity feeds on their actual or alleged being" (Gerth and Mills 1964, 276). In religious terms, the elite believe that they have been blessed by God or the gods. Frequently, the possession of great resources comes linked with the ethical responsibility to use these resources in the service of others and society as a whole. Religious teachings that mandate acts of charity and outreach to the poor and needy become more central among the elite. Moreover, instead of placing an emphasis on guilt and sin—either one's own or one's ancestors'—a theodicy of dominance affirms the ways of life enjoyed by elite as evidence of righteous living or as a lifestyle to be upheld. You may remember that we talked about a similar concept in Chapter 2. Members of the Indian Brahman caste who fulfill their responsibilities as elites in society expect to enjoy continuing good fortunes in future lives.

The importance of Weber's theodicies is that they link religious beliefs and practices to specific social groups in society. Theodicies recognize that even when people all belong to the same religion they may worship differently from one another, their theologies and beliefs may emphasize different things and in some cases be radically different, and they may experience the sacred in different ways. Now, Weber did not want us to think that religious beliefs were inevitable reflections of economic class differences or that they inevitably supported only the interests of the privileged as Marx's formulations did. However, Weber did acknowledge that religion has the potential both to support the status quo of inequality and to challenge it at specific times and in specific places in history.

Weber's ideas about religion also laid the groundwork for contemporary studies of religion and social change. Incorporated in the theoretical links he made between theodicies and different class and status groups is the idea that religion, especially for the nonprivileged, can be the basis for expressing those groups' frustrations and resentments at the injustices they experience. Unlike Marx, Weber held that the theodicies of the poor or lower classes were not always a drug to comfort and divert them. Instead, their theodicies could encourage them to work to try to change their world. Theodicies of suffering, Weber observed, also bring with them the idea that the religion of the poor includes "a special mission," an "ethical imperative," and a "'task' placed before them by God," to bring the social order back in line with the divine will by prophetic social action in this world. As we will see, religious beliefs and practices include prophetic calls for social and economic justice in this world, not just promises that it will exist in the next. Throughout history, religion has played a role in maintaining the existing structure of society and has also given birth to a wide range of social movements and reform efforts that have literally changed the world.

THE LESSONS FROM STUDYING SOCIAL MOVEMENTS

Much of the sociological work on religion, forms of economic and social inequality, and social change has been based on the two perspectives provided by Karl Marx and Max Weber. Many studies conducted during the 20th century tried to address the theoretical binary of "religion as opiate" versus "religion as mobilizer." Over the last two decades, the study of social movement activism has produced a great deal of evidence to demonstrate that the relationship between religion and social change is never "either/or." It is always "both/and." Religion provides a set of resources that are important to all efforts to create social change.

Christian Smith's *Disruptive Religion* represents the only attempt by a sociologist to systematically categorize all the possible resources available from religious institutions that are significant for social movement activism, though other scholars focus on subsets of these resources (1996a, 9). (See Table 7.1.) In all, Smith notes 21 separate "religious assets" that make up six basic types of resources, which are useful for activism, some obvious, and others less so. Religious resources are divided into motivational, organizational, identity-constructing, social and geographical positioning, privileged legitimacy, and institutional self-interest.

Among the most important assets that religion can bring to social movements is a reason or motivation for a person to participate in the movement and put himself or herself at risk in fighting for social change. The idea that justice and freedom are God's will for humans here on earth, so fighting for these causes is a moral commandment, not only gets people to act, but also provides strength and courage, rooted in the sacred, that allows participants to face police brutality, jail, torture, and even death for the cause of justice. For example, religious teachings that mandate social and economic justice, paired with familiar Biblical stories, are powerful means to motivate people to action (Gutterman 2005, Swarts 2008). On the basis of these teaching, religious leaders have the authority to tell their members what to do—which causes they should support and which they should oppose. Sometimes this authority can also be used to challenge or even condemn people in power when they are perceived to be violating a religion's moral teachings (deviance-monitoring). Music, songs, and personal testimonies can also motivate people to fight back in spite of the dangers they are likely to encounter in doing so (Gutman 1966, Halker 1991, Mirola 2003a). Among other religious resources that Smith noted are useful for social activism are financial support, meeting space, access to computers and copiers for communicating information and making flyers and leaflets, and established organizational networks that link local congregations to national and international religious bodies. Sharing a religious tradition often can get people to work together for a common cause in a way that no other shared identity could (Swarts 2008).

The Emergence of Religious Activism

So, now you know something about the complex ways that religion simultaneously can inhibit and empower social activism. But now a new question emerges: "What conditions

---

TABLE 7.1   Religious Resources That Are Available for Social Movements (Smith 1996a)

I. Transcendent Motivation Assets
   A. Legitimation for protest rooted in the ultimate or sacred
   B. Moral imperatives for love, justice, peace, freedom, and equity
   C. Powerfully motivating icons, rituals, songs, testimonies, and oratory
   D. Ideologies demanding self-discipline, sacrifice, and altruism
   E. Legitimation of organizational and strategic–tactical flexibility

II. Organizational Assets
   A. Trained and experienced leadership
   B. Financial resources
   C. Congregated participants and solidarity incentives
   D. Preexisting communication channels
   E. Preexisting authority structures and deviance-monitoring mechanisms
   F. Enterprise tools
   G. "Movement midwives"

III. Shared-Identity Assets
   A. Common identification among gathered strangers
   B. Shared superidentities nationally and internationally
   C. Unifying identity against outside threats

IV. Social and Geographic Positioning
   A. Geographical dispersion
   B. Social diffusion and cross-cutting associations
   C. Transnational organizational linkages

V. Privileged Legitimacy
   A. Political legitimacy in public opinion
   B. The protection of religion as a last "open space"

VI. Institutional Self-interest
   A. Institutional resistance to state encroachment

---

shape whether any particular religious tradition will generate activism for social change and whether it will maintain the status quo?"

Let's think about the answer to this in two ways. First, we need to explore this question from the standpoint of religious groups and congregations themselves, what we might call "religious activism." For them, the question is best reframed to address those occasions when whole denominations or religious groups engage in social and political change efforts or movements. Familiar evidence for this can be seen today in the pro-life movement, in which evangelical Protestants, Roman Catholics, and many congregations from socially conservative religions have mobilized their resources to call for greater regulation of abortion procedures and to attempt to overturn *Roe v. Wade*, the Supreme Court case that made abortion legal in the United States.

A less familiar example comes from the ways in which congregations in countries like Poland and East Germany became the organizational base for their respective national movements to end the Soviet-backed socialist government in their countries. In 1989, every Monday night, thousands of people gathered at the Church of Saint Nicholai in the East German city of Leipzig for prayer services that were also political demonstrations led by Pastor Friedrich Magirius. In these, as well as many other instances, congregations and their leaders have mobilized around a wide variety of social changes. But the question remains: Why does this seem to happen around some social changes but not others?

Of course, one key reason this happens comes back to the content of these religious groups' theologies and their histories of social and political engagement. Most congregations will not become politically involved overnight. Most religious traditions have theological understandings of secular politics and social change that shape whether the members of these groups will make efforts to try to change aspects of the secular world. Many fundamentalist Christian congregations, for instance, believe that the world is too sinful to be changed for the better. Such an approach leads them to retreat from contact with the world and to focus on holy living while waiting for Jesus to return, destroy this world, and create a new one. Many U.S. Evangelical and mainline Protestant religious groups have had more open social theologies that go back to the fight to end slavery in the American South and earlier still to battles for freedom of religion and for the separation of church and state following the Revolutionary War (Smith 1998). Today, mainline Protestants and Roman Catholics who were radicalized by the Civil Rights movement of the 1950s and 1960s continue to be more engaged than members of some other denominations in fights around racial equality, poverty, employment, and many other related issues. Black Pentecostal clergy and congregations that have not been engaged in political activism are increasingly drawing on their own racial and religious histories to mold new ways of generating congregationally based activism (McRoberts 1999). Consequently, when a new issue comes along, such as immigrant rights or neighborhood development, these types of congregations can draw from their tradition of beliefs and practices and apply those ideas to the new issue (Craig 1992, Wuthnow 1988).

But a historical tradition of activism is not enough to predict whether or not religion will become a force for social change. A classic 1942 study by Liston Pope examined the role of local churches in shaping labor reforms in the textile mills of Gastonia, North Carolina, in the 1930s. In their introduction to the study, Peterson and Demerath (1942, *xxxii-xl*) argue that five principal conditions shape the likelihood that religious groups will become forces for social change. (See Table 7.2.) These include the type of issue itself and how the congregation's members feel about it, the degree of actual congregational involvement, the structure of the denomination, the level from which a religious group is calling for involvement, and the background of the minister.

Of course, not all social issues engage religious groups equally. In our own recent history, we have seen that issues related to gender and sexuality generate great interest and concern in congregations from many religions. Issues related to life and death, such as abortion, war, the death penalty, stem cell research, and euthanasia all have mobilized religious groups to work politically in both support of and in opposition to them. But think for a minute about environmental activism, the antiglobalization, or anti–nuclear power movements. Religious groups or leaders do not figure as prominently in these social movements. We'd be wrong to think that religious groups are unconcerned about these movements and their causes, or even that they have not taken stands or worked politically either to support or oppose any goals of these movements. Yet it is rare for entire religious organizations with their members to participate in social activism around these issues.

However, as Peterson and Demerath suggest, the more frequently and deeply members of churches do get involved with such issues, the more likely it will be for the religious group or denomination as a whole to do so. A clear example of this tendency is the environmental movement. Until recently, it was rare to hear religious leaders speaking out about environmental degradation or the need to expand conservation efforts. Today, because many of their members have become interested in the environment and motivated to protect it, many groups have developed entirely new theologies around the environment and the proper role of humans in caring for it. When we get to Chapter 14, you'll see how this happened among Evangelical Christians.

More important than the issues that attract the interest and activism of religious groups, though, is the internal political structure of the religious group. Religious groups have different kinds of decision-making and governing structures. Some groups are hierarchical with formal pronouncements about what members of a faith ought to do or think about issues being handed down from those with authority at the top of the organization. For instance, the Roman Catholic Church has issued "encyclicals" and other formal statements from the Pope regarding the Church's position on various social issues. In 1891, Pope Leo XIII released *Rerum Novarum*, "On the Condition of Workers," in which he officially called on all Catholics to support the labor movement's efforts to achieve collective bargaining rights, living wages, shorter hours, and other reforms. The encyclical also formally permitted Catholics to join labor unions. Likewise, in 1968 Pope Paul VI issued his encyclical, *Humanae Vitae*, which became a contemporary basis for Roman Catholic involvement with the pro-life movement. But not every religious group is hierarchical. Some are arranged so that each member has a say or a vote in making decisions or crafting policies. In these cases, whether a religious group becomes involved in social change, and whether the group works for or against change, rests solely with the congregation itself. When James Wood studied which types of church-governing structures were most likely to support national civil rights policy *as churches*, he found that those with hierarchical structures were most likely to do so and those with more congregational (member-based) structures were least likely to do so (Wood 1970). The reason for this finding has to do with the way the political structure of the denomination or congregation buffers clergy who wish to take action on an issue from a disapproving or apathetic congregation. In a hierarchical structure, a minister's authority to openly engage social and political issues is recognized, even if church members disapprove of the involvement. In a congregational structure, because the minister serves at the will of the congregation, disapproving members of such congregations can "veto" a minister's wish to become publicly involved in any particular social issue by threatening to rescind that minister's call to lead them.

Of course, decisions by those at the top of a religious structure to take a political stand on some issue—regardless of the governing structure of local congregations—may not result in local congregations actually doing so. For instance, the national governing bodies of many mainline Protestant denominations have issued statements calling on members and local congregations to actively work for economic justice around the world by supporting campaigns for a higher minimum wage, the right to organize unions, and employer-provided health care and other benefits. However, as Pope (1942) and others have demonstrated, just because the leaders of a denomination call people to action doesn't mean that that they will actually work for these issues locally. When the national Episcopal Church voted to approve the ordination of female priests, some local congregations and regional dioceses simply ignored the issue, and a few continue to do so to the present day. The point here is that the further removed an official call for social action or involvement is from local members of religious groups and their concerns, the less likely these religious pronouncements in support of change are to translate into action.

Finally, whether a religious group will engage in social activism depends to a great extent on the characteristics and background of the group's religious leaders. As Peterson and Demerath (1942, *xxxvii*) observed, the level of activity is related to a minister's age, the minister's social status (in the sense of prominence), the amount and quality of his or her education, the location of the congregation (rural, urban, or suburban) a minister serves and whether he or she was brought up in these areas, and whether the minister has "tenure," or some degree of protection from members who disagree with him or her. Younger ministers, those with more personal social prominence in their background, those with university educations (as opposed to a Bible college training), and those from more urban and cosmopolitan backgrounds all are more likely, as Peterson and Demerath said in 1942, "to be more independent and more adventuresome" when it comes to working for social and political change in their communities. Similar patterns have been found among today's clergy.

Using data from the first wave of the National Congregations Study in 1998, several sets of researchers found relationships between education or social class and clergy social activism. Among Evangelical clergy, the amount of education had no effect, but among mainline Protestants and Black Protestant clergy, higher education was associated with the clergy being more politically engaged (McDaniel 2003, Guth et al. 2003, Smidt et al. 2003). The higher the social class, the more likely clergy were to support social- and gender-related public issues while remaining neutral on or opposing issues that touched on economic justice. This finding reflects a long-standing effect of how class mediates religious convictions for making the world a better place, which has appeared in many studies of religion and social reform (Hart 1992, McCloud and Mirola 2008, Olson 2000).

Race and gender also play roles in shaping clergy activism. As a group, Black clergy are theologically conservative but can be politically liberal and are more likely to be

---

TABLE 7.2   Factors Influencing Religion to Become a Force in Social Change Movements

1. The type of issue and the degree of congregational interest and commitment to it
2. The extent of congregation members' involvement in social issues
3. The governing structure of the congregation and/or denomination
4. The level of the religious organization's hierarchy from which a statement is issued
5. The background characteristics of the religious leaders in congregations

---

Source: Peterson and Demerath in Pope's *Millhands and Preachers* (1942, *xxxii–xl*)

1. A preponderantly religious world view among revolutionary classes
2. Theology at odds with the existing social order
3. Clergy closely associated with revolutionary classes
4. Revolutionary classes united in a single religion
5. Revolutionary classes' religion different from the religion of the dominant class
6. Alternative organizational structures and political access not available

---

Source: Robinson (1987, 53)

politically engaged on many other issues besides theology (Olson 2000). In her study of 10 Black churches in Philadelphia, Katie Day (2001, 184) found that Black pastors were in positions in their communities where almost daily they had to "confront the urban policies of city, state, and federal agencies as well as banking, commercial, and philanthropic communities . . . Once again, if the black Church doesn't do it, who will?" Heidi Swarts (2008) notes that urban congregations, especially Black Protestant, mainline Protestant, and Roman Catholic churches, are among the few organizations that remain in many inner cities across the country. Their location makes them prime candidates for institutions to work on social activism, especially on poverty, housing, and urban development issues, because they witness the economic and political forces that cause these problems on a daily basis.

Women clergy are more likely to express their interest in political engagement as a living out of their religious convictions. However, there is still a debate about whether women ministers are more actively engaged than their male counterparts. Laura Olson's 2000 study of Milwaukee Protestant clergy included four women pastors. She found that the three women serving in mainline Protestant churches felt unable to be vocal about or personally involved with political issues because of pressure from their congregations to avoid these issues. The single woman she interviewed who served a Black Protestant congregation, in contrast, addressed political issues in her preaching and in her ministerial role, although she was nrither personally nor practically involved with political efforts to change the conditions of life in her inner-city neighborhood because those efforts were not the focus of the senior male pastor in the congregation.

When Activists Get Religion

Examining what factors push religious groups from within to work for social change is only one part of the story. Secular social movements and their organizations often attempt to mobilize religious resources as well. In these cases, movements see benefit to building coalitions with congregations or religious individuals in communities to tap their resources. While social movements seeking support from religious groups see benefits in forging these associations, they are not trying to make their movements "religious." More often, they are trying to use religion to gain the support of a religious general public, to build solidarity within their movement when activists themselves hold strong religious values, or to appeal to individuals or groups in power to grant their desired changes or reforms.

Leland Robinson (1987) outlined a set of conditions that shape the likelihood that religion will become a tool for social movement activism in the way we have described. (See Table 7.2.) Although Robinson was interested in revolutionary movements that were aimed at radical national and political change specifically, it is useful to think about these conditions as they apply to less extreme forms of social movements. Two of these conditions focus on the religious beliefs of the groups mobilizing for social change.

Robinson argues that religion is likely to be used as a source for social movement resources when movement participants themselves maintain a view of reality that is specifically rooted in religious tradition and when these participants also share the same religious tradition. In other words, religion is important when there is a shared religious culture among the people who are fighting for change. For example, Southern Black churches have been the cornerstones of community life for African Americans since the end of slavery. Because African Americans in the south joined a rather small number of different Protestant denominations, they tend to share a similar religious culture that ultimately made the interweaving of the civil rights message with religious ideas logical and fairly straightforward for the movement. Today, it is still true that any social movement that seeks to engage the African American community must first gain the approval of Black churches and their clergy (Swarts 2008, Wood 2002).

But sharing a similar religious culture with potential supporters is not in itself a sufficient basis for movements to "get religion." Robinson also noted that the beliefs and practices of a religious group must truly oppose the ones that the social movement is opposing. Because the elite often use religion to justify their power, those who are trying to challenge elite power may be suspicious of people who are religious. However, when alternative religious beliefs link God's will, themes of justice, and liberation to legitimate a movement's critique of the existing social order and the need for concrete social reform—and even radical change—religion will become revolutionary. *Theologies of liberation*, constructed by religious activists living among the poor in developing countries, provided oppressed groups in these places with a foundation for their resistance and reform efforts. These beliefs became alternatives that allowed marginalized and poor people to reject other religious beliefs that would have kept them in their place. Furthermore, this distinct separation between the religious beliefs of the groups who are fighting for change and those of the group with power becomes another way to reinforce the "us versus them" distinction between groups in conflict. The groups that are fighting for change ("us") have God on our side, are Right, are Good, are fighting for Justice, and will eventually be victorious, while their opponents ("them") by definition are Wrong, are Evil, are Unjust, and will eventually lose.

Religion also is likely to play a role in social movements when religious leaders themselves, in their personal lives, have close ties to movement participants. These ties may emerge from *physical proximity*, in which participants of a social movement are members of their congregations or when clergy witness the objective conditions that affect movement participants, such as unemployment, hunger, disease, poverty, or military repression. Both of these conditions obtained when Roman Catholic priests and nuns stood up for the poor and indigenous peoples throughout Latin America after directly experiencing their living conditions (Lernoux 1982). This closeness may also emerge when religious leaders are members of the group fighting for social change and would benefit directly from its success.

Finally, Robinson argues that, in order for religion to be seen as a practical resource for social change, movement participants must lack alternative resources, organizations, and means for generating social change. Religious resources, in other words, often are the only ones available. But let's be clear about this. We are not saying that religion is a choice of last resort. For groups that lack access to political, economic, and other sorts of power, using religion not only makes sense for the reasons we have noted, but it is one of the only sources of resources available to support a mass movement. An examination of the many social movements around the world in history confirms that groups fighting for social changes are also systematically denied access to political power, economic resources, media resources, and just about any other set of resources. In these cases, religious resources become, at least initially, the only ones available to support social activism. Congregations become political-organizing locations because they are the one physical space where movement participants can gather free from observation by the powerful. The collection plate on Sunday mornings becomes the means for collecting scarce finances among the poor. Sermons call for social change in practical terms that are supported by religious teachings, symbols, and traditions. When some groups in society are blocked from using formal mechanisms to achieve social change, or when those in power resist the change that the public demands, religion is likely to enter the struggle as a force for change.

But more than anything else, movement activists see religion as a strategic source of resources apart from the fact of the activists holding religious worldviews or lacking access to the political process. Movements "get religion" because they believe that doing so can and will help them win the tangible goal of social change.

ANY LIMITS OF RELIGION'S INFLUENCE ON CHANGE?

In a word, yes. It's important to know about the conditions that turn religion into a force for social change or open up religious resources as tools for secular social movements. However, believers and activists alike sometimes assume that religion is without limits in its abilities to change the world once it is mobilized to do so. Nevertheless, the histories of many social movements include a subtext that hints at the structural challenges that limit the powers of religious groups and leaders once they become part of social movements.

Religious beliefs themselves can be an obstacle to mobilizing groups for change. Though many religious traditions have social teachings regarding justice, equality, and fairness with which most people would agree, these same groups also have beliefs with which many would disagree. For example, Roman Catholics have a strong tradition supporting peace and social justice, but Catholic teaching that opposes abortion is equally central. Since Roman Catholicism teaches that all the beliefs of the church are absolute and not open to compromise, this combination of teachings can pose a potential problem for movements that seek the support of Catholics. Activists who are working to alleviate poverty, hunger, or war may see Catholics as easy allies because of their peace and justice traditions. But—and here's the key—what happens to movement unity and cooperation when those same activists also want to fight for same-sex marriage rights, abortion rights, or population control? For non-Catholics, all of these issues are clear social justice issues, but Catholics may see them as violations of their Church's teachings on family, marriage, and the life of the unborn. This example illustrates how the process of building movement relationships and coalitions that are religiously diverse or that bring together religious and nonreligious activists can break down over religious beliefs, dividing a movement before it even begins to mobilize the unity it needs to achieve its goals.

Religion's impact on and within social movement activism is further limited by the characteristics of the religious activists themselves. Differences among these activists in class, race, gender, neighborhood, and even official roles within the religious group can disrupt the ability of religion to create a united front to achieve change. Social class divides between, say, different groups of religious activists, or movement leaders and the rank-and-file members, can create conflict with movements. Middle-class churchgoers often come from religious and class cultures that are more reserved and that emphasize respectability, while parishioners who are working class, poor , and members of minority cultures are often accustomed to being more emotionally involved in church services. For example, they may be accustomed to "call and response" services in which congregations shout out their agreement with the minister's or other leader's statements. It can be difficult for members of these two different types of churchgoers to join forces to verbally challenge the elite. In a 2008 study of congregation-based community organizing, Swarts recounts an event hosted by the Saint Louis-based Metropolitan Churches United. A state senator's aide at the event was booed by 2500 church members, most of whom were poor, for not being prepared to discuss a piece of legislation that was the focus of the meeting. The priest who was chairing the meeting allowed the booing to go on. In hindsight, the priest felt badly about allowing the aide to be booed. Swarts (2008, 10) notes, "The priest's understanding of Christian behavior influenced his etiquette of contention: he was reluctant to polarize the conflict and cast the aide as an opponent. But to his organizers, the moment of empowering the disempowered enacted a higher justice." Class differences in forms of contention and disagreement vary widely, leading to intramovement divides between middle-class leaders and rank-and-file participants or their working class counterparts.

Differences in race and ethnicity also can undermine religiously based activism. White congregations and religious leaders on the whole think about social justice and how to achieve it differently from the ways that African-American congregations do. White conservative Protestants, for example, tend to focus on individual rather than structural factors in their understanding of social inequalities. If a person is poor, they believe that the solution is to improve the person's skills and abilities and to limit any individual behavior or morality that may be blocking them from achieving economic well-being (Emerson and Smith 2000). In African-American congregations, individuals are more likely to take a structural or policy approach to addressing social problems, focusing less on the individual and more on the economic and political policies that maintain inequalities. African-American congregations are also more likely to be involved in local neighborhood issues, community issues, and civil rights activities. Racial differences can play out as religious leaders and their congregations decide what kinds of movements for change "make sense."

Gender differences also can cause controversy, especially with regard to the leadership of social movements. For example, women ministers from Black and mainline Protestant congregations and women rabbis from Jewish congregations may not be recognized as legitimate religious leaders by other clergy or by conservative Protestant or Roman Catholic activists (Olson 2000).

Religion is also limited in its ability to mobilize mass movements when religious and secular activists work in the same social movement organizations and must agree to strategies and tactics for action. Sociologists who study social movement activism observe that the unique cultures of religious groups do not always work well with the cultures of other social change groups, such as unions, political parties, or secular community organizing groups like the Association of Community Organizations for Reform, more commonly called ACORN (Rose 2000, Simmons 1994, Smith 1996b, Swarts 2008, Wood 2002). Religious groups tend to enter social movement activism and coalitions with less focus on top-down decision making and action within hierarchies and more focus on building inclusiveness, supporting equality, allowing democratic participation, and operating by consensus. Unions, political parties, and other similar groups with whom these religious groups may partner are hierarchical organizations whose leaders tend to determine the strategies and tactics and whose rank-and-file members are expected to carry them out. Religious groups may want to focus on process and on building consensus before taking action, whereas secular groups want to act quickly. Religious activists see their role as building and extending a moral force for change that requires strong relationships. Secular activists are more likely to focus on doing what is necessary to win. These fundamental differences in group process and culture can breed frustration and alienation between would-be allies.

When a social movement uses militant tactics, religious activists often are less willing to engage, even when the tactics are used in the heat of intense conflicts. In William Mirola's study of church–labor coalitions in the 1995 strike of 2500 newspaper employees against the *Detroit News* and *Detroit Free Press*, religious leaders and lay supporters were extremely put off by the use of derogatory and profane language on picket lines, in conflicts with replacement workers, and with the police (2003b, 455). One religious activist noted,

> We had a hard time in being involved in some of the union face-offs where the Teamsters would show up with sling shots and hide behind one another and zap the guards. We were trying to make a public impression that the guards were acting out, which they were, and expose it, but not this sleight of hand thing, where you are doing the same bullshit but you're just exposing the opposition. We'd like to see a consistent ethic across the board."

Conflicting definitions of what constitute appropriate or legitimate forms of protest between congregation-based and secular participants in a social movement can undermine their ability to work together. Perceptions that tactics have "gone too far" can bring a halt to religiously motivated activism (Cousineau 1998). Religious activists often withdraw from these conflicts under such circumstances. Secular activists may learn from the experience that religious resources are more trouble than they are worth to organize and may be reticent to build coalitions with congregations in future conflicts.

CONCLUDING THOUGHTS

In this chapter, we have explored the complex ways that religion works to maintain the structures of power and inequality in the social world. We also have explored how religion can challenge those structures and work to change them. Because religion so often emphasizes the importance of order, harmony, patience, meekness, and service, religious leaders and their teachings have consciously and unconsciously helped to support the powerful. The teachings tell members of society who are on the bottom rungs of the social ladder to obey their rulers and to be content with their current circumstances, awaiting a better world in the afterlife. In more extreme cases, clergy support the political and economic elite with their silence because they benefit from the patronage of those with power. Yet we have also seen that, under certain circumstances, religion generates movements for change. It mobilizes people to be willing to risk what little they have, including their lives, to fight for an end to exploitation, oppression, military rule, and a host of other social injustices.

Religion is never simply on one side or the other of social conflicts. More often than not, we see religion on both sides simultaneously. The same beliefs, rituals, traditions, and leaders are deployed in the interests of both those with power *and* their challengers. While sociology helps us to understand why religion can both motivate and hinder social changes in our world, it also helps us to consider the unintended consequences of religious activism for religious groups and for secular social movements that try to mobilize religious resources. It may seem as though religion should be an obvious source of resources for social movements, but instead the legacy of social movement successes and failures underscores the need for movements to be aware of the challenges that the involvement of religion can bring to a movement. Likewise, religious leaders are wary of being used by secular movements for the resources that they may provide. If you are a member of a religious group that has become involved in social activism, or if you are an activist for a secular cause considering whether or not to try to mobilize religious resources to achieve your goal, be aware that religion is always both a conserving and a transforming force in social life. But whether religion exerts more of a conserving or more or a transforming force will depend on both the religious and political context in which it operates.

SUGGESTED READING

Craig, Robert H. 1992. *Religion and Radical Politics: An Alternative Christian Tradition in the United States*. Philadelphia: Temple University Press.

Hart, Stephen. 1992. *What Does the Lord Require: How American Christians Think about Economic Justice*. New Brunswick: Rutgers University Press.

Lindsay, D. Michael. 2007. *Faith in the Halls of Power*. New York: Oxford University Press.

Olson, Laura. 2000. *Filled With Spirit and Power: Protestant Clergy in Politics*. New York: SUNY Press.

Pope, Liston. 1942. *Millhands and Preachers*. New Haven: Yale University Press.

Smith, Christian. 1996a. *Disruptive Religion: The Force of Faith in Social Movement Activism*. New Brunswick, NJ: Rutgers University Press.

Swarts, Heidi J. 2008. *Organizing Urban America: Secular and Faith-based Progressive Movements*. Minneapolis: University of Minnesota Press.

CHAPTER

8

Give Us Our Due

Religion and the State

1. Why do religious groups seek political influence?
2. Under what circumstances is close entanglement between church and state most problematic?
3. What is *freedom of religion*, and how does it play out in democratic states?
4. What is the boundary between *freedom of religion* and *freedom from religion*?
5. What are the advantages and disadvantages of 'separation of church and state' for religious groups?

In the United States and around the world, religion and politics are a volatile mixture. Presidential candidates in the United States are vetted on their religious beliefs, and it caused quite a stir in 2007 when Keith Ellison, U.S. Representative from Minnesota and also a Muslim, swore his oath of office on the Qu'ran rather than the traditional Bible. Even more uproar surrounded the 2008 presidential campaign, during which the religious beliefs of candidates and their pastors were explored in depth. Around the world, there are secular governments resisting the involvement of traditional religious authorities, religious sects fighting for control over government, and religious and secular groups sparring.

These struggles are nothing new. Back in the late 1970s, a Muslim cleric—the Ayatollah Khomeini—replaced the Shah of Iran as the country's political leader. In the process, Iran was unexpectedly transformed from a secular state in which religious leaders had no special influence or role in government—indeed, it was a state that resented and resisted the influence of religious leaders—to a theocratic state that was based on Islamic law. Meanwhile, during the same period in some Central American countries, including El Salvador and Nicaragua, Catholic priests aligned on either side of political revolutions. For example, while some in the Catholic Church in El Salvador supported the status quo of a repressive government that protected the interests of large landholders, others—including Archbishop Oscar Romero—aligned with an uprising against the government. Also in the late 1970s, there was a resurgence of involvement by fundamentalist and evangelical Christians in U.S. politics, a trend that first became apparent with the election of Jimmy Carter, an avowed Born-Again Christian. Carter's surprising ascent to the U.S. Presidency was due partly to a national mood of disillusionment after the Watergate scandal. But it also signaled the reemergence—decades after the humiliation of the Scopes trial—of fundamentalist and evangelical Christians in the public arena. These groups came out with a bang, organizing via groups including the Moral Majority, Focus on the Family, the Christian Broadcasting Network, and the Heritage Foundation. These late-20th-century entanglements between religion and politics simply continued a long and worldwide tradition of interaction between religion and politics, church and state.

Some observers are perplexed by religion's resilience and its ongoing efforts to influence government, law, and politics. How, in a secularizing world, does a state revert back to theocracy, as happened in Iran? Why have conservative religious groups reemerged as powerful political actors in the United States and elsewhere, including Turkey, India, and Japan? Why do strong ties between religion and government remain around the world? Throughout much of the world, it seems that governments and politicians, along with religious groups and their leaders, are not buying into secularization. They have conceded neither the inevitability nor the irreversibility of the modernizing trend of paring religious influence back from the state and its politics. Instead, religious groups have resolutely planted themselves in the middle of the public square.

RELIGION AND POLITICS IN THE UNITED STATES

Observers of the American political system can hardly miss the interaction between religion and political behavior. Political issues—including war, education, government funding, and abortion—are frequently presented in a context that integrally connects them to voters' religious beliefs. And opinions on these issues often form along religious lines, as do preferences for particular candidates and political party affiliations. For example, in the 2008 U.S. presidential election, voter preferences broke along clear religious lines. In particular, white evangelical Protestant voters favored the McCain–Palin ticket by more than two to one, while those with no religious affiliation preferred the Obama–Biden ticket by about the same proportion (Pew Forum on Religion and Public Life 2008b).

Religion also plays a role in political behavior at the state and local level. For example, in a number of battleground states in the 2004 presidential election, state ballot referendums that banned gay marriage resulted in large voter turnout, especially among conservative Christian voters. The question of whether to legalize gay marriage was explicitly framed by its opponents as being religious in character; opponents of gay marriage provided Biblical references and appeals to religious tradition to make their case. On occasion, religion has also affected the outcome of local and state school board elections. In some well-publicized cases, disputes about how to approach the teaching of evolution have been the impetus for religious candidates to run for local or state office—and for others to oppose them. A case in point: After the Dover, Pennsylvania, school board introduced intelligent design theory into science classrooms in public schools, each of the eight school board members who had supported the policy was voted out of office and replaced by candidates who opposed the policy (Goodstein 2005).

Research by sociologists and political scientists confirms our intuition that there is a connection between religion and political behavior in the United States: Religious tradition and worldview both influence political behavior, including voting in national, state, and local elections—and, for members of legislative bodies, participating in roll-call votes. For example, sociologists Clem Brooks and Jeff Manza (1997) analyzed presidential voting patterns from 1960 to 1992 and found that, after they controlled for a variety of other factors, religious tradition remained a significant predictor of political behaviors, including candidate choice, turnout, and party affiliation. In particular, conservative Christians were more likely to be registered and vote as Republican. Because their study spanned more than 30 years and nine presidential elections, Brooks and Manza were able to examine whether the affinity between particular religious traditions and political behaviors changed over time. Interestingly, they found relatively little change over time. The most significant shift was a modest, but steady, erosion of mainline Protestant support for the Republican Party. Among other groups, however, change was minimal: Conservative Christians remained mostly Republican in their affiliation and voting, and Catholics remained largely Democrat. The findings that link religious worldview with political activity have been echoed by a variety of other social science researchers (Kellstedt and Green 2003, Kellstedt et al. 1994).

Brooks and Manza also noted the magnitude of the political cleavage among religious groups. Because they have studied how a variety of voter characteristics affected voting patterns, they were able to compare the size of the religious effect with the size of factors such as social class and gender. They found that the effects of religious tradition on political behavior were *twice* as large as the effects of social class and *four times* as great as the effects of gender. Religion certainly does matter in U.S. presidential elections!

Religion also matters with respect to roll-call votes in legislative bodies. Chris Fastnow and colleagues (1999) found that religious tradition affects the voting of U.S. representatives in Congress both on the specific issue of abortion and on voting more generally. That is, representatives from more conservative religious groups (e.g., Mormons, Catholics, and Evangelicals) are more likely to vote pro-life on abortion measures and to vote more conservatively on a wide range of other issues. These relationships hold even when party affiliation in controlled.

The patterns are not, however, set in stone. For example, although Evangelicals remain consistently conservative, Mormons and Catholics have become more conservative in their voting patterns since the late 1950s. This finding reflects the new alignment in religion that sociologist Robert Wuthnow (1988) so astutely described in *The Restructuring of American Religion*. No longer is the nation divided by religious affiliations such as Protestant, Catholic, and Jewish. Instead, religions increasingly align along dimensions of liberalism or conservatism, which creates new bedfellows such as those found in Fastnow et al.'s research. Fastnow and her colleagues also found that the effects of religion on abortion-related votes have dissipated over time as the effects of party affiliation have grown. One way to understand this is that religious differences on abortion have been absorbed into political party ideology. That is, pro-life Democrats are hard to find, as are pro-choice Republicans. This fascinating trend illustrates why it is naïve to assume that religion and politics are ever truly separate from each other.

WHY POLITICS?

At its heart, politics is the struggle for control over government and its functions. So, what's the big deal? What does government *do*? A lot, as it turns out.

To begin with, governments set national policies and priorities. They decide—with more or less input from the people, depending on the political system—what overall goals the society will pursue, which societal issues will be addressed, and how to approach them. The state decides whether building up the military will take precedence over researching health or mitigating environmental problems, whether teachers or tests will determine how much kids have learned in school, and whether incentives or punishments will be used to change the frequency of certain behaviors. During President Franklin Delano Roosevelt's administration, for example, a priority was placed on creating a social safety net for many Americans and for building federal government infrastructure: That priority has had implications for American government and American society far past the end of Roosevelt's presidency.

In any political system, religious groups are likely to have preferences about national priorities and policies, preferences that they express through active engagement in the political process. The U.S. Civil Rights movement, driven in large part by religious groups, saw its priorities encoded in the 1964 Civil Rights law, and the religiously based U.S. pro-life movement has seen its priorities increasingly embedded in U.S. government policy, including international population control programs and medical practices in the United States.

National priorities are represented in part by tax policies and the redistribution of money via the tax system. As former Secretary of State Colin Powell noted during the 2008 presidential election, "Taxes are always a redistribution of money." (You can watch him say this on You Tube at http://www.youtube.com/watch?v=Nh_c5bbvmqc, about two minutes into the video.) When children are valued, governments may provide tax breaks to parents and fund elaborate educational systems. Likewise, a society that wants to encourage investment in private firms may lower or eliminate the tax rate on investment earnings. And, of course, the tax system in the United States allows people to deduct charitable contributions to churches and other religious organizations from federal (and often state) taxes, another example of using the tax system as a way of supporting certain endeavors.

Once taxes are collected, modern welfare states redistribute funds through government programs. Many groups benefit from such redistribution—farmers, college students, suburban drivers, nonprofit groups, families with children, senior citizens, military contractors, and other industries and corporations. In the United States, billions of dollars are at stake each year: It's no surprise that religious groups try to influence government to shape funding priorities and tax policy, and perhaps even to secure a share of these funds for themselves and their causes.

Faith-based organizations secured better access to U.S. government funding for their social service activities because of former President George W. Bush's faith-based Charitable Choice initiative. Though this initiative was limited in its implementation, the

Christian groups that benefited from it nonetheless viewed it as a victory. Interestingly, other religious groups were more reserved in their opinion of it. Why? We find a clue in a 2006 investigation by the *Boston Globe*: Reporters found that 98.6% of this program's funds were distributed to Christian groups (Kranish 2006). The program did not represent the diversity of religion in the United States! Upon taking office in 2009, President Obama retained this policy initiative, though he reorganized it into the White House Office of Faith-based and Neighborhood Partnerships and placed it within his Domestic Policy Council. It remains to be seen how Obama's version of faith-based initiatives will be implemented and whether these partnerships will include non-Christian religious groups.

Governments also decide who is in or out, in terms of citizenship or full membership in a society, and who will receive which benefits of membership. In the United States, the right to vote was not universally guaranteed to African Americans until the passage of the 15th Amendment in 1870 or to women until the passage of the 19th Amendment in 1920. Even then, local governments devised strategies, including literacy tests and poll taxes, to limit the voting rights of Blacks. Religion has also been used as a criterion for citizenship: For example, as nation–states formed in Europe in the 1800s, Jews often had to renounce their religious beliefs in favor of Christianity in order to become full citizens of these newly emerging states (Sacks 1999). And in a recent case in France, the State Council denied citizenship to a Moroccan woman who had lived in France for eight years, who spoke French, and whose three children were French citizens. They ruled that she was insufficiently integrated into French life. Her devout and orthodox practice of Muslim faith was singled out and deemed "incompatible with the essential values of the French community, notably on the principle of equality of the sexes." A government attorney detailed her offense: "According to her own statements, Faiza M. leads a virtually reclusive life, cut off from French society . . . She has no idea about secularism or the right to vote. She lives in total submission to the men of her family" (Field 2008). And, yes, she wore a burqa to her interviews with French immigration officials.

Governments also make rules and laws for their citizens. For centuries, governments have had basic laws protecting human life and private property. With the rise of modern welfare states, however, governments increasingly regulate everyday behavior. We face state-created restrictions on what we eat and drink, how we may advertise goods or services, what safety equipment we must use, what teachers can say to kids in school about topics ranging from sex education to evolution, and what doctors can say to women about their options if they are pregnant. Zoning laws that are enacted by local governments regulate what you can do with and on your property. Child-protection laws restrict how you can treat your children: whether you can spank them, what constitutes an appropriate diet for them, and whether you can remove them from public schools. Drug laws outlaw the sale of certain substances and regulate the sale of many more.

To many of us, this seems like a good thing. Government is looking out for us and keeping our best interests at heart. Certainly, each of these restrictions has its advocates! But sometimes there is a clash between what government allows and what religious groups require. For example, governments may outlaw practices that are integral to the ritual life of certain religious groups. In 1987, the City of Hialeah, Florida, passed an ordinance that outlawed animal sacrifice. This prevented a religious group called Santeríans from engaging in a ritual practice that was important to them. This ordinance was most likely intended to protect the sensibilities of non-Santeríans, as it did not outlaw commercial animal slaughter, hunting, or other forms of killing animals. It singled out animal sacrifice. In 1993, the U.S. Supreme Court ruled the ordinance unconstitutional (United States Supreme Court 1993). Along the same lines, smoking and burning candles and incense are forbidden in college dormitories by many local fire codes. This rule creates problems for Native American students whose religious tradition requires smudging or the burning of sage, cedar, or sweetgrass as part of prayer or as a blessing (Stokes 2001). More recently, the Macon–Bibb (Georgia) County Commission banned human burials without a "leak-proof casket or vault." Who might want to be buried *au naturel*? Environmentalists come to mind. So, too, do Muslims: Islamic burial traditions do not include caskets (Shishkin 2009). And the well-publicized practice of polygamy among Fundamentalist Latter-day Saints brought the laws of the state into direct conflict with a religion in which multiple marriage and large families were integral to the original theology of the religion and expected by the community. These are but a few examples of how government regulations that are designed to protect people can also restrict the practice of religion. It is worth noting that in each of these examples the conflict pits minority religions against the state. Members of majority religions, on the other hand, are unlikely to find themselves in the midst of such conflicts. Later in this chapter we will explore why that is so.

Given the role of government in setting and pursuing national priorities, redistributing wealth, defining citizenship and its benefits, and regulating our behavior, it is not surprising that religious groups seek a voice in politics. What varies across societies is how the relationship between religion and government plays out.

"PRINCES, GOVERNORS, AND OPPRESSORS": VARIETIES OF RELATIONS BETWEEN RELIGION AND GOVERNMENT

> *Know that you can have three sorts of relations with princes, governors, and oppressors. The first and worst is that you visit them, the second and better is that they visit you, and the third and surest that you stay far from them, so that neither you see them nor they see you.*

—ABU HAMID MUHAMMAD AL-GHAZZALI (B. 1058 A.D.)

Muslim theologian and scholar Abu Hamid Muhammad al-Ghazzali lays out a broad schema for how religion and politics may relate to each other. Many centuries later, his typology is still relevant! Before we explore why, let's dissect his quote.

Al-Ghazzali's use of the term "visit" is best understood as a signal of who is the supplicant or dependent: The one doing the "visiting" is the weaker party and the one who receives the visit is stronger. In addition, al-Ghazzali writes from the perspective of the religious leader: When he says "us," he means religious individuals, and when he says "them," he means politicians (i.e., "princes, governors, and oppressors").

In al-Ghazzali's view, one possibility is that *politics will dominate religion,* using religious institutions to pursue political ends: "You [the religious individual] visit them [political leaders]." Another possibility is that *religion will dominate politics,* with political rule emanating from a deity mediated by religious leaders: "They [political leaders] visit you [the religious individual]." Lastly, there may be a *separation between religion and politics*: "Neither you see them nor they see you." We will consider each of these cases in turn.

Religion as a Tool of the State: "You Visit Them"

On occasion, rulers have coopted religion to strengthen their position of power. They have used religion "for [their] own purposes, most frequently to legitimate political rule and to sanctify economic oppression and the given system of stratification" (Casanova 1994, 49). This function of religion was Marx's focus: "the opium of the masses" and the justifier of inequality and suffering that stifled rebellion by the oppressed classes.

A classic example of this scenario is Henry VIII's rebellion against the Pope in the 16th century. Denied an annulment of his marriage by the Pope, Henry was thwarted in his efforts to wed a new wife who would presumably produce a male heir. He responded by breaking from the Roman Catholic Church, rejecting the Pope's authority over him and his nation, and establishing his own church, the Church of England. This act was about more than just whether and whom the king of England could marry. It also consolidated both political and religious power in the monarchy and created a state religion that legitimated the monarch's rule and actions.

We find more contemporary examples of politics coopting religion for its own purposes in Central America in the 20th century. Dana Sawchuk (1997) observed that in Nicaragua, up until the 1970s, "the institutional [Catholic] church had given its uncritical support to the country's dictatorial elites." In the same era, former Catholic priest Phillip Berryman (1984) observed that the repressive regime in El Salvador was supported by that country's central Church structure even though local priests had joined the reform movement. When Oscar Romero was selected as Archbishop of El Salvador in 1977, government officials considered him to be a "safe" choice. "Conservative, timid, spiritual and in poor health," he was expected to toe the line for the government, supporting large land owners and resisting economic and political reforms. In this respect, however, Oscar Romero was a disappointment to the government of El Salvador. He became that nation's highest Church official to work for reforms and, when he was assassinated in a church by a government soldier, to die for that movement. Romero's defection came as a surprise to the government, which expected the Catholic Church to support it and continue to legitimate economic inequality and political repression. That is the nature of Al-Ghazzali's notion of "you visit them": Religious leaders are expected to kow-tow to politicians.

Al-Ghazzali suggests that this is the least desirable of the possible relations between religion and politics. From the perspective of rulers, of course, benefits accrue when religious leaders always agree with you! In particular, it typically solidifies the legitimacy and power of rulers. But, as American legal scholar Stephen Carter has argued, such consolidation is often not good for society as whole. In particular, it impedes democracy. In his book *The Culture of Disbelief*, Carter argues that religion best serves democratic societies when it operates as an independent and collective source of conscience that can stand up against the state:

> Religions are communities of corporate worship, or . . . groups of believers struggling to come to a common understanding of the world . . . the group, moreover, will often be engaged in . . . acts of resistance . . . interposing the group judgment against the judgment of the larger society . . . When the state tries to block that process of discernment in a faith community, it is acting tyrannically by removing potential sources of authority and meaning different from itself. (1993, 142)

While politicians undoubtedly prefer the support of religion, independent religions can dissent from the government. They can say, "This is wrong and it must change." A number of religious groups dissented, for example, from the institution of slavery in the United States and from the racial segregation and discrimination that predominated in the century following the end of the Civil War. Today, some religious groups dissent from the use of the death penalty by the criminal justice system, and some dissent from the practice of abortion. These groups are offering a religiously informed moral vision that diverges from the official policy of government. Similarly—although they were slow to come to nations like El Salvador—Central-American political reforms were facilitated by the growing independence of the Catholic Church from repressive regimes. Religious claims do not always prevail, but they can be heard and considered. They can shape the moral direction of a nation. In so doing, independent religion stands a chance at reining in some of the most destructive tendencies of powerful governments.

Theocracy: "They Visit You"

During the 2008 U.S. presidential election, Republican candidate Mike Huckabee gave a speech in Michigan in which he argued that "it's a lot easier to change the Constitution than it would be to change the word of the living God, and that's what we need to do . . . amend the Constitution so it's in God's standards rather than try to change God's standards" (Montanaro 2008). These were provocative words from the Southern Baptist minister and former governor of Arkansas. Huckabee's comment drew praise from conservative Christians, who understand religious law to be primary, absolute, and unchanging. Secularists and others, however, were dismayed at Huckabee's implication that secular law should conform to religious law.

Systems dominated by explicitly religious law and governed by religious elites are often referred to as theocracies. In theocracies, sacred deities rule by acting through human intermediaries (e.g., clerics, priests, and the like). The Vatican, which is the political seat of the Roman Catholic Church and an independent state, is a theocracy under the religious and political leadership of the Pope.

Historically, theocracies are not unknown in the United States. As sociologist Rick Phillips (1999) writes, as late as the mid-1800s Mormons sought to establish a theocracy in the Utah territory by choosing almost exclusively from among church leaders for political positions and by vesting a combination of "political, judicial and ecclesiastical authority" in Brigham Young and other church officials. As a result, church officials made religious, judicial, and political decisions, including vital rulings on water rights, and set penalties, including liens on property. Phillips called the Mormon Church the "de facto state religion" of the Utah territory.

Iran is an important example of a modern theocracy. Religious rule dates back centuries in Iran, but during the 20th century it was gradually dismantled, culminating in the secular regime of the Shah of Iran, Muhammed Reza Pahlavi. The Shah's "secularization project" had stripped religion from a wide range of social institutions: Land ownership by religious institutions was limited; family law was modernized, especially with respect to the rights of women; the government took over the publishing of religious textbooks from clerics; clerics lost control over courts and schools; and constitutional provisions that had allowed clerics to veto governmental rules or regulations they deemed "un-Islamic" were ignored (Kazemipur and Rezaei 2003). Secularization had not been embraced by all religious leaders, however, and during the 1979 Islamic Revolution, Muslim clerics regained control of the government and turned back many of the earlier changes. According to Kazemipur and Rezaei,

> [T]he new regime launched a heavy "Islamization" project, making drastic changes in political, legal, cultural, and, less dramatically, economic domains, in order to make them reflect the so-called Islamic principles. Shortly after, it began an ambitious "cultural revolution," aiming to transform the higher education system. The Islamization project eventually reached its climax by touching upon subtle issues such as the designation of seats in public places (public transit system, classrooms, offices, etc.), a restrictive dress code as an embodiment of the Islamic rules governing modest dressing, and the banning of a wide range of music styles as corrupt and "westoxicated." (2003, 348)

So how can we tell the difference between religion used for political purposes ("they visit us") and political structures that are based on religious belief ("we visit them")? In *The Culture of Disbelief,* Carter (1993) helps explain the distinction by describing the ways in which religion and politics typically intermingle:

> Religions are moral forces in the lives of their adherents, which means, inevitably, that they are moral forces in the political world. And, as with all institutions, a degree of cross-pollination between religion and politics is inevitable. But when secular political considerations become prior to, rather than subsequent to, religious considerations, the result is not cross-pollination but pollution.

At issue is the *source* of our reasoning and the *use* to which we put religion. In the case of theocracy, religion provides the moral foundation for government and government decisions are based on religious considerations. As Carter notes, religion comes first and politics follows. The alternative is less appealing to Carter and, it appears, to Al-Ghazzali. When religious belief is shaped to support government actions or policy then religion is being used in strategic and instrumental ways to support political rule. In this case, religion is second to politics.

By this standard, Iran offers an example of "they visit us": Only the most cynical person would argue that religion in Iran is simply being used in strategic and self-serving ways to maintain the political and economic position of political rulers. Instead, Islamic religious belief provides the moral basis for political rule. In theocracy, sincere religious belief drives political decision making, be it voting or policy making. You might disagree with the religious basis for the politician's actions: It may not reflect *your* own beliefs. Or you might not want religion to be used in political decision making at all. But the religious belief that is guiding decisions appears to be sincere.

When religion is used for political purposes, however, the sincerity of the religious belief is most certainly in question. As Carter notes, when religion conveniently supports all of an individual's political positions, one might reasonably wonder whether the religion or the political positions came first. In the case of theocracy, the religious belief comes first. When political systems coopt religion for their own purposes, the political positions come first. Both systems are, however, inherently conservative in that the entanglement of religion and the state tends to inhibit rather than encourage social change.

As we mentioned at the beginning of the chapter, the swing *back* to religious rule in Iran came as a surprise to many who viewed secularization as an irreversible historical process and believed that the freedom of government from the influence of religion was inevitable social progress. But in her book *The Battle for God,* Karen Armstrong argues that those who were surprised were perhaps not paying enough attention:

> For decades, the more conservative religious people who felt, for different reasons, slighted, oppressed, and even persecuted by their secular governments, had been seething with resentment . . . In their view, history had taken a fatal turn; everything was awry. They now lived in societies which had either marginalized or excluded God, and they were ready to re-sacralize the world. (2000, 279)

The interest in resacralization is not limited to Iran. We also saw this movement in the United States when fundamentalist Christians retreated from the public sphere after the Scopes trial in 1925. The trial, which pitted creationists against evolutionists, was decided in favor of religion, but the battle itself was humiliating for fundamentalist Christians, who were disdained and mocked as backward, premodern, and irrational. Although fundamentalists retreated, they did not go away: Instead, as we mentioned earlier, they reemerged in the public square with significant political clout in the mid-1970s. The political power of fundamentalists coalesced into a powerful political base for George W. Bush during his two terms in office and was energized again by John McCain's selection of Sarah Palin, governor of Alaska and a member of a Pentecostal Christian church, as his 2008 Vice Presidential pick. In the United States we have not gone to the extent of creating a theocracy, but we do see backlashes against secularization from time to time.

The citizens of many Western countries are deeply uncomfortable with the notion of theocracy, worrying about what would happen if their government shifted towards religious rule. We see this in the concerns raised about presidential candidate Mike Huckabee's comments on man's law and God's law, and in the suspicions about what Sarah Palin's religious beliefs suggest about her worldview and politics. Many fear that religious involvement in political affairs would lead ultimately to the imposition of someone else's religious belief on them and that their individual rights, including freedom of religion, speech, or assembly, would be limited. Westerners are also concerned about working with other nations that are ruled by theocrats, worrying that religious differences will interfere with peaceful or productive relations or that overtly religious states will act in unpredictable or seemingly irrational ways.

Recent events in Western Europe suggest that these concerns are not unfounded. In 2008, *The Wall Street Journal* reported that Amsterdam police had arrested a Dutch cartoonist whose pseudonym is Gregorious Neckschot. His offense was to publish distasteful political cartoons that mocked Muslims and elements of Muslim faith (Higgins, 2008). Prior to the arrest, similarly offensive political cartoons had been published in Denmark and had provoked protests and violence. Are such cartoons free speech or criminally punishable offenses? Politicians, journalists, religious groups, and secularists are trying to sort out this issue. The outcome is likely to make at least one group very unhappy. This conflict is an unfortunate, but predictable, consequence of diversity in religious and political beliefs.

Under what circumstances does religious rule raise the greatest concerns? Consider a society in which religious belief and practice is identical among the whole population.

In this place, people believe in the same gods, hold the same views about morality, understand one another's roles in society, and share consistent patterns of behavior. In that kind of society, if religion reinforced government and if government drew its roadmap from religion, people might not have any significant concerns: Few persons, if any, would be left out. Historically, this sort of society is not all that unusual. Anthropologists have noted that theocracy—the integration of religion and politics under the rule of a "sacrosanct group, ultimately 'priest-kings'" (Webster 1976)—was a typical mode of governance, especially in early complex societies. And in this sort of situation, theocracy does not raise the kinds of worries about human or civil rights that pervade religiously diverse Western societies today, in which a multitude of beliefs, moralities, and patterns of behavior coexist.

Large-scale social changes including urbanization, industrialization, wide-scale immigration, and improved communications and transportation networks have produced societies with complex and diverse religious and ethnic cultures. Theocracy as a form of rule encounters distinct problems in societies that have high levels of religious, ethnic, or cultural diversity. That is, theocracy may work well for those who share the beliefs and behavioral expectations of religious rulers. But for people whose backgrounds, experiences, or beliefs differ from those of the rulers, theocracies may enforce rigid doctrinal and behavioral expectations. Combining the power and legitimacy of the state with that of the dominant religion can create an inexorable and oppressive society. And depending on the size and influence of the nonbelieving group or groups, imposing theocracy on a religiously diverse society may also create social instability as minority groups assert their right to freedom from the constraints of someone else's religion. Carter also notes this danger and its consequences for the minority religion and the larger society:

> A more practical danger also lurks, one that the legal scholar Frederick Mark Gedicks has noted: 'Without exemption, some religious groups will likely be crushed by the weight of majoritarian law and culture. Such groups pose no threat to order. However, majoritarian dominance could radicalize some believers into destabilizing, antisocial activity, including violence.' Of course, the dominant culture can do what it has always done in the face of threats to order, especially threats from people the nation itself has oppressed, such as Native Americans and slaves: It can declare the marginalized group and violent dissenters to be criminals, and thus rid itself of them, their movements and the religions all at once. (1993, 129)

Transforming religious dissent into criminality is, however, a hallmark of repressive political regimes, albeit of both the theocratic and the secular variety.

The broad social forces that lead to cultural, religious, and ethnic diversity affect almost all societies, including ones like Iran that attempt to reimpose theocracy after decades of secular rule. As a result, efforts by Muslim clerics in Iran to control government and implement religious rule have been complicated by the significant amount of modernization that had already occurred in that nation, and many skeptics argue that it is not possible to put that genie back in the bottle, not at least without significant political and religious repression.

It may be somewhat self-serving for al-Ghazzali to prefer the primacy of religious over political rule. After all, he writes as a religious, and not a political, personage. But his ultimate preference—that politics and religion keep out of each other's way—is illuminating and shows great foresight for someone who wrote many centuries ago. For much of the last century, this separation of religion from politics—the notion of "separation of church and state" and the principles of "freedom of religion" as well "freedom from religion"—has characterized the American political landscape, the recent resurgence of political engagement by conservative Christians notwithstanding. But what does separation of church and state look like in the real world?

SEPARATE SPHERES: IMPLICATIONS OF SEPARATION OF CHURCH AND STATE

When all or the vast majority of people in a society share the same religious beliefs, religion may be fairly easily incorporated into governmental structures, laws, and everyday life. The situation is quite different, however, in societies that have high levels of religious diversity, in which a variety of groups espouse a range of beliefs, many of which do not overlap. In religiously pluralistic societies like the United States, diverse groups jockey with each other for influence, seeking to have their particular religious beliefs and practices more broadly inform laws and government policy. As Robert Wuthnow reports in his 2005 book *America and the Challenges of Religious Diversity*, America is a religiously diverse society. Most Americans report that they are Christians, but a sizeable minority belong to other religions: Judaism, Hinduism, Buddhism, Islam, and varieties of other non-Christian religions. In addition, Americans have a variety of views of other religions. Many are "Christian exclusivists" who believe that there is one right way, theirs. Other Christians are what Wuthnow describes as "Christian inclusivists" who espouse Christianity but concede that other religions also have validity. Yet other Americans are "spiritual seekers" who piece together their faith from a variety of religious and spiritual traditions. Spiritual seekers not only accede to the validity of other religions but find much of personal value in them. Still others espouse any of a variety of non-Christian faiths. Although religious fervor is lower in European countries than in the United States, immigration has ensured that there are similarly high levels of religious diversity in much of Europe, not only among new arrivals but also among second-generation and later non-Christian immigrants.

In democratic societies, religious diversity is often understood as a result of "religious freedom." But, as we will discuss, even "religious freedom" is an amorphous term. Does it mean freedom *of* religion, that is, the freedom to practice your religion without constraint? Or does it mean freedom *from* religion, freedom from being impinged upon by others' religions or by any religion at all? This distinction matters. Political tensions arise among diverse religious groups. But there are also significant tensions between religious and secular persons and groups.

The U.S. Interpretation of Religious Freedom

Americans' notion of freedom of religion comes from the First Amendment to the U.S. Constitution. The first clause reads, "Congress shall make no law respecting an establishment of religion, or prohibiting the free exercise thereof." As this text indicates, there are two parts to our notion of religious freedom, at least in theory. First, the state cannot establish a religion—not for some of us, and not for all us. The state must stay out of the religion business. Second, government cannot interfere with an individual's belief or religious practice. It cannot tell us what to believe or not believe or how to practice our religion.

Freedom of religion is an individual right—persons are free to believe and practice as they see fit with respect to religion. But, as we argued in Chapter 1, religion itself is a collective activity that exerts power among groups of people. As a result, freedom of religion is best understood as a right that extends beyond just individual freedoms. It also encompasses the freedom or autonomy of religion as an institutional sector. Thus, we begin our discussion with the institutional autonomy of religion.

The Disestablishment Clause and the Institutional Autonomy of Religion

The first element of the separation of church and state in the U.S. Constitution is often referred to as the antiestablishment clause. It refers to the independence of religion as an institutional sector. The framers of the U.S. Constitution were strongly opposed to an official or state religion in the form of a theocracy or even a state-sponsored church. In particular, they did not want the government to grant privileged status to any one of the varieties of Protestantism—Anglicanism, Congregationalism, or Presbyterianism—that dominated early colonial society. As a result, from its founding the United States has not had an "official" church or denomination.

Nonetheless, a generalized form of Protestantism dominated early American society. In *Public Religions in the Modern World* (1994), political sociologist José Casanova writes that the disestablishment of religion in the United States did not happen all at once. Nor did it happen just by constitutional edict. The First Amendment laid the groundwork for freedom of religion, but in practice that freedom evolved in three distinct historical phases through social and cultural shifts.

The first phase is obvious: the formal disestablishment of religion as embodied in the U.S. Constitution. The ban on state-sponsored religion did not, however, prevent a homogenized Protestantism from being the culturally dominant religious tradition in the country although future developments would slowly chip away at its hold on American culture and society.

The second phase was more cultural and social in nature. It began prior to the Civil War and had two distinct components: (1) the rise of secular or nonreligious common schools, colleges, and universities whose primary purpose was not the moral education of citizens but the training of productive workers for an emerging industrial economy, and (2) the fracturing of an already fragile union of diverse Protestant traditions, especially along northern and southern lines in response to the moral crisis of slavery. In practice, these two trends—the rise in the number of secular schools and the dissolution of the earlier unity in American Protestantism—served to weaken the cultural grip of Protestantism on American society as a whole.

The final blow, or third wave of disestablishment of Protestantism in the United States, occurred in the early to mid-20th century. During this time, what Casanova refers to as "Protestantism as the American way of life" receded: "The disestablishment of the Protestant ethic brought about the secularization of public morality and the emergence of a pluralistic system of norms and forms of life" (1994, 145). This era saw the rise of a sort of cultural relativism in which cultural, ethnic, and religious groups brought diverse notions of morality into the public sphere, eroding the early monopoly of a generalized Protestantism.

The end result was that although American culture has been dominated by general precepts of Protestantism, today there is a wide range of religious groups in the United

States, each functioning independently of the state. While any one religious tradition might be strengthened if it received sponsorship from the state, some scholars have persuasively argued that religion as a whole—the sector that contains a wide diversity of religious traditions and organizations—has benefited from freedom from state influence and sponsorship. Indeed, sociologists Roger Finke and Rodney Stark (2005), among others, have demonstrated that the independence of religion as an institution in the United States—its legal, social, and cultural disestablishment—has produced a vibrant and diverse marketplace of religions. The U.S. has unusually high levels of religious fervor and participation, levels that are much higher than societies with state-established and supported churches.

Despite the religious fervor that characterizes America's past and present, religion's disestablishment from the state has led to its segregation into a distinct and separate sphere of social life. This trend has had costs for religious groups and their adherents. Religious scholar Peter Beyer (2003) notes that religion's independence as an institution also puts religion in direct competition with other institutions, and in these cases religion may not prevail. In some sectors, there are ways to accommodate religious belief that dissents from the state. For example, the military has a process for adjudicating claims for conscientious objector status when such claims are based on religious opposition to war. But competition persists in other sectors.

The role of religion has been vigorously contested in schools, institutions viewed by many to have responsibility for the moral as well as the intellectual development of children. Prayer and study that leads to religious development is not permitted in public schools in the United States, and in Canada the influence of religion in the schools has waned in recent years. Religion's exclusion from public schools is the price that it pays for independence from the state.

In a similar vein, modern medicine—which may call for procedures that some religious groups find objectionable—often prevails over religious belief in court battles over the medical care of children. Christian Scientists' beliefs prompt them to reject Western medical care, and Jehovah's Witnesses may wish to decline blood transfusions, but they may not legally be allowed to refuse this care for their sick children. And when they decline medical interventions for themselves, adults are often viewed as irrational. As social institutions, medicine and science tend to dominate religion. In a society in which religion was integrated into the governance structure, such competition would be moot: Religion would not have an independent voice that competes with or dissents from other voices.

Despite these costs of disestablishment for religion, however, religion also benefits from its institutional independence. We noted earlier that systems in which religion and politics are closely intertwined tend also to be fairly slow to change. Such societies lack independent religious voices, ones that are positioned to make strong cases for social change. They also lack independent religious institutions that are equipped to mobilize for change. The value of keeping religion independent from the state is clear when we consider the experience of Poland under Soviet-imposed communism. As Casanova (1994) chronicles, Catholicism in Poland had a strong presence in Poland long before communist rule. Despite attempts by communist rulers to weaken the Church and impose atheism, Catholicism remained a strong, unifying national force in Poland. It constituted a powerful independent source of dissent from communist rule and played a major role in the eventual decline of the communist regime in Poland in the late 20th century. It is not clear that any other actor or institution in Poland could have been nearly as effective in its dissent if Catholicism had not been present. It is not a coincidence that Poland was the first of the Eastern Bloc countries to effectively rebel against communist rule.

Free Exercise and the Privilege of the Majority's Religion

The U.S. Constitution also guarantees an individual's right to free exercise of religion—the right to believe the tenets of your religion and to practice your religion without interference from the state. This right is often what people envision when they hear "freedom of religion": that government cannot dictate what you think. Nor can it interfere with your religious actions, including rituals and practices. If you believe that God is a grandfatherly figure who resides in the skies above, that is your right. If you believe that spirits inhabit inanimate objects like trees and rocks, well, that, too, is your right. If you believe that your good acts in this life will reflect well on you in the next, live and let live! Ideally, actions undertaken for religious reasons are also protected, including practices such as the Jewish Seder, Christian baptism, Muslim burqa, polygamy on the part of the Fundamentalist Latter-day Saints, and animal sacrifice by Santeríans and the Hmong from Laos.

Does this mean that religious beliefs and practices are always accepted and respected in the United States? Of course not. To begin with, religious beliefs and practices, especially those, which are out of the mainstream, are vulnerable to informal censure from others in the broader community. The First Amendment speaks to the state's position on religion, not your neighbor's personal response to religion. More important, however, the state itself struggles to accept religious beliefs and practices that are outside the mainstream. Indeed, sociologist Lori Beaman (2003) and legal scholar Stephen Carter (1993) have both noted that the way a person experiences freedom of religion often depends on what that religion is and, especially, whether it is the majority religion.

There is a distinct advantage to being a member of the majority religion because often that religion, its beliefs, and its practices are taken for granted as "normal" by the law and by government policies. Meanwhile, minority religions—those whose adherents do not make up the majority in a given society—are more likely to find that existing legal, political, and social structures are not designed to accommodate their beliefs and practices. As it turns out, in the United States the constitutional protection of the full range of religious beliefs and practices does not always result in true freedom of religion, particularly in the case of minority religions. Instead, tenets of the majority's religion, along with impediments to minority religions, sometimes creep into laws and government policy.

Sometimes this happens in obvious ways, as when animal sacrifice—a religious ritual associated with the minority religion of Santeria—was banned by the city of Hialeah, Florida. Or when polygamy, a practice in the early Mormon church, was explicitly outlawed by the state. In these cases, no effort was made to hide the animus (if you'll excuse the expression) towards the minority religion and its practices. The city ordinance against animal sacrifice was squarely aimed at stopping the religious practices of the Santeríans, and it was ruled unconstitutional by the U.S. Supreme Court for just that reason. Polygamy remains illegal, and much disdained, in the United States.

But often the granting of privileged status to the majority religion and its practices—and the concurrent placing of minority religions at a disadvantage—is more subtle and may go unnoticed except by members of the minority religion (and alert observers). Take, for example, the case of peyote. Peyote is a hallucinogenic drug that is illegal in the

United States. It has been used for generations in Native American religious rituals. In 1993 the U.S. Supreme Court ruled that state employees who were fired for using peyote in religious ceremonies were fired for "cause" and were thus ineligible for unemployment compensation. (See Pavlik 1992 for a discussion of the meaning of freedom of religion in this case.) The state employees had requested exemption from the prohibition on the use of peyote because they were using it as part of a Native American religious ritual. Their state government denied their request and in so doing failed to accommodate their religious beliefs and practices. The U.S. Supreme Court sided with the state government, ruling that the *individual* request of particular religious believers to use this illegal substance for religious purposes did not outweigh the overall public good of fighting what the government termed the "war on drugs." In this case, the free exercise of religion for this group lost to what was deemed a more important societal priority.

Of the many issues in play here, two concepts are particularly important for our discussion of the free exercise of religion. First, the employees who asked for an exemption were treated as individuals asking for an exception to a law rather than as members of a religious group for whom the law presents an undue burden. As Stephen Carter (1993) has noted, they were treated as if their religious practice was a choice and as if they could simply go out and find a legal substance to substitute for peyote to continue the practice of their religion. Carter heartily disagrees with the notion that religion and its practices are a choice: He argues that religious believers most commonly experience their religion as an imperative from a higher power that they deviate from at great risk. And the state, he argues, should be very cautious about limiting the exercise of religion in a society that holds free exercise as an ideal.

Second, and importantly, these employees were treated differently than members of the majority religion were treated in an analogous situation that occurred more than 50 years earlier. We refer to Prohibition, a 15-year period in U.S. history during which the 18th Amendment to the U.S. Constitution barred the manufacture, export, and import of alcohol. However, Congress exempted *religious* uses of alcohol, allowing Christians to continue to use wine in their religious rituals. The religion of the majority, Christian religion, was privileged and exempted from the constitutional ban on alcohol on the grounds that the ban would be too disruptive to religious practice, while in a separate and later case indigenous religion was subordinated to what was framed as the larger good. The ban on peyote was, apparently, not too disruptive, at least not to followers of the majority religion!

Since then, federal law has changed to create an exemption for peyote, but the case is a good example of how the law is often constructed to privilege (keep legal) the practices of the dominant religion while outlawing the practices of minority religions, all in the name of the "public good." The result is interference by the state in religion, the sort of interference that Stephen Carter sees as problematic for the ideal of freedom of religion.

SEPARATION OF CHURCH AND STATE: FREEDOM *FROM* RELIGION?

Although the U.S. Constitution never uses the phrase "separation of church and state," we derive that concept from the First Amendment. To some people, separation of church and state refers to a wall that protects government and politics from religious influence. They believe that the public sphere, including politics, should be free *from* religion. Some of them worry that a politician with a clear and specific religious commitment—be it a faith tradition or a policy position based on religion—might be elected to public office and proceed to impose that belief on the rest of us either through law or government policy. Many feminists, for example, worry about conservative Christians securing elected office because they are concerned that women's rights might be abridged by those whose theology is more patriarchal. They worry that abortion rights, antidiscrimination laws, and social services to support women in the workplace might erode if individuals who follow this particular religious tradition have power.

Legal scholar Stephen Carter offers a different interpretation, however. He argues that religious persons have as much right as anyone to express political opinions and advocate for particular political positions. Voters can decide for themselves whether or not to support religious candidates and the positions they espouse on the merits of the positions. In Carter's view, the separation of church and state was not intended to protect government and politics from religious influence so much as to protect religion from interference from the state and to preserve religion's independence as a source of belief and conscience for its followers. For example, Carter argues that the government should not step in and tell the Catholic Church that it must allow women to become priests. The restrictions on gender for pastoral leadership in the Catholic Church are rooted in its theology, and the government can neither rewrite that theology nor insist that the Catholic Church disregard it. It is important to note that Carter does not agree with the Catholic Church's teachings here. But he believes that the autonomy of religious groups to hold and practice their beliefs is more important than the details of individual cases. Thus Carter advocates for a one-way wall that keeps the state out of religious belief and practice but still allows religious belief and practice—as sources of individual and group conscience—to find their way into the political sphere.

There is, however, no consensus on the role that religion should play in politics, especially in diverse societies. The question becomes even more critical when we consider two concurrent trends. First, as we have argued throughout this text, around the world as well as in the United States, religion is not going away quietly. Rather, religion remains a strong basis for individual and group identity and a basis for social action. Second, and equally important, both the U.S. and other governments around the world are constantly expanding the scope of their activities. As sociologist Michael Hechter (2004) argues, when the government becomes a welfare state—taking responsibility for more and more of the day-to-day concerns of its citizens—government and politics become the terrain on which cultural differences, including religious differences, are played out. Not wanting to be left behind in law or government policy, especially now that such policy reaches into all corners of our lives, religious groups enter into the fray of politics.

Islamic scholar al-Ghazzali's ideal relationship between church and state is one in which "neither you see them nor they see you." His argument for separate spheres for religion and politics is reasonable, especially considering the problems that are inherent in theocracies or states that appropriate the blind support of religion. But now we live in a different context. Religion and politics, and church and state, frequently bump up against each other. It is this modern social context—the continuing importance of religion, the rising diversity of religion within individual societies, and the rise of a powerful welfare state—that make this interaction so complicated and consequential.

SUGGESTED READING

Beaman, Lori. 2003. "The Myth of Pluralism, Diversity and Vigor: The Constitutional Privileging of Protestantism in the United States and Canada." *Journal for the Scientific Study of Religion* 42 (3): 311–325.

Carter, Stephen. 1994. *The Culture of Disbelief.* New York: Anchor.

Casanova, Jose. 1994. *Public Religions in the Modern World.* Chicago: University of Chicago Press.

Finke, Roger, and Rodney Stark. 2005. *The Churching of America, 1776–2005: Winners and Losers in Our Religious Economy* (2d ed.). New Brunswick, NJ: Rutgers University Press.

Pavlik, Steve. 1992. "The U.S. Supreme Court Decision on Peyote in Employment Division vs. Smith: A Case Study in the Suppression of Native American Religious Freedom." *Wicazo Sa Review* 8 (2): 30–39.

Wuthnow, Robert. 2005. *America and the Challenges of Religious Diversity.* Princeton, NJ: Princeton University Press.

CHAPTER

9

Adam, Eve, and Steve
How Religion Intersects with Gender and Sexuality

1. Is religion essentially a woman's institution?
2. What roles does religion play in shaping gender relations in society?
3. Does religion change when women are in charge?
4. Sex, sex, sex . . . why does it always seem to come back to sex?
5. Can the roles of women, gays, and lesbians in society change in the absence of a concurrent change in religion?

In July 2008, the bishops of the Church of England made a historic decision. After many years of debate, they voted to allow women to become bishops, a position that was previously denied to women even though they could serve as priests and deacons. Now, depending on your point of view and your religious tradition, this decision is either the biggest non-news event of the year or something that is revolutionary—and not necessarily in a good way. What made this decision trickier is that it came just before the once-a-decade Lambeth Conference, when all Anglican bishops from around the world meet in England to talk about policy, mission, and other important global issues. This time, it wasn't just any ordinary meeting. Many feared and expected that during this meeting the worldwide "Anglican Communion" would split apart. But why? What could make something like that happen after it had existed for 500 years?

In 2003, the American Episcopal Church voted to approve the consecration of the Right Reverend Gene Robinson as the new Bishop of New Hampshire. Again, we hear you yawning, "So what?" Well, Gene Robinson is an openly gay man, and despite the objections of many Anglicans around the world who reject the idea that openly gay men and lesbian women can serve in any position in the Church, American Episcopalians have refused to change their minds and retract Bishop Robinson's appointment. This has resulted in Anglican leaders around the world calling for the censure of the American Church for what they believe to be outright heresy. Episcopal proponents of gay and lesbian accept- ance, however, see this international Anglican condemnation as rooted in ignorance and as an attitude that should be dismissed as irrelevant to life in the American Church today.

These highly publicized battles over gender and sexuality in religion are hardly unique. Just read the news. Increasingly, coverage of religion veers into conversations about sex, gender, or both! Sometimes it seems that American religious groups have made negotiating the complexities of human relationships—between men and women, women and women, and men and men—a centerpiece of their theological, political, and cultural missions. At the same time, somewhat ironically, believers bemoan that so much attention is focused on gender and sexuality. They want to know, "What about other vital issues like poverty, war, or racism?"

While these other issues are important, too, gender, sexuality, and the conflicts over them seem to have become central to many religious groups. Some religions make efforts to reinforce clear boundaries in the division of labor between men's and women's roles in the congregation and in the home. So, for example, Evangelical Christian groups like Promise Keepers help men stay focused on their God-given responsibilities as husbands and fathers. And in some Muslim circles, women debate the practice of wearing the hijab. To some people, this veil is a symbol of women's second-class status in Islam. Others counter that the veil frees women from Western cultural pressures regarding their appear- ance and that it empowers women. There is no consensus in sight. Debates over the role of women as religious leaders also continue. Can women lead worship services, as men do? Can they fully participate in religious rituals? In addition to facing issues of gender, Christian, Jewish, and Muslim groups around the world are confronting shifts in our understanding of human sexuality, especially as gay, lesbian, bisexual, and transgendered people and relationships become more visible inside and outside religious groups.

But before we go any further here, it is important to define our terms. In Box 9.1, we include some basic, perhaps familiar, definitions at the start of this chapter simply because we need to be clear about the analytic differences between terms such as "sex" and "gen- der" and between "sexual orientation" and "sexual identity." Often the term "gender" brings to mind women and their issues, as if gender is only about women. But gender refers to men's issues, too. Both men and women feel pressure to conform to society's gender roles, and both men and women are affected by disparities that arise out of gender. The same is true of "sexuality": It often suggests orientations other than heterosexual. But the concept of sexuality encompasses the full range of sexual identities and orientations that can only be understood in the context of a larger social system. If we think of sexual identity and orien- tation as only a "gay thing," we miss the larger picture of how social institutions like religion are central to defining and limiting sexuality for everyone, including heterosexual people. Thus, to understand the complexities of religion and gender, we must examine how reli- gion shapes—and is shaped in turn by—the experiences of men *and* women.

In this chapter we explore the intersections of religion, gender, and sexuality in the United States and worldwide. Sociologists have especially focused on the construction of these identities. They study how men and women learn what it means to be a man or woman in light of the teachings and history of their religions. Likewise, those who study sexuality examine how gays and lesbians construct their religious identities in the face of widespread condemnation even within their own traditions.

BOX 9.1

Now, in Case You have Forgotten:

Sex: *The biological and anatomical categories of being male or female.*

Gender: *The social categories of what it means to be a male or female in a particular society in specific times and places. A person's gender is not always identical to that person's sex.*

Gender Roles: *Society's "scripts" or expectations for how males and females are supposed to behave, how they should look, what their attitudes should be, what jobs are appropriate for them, and so on.*

Sexuality: *The totality of categories that individual societies construct around our bodies' sensual feelings, desires, fantasies, behaviors, and emotions.*

Sexual Orientation: *How society defines specific sets of feelings, desires, fantasies, behaviors, and emotions to express what is expected from particular sexual categories.*

Sexual Identity: *How an individual identifies his or her own sexuality as male, female, or something in between, possessing unique sets of sexual feelings, desires, fantasies, behaviors, and emotions.*

But gender and sexuality are more than just identities. They are also structures of power and privilege. Thus, we also examine how religion and religious organizations shape power dynamics between men and women, as well as among people whose sexual identities span a spectrum. We consider two significant structures of power: patriarchy and heterosexism. Patriarchy is a system in which men enjoy the privileges and control the resources of the society. They make the decisions. They set the policies. It's a man's world. Heterosexism works in the same way and sometimes is closely connected with patriarchy. Heterosexism is a system in which heterosexuals enjoy the privileges and control of social resources. In this case, it's a straight world.

Within patriarchy, certain gender roles, behaviors, attitudes, and experiences are defined as normal or "divinely ordained." For example, within patriarchy, men are expected to be heads of the household, women and children are expected to be obedient, boys must be adventurous, and girls must be nurturing. Those who do not adhere to these norms or who do not behave or believe as they are expected to do, are seen as "others" (or outsiders). A man who stays home with his children, a woman who makes family financial decisions, girls who play football, and boys who love Broadway musicals are identified as "different," sometimes "sinful," or just plain "weird." Remember, within a patriarchy, gender roles are constraining for *both* men and women. Likewise, heterosexism posits male–female relations as "normal," and those who fall outside this norm—gays and lesbians, bisexuals, single people, even polygamists—are marginalized, derided, and viewed as odd.

As we will explore further, religion plays a central role in the support and maintenance of patriarchy and heterosexism. It reinforces power differences and inequalities between men and women and between heterosexuals and gay, lesbian, bisexual, and transgendered people.

BUT ISN'T A WOMAN'S PLACE IN . . . RELIGION?

Sociologists concur: In general, and across time and place, women are more active in religion than men. More women than men belong to religious organizations, women's religious belief is stronger, religion is more important to women and their identities, and women engage in more religious behaviors than men.

According to the Pew Forum on Religion and Public Life (2008a, 64), women make up more than half of all Christian groups, 60% of Black Protestants and Jehovah's Witnesses, and 56% of Mormons. (See Table 9.1.) More women than men espouse "alternative" spiritualities, especially New Age, neopagan, and holistic spiritualities (Woodhead 2008). Jenkins (2006) argues that women have played a key role in the spread of Christianity worldwide. They are converts themselves, but they are also channels through which entire families are brought into Christian communities in Asia, Africa, and Central and South America. Men do predominate in the main non-Christian religions in the United States: Judaism, Islam, Buddhism, and Hinduism. But men also are more likely than women to claim no religious affiliation; nearly three-fifths of those with no affiliation are men. Even more striking, men make up two-thirds of those who say they are agnostic and 70% of those who are atheist.

Religion is also more important to women than men. (See Tables 9.2–9.5.) They believe more strongly in a personal God, they attend church more regularly, and they pray

TABLE 9.1   Gender Distribution within Major Religious Traditions

	Men	Women
Total Population	**48%**	**52%**
Protestant	46	54
Evangelical churches	47	53
Mainline churches	46	54
Historically Black churches	40	60
Catholic	46	54
Mormon	44	56
Jehovah's Witness	40	60
Orthodox	46	54
Jewish	52	48
Muslim*	54	46
Buddhist	53	47
Hindu	61	39
Unaffiliated	59	41
Atheist	70	30
Agnostic	64	36
Secular unaffiliated	60	40
Religious unaffiliated	52	48

*Due to rounding, figures may not add to 100.

Source: Pew Forum on Religion & Public Life 2008, 64, Pew Research Center 2007.

TABLE 9.2   Gender Differences in Importance of Religion to Life by Religious Affiliation

	Total	Men	Women
Total Population	**56.0%**	**49.0%**	**63.0%**
Protestant	70.0	64.0	75.0
Evangelical	79.0	74.0	83.0
Mainline	52.0	44.0	58.0
Historically Black	85.0	80.0	88.0
Catholic	56.0	48.0	63.0
Mormon	83.0	83.0	83.0
Orthodox	56.0	53.0	60.0
Jewish	31.0	23.0	39.0
Muslim	72.0	66.0	77.0
Buddhist	35.0	31.0	40.0
Hindu	45.0	49.0	60.0
Unaffiliated	16.0	13.0	19.0
Atheist	3.0	2.0	6.0
Agnostic	6.0	5.0	7.0
Secular unaffiliated	0	0	0
Religious unaffiliated	40.0	38.0	42.0

Source: Pew Forum on Religion and Public Life 2008a, 24.

TABLE 9.3   Gender Differences in Beliefs in a Personal God by Religious Affiliation

	Total	Men	Women
Total Population	**51.0%**	**45.0%**	**58.0%**
Protestant	65.0	60.0	69.0
Evangelical	73.0	69.0	77.0
Mainline	52.0	46.0	58.0
Historically Black	67.0	62.0	70.0
Catholic	48.0	43.0	53.0
Mormon	85.0	86.0	85.0
Orthodox	43.0	33.0	51.0
Jewish	17.0	14.0	20.0
Buddhist	12.0	11.0	13.0
Hindu	22.0	22.0	22.0
Unaffiliated	19.0	15.0	24.0
Atheist	3.0	3.0	3.0
Agnostic	7.0	6.0	9.0
Secular unaffiliated	9.0	8.0	12.0
Religious unaffiliated	38.0	33.0	43.0

Source: Pew Forum on Religion and Public Life 2008a, 29.

TABLE 9.4   Gender Differences in Worship Service Attendance by Religious Affiliation

	Total	Men	Women
Total Population	**39.0%**	**34.0%**	**45.0%**
Protestant	50.0	46.0	54.0
Evangelical	58.0	54.0	62.0
Mainline	34.0	31.0	38.0
Historically Black	42.0	36.0	45.0
Catholic	42.0	36.0	45.0
Mormon	75.0	75.0	76.0
Orthodox	34.0	30.0	38.0
Jewish	16.0	16.0	16.0
Muslim	40.0	48.0	30.0
Buddhist	17.0	20.0	14.0
Hindu	24.0	19.0	30.0
Unaffiliated	5.0	5.0	5.0
Atheist	4.0	4.0	5.0
Agnostic	2.0	3.0	1.0
Secular unaffiliated	1.0	1.0	0.0
Religious unaffiliated	11.0	12.0	10.0

Source: Pew Forum on Religion and Public Life 2008a, 38.

TABLE 9.5   Gender Differences in Frequency of Prayer by Religious Affiliation

	Total	Men	Women
Total Population	**58.0%**	**49.0%**	**66.0%**
Protestant	69.0	62.0	76.0
Evangelical	78.0	71.0	83.0
Mainline	53.0	43.0	62.0
Historically Black	80.0	76.0	84.0
Catholic	58.0	48.0	66.0
Mormon	82.0	80.0	84.0
Orthodox	60.0	51.0	67.0
Jewish	26.0	22.0	30.0
Buddhist	45.0	46.0	46.0
Hindu	62.0	56.0	72.0
Unaffiliated	22.0	17.0	29.0
Atheist	5.0	3.0	7.0
Agnostic	9.0	6.0	14.0
Secular unaffiliated	11.0	8.0	15.0
Religious unaffiliated	44.0	37.0	51.0

Source: Pew Forum on Religion and Public Life 2008a, 46.

more often. Among non-Christian groups—Jews, Muslims, Buddhists, and Hindus—women surpass men on most of these measures. For example, only in Islam and Buddhism do men attend religious services more frequently than women.

Why are women more religious than men, on so many dimensions and across so many different traditions? This is not a new question. In the 19th century, Christian clergy bemoaned how few men were in their churches. One study of Methodists in upstate New York in the early 1800s found that the focus on the spiritual rather than on the practicalities of business deterred most men from joining and participating (Johnson 1989). Most men at this time, especially men from the upper and middle classes, resisted any attempt by religious or any other authorities to limit their personal freedom. Consequently, some clergy tried to create environments that would appeal to a more "masculine" audience. Late in the 19th century, for example, the Men and Religion Forward Movement was organized to address the religious dimensions of masculinity and fatherhood in a manner that would bring men back to church (Curtis 1991).

A century later, the head coach for the University of Colorado turned his vision for "a revival among Christian men who were willing to take a stand for God in their marriages, families, churches, and communities" into a movement known as Promise Keepers. Their first conference in 1991 drew 4200 participants to address the question: "Where are the men?" (Promise Keepers 2008). This group remains strong.

Some have argued that women are naturally more emotionally expressive, nurturing, willing to meet others' needs before their own, and more inclined to build and maintain relationships. In contrast, men are naturally less emotional and more instrumental, more aggressive and active, and more concerned with accomplishing practical tasks. Thus, the reasoning goes, women are better suited to the comforting and community-building aspects of religion. Take, for example, Christianity, which places high value on taking care of the needy, engaging in self-sacrifice, and being in solidarity with others. It sometimes seems literally made for women! (Or, at the very least, made for patriarchy's image of the ideal woman.) Sociologists are, however, suspicious of attributing social behaviors to inborn traits. We question the assumption that these traits are fixed orientations arising out of inborn differences between men and women. Is it not just as likely that religion shapes the identities of men and women to feature such distinctions in traits?

Women's disproportionate commitment to religion is especially perplexing because most contemporary religious traditions around the world continue to embrace doctrines and practices that *reinforce* the inferior status of women. Let us examine in brief several examples of such doctrines and practices.

In the Hebrew sacred texts of the Torah, women are ritually and socially inferior to men. In the Ten Commandments, a man's wife is listed as a piece of property that others are forbidden to covet (Exodus 20:17). The same chapter of the Old Testament notes that a man may sell a daughter as a slave . . . and the text does not read "if," but "when," he does so (Exodus 21:7)! Jewish women, who were considered ritually unclean during their menstruation, were segregated during this time to prevent them from touching others and making them unclean (Leviticus 15:19–24). Women also were segregated after giving birth to a child. The duration of the segregation was based on the sex of the child. If a woman gave birth to a boy, she was considered unclean for 40 days. During that time, she couldn't touch anything holy or to enter the sanctuary. But if she had a girl, she was unclean for 80 days (Leviticus 12:1–8). Although not many Jews embrace these rules today, they still shape the patriarchal nature of Orthodox and Hasidic Judaism. For example, in contemporary

Orthodox Judaism, women must be seated apart from men, they cannot lead services, and they are not counted as part of a *minyan*, a minimum of 10 male adults who must be present in order to conduct public services.

The Christian New Testament also contains passages that relegate women to subordinate positions in society and church. In his writings to Christians throughout the Roman Empire, Paul laid out a clear gender hierarchy: The head of a woman is her husband (I Corinthians 11:3) and women were created for men (I Corinthians 11:8). He taught that

> The women should keep silence in the churches. For they are not permitted to speak, but should be subordinate, as even the law says. If there is anything they desire to know, let them ask their husbands at home. For it is shameful for a woman to speak in church. (I Corinthians 14:34–35).

Paul also reminds wives to "be subject to your husbands, as to the Lord," and he writes that "wives also be subject in everything to their husbands" and advises, "let the wife see that she respects her husband." (Ephesians 5: 21–33). In his first letter to Timothy, Paul writes,

> Let a woman learn in silence with all submissiveness. I permit no woman to teach or to have authority over men; she is to keep silent. For Adam was formed first, then Eve; and Adam was not deceived, but the woman was deceived and became a transgressor. (1 Timothy 2:11–14).

He encourages Titus to train "young women to love their husbands and children, to be sensible, chaste, domestic, kind, and submissive to their husbands" (Titus 2:4–5). These are a small sample of Christian teachings related to women, though hardly the only ones.

Some feminist scholars argue that Jesus never supported these subordinate roles for women. To the contrary, Jesus treated women in a more egalitarian way, especially given the cultural norms of the day. In addition, historical evidence suggests that women held positions of prominence in the first millennium of Christianity as abbesses. An abbess was the female head of a community of nuns and had full authority over the running of her nunnery. The medieval church was, nonetheless, a strictly patriarchal institution. Even today, there is not much change in some denominations. Among Catholics, "women cannot be priests, so the argument goes, not because of any lack of appropriate skills or ability, but because their femaleness makes it impossible for them to resemble Christ in the Eucharist" (Chaves 1997, 88). Similar arguments are put forward by some Protestant denominations.

Buddhism's principles have also been used to undermine the position of women. Buddhism teaches that there are "five impediments" to reaching enlightenment: desire, anger, drowsiness, restlessness and remorse, and doubt. In most Buddhist traditions, these impediments confront men and women alike. In some branches, however, especially in Japan, these impediments are understood to apply *especially* to women, who by their very nature are burdened with these obstacles. No matter what they do, women will not be able to reach enlightenment.

CHANGING GENDER ROLES, CHANGING RELATIONSHIPS TO RELIGION

Men and women continue to renegotiate gender roles and their understandings of masculinity and femininity. Religion often plays a substantial role in this process. Sometimes it is the authority against which people rebel, such as when men and women outright reject religious authority during their sorting out of appropriate gender roles. Other people hold to traditional religious teachings about gender in the face of secular trends towards equal treatment and access to leadership and other social resources for men and women. Some people fall in the middle between these two positions. They attempt to modify traditional religious beliefs and practices to accommodate a more equitable distribution of power, but do not reject the beliefs and practices altogether.

Still other men and women move to new religious movements, sometimes framed as "spiritual practices," that hold gender equality as a key tenet. In a world where "religion" is often understood to mean intellectual belief and practices that exist in male experience, these women's spiritual practices sometimes fly below the radar. That is, sometimes they do not count as "real." Consider Susan Starr Sered's (1994, quoted in Woodhead 2007, 565) comparative study of religious groups in which women predominate:

> Women's religions tend to be characterized by greater concern for this-worldly matters including bodily and emotional wellbeing (health and healing) and the quality of intimate and family relationships, and to be more centered around home, food preparation and sometimes the natural world.

But because the concrete expression of women's spirituality compared with men's spirituality tends to involve New Age, neopagan, and holistic health and well-being practices, they are routinely subsumed under the categories of "folklore," "superstition," "syncretism," "heresy," or simply, "ladies' auxiliary," but not considered to be *real* or legitimate expressions of religion (Sered 1994, 286 quoted in Woodhead 2007, 565). Negotiating religious and gender identities individually or collectively remains a complicated business!

Linda Woodhead explored how women make sense of male-dominated traditional religions. She views religion as a power structure, itself a product of broader gender-based power inequalities: "The structure of male privilege and power relations exists at the macro level but then power is negotiated in the small, ceaseless, real-time interactions between individuals" (2007a, 551). Women and men constantly respond to these power differentials as they construct gender and religious identities within faith traditions.

Woodhead argues that, in part, women derive identity from their religious faith. "Mainstream" refers to women who belong to religious groups with power structures that privilege men over women. In contrast, "marginal" refers to women who belong to religious groups that offer alternatives to a male-dominated structure. Religious groups and the identities that they foster may affirm and reinforce existing inequalities in power that are based on gender ("confirmatory"). Or, they may challenge these inequalities ("challenging"). These labels are *not* interchangeable with our familiar ideas of religiously conservative or liberal people and groups. It is never that simple. Evangelical groups may challenge gender inequalities, and Liberal Protestantism may confirm them.

Figure 9.1 shows four potential associations of religion and gender that may affect religious organizations and individuals. With respect to male privilege, religious groups and identities may be consolidating, tactical, questing, or countercultural.

Consolidation occurs when religious groups and identities generally affirm existing structures of gender inequality and legitimize traditional gender roles. This outcome often occurs in the face of liberalizing cultural forces and growing gender equality in the broader society. Organizations like Promise Keepers serve a consolidating function for men by trying to maintain the traditional male roles as the head of the household and

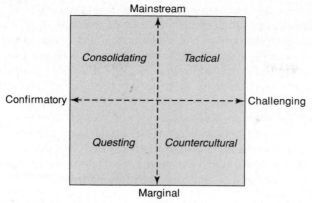

FIGURE 9.1 Gender and responses to religion and male power and privilege.
Source: Woodhead 2007.

protector of the family. Along similar lines, religious organizations may cite scripture to assert that housewife and mother are the only appropriate roles for women.

Remember, both men and women enact these gender roles and are affected by them. Consolidation is an active process of balancing religious beliefs against the countervailing force of a secular society that does not share these beliefs. Mary, an evangelical traditionalist who was a respondent in Lori Beaman's (1999, 28) study of evangelical women, embodies this approach. She recounts her ideas about men's and women's roles:

> I feel that the man should have a stronger, how should I put it? . . . well, he's the leader in the home and I just feel that . . . I know in some homes a wife can balance the checkbook much better than the husband can, and so I think those things, I'm not saying he has to be the head of everything. But I think when it comes to . . . well, like buying a new car—I want a certain kind, and he feels another kind would be more for our budget and more economical, so I think his word has to be the final word.

In religious contexts that are consolidating, traditional beliefs about proper gender roles are not "false consciousness," in which women like Mary are blinded by their faith to other options. Instead, clear-cut traditional roles provide an alternative to the confusion, complexity, and frustration that women face when they juggle domestic duties, a career, and community life. In *The New Faces of Christianity,* Philip Jenkins makes a similar point. He notes that North Americans or European Christians might see the decision to follow traditional roles as an uncritical acceptance of Biblical texts. But these roles may actually protect women who regularly face the prospects of rape, incest, sexual abuse, and abandonment in patriarchal societies. Literal readings of the Bible provide women with the means to regulate men's behavior, especially within homes and extended families. Biblical literalism also allows women to use the many powerful women in the Bible as examples for their own roles in their families and their communities.

Mainstream religious groups may also adopt a *tactical* approach to interacting with patriarchal gender structures. Women in tactical religious contexts tend to create "parallel religious associations in which women-only groups, which meet on a regular weekly or more-than-weekly basis, are the basic social unit" (Woodhead 2007, 557). Women in these associations do not directly challenge the male power structure. Instead they are empowered by meeting and interacting with other women free from male supervision and direct control. Over time, such spaces may allow the emergence of a women's movement to challenge male dominance. For centuries, women's religious orders have provided a space where women were educated, held positions of some power, and escaped the traditional social pressures to be wives and mothers.

Tactical opportunities allow individual women in mainstream religious contexts to pursue the "personal and emotional benefits" of being in women-only religious spaces (Woodhead 2007, 559). Women's groups in conservative and mainline churches allow women to interact on their own terms and develop social bonds. Evangelical women may work together through organizations such as Women's Ministries Unlimited (Assemblies of God), Wesleyan Women, Women's Aglow International, and Women's Missionary Union (Southern Baptist), among many others. Groups like Episcopal Church Women, Women of the ELCA (Lutheran), and Presbyterian Women serve similar purposes in mainline Protestant denominations.

These contexts also provide opportunities for women to discuss and debate Biblical texts and religious teachings about gender roles. Research shows that there is only a loose relationship between believing church teachings and conforming to them completely in daily life. Consider, for example, the Southern Baptist women in Pevey, Williams, and Ellison's (1996) study of the Ladies Bible Class at the Shady Grove Baptist Church. While these women know and accept Southern Baptist teachings about a wife's duty to submit to her husband, they also claim a fair amount of independence in their marriages. One of them, Susie, definitively described her relationship with her husband:

> I'm not afraid to speak up and I mean I am [a] very assertive woman and so it wouldn't bother me to be pretty adamant, you know if I felt really strong about something. And of course I would. I think that I could prevail upon [my husband] if I felt [a decision] was not in his best interests . . . And he will have to listen to me. You know we're a team.

Another woman in the group, Ruth, explains that her willingness to submit to her husband is due to their unique relationship, not to a decision to follow Biblical principles:

> A lot of my willingness to [submit] is his personality and how confident I am in our relationship and I don't know that I'd necessarily do that with someone else . . . I don't know if I would be willing to take that submissive role in another situation, even though I think the Bible very strongly says that is our role.

Jenkins (2006, 159) sees the same basic pattern at work in religious communities in Africa, Asia, and Central and South America:

> Women's organizations and fellowships, such as the Mothers' Unions . . . allow women's voices to be heard in the wider society. So do prayer fellowships and cells, which can be so independent as to unnerve official church hierarchies. Female believers look to the churches for an affirmation of their roles and interests, and they naturally seek justification in the scriptures, which provide a vocabulary for public debate.

Thus, religion can become a tactical means of empowerment for women. It can also allow them to challenge men's power in religion and society. For example, Mark Chaves (1997) found that religious groups with autonomous women's organizations were two and a half times more likely to ordain women. These groups are integral to organizing change within religion.

Questing is a third way that religion may intersect with gender. Such groups and identities are on the fringe of the religious landscape and of society in general. Questing provides individuals with ways to improve their spiritual, physical, and emotional wellbeing within the existing social order. New Age spirituality is one of the most familiar forms of questing. (It may seem contradictory to describe this as both religion and spirituality, but for our purposes here, we are including all things spiritual under the umbrella of religion.) As we noted in Chapter 3, there are many variants of New Age spirituality, including yoga, various kinds of meditation, alternative and herbal medical practices, Reiki (a combination of healing and massage), aromatherapies, sweat lodges, rituals that use crystals, astrology, and tarot card readings. These spiritual practices also are "holistic," addressing mind, body, and spirit as one. As we also noted earlier, these practices are usually dismissed as superstition. Nevertheless, they are widely practiced, often alongside more traditional religious forms. Questing religion typically focuses on the sacred *within* an individual and the vast majority of participants are women (see also Glendinning and Bruce 2006). Sointu and Woodhead (2008, 269) suggest that, because holistic spiritualities are inherently relational, they validate women's traditional work of relational, emotional, and bodily care. Like consolidating religion, questing religion provides a means to cope with the dominant gender order without challenging it.

Finally, *countercultural* religion uses "sacred power as a central resource in the attempt to establish more equal distributions of power between the sexes" (Woodhead 2007, 560). It includes religions that replace a male orientation with a female one, like Wicca. In these religions, women identify with the Goddess, Her power, and Nature, and they reject the worship of a supreme male God who is separate from the natural world, as in the Judeo–Christian tradition (Christ 2007). These women (and some men who also follow this religious tradition) challenge what they believe to be the root cause of women's oppression and of environmental degradation: separating the divine from the physical world on which all life depends and not seeing the natural world as sacred (Griffin 1995).

Men who follow these religious movements also use the beliefs as a way to critique men's traditional gender roles. In Mary Jo Neitz's (2005, 270) study of Goddess movements, practitioners see their beliefs and practices as liberating for men as well as women. One woman she interviewed expressed it this way:

> Patriarchy is just as crippling for men as for women. It's just that most men don't understand that. They are in a gilded cage, so they think it's a nice cage. The men who are in the Craft (Wicca) are aware that it's a cage . . . and they are trying to find a way out . . . There are men now who are trying, for their own reasons—for their own healing, for their own sense of wholeness. I know men who feel that they have been robbed of having a feminine half, and being told culturally that any kind of female behavior was wrong for them, and they are reclaiming their right to have a feminine side. But they are also now freer to find an expression for their masculine energy that makes them feel comfortable and find an expression for their female energy that is more balances and more true to themselves.

Wicca and the broader Goddess movement are countercultural because they provide a collective basis for both men and women to challenge and reshape existing gender roles. These movements have empowered women to organize politically for religious and social change.

Religion is integrally tied to the structures of power and privilege that shape the lives of both men and women. These structures are changing, however. As they change, individual men and women find new ways to redefine gender identities, often drawing on religion for guidance. For women, defining their gender identity may mean holding on to an older form of identity, creating a new one, or fighting politically for wholesale changes in the roles of men and women in broader society. Religion also guides men's understanding of what masculinity means in the face of trends that include the growing political and economic power of women, metrosexuality, and the rise of an LGBT (Lesbian, Gay, Bisexual, or Transgender) movement.

DOES RELIGION CHANGE WHEN WOMEN ARE IN CHARGE?

Approximately 44 Christian denominations permit women to be ministers. Some have ordained women since the early 1800s. Others have only allowed women to be clergy within the last 10 or 20 years. Interestingly, several large conservative Evangelical groups such as the Church of the Nazarene and Assemblies of God have been ordaining women for over 75 years or more, while more liberal mainline Protestant groups like the Lutherans and Episcopalians only began ordaining women in the 1970s.

Data on women clergy in the United States are scant. We do know that women made up approximately 34% of all Protestant seminary students in 2006 and composed 38% of those who were specifically pursuing a Master's of Divinity Degree. Women also make up more than half of all students in nondegree programs and 22% of all full-time faculty members in seminaries (Association of Theological Schools 2007, 8, 11). In specific denominations, the number of ordained women continues to grow. They make up 18.5% of clergy and 22% of bishops in the United Methodist Church. In the Episcopal church, they compose 31% of all active clergy and 46% of the newly ordained. In contrast, Reverend Jeren Rowell (2003) noted that less than 3% of Nazarene clergy were women, a drop from 20% in 1908. Within Judaism, there were 495 rabbinic alumnae from the Hebrew Union College–Jewish Institute of Religion, constituting approximately 18% of all rabbinical alumni of the institution. And although women are not officially permitted to be priests in the Catholic Church, Catholic women carry out many leadership roles in local parishes as "pastors" and women make up 80% of nonpriests serving in paid Catholic ministries, not including teachers (Chaves 1997, 24).

There is evidence of occupational segregation by gender in religious organizations. In a study of Episcopal and Unitarian–Universalist clergy, Nesbitt (1993) found that women were more likely to be segregated into positions as "permanent deacons," which focus on community service and outreach. Such positions are often unpaid, so the women who fill them often also work full-time jobs. Among Unitarians, women often worked as Ministers of Religious Education. Women in the clergy role of "pastor" or "priest" were most likely to hold jobs as assistants or associates, reporting to a male rector or head pastor. Women were also more likely to lead congregations that were smaller, that were located in rural areas, and that operated with smaller budgets. Some scholars have described the obstacles that women face in advancing to high-profile, high-prestige leadership positions in the church as a "stained-glass ceiling."

Many sociologists wonder whether women lead congregations differently than men. Research suggests that women do exercise their power as ministers differently than do men. Ruth Wallace (1993) found that, among Catholic congregational leaders, women were more likely to use collaboration, and men were more likely to use hierarchical power, to get things done. That is, female pastors focus more on building relationships with other lay people and on using their knowledge and abilities to help lead, whereas men rely more on the authority of their positions. Women leaders also have different priorities for the social focus of the church. Wallace found that female clergy are often more liberal on issues such as abortion rights or gay rights. They are also more likely to be more engaged with broader issues of peace and social justice.

Much of women's ability to exercise power within religious organizations depends, however, on the religious context and on women's relative position in the authority structure. For example, Olson (2000) argues that, despite their personal political views, women find it more difficult to exercise moral authority in the political arena. The uphill battle simply to become a minister in a congregation is draining. Encouraging a congregation to engage in political action is often risky: Political action is needed precisely in the areas where there is resistance to change. Put together, these challenges represent a substantial barrier blocking many women clergy from pushing their congregations towards political activism. Olson's interviews of four female clergy in Milwaukee revealed that three of them had strong personal political convictions but were not politically engaged as clergy. One African-American female pastor preached about the importance of political engagement. She was limited from becoming more politically engaged herself, however, because "the senior (male) pastor of her church stressed day-to-day survival issues, rather than politics, as the top priority for his staff" (40).

Again, we see that power structures are inherent both in religious organizations and in society's gender roles. But male dominance is not just built on abstract ideas about gender roles for men and women. It also rests on beliefs about sexual identity (Pharr 2001). It is time to turn our attention to sex!

SEX, SEX, SEX . . . WHY DOES IT ALWAYS COME BACK TO SEX?

"The Homosexual Agenda!"

If you pay attention to the news, you know that the debate over sexuality is rocking many religious organizations as well as broader society. The diversity in sexual identities is a pretty complicated business. Although most people are attracted to members of the opposite sex, others are attracted to members of the same sex and still others are attracted to both. The sexual revolution that began in the 1960s also raised the possibility that even within the sexual-identity categories of "straight," "gay," "lesbian," and "bisexual," there is further diversity in the way that people actually live in sexual and emotional relationships with others over their lifetime. Out of this complexity, political conflicts have emerged over gay and lesbian rights, same-sex marriage, and antidiscrimination laws. These debates have serious implications for religious groups because religion often provides the rationale behind opposition to the rights of alternative sexualities. So it is no surprise that religion continues to play a key role in shaping our debates over human sexuality.

Conflicts over sexuality occur within religious groups, among them, and between them and other institutions in society. How do the world's religions understand human sexuality and behavior? How have religious groups and believers responded to this touchy and sometimes uncomfortable subject? What do they do with their religion's teachings about sexuality? And finally, how have gay, lesbian, bisexual, and transgendered persons responded to religion?

Given how contentious these issues are today in the United States, it may surprise you to learn that we do not know a lot about how most of the world's religions view human sexual diversity—and perhaps this is for good reason. Historically and cross-culturally, societies have not divided human sexuality into heterosexuality and homosexuality. These terms developed in the early 20th century as clinical psychological labels. Behaviors associated with these labels existed, of course. But people were not organized into significant social and political groups on the basis of "who they partnered with." Instead, for most of human history, the social meaning of sexual behavior has focused on procreation within family units to ensure that people had children.

In the premodern world, men and women were obligated to reproduce to maintain the extended family as an economic and political unit. Among elite members of society, women's sexual behavior was highly controlled. Virgin daughters were valuable to their families because they could be given in marriage as part of political treaties, to connect two already powerful families, and to build a family's economic wealth (Boswell 1994). For elite men, things were different. Their sexual behavior was less tightly controlled. Although the broader society might discourage promiscuity, men could have sex with women, other men, girls, boys, and servants, just as long as they produced male heirs with their wives—heirs who could inherit family property and keep political power in the family. For people who did not have political power or wealth, sexual behavior was much less tightly controlled. Peasants might enter into a common-law marriage, but the relationship was local and informal, not a concern of the church or the state.

Prior to the modern era, people developed gender identities, for sure, but there were no distinct *sexual* identities for people to claim. Today, especially in North America and Europe, men and women can identify themselves as "straight," "gay," "lesbian," "bisexual," or "transgendered." The development of these identities has prompted new forms of political, psychological, and religious regulation. In her analysis of homosexual behavior prior to World War II, Urvashi Vaid (1995, 39) points out that widespread "public morality campaigns, police crackdowns on homosexual solicitation, and increased enforcement of criminal laws" were a backlash against the "sexual anarchy" of the 1890s and early 1900s. In that era, gays and lesbians were pressured to remain invisible on the fringe of social life.

More recently, an organized gay and lesbian rights movement has worked to overturn political regulations in the United States, including laws that criminalize "sodomy." The American Psychological Association no longer labels homosexual behavior and identity as a clinical disorder. As a result, religion is now the principal source of sexual regulation. Beginning in the 1970s, many Christian denominations found themselves in the sometimes awkward position of talking about sex. That is, they developed official policies and taught more directly about sexual behavior of all kinds (Wilcox 2003).

In the Jewish and Christian traditions, seven Biblical references are used to justify opposition to sexual behavior that is oriented toward others of one's own sex. In the story of Sodom and Gomorrah, God sends two angels to Sodom to see whether it is as wicked as its reputation suggests. When the people of Sodom try to gang rape the angels, God destroys the city. This tale is traditionally used to show "what God thinks" of homosexuality (Genesis 19:1–28). Other Biblical references include injunctions from the Torah that "You shall not lie with a male as with a woman; it is an abomination" (Leviticus 18:22), that "If a man lies with a male as with a woman, both of them have committed an abomination; they shall be put to death, their blood is upon them" (Leviticus 20:13); and, presumably to address "drag" in the ancient world, "A woman shall not wear anything that pertains to a man, nor shall a man put on a woman's garment; for whoever does these things is an abomination to the Lord your God" (Deuteronomy 22:5). In the New Testament, Paul refers three times to what is presumably homosexuality:

> For this reason God gave them up to dishonorable passions. Their women exchanged natural relations for unnatural, and the men likewise gave up natural relations with women and were consumed with passion for one another, men committing shameless acts with men and receiving in their own persons the due penalty for their error. (Romans 1:26–28)

> Do you not know that the unrighteous will not inherit the kingdom of God? Do not be deceived; neither the immoral, not idolaters, nor adulterers, nor sexual perverts [traditionally translated as "homosexuals"], not thieves, nor the greedy, nor drunkards, nor revilers, nor robbers will inherit the kingdom of God. (I Corinthians 6:9–10)

> Understand this, that the law is not laid down for the just but for the lawless and disobedient, for the ungodly and sinners, for the unholy and profane, for murderers of fathers and murderers of mothers, immoral persons, sodomites, kidnappers, liars, perjurers, and whatever else is contrary to sound doctrine. (I Timothy 1:9–10)

These verses have been used repeatedly to argue that being Christian is incompatible with being gay or lesbian. In turn, this has reinforced a religiously based sexual ideology that privileges heterosexuality.

So, for example, the Roman Catholic Church teaches while there is nothing inherently sinful about *being* homosexual, any same-sex sexual *behavior* is a mortal sin. So too is sexual activity outside of heterosexual marriage. Other Christian traditions argue likewise. Representing an extreme case, the Reverend Fred Phelps and the members of his small Baptist church in Topeka, Kansas, publicly proclaim that "God Hates Fags." Phelps is notorious for organizing antigay demonstrations during gay and lesbian pride celebrations and at the funerals of celebrities who have died from AIDS. Phelps and his followers protested at the memorial service held for Matthew Shepard, the gay University of Wyoming student who in 1998 was brutally beaten and left to die hanging on a barbed-wire fence along a country road. Although most Christian traditionalists distance themselves from Phelps and his actions, they nonetheless concur that expressions of sexuality other than heterosexuality are morally wrong and should be formally opposed.

A recent Pew survey asked respondents whether they thought homosexuality was acceptable or whether it should be discouraged by society. (See Table 9.6.) About 50% of the

TABLE 9.6 Differences in Attitudes about Whether Society Should Accept or Discourage Homosexuality, by Religious Affiliation

	Accept	Discourage
Total Population	**50.0%**	**40.0%**
Protestant	38.0	51.0
Evangelical	26.0	64.0
Mainline	55.0	34.0
Historically Black	40.0	46.0
Catholic	58.0	30.0
Mormon	24.0	68.0
Jehovah's Witness	12.0	76.0
Orthodox	48.0	37.0
Jewish	79.0	20.0
Muslim	27.0	61.0
Buddhist	82.0	12.0
Hindu	48.0	37.0
Unaffiliated	71.0	20.0
Atheist	80.0	14.0
Agnostic	83.0	10.0
Secular unaffiliated	74.0	17.0
Religious unaffiliated	59.0	29.0

Source: Pew Forum on Religion and Public Life 2008a, 92.

TABLE 9.7 Impact of Religious Belief and Practices on Public Opposition to Homosexuality for Selected Groups

	Total	Attend weekly or more	Religion is very important	Pray at least daily	Absolute belief in personal God
Total Population	**40.0%**	**57.0%**	**52.0%**	**49.0%**	**51.0%**
Protestant					
Evangelical	64.0	75.0	70.0	69.0	69.0
Mainline	34.0	44.0	42.0	39.0	39.0
Historically Black	46.0	54.0	49.0	49.0	50.0
Catholic	30.0	37.0	35.0	33.0	34.0
Mormon	68.0	76.0	75.0	74.0	71.0
Orthodox	76.0	57.0	47.0	48.0	44.0
Jewish	20.0	N/A	27.0	32.0	24.0

Source: Pew Forum on Religion and Public Life 2008a, 94.

35,500 respondents felt that homosexuality was acceptable. Opposition to homosexuality broke down along religious lines. Mainline Protestants and Catholics were most support-ive of public acceptance of homosexuality; 55% and 58% of them, respectively, said that it was acceptable, while about a third of respondents in each group opposed public ac-ceptance. Among Protestants, Evangelicals were the group that felt most strongly that ho-mosexuality should be discouraged (64%). Black Protestants were torn, with 40% report-ing that they saw homosexuality as acceptable while 46% reported that it should be discouraged. Three-quarters of Mormons and two-thirds of Jehovah's Witnesses opposed homosexuality. American Buddhists (82%) and Jews (79%) were the most accepting of it, while Muslims were the least accepting (27%).

A number of factors correlate with opposition to public acceptance of homosexual-ity: an absolute belief in a personal god, weekly attendance at religious services, daily prayer, and a strong sense of religious identity. (See Table 9.7.) Among Mormons and Evangelical Christians, those who are most devout are also more likely to oppose homo-sexuality. Similar patterns hold for the other groups as well. Even among Jews, who are generally accepting of homosexuality, religious devotion increases the likelihood of op-position: Jews who reported praying at least once daily were four times as likely as other Jews to oppose public acceptance of homosexuality.

Religion shapes and supports heterosexual "privilege" in other ways as well. Some religious organizations prohibit openly gay and lesbian people from belonging to or hold-ing positions of power in congregations. Some religious groups work politically to oppose laws or policies that they believe give societal approval to sexual behavior outside hetero-sexual marriage. Mainline Protestant denominations have struggled to define appropriate institutional roles for openly gay and lesbian parishioners. The United Methodist General Conference passed a statement in 1984 that prohibits the ordination of gays and lesbians. It also formally prohibits the church from funding groups that are deemed to support or promote homosexuality (United Methodist Church 2004). The Presbyterian Church (U.S.A.)'s *Book of Order* forbids the ordination of sexually active gays and lesbians (Presbyterian Church U.S.A. 2008). Facing a denominational split, however, it adopted a resolution in 2006 that allows some presbyteries to opt out of this prohibition on the basis of the Church's Theological Task Force Report that concluded that "sexual orientation is not, in itself, a barrier to ordination" (Presbyterian Church U.S.A. 2006, 20).

The U.S. Episcopal Church has been wrestling with whether open gays and les-bians, especially those who are in relationships, should be ordained as priests and con-secrated as Bishops. In 1996, retired Bishop Walter Righter was accused of heresy, but was later acquitted of the charge, for ordaining an openly gay man as a priest. His ac-tion ran contrary to a 1979 Church resolution, which stated that it is not appropriate to ordain noncelibate gays and lesbians. In 2003, the General Convention of the Church voted to approve the consecration of the Reverend Gene Robinson as Bishop of New Hampshire. Robinson is an openly gay man who is in a long-term relationship. Although the national Episcopal Church has effectively accepted open gay and lesbians in positions of power, this move puts Americans in conflict with other Anglican Churches around the world (although not so much in Canada because the Anglican Church of Canada does not exclude gays and lesbians on the basis of their sexual orientation alone from serving as priests and deacons)) that consider homosexuality to be sinful and criminal. As we noted at the beginning of this chapter, this decision along with the 2009 resolution allowing gays and lesbians who are in life-long, committed relationships in all levels of ordained ministry may well lead to a schism in the world-wide Anglican community.

In contrast to these fiery debates in mainline Protestant denominations, most Evangelicals, Roman Catholics, and Eastern Orthodox Catholics prohibit openly gay people from being ordained. For Evangelicals, this is a nonissue because they follow a literal interpretation of the Bible and associate homosexuality with evil. In the rare cases in which an evangelical congregation supported gays and lesbians, the parent organization typically responded by expelling the congregation. In 1992, for instance, the North Carolina State Baptist Convention "dis-fellowshipped," or expelled, the Olin T. Binkley Memorial Baptist Church in Chapel Hill, North Carolina, for fully including LGBT members in the life of the congregation and for approving John Blevins, an openly gay man, to preach as a step towards ordination (Hartman 1996). Following this episode, the Southern Baptist Convention decreed that all Southern Baptist congregations were required to oppose homosexuality.

Roman Catholic policy also officially bars LGBT people from being ordained. In 2005, Pope Benedict XVI reaffirmed the Vatican's longstanding policy that homosexual men should not be admitted to seminaries even if they are celibate:

> [The Church] . . . cannot admit to the seminary or to holy orders those who practice homosexuality, present deep-seated homosexual tendencies or support the so-called "gay culture." Such persons, in fact, find themselves in a situation that gravely hinders them from relating correctly to men and women. One must in no way overlook the negative consequences that can derive from the ordination of persons with deep-seated homosexual tendencies.

This ban also applies to religious orders.

Eastern Orthodox Churches have a similar policy:

> The Orthodox Church believes that homosexuality should be treated by religion as a sinful failure . . . correction is called for. Homosexuals should be accorded the confidential medical and psychiatric facilities by which they can be helped to restore themselves to a self-respecting sexual identity that belongs to them by God's ordinance. (Harakas 2005)

Many non-Christian traditions also condemn alternative sexual behavior. Islam resembles conservative Christianity and Orthodox Judaism in its rejection of homosexual behavior as inherently immoral. The Qur'an and the Hadith, a collection of actions and teachings attributed to Muhammad, both contain condemnations of sexual relationships between men:

> We also sent Lut: He said to his people: "Do ye commit lewdness such as no people in creation (ever) committed before you? For ye practice your lusts on men in preference to women: ye are indeed a people transgressing beyond bounds. (*Qur'an* 7:80–81)

> What! Of all creatures do ye come unto the males, and leave the wives your Lord created for you? Nay, but ye are forward folk. (*Qur'an* 26:165)

The Hadith recommends that men who engage in homosexual behavior be punished by death. Similar opposition to homosexuality is found in other religions.

The effects of these ideologies are not limited to what happens *inside* congregations. They also drive political action by religious groups in broader society. The Roman

Catholic Church opposes the marriage of same-sex couples. The Congregation for the Doctrine of the Faith (2003) stated,

> In those situations where homosexual unions have been legally recognized or have been given the legal status and rights belonging to marriage, clear and emphatic opposition is a duty. One must refrain from any kind of formal cooperation in the enactment or application of such gravely unjust laws and, as far as possible, from material cooperation on the level of their application. In this area, everyone can exercise the right to conscientious objection . . . When legislation in favor of the recognition of homosexual unions is proposed for the first time in a legislative assembly the Catholic law-maker has a moral duty to express his opposition clearly and publicly and to vote against it. To vote in favor of a law so harmful to the common good is gravely immoral.

Why is *this* issue so important to conservative religionists today? Part of the answer lies in the central role of the Bible or other sacred texts as a source of moral authority. If we dismiss the Bible's rules on sexuality as being historically or culturally based and thus no longer applicable to today's society, rather than regarding them as universal and absolute, then what stops us from dismissing all its other rules and commandments in the same fashion? People who take a religiously conservative approach to sexuality argue that if the Bible isn't absolutely, literally true for all times and places, then maybe none of it is true. At what point do you draw the line? If we disregard the text's codes of conduct regarding sexual behavior, then why believe that the Bible's call to feed the hungry, not to kill, or not to steal are relevant in today's world either? Of course, redefining gender and sexual norms also challenges religious ideas about family, the structure of authority in marriage, and the raising of children. The point is that opposition to homosexuality, gay rights, or same-sex marriage is based on more than just ignorance or fear. Opponents are fighting for larger religious principles here.

Despite the condemnation of homosexuality by some religious groups, a growing number of groups are embracing the idea that sexuality is a part of the divine ordering of creation. Consequently, *sexual identity* is a relatively fixed and neutral aspect of one's being that is out of one's control. Because it is God-given, it is not an appropriate basis for moral evaluation. Many liberal mainline Protestants, Roman Catholics, Reformed Jews, Reconstructionist Jews, and even Conservative Jews have adopted this official position. Because they understand sexual identity to be an inherent quality rather than a choice, these groups condemn discrimination on the basis of sexual identity. Tensions linger, however, when discussions turn to sexual *activity*. Same-sex marriage is at the heart of the most charged debates.

While the idea of marriage may seem straightforward to you, it is actually complicated, and that's part of the problem here. Marriage as a *civil institution* is the recognition by the government and the law of the intimate and sexual relationship between a man and a woman that makes them a couple. Civil marriage is a contract that brings with it many legal and social benefits, including access to certain tax breaks, hospital visitation rights, and power of attorney. Marriage as a *religious institution*, however, is a recognition of a couple's relationship by a religious authority figure and "in the eyes of God." In the United States, civil and religious marriage are not the same. Couples may be married by a Justice of the Peace and never have their marriage recognized by a religious group.

But it doesn't work the other way around. In order for a marriage to be legally valid, the couple must sign a marriage license issued by the state government. This is why, at the end of every wedding conducted in a church, you will here the words "In the name of the state of [insert whatever state you like], I now pronounce you husband and wife." The couple marries in a religious ceremony, and then the government—by the authority it has given the church official performing the ceremony—recognizes the marriage as a legal act.

There are, of course, alternatives to marriage that have emerged as a result of LGBT struggles for recognition. "Civil unions," sometimes called same-sex unions, are a parallel to civil marriage. In Vermont, New Jersey, and a few other states, gay and lesbian couples may have their relationships recognized by those state governments and receive all the legal benefits to which married heterosexual couples are entitled. The difference between a civil marriage and a civil union is that the gay or lesbian couple's relationship would be recognized only by a state that makes such allowances for same-sex couples. Gay marriage advocates argue that the term "marriage," not "civil union," should apply to gay and lesbian couples as well as to heterosexual couples. Their opponents, however, see marriage as a relationship that can exist only between a man and a woman. While only a few states provide legal recognition for gay couples, even fewer religious groups do.

Mainline Protestant denominations have taken varying approaches to sanctifying same-sex unions. In 2003, the U.S. Episcopal Church began allowing—though not encouraging or requiring—local congregations to bless same-sex unions. ELCA Lutherans neither prohibit nor sanction the blessing of same-sex unions. The most proactive Protestant group is the Unitarian denomination, which encourages congregations to "take an affirmative position in support of the value of marriage between any two committed persons, whether of the same or opposite sexes, and to make those positions known in their home communities." The United Church of Christ takes a similar stand.

Sometimes, local churches are more progressive than national bodies. Increasingly, ministers across denominations have moved forward on their own to assist gay and lesbian congregants. Some congregations set themselves apart by joining denominational movements for inclusivity. For instance, ELCA Lutheran congregations that welcome LGBT members label themselves "Reconciled in Christ" congregations. Similarly, United Church of Christ churches are "Open and Affirming," United Methodists are "Reconciling," and American Baptists are "Welcoming and Affirming" churches (Wilcox 2003).

A number of religious groups and organizations have emerged, led by LGBT individuals, to meet the needs of homosexuals and to create a safe and inclusive sacred space for them to find a spiritual home. The Universal Fellowship of Metropolitan Community Churches (MCC) is a worldwide federation of over 300 churches and 43,000 members in 22 countries that serve the LGBT communities. A central part of the MCC mission is for the federation members to be "leaders in the world about the union of *spirituality* and *sexuality* by articulating our message and spreading it effectively" (United Federation of Metropolitan Community Churches 2005). Other groups that attempt to meet the spiritual needs of LGBT people include Dignity (Roman Catholic), Integrity (Episcopal), Lutherans Concerned (ELCA Lutheran), the National Gay Pentecostal Alliance (Pentecostal),

Affirmation (Latter-day Saints/Mormon), AXIOS (Orthodox), and al-Fatiha (Muslim) (Wilcox 2003).

In spite of the LGBT groups that exist in various denominations, sexual identity and activity among those who are not in heterosexual marriages—single people, gay or lesbian people, divorced individuals, widows and widowers, bisexuals, and transgendered people—are not yet on the radar screen of most religious groups. The theology and policies of Christian denominations remain oriented around the norm of heterosexual marriage. Moreover, to gain acceptance in religious settings, gays and lesbian often are forced to mirror the behavior of heterosexuals, even in progressive religious groups. This situation obscures the different role that sex plays within gay and lesbian communities and cultures. Among gays and lesbians, sexual activity is more likely to be understood as a means of social or political expression among gays and lesbians. It is not *just* a private relationship (Vaid 1995).

In the United States today, most religious groups and people fall somewhere between the extremes of opposition to and support for homosexuality. A consensus remains unlikely. Most people agree that human sexual identity and orientation will remain a central dilemma facing American religion well into the 21st century. And within most religious groups the debates rage "over the heads of LGBT people themselves . . . despite the presence of a small number of very vocal LGBT activists" (Wilcox 2003, 44).

NEGOTIATING LGBT IDENTITIES WITHIN RELIGIOUS INSTITUTIONS

It often seems contradictory to be a person of faith *and* an open lesbian, gay man, bisexual, or transgendered person. How do such people manage the tension between their religious and sexual identities? Ethnographic studies have explored how LGBT people make sense of their place in religious groups (e.g., Mahaffy 1996). Until recently, there were few ways to negotiate these conflicting identities. One could remain silent about one's sexuality. One could actively attempt to change into a heterosexual person. Or one could compartmentalize the two identities, keeping them separate in daily life. Each of these approaches, however, "consolidates" heterosexist power and privilege (to borrow a term from Linda Woodhead, 2007). That is, these approaches maintain heterosexuality as the norm in the face of a rapidly changing culture. In Randal Schnoor's study of gay Jews (2006, 49), Saul, a traditional Jew, said,

> If I weren't Jewish, I might be out there fighting for gay rights, but my Jewish identity is far more important to me than my gay identity. And that's something I know right from [the start]. I did not want to allow my same-gender romantic orientation to affect my passion for Judaism and Jewish life and the Jewish people. I never wanted that to impinge on it, to steal time from it and to even affect it.

Schnoor reports that other respondents adopted an ultrareligious life to "purge" themselves of their homosexuality.

To integrate their religious and sexual identities, LGBT people often reinterpret the Bible verses and religious traditions that have been used to condemn gay people (Rodriguez and Ouellette 2000, Schnoor 2006, Thumma 1991, Wilcox 2002 and 2003,

Yip 1997). Historical and cultural analyses reframe the texts. So, for example, Paul's injunctions against same-sex activity are reinterpreted to refer to man–boy sexual contact, which was common in parts of the ancient world, or to the practice of temple prostitution. New meanings emerge from an examination of different translations of texts. And as we have already observed, the reality of living with an LGBT *identity* did not exist in the ancient world. Men and women who engaged in homosexual behavior had no language to describe this behavior as some kind of unique sexual identity. Sex was sex. People's sexual partners, when they had sex, and whether their behavior was okay or taboo depended on whether they were men or women, elites or peasants, free people or slaves. Each society in human history has had its own unique cultural norms for defining human sexuality. Consequently, gay rights advocates within religious groups argue that Biblical texts, like the ones we have cited, cannot be used to condemn contemporary sexual identities and behavior. Likewise, it would be wrong to say that an individual from the past, like the Greek philosopher Plato, was gay just because he engaged in sex with male students. Our cultural norms and the meaning of sex and sexual identities are just too different to be applied to people from earlier eras.

Such reinterpretation is nearly universal among religious LGBT individuals. It mirrors Woodhead's (2007) tactical approach by ignoring or challenging the "sanctified" sexual order that is posited by official church teaching. Research shows that LGBT believers are more likely to alter their religious beliefs than their sexual identity in order to resolve the tension between the two. Mahaffy (1996, 397) notes that more than half of the lesbians in her study adjusted their religious views by "reading about other gay Christians' experiences, meeting other gay Christians, participating in therapy, recognizing that spirituality and religion are separate entities, and disregarding the portions of Scripture that are condemning while affirming beliefs and traditions that embrace homosexuals." Andrew Yip (1997), in his study of Roman Catholics, shows that although Roman Catholicism continues to teach that homosexual behavior is a disorder and is morally wrong, gay and lesbian Catholics in Britain reject their church's label of deviance. They feel that their sexual and religious identities are compatible despite Church teaching. More important, many gays and lesbians in his study were active Catholics who remained committed to their Catholic identity. Similar patterns are reported among LGBT Seventh Day Adventists, Evangelicals, and Jews (Drumm 2005, Schnoor 2006, Thumma 1991).

LGBT people also negotiate their religious and sexual selves through what Woodhead calls "questing": the acceptance of the dominant (hetero)sexual order while simultaneously seeking an individual or group position within it that confers well-being (Woodhead 2007, 559). LGBT people who reject traditional organized religion have embraced New Age spirituality, neopagan traditions, and other forms of alternative spiritualities. Many lesbians have been attracted to the goddess-centered spirituality of Wicca and to other forms of neopagan religion. These traditions emphasize gender equality and balance as central themes (Neitz 2005). The use of magic and ritual to access spiritual power and social empowerment attract some LGBT individuals to a spiritual quest. Many LGBT Buddhists also engage in questing: Meditation and "practicing mindfulness and compassion in daily life . . . helps to stop the suffering of ourselves and of all beings" (Cadge 2005, 144).

In a more conventional form of questing, Peter Savastano (2005) describes how gay Italian Catholic men in Newark, New Jersey, become devotees of Saint Gerard Maiella, a popular Saint among Southern Italian immigrants to the United States. Saint Gerard is the official patron saint of mothers, infertility, and childbirth, but gay followers recraft him as the patron of

> fecundity—the fecundity of romantic and sexual relationships with all of the emotional, spiritual, and physical fulfillment such relationships can bring— and with a new and creative configuration of family that extends beyond traditional patriarchal family structure. (Savastano 2005, 184)

Gay devotees tap into the spiritual energy of Saint Gerard by participating in processions, prayers, novenas to the Saint, and an annual *fiesta* in Newark's Little Italy. In all these examples, the negotiation of religious and sexual identities takes place outside the confines of tradition religion.

Finally, some LGBT individuals respond counterculturally by constructing new religious organizations and traditions that oppose heterosexist structures in religion and the broader society and that provide alternatives to them. The Universal Fellowship of Metropolitan Community Churches, an international denomination created by and for the LGBT community, is a case in point. Its goal is to create a new inclusive community that supports all people regardless of their gender or sexual identity. MCC is a space where LGBT people are free to build integrated identities that can move beyond church walls to be a model for the rest of society. MCC also plays an active political role in organizing various forms of social action and is a leader within the LGBT movement. MCC states, "Working to talk less and do more, we are committed to resisting the structures that oppress people and standing with to those who suffer under the weight of oppressive systems, being guided always by our commitment to Global Human Rights" (United Federation of Metropolitan Community Churches 2005). Religious beliefs and practices become the basis for this organization's political work to challenge heterosexism in all aspects of society.

CHALLENGING AND TRANSFORMING RELIGIOUS IDEAS ABOUT GENDER AND SEXUALITY

Gender, sexual identity, and religious identity often conflict with one another. These conflicts occur at the institutional level but also within individuals. And religion matters here. It is the main source of opposition to full equality for women and the acceptance of alternative sexualities, and it plays a vital role in determining the treatment of gays and lesbians as well as women in society.

As you have seen, people actively engage religion to construct religious and gender identities that make sense to them and meet their needs. We expect that American women will continue to reject some forms of organized religion and embrace others as they negotiate changing gender roles. And in parts of the world where religion relegates women to subordinate positions, women will continue to draw on religion to cope with these realities as well as to fight to change them.

The integration of gays and lesbians into mainstream American religion (or the failure to integrate them) has important implications for all Americans. Religion has historically been used to justify intolerance toward poor people, racial minorities, and women and to deny them access to resources in religious groups and broader society. Today religion is used to deny gays and lesbians full inclusion in society. In some parts of the world, gays and lesbians are imprisoned and killed by governments that base their civil law on Biblical and Qu'ranic injunctions against homosexual activity. Controversies about sexuality and gender issues in religion extend beyond the academic or theological realms. They are political: Religious movements around the world help to maintain patriarchy and heterosexism and also mount challenges to them.

SUGGESTED READING

Bagley, Kate and Kathleen McIntosh (eds.). 2007. *Women's Studies in Religion: A Multicultural Reader.* Upper Saddle River, NJ: Prentice Hall Publishers.

Beaman, Lori. 1999. *Shared Beliefs, Different Lives: Women's Identities in Evangelical Context.* St. Louis: Chalice Press.

Boswell, John. 1980. *Christianity, Social Tolerance, and Homosexuality.* Chicago: University of Chicago Press.

Boswell, John. 1994. *Same-Sex Unions in Premodern Europe.* New York: Villard.

Brown Zikmund, Barbara Adair, T. Lummis, and Patricia M. Y. Chang. 1998. *Clergy Women: An Uphill Calling.* Louisville: Westminster John Knox Press.

Fetner, Tina. 2008. *How the Religious Right Shaped Lesbian and Gay Activism.* Minneapolis: University of Minnesota Press.

Hartman, Keith. 1996. *Congregations in Conflict: The Battle over Homosexuality.* New Brunswick, NJ: Rutgers University Press.

Nesbitt, Paula D. 1997. *Feminization of the Clergy: Organizational and Occupational Perspectives.* New York: Oxford University Press.

Sered, Susan Starr. 1994. *Priestess, Mother, Sacred Sister. Religions Dominated by Women.* New York: Oxford University Press.

Thumma, Scott and Edward R. Gray. 2005. *Gay Religion.* New York: Altamira Press.

Wilcox, Melissa M. 2003. *Coming Out in Christianity: Religion, Identity, and Community.* Bloomington, IN: Indiana University Press.

Woodhead, Linda. 2007. Gender Differences in Religious Practice and Significance. In *The Sage Handbook of the Sociology of Religion,* edited by James Beckford and N. J. Demerath, III, 550–570. Los Angeles: Sage.

10

The (Not So Great) Color Wall of the United States

Race and Religion in Contemporary Times

1. How much racial separation is there in American religion?
2. Why does racial separation in religion exist?
3. Does racial separation in religious life matter, and if so, how?
4. What do we know about multiracial congregations?
5. How can they help us understand religion and race?

A few years ago, Bishop Fred Caldwell, pastor of the Greenwood Acres Full Gospel Baptist Church in Shreveport, Louisiana, a large African-American congregation, offered a unique proposal. He offered to *pay* non-Blacks to attend his church. So adamant was he that his church should not be segregated that Bishop Caldwell announced that for at least one month he would pay non-Blacks $5 per hour to attend the multiple-hour Sunday morning service and $10 an hour to attend the church's Thursday night service. And he would pay this money out of his own pocket. Bishop Caldwell told the Associated Press, "This idea is born of God. God wants a rainbow in his church." He said that the inspiration came to him during a sermon. "Our churches are too segregated, and the Lord never intended for that to happen," Caldwell told *USA Today*. "It's time for something radical. . . . I just want the kingdom of God to look like it's supposed to" (Boston 2003, Maxwell 2003).

Pay people to attend worship services? When we asked people what they thought of Bishop Caldwell's offer, we certainly got responses! To many people, paying people to worship was outrageous. Others thought the idea was brilliant and a good way to draw attention to racial segregation in houses of worship across the nation. Still others thought that the Bishop should not focus on the race of the people who attended his church, but merely minister to whoever attended. They found his "religious affirmative action" deeply troubling. Discussion spread beyond the Bishop's simple offer to whether the racial makeup of congregations matters. Does it? And are religious places of worship really racially segregated? Let's look at this in more depth.

HOW SEGREGATED ARE RELIGIOUS CONGREGATIONS?

For a long time, when people studied race relations and inequality, they did not consider religion. But since well over 100 million Americans attend religious services each week, and since 90% of Americans say they have a religious faith and believe in a higher being, it seems like we ought to consider the role of religion in race relations.

Although many people have noted that our society is most segregated when people meet to worship, when we first tried to find out exactly how segregated it is, the only answer we heard was "very." So my colleagues and I (Emerson) set out to find a more precise answer.

To do so, we decided to study segregation in two ways. First, we defined homogenous congregations as ones in which 80% or more of the congregation is of the same race and mixed-race congregations as those in which no one racial group makes up 80% or more of the congregation. We used this cut-off of 80% because research that was done with other organizations—such as businesses—found that until a group composes 20% or more of an organization, it lacks the critical mass to make any significant changes in the organization (Kanter 1977, Pettigrew and Martin 1987).

Armed with these definitions, we used data from a national random sample of congregations. We found that *over 90%* of congregations are racially homogenous. You have to look hard to find a racially mixed congregation in the United States. (See Figure 10.1.)

But where you look is important. As Figure 10.2 shows, the faith tradition matters. Protestants are the least likely to have racially mixed congregations—just over 5%. Catholic congregations are nearly three times more likely to be racially mixed than are Protestant congregations. Because of the small size, we had to combine all the congregations of all other religious traditions—such as Buddhist temples, Muslim mosques, and Jewish synagogues—into one category. When we do that, we find that over a quarter of

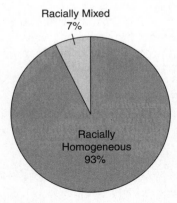

FIGURE 10.1 Racial composition of U.S. congregations.
Source: National Congregations Study.

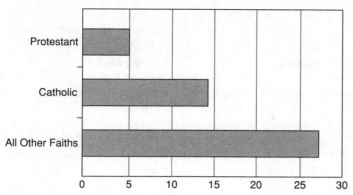

FIGURE 10.2   Percentage of congregations that are racially mixed, by faith tradition.
Source: National Congregations Survey.

them are racially mixed. Why this variation? We found that the larger the religious tradition—that is, the larger the number of people who are involved in that faith and the number of congregations they have to choose from—the more segregated it is. To put it most bluntly, the more choices people have of places to worship, the more they choose to be with people who are racially similar to themselves.

We have a more sophisticated way to study congregational segregation. Instead of just studying whether a congregation is racially mixed, we can examine how diverse congregations are by asking *What is the probability that any two randomly selected people in the congregation will be of different races?* In other words, if you were to walk into a congregation, write the name of each person in attendance on a little slip of paper, put those slips of paper into your hat, mix them up, and then, with your eyes closed, draw out two people's names, how often will they be people of different racial groups (according to social definitions of race)? Fifty percent of the time, perhaps, or maybe 30 percent of the time?

Rather than using a hat and slips of paper, we used a statistical formula and a computer. We found that that the average (median) diversity of a congregation in the United States is *only .02.* That means that the probability that any two randomly selected people in a congregation will be of different races is only 2%.

To put that number is context, we did the same calculations for the nation's neighborhoods and schools, both of which are themselves highly segregated. We found that the probability that two randomly selected people from a U.S. neighborhood would be of different races was .20 (20%). In U.S. schools, the probability is .40 (40%). Thus, religious congregations are *10 times less diverse* than the neighborhoods in which they reside and *20 times less diverse* than the nation's public schools. When Martin Luther King, Jr. said that religious congregations are the most segregated institutions in the United States, he wasn't kidding. Forget the color line. When it comes to religion in the United States, we have a color wall. Just as China has its Great Wall, so does the United States (Emerson 2006).

SO WHAT IF RELIGIOUS CONGREGATIONS ARE SEGREGATED?

Most of us know intuitively that houses of worship are segregated. We now know just how segregated. But the next logical question is, "So what?" Does it make any difference for race relations and inequality? It does, dramatically so.

Religion has a great deal of potential for mitigating racial division and inequality. Most religions teach people to love and respect one another and to support the equality of all people. They usually teach that racial prejudice and discrimination are wrong. They often proclaim the need to embrace all people. They speak of the need for fairness and justice. They often teach that selfishness and self-serving behaviors are counter to the will of the divine. In the United States, religious faith motivated the fight against slavery. It played an essential role in the Civil Rights movement. It directs people to value openness and diversity. It motivates believers to take action to reduce racial separation and injustice, for example, by voting in ways that will overcome racial inequality, by volunteering for groups that work against racial hate and discrimination, by forming organizations that are intent on reducing inequality and strengthening justice, or by donating money to such organizations.

Stories about the positive actions of religious people and organizations to combat racial division and inequality abound. But despite all those efforts, congregations themselves remain segregated. That segregation creates a powerful countervailing influence that limits, and sometimes even undoes, much of the good work we have just described.

Keep in mind that there is a difference between macro and micro effects. In a way, religion plays a contradictory role by strengthening microlevel ties among people but weakening macrolevel ties. Shared religious belief and practice strengthens microlevel bonds among individuals in the group and reduces diversity within groups. But while religion strengthens the group internally, it simultaneously heightens the group's isolation from other groups. It creates a social distance between members of the religious group and outsiders. This in turn reduces opportunities for members of a given religious group to form macrolevel bonds with outside individuals or groups. Forming those macro bonds is essential if we are to racially integrate society as whole. Though many religious groups vocally support racial integration and equality, they do not *practice* it.

Why does this matter? The racial segregation of religious groups inhibits movement between groups. It also increases the importance of group boundaries and social differences. When congregations are racially segregated, there is less opportunity for intergroup mobility (through intermarriage, for example) and more importance is placed on racial boundaries, separate racial identities, and other differences between groups. So, though many in the religious community call for and work toward an end to racial division, the very organization of religion into segregated congregations undercuts their efforts.

Racial segregation of religious groups affects how we see ourselves and others. The separate groups that are produced by the segregation of congregations end up representing categories as each group seeks to define its own identity and finds that it defines itself not only by religious and other views, by also, perhaps without direct intention, by race. According to scholars David Hamilton and Tina Trolier (1986, 188), categorization has important implications:

> The social categories we develop are more than convenient groupings of individuals that simplify the actual diversities among the people we observe and encounter. They are also categories that can bias the way we process information, organize and store it in memory, and make judgments about members of those social categories.

We all consistently engage in social comparison (Am I smart? Who is good looking? Who has money?), and research links this categorization process to at least seven biases

(Hewstone, Jaspers, and Lalljee 1992; Hogg and Abrams 1988; Howard and Rothbart 1980; Linville, Salovey, and Fischer 1986; Tajfel 1978; Taylor 1981; Wilder 1981):

1. Our brains exaggerate the similarities of in-group members to one another and their differences from out-group members. We see ourselves as more like other group members than may be true and very much unlike those who are outside our group.

2. Because people recognize the out-group by its perceived differences, out-group members are identified by those differences, overly homogenizing them. That is, we often overlook the diversity that exists outside our own group, instead assuming that all of "them" are alike.

3. Even when they perform exactly the same actions, in-group members are evaluated more positively and out-group members are evaluated more negatively. For example, if members of both groups build houses that look exactly the same, we tend to evaluate the house built by our in-group member as superior to the one built by the out-group member. In-group favoritism causes us to see the members of our group as better organized, more skilled, more cooperative, and simply more gifted at all tasks.

4. We attribute positive behavior of in-group members to internal traits such as intelligence and excuse negative behavior as a result of external causes such as a poor home life. We do exactly the opposite for out-group members, attributing positive behavior to effects outside the person's control and blaming negative behavior on personal characteristics.

5. Cognitive psychologists find that we have better memories for negative out-group behaviors than for negative in-group behaviors. For instance, we tend to remember when someone belonging to an out-group sings badly, but we forget when members of our own group do so.

6. Because our brains tend to overly homogenize out-groups, a negative behavior by an out-group member is likely to be perceived as a characteristic of the entire out-group. We make the leap from "James of Group X shoplifted" to "Group X shoplifts." We are less likely to do that if James is a member of our own group.

7. Once people have preconceived stereotypes of an out-group, they tend to recall only information that confirms their stereotypes and to dismiss contradictory evidence as an exception. We might have a relative, for example, who maintained that African Americans were lazy, shiftless liars, even though one of the closest friends of this relative was African American. The relative's explanation? Her friend was not like other African Americans; she was the exception.

Religion contributes to racial division and inequality because it creates the very condition—racial segregation in an important social setting—that feeds the practice of racial categorization and the errors in perception that follow from it.

Racial segregation of religious groups also affects with whom—and how—we interact by creating another sort of bias, the ethical paradox of group loyalty. The paradox is that even if a group of people is composed of loving, unselfish individuals, the group transmutes individual unselfishness into group selfishness with respect to the outside world.

What does that mean in English? Imagine two groups. Each member is a deeply committed religious person, full of love and concern for others, and each has developed a friendship or two with people of other groups. For historical reasons, one group has more social goods—income, wealth, education, and power—than the other group.

Although they are both composed entirely of unselfish individuals, the two groups will continue to be divided and unequal. How can this be?

This question was explored by Reinhold Niebuhr way back in 1932 in his book, *Moral Man and Immoral Society.* He wrote that direct contact with members of other groups is limited—it's always less than the amount of contact one has with members of one's own group. People thus know the members of their own group and their needs more deeply, fully, and personally than they know the members and needs of the other groups. Therefore, they attend to the needs of their own group first, precisely because they are moral and loving. How can they turn their backs on the needs of their own group in favor of another group? At the individual level, selfishness is usually considered negative, but at the group level, when it results in ranking the needs of in-group members over those of out-group members, it is considered moral and just. Indeed, at the group level, it is not selfishness, but morality, service, sacrifice, and loyalty.

We find evidence of this phenomenon every day. Consider families. Although people are considered to be selfish if they always look out for their own individual needs first, it is considered wrong and immoral for them not to consider the needs of their own families first, ahead of other families. Parents would be considered immoral if they did not put food on the table for their own children first, before caring for outsiders. Only if they had extra money would it be reasonable for them to consider helping other children.

So the members of the over 300,000 congregations in the United States are busy creating their group identities and forming moral persons. Those moral persons, acting ethically, help their own families and the members of their own congregations first, making sure those needs are met before looking elsewhere to see which other people might need help. Because of racial segregation in congregations, this practice means that we largely help people of our own race. Whites help whites, African Americans help African Americans, Asians help Asians, Latinos help Latinos, and so on.

The problem with this pattern is that it maintains the inequality among groups. Members of groups who have the most resources share them with others who belong to their own group. Members of groups who have the least are busy trying to meet the needs of others in their group, which, because the group as a whole has less, are typically bigger needs that members are trying to meet with less. It is a nasty cycle, even though the people involved are doing their best.

We also have another problem, according to Niebuhr. Because the members of a group cannot understand and appreciate the needs of another group as completely and deeply as they do the needs of their own group, it is practically impossible for love, compassion, and persuasion to overcome group divisions and inequalities. For this reason, relations between groups are mainly political rather than ethical or moral. (Wow, reflect on this statement—it's a doozy.) As Niebuhr (1932, *xxii–xxiii*) says, relations between groups "will always be determined by the proportion of power that each group possesses at least as much as by any rational and moral appraisal of the comparative needs and claims of each group."

The facts that we have just considered have important implications for the perpetuation of racial inequality and stratification. The logic is straightforward. (1) In the United States there is racial inequality in access to valued resources (e.g., white Americans have about 10 times the average wealth of Black and Latino Americans). (2) Access to valued resources—such as jobs, prestige, wealth, and power—is gained in significant part through social ties (Hechter 1987). (3) For reasons such as social categorization, comparison, and the paradox of in-group loyalty, people have positive bias for their in-group and negative bias for out-groups. These three facts suggest that—other factors being equal—any social structure or process that both increases the saliency of group boundaries and reduces interracial ties necessarily reproduces racial inequality. Because the organization of religion in the United States heightens the salience of racial boundaries and reduces interracial ties, it necessarily reproduces racial inequality (Emerson and Smith 2000).

CAN WE FIND A SOLUTION?

So is that it? Can religion really only entrench and amplify the racial divisions and inequalities that already exist? That would be a pretty disappointing conclusion. But that is not the final word. Consider for a moment: How could religion change so that it could actually move toward reducing racial division and inequality?

If all the evidence against positive effects of religion is built on the foundation of segregated congregations, what if congregations were not segregated? Could positive changes for racial division and inequality result?

My colleagues and I spent a number of years trying to figure this out. We did so by studying multiracial congregations (the 7% of congregations from Figure 10.1). For comparative purposes, we also studied racially homogenous congregations. We conducted telephone interviews, mail surveys, and face-to-face interviews, and we spent lots of time in congregations across the country. Emerson even spent nearly six years in one congregation as it transformed from an all-white congregation to one that no longer had a majority racial group and that included members from well over 40 nations.

Social Ties

The first difference we noticed between racially mixed and segregated congregations was just how many more friendships across race there were among the people in racially mixed congregations. An African-American woman from Chicago who was a member of a multiracial congregation called Crosstown said,

> I grew up in a predominantly black church and neighborhood. Crosstown has taught me about other races of people. [The diversity at Crosstown] helped me to develop relationships with people outside my race where I felt they were my friend and we share Christ in our life and that they have the same struggles as I do. . . . I've gotten to know other people on that more personal level.

To test more systematically whether these interracial friendships occur in racially mixed congregations, we conducted a national survey that included several questions about the racial composition of people's friends and acquaintances. We classified respondents into three groups: those who were attending racially homogenous congregations, those who were attending racially mixed congregations, and those who were not attending any congregation. One of our questions asked people to think of their circle of friends, the people with whom they like to spend time with whom they keep in regular contact (friends from their congregation, neighborhood, work, childhood, etc.). Were all, most, about half, some, or none of the people in their circle of friends the same race as they were?

What did we find? Of the respondents who were attending racially homogenous congregations, 83% said that most or all of their friends were the same race as they were. Of the respondents who were not attending any congregation, 70% said that most or all of their friends were the same race as they were. Here we see a general pattern: Religion often serves to intensify general patterns in larger society. If society is segregated, religion can intensify that segregation through a variety of ways, but certainly by providing yet another plane of segregation—its congregations.

What about people attending racially mixed congregations? We found a dramatic difference in their replies. Whereas 83% of people from homogenous congregations and 70% of people who did not attend a congregation said that most or all of their friends were the same race as they were, only 36% of people who were attending racially mixed congregation said that most or all of their friends were the same race as them. And we found that those 36% who did say that most of their friends were their own race were relatively recent arrivals to their racially mixed congregations.

This same pattern recurred for every question that we asked about people's relationships with other people. People who were not attending congregations were more likely to be interracially married, to have a best friend of a different race, and to have diverse social networks then are those who attended racially homogenous congregations. But both groups' level of racial diversity in relationships paled greatly compared with that of people in racially mixed congregations.

As mechanisms for punching holes in the color wall, racially mixed congregations seem to be promising. But we shouldn't get ahead of ourselves. For all we know at this point, the folks attending these types of congregations formed their friendships before they joined their mixed congregation. For that matter, perhaps they ended up in such congregations precisely because they had racially diverse friendships in the first place.

So we again set out to find the answer. We went around the country and interviewed about 150 people who were attending racially mixed congregations and, for comparison, about 50 people who were attending racially homogenous congregations. We discovered that people who attend mixed congregations are somewhat more likely to have attended a racially mixed school or lived in a racially mixed neighborhood at one time in their lives. But over 80% of the people in racially mixed congregations said that most of the racial diversity in their friendships came *because of* their involvement in their congregation. Indeed, when we did a fancy statistical analysis called logistic regression, we found that by far the most important factor among people who have racially diverse relationships is whether they attend racially mixed congregations. One Salvadoran immigrant who was living in Los Angeles and attending a racially mixed congregation said that that perhaps 10% of the people she knew before she started attending her church were of different races, but now, "since I have been at this church the majority of my friends are of different races."

This pattern happens for a couple of reasons. First, of course, people make friends with others in their congregation, and if the congregation is racially mixed, the friendships are likely to reflect that diversity. But the effect of these types of congregations goes further. Once they started forming interracial friendships with other members of their congregation, people often met other people in their new friends' networks. For example, Chanel, an African-American woman who attends a racially mixed congregation in the South, met Rosita, a Latina woman who attends the same congregation, through a women's group at the church. They soon became friends. Rosita began to invite Chanel over to her place for birthday parties or other gatherings. Chanel met and got to know an extended network of other Latinas through Rosita. Chanel also invited Rosita to her place for family gatherings, where Rosita met and became friends with an extended network of other African Americans. Their children too became fast friends, and they often got together so that their children could play together. We found that this sort of pattern made people more confident and comfortable getting to know still others of different racial groups. As one man from the Northeast who attends a racially mixed congregation said, "Being in this church has really opened me up to people of all different backgrounds. Now when I meet people of different races at work, I don't just say hello and move on. I am comfortable to get to know them. I've made new friends at work this way."

Attitudes

Families and friends were attending a celebration service as the culmination of a weekend of youth events at a Baptist church in the Deep South. Sixteen-year-old Chase—white and, due to an accident, in a wheelchair for life—was one of the youths in attendance that weekend. He had not attended any congregation prior to this event, but he had been invited to this youth weekend by a white classmate who belonged to the church. That Sunday, moved by what he had experienced over the past few days, Chase shared with the congregation the fact that he had found a purpose in this congregation: He had made friends with youths of many different races who didn't seem to treat him differently just because he was in a wheelchair. Having talked it over with his parents the day before, he announced, through tears, that he had found a home and that he wanted to become a member of the congregation.

Also in attendance that day were his parents and his older brother, Tre. Tre was a long-time devout skinhead. His head was shaved nearly clean, he had swastika tattoos all around his upper arms, he had a skinhead symbol tattooed on his chest, and he had a noose tattooed on the full length of his left thigh. He didn't like nonwhites at all: "They're whiners, they steal jobs that belong to us, they're lazy, steal, and they have the government always givin' 'em stuff." He was particularly upset at this church that he had come to in support of his brother, Chase. The senior pastor was African American, and the associate pastor was Latino. In fact, in his view the entire congregation was a sickening mix of the different races—black, Latino, Asian, and worst of all, whites. What are whites doing here with these people? he thought. He felt ill at the sight. Why hadn't his brother told him what this congregation was like? And now there was his brother, up at the front, saying that he wanted to become part of this God-forsaken place, even enjoying the support of his parents. UNBELIEVABLE! he thought. He felt angry and claustrophobic. He just wanted to get out of the place. But as he described it to us, then something happened to him.

> Seein' the people all come up to hug my brother, seein' his happy face, seein' all these different people singin' together, feelin' the power in that, it was somethin' I ain't never seen or felt before. Not sure how to describe it, just that it felt real, like it was the way things was supposed to be. I felt like some real bad stuff broke inside of me that day. These people weren't all bad people. They were carin' for my brother.

Two weeks later, through tears of his own, Tre joined the church as well and asked the African-American pastor to come with him later that week to get his white supremacy tattoos removed.

Few stories about change in racial attitudes are as dramatic as this one. But researchers have found that there is a pattern of change in the direction of more positive racial attitudes among people who attend these mixed congregations. This change has been found in all racial groups, but especially among whites (Yancey 2001). They are the ones who most often had significant changes in their views, and they are the ones who differ the most from their peers of the same race who are in homogenous congregations. These changes in attitudes seemed to come about due to their newly formed friendships, the lessons they heard in sermons and teachings, and the experience of working with people of different races on common tasks.

These differences between people who attend racially mixed and racially homogenous congregations are found across religious traditions.

Not all multiracial congregations are free of strife, of course. One multiracial mosque in the Midwest had to deal with a serious problem. Members of the congregation included people from nations who thought that you must *always* remove your shoes when you enter the mosque, and people from others nations who thought that you must *never* insult Allah by removing your shoes when you enter the mosque. Pretty easy to see we've got a conflict here. Folks took the shoe issue very seriously, because it was tied to what they saw as the proper way to worship. And because the shoe issue was related to nationality, ethnicity, and race, the problem quickly became destructive. People in one group took such offense at the other group's behavior that the mosque leaders decided to put up a screen to divide the shoe removers from the shoe wearers, even though this also divided people by ethnicity and race. But they did not intend to keep the screen there permanently. After the screen was installed, the imam began to teach that Allah calls all Muslims to be together, regardless of race, ethnicity, and worship approach. He urged them therefore to find a way to unite in their mosque. They would all have to remove their shoes, all wear their shoes, or—the solution he proposed—all accept that whatever other people in the congregation do, they do out of reverence for Allah, not because they are from an inferior ethnicity or culture. Over time, the worshippers came to accept this view, and the screen was eventually removed, even though some people continued to remove their shoes and some continued to wear their shoes. Friendships across cultures formed, and the attitudes that people held about the different groups attending their mosque became more favorable.

Raised Status

This example is related to yet another difference that we have found between mixed congregations and homogenous ones. The congregation that Emerson spent years studying made a commitment to go on mission and service trips to each of the nations from which members of the congregation hailed. The appointed leaders of each trip were the people from that particular country. The senior pastor of the congregation told us that this system worked wonders to broaden the views of his congregants. A Guatemalan cleaning lady who can barely speak English may be easy to marginalize in the U.S. context, but when she was the leader on the trip to Guatemala, she became the person who was fluent in the language, who knew the lay of the land, who had the social connections, who knew what to eat and what to avoid. She came to be seen—this pastor and his congregants told us—in a substantially new light. She was important, she had skills they did not have, and they were dependent on her. As a result of evening discussions while they were on these trips, the congregants came to conclude that social context, not a person's essence, shapes other people's views of that person's worth and skills. Within multiracial congregations, we found, the status of racially different individuals is often raised in the eyes of their fellow worshippers.

As you will recall, segregated congregations contribute to maintaining socioeconomic inequality. But we found that there was a different pattern in many mixed-race congregations. Because of the social ties that existed between people and their more inclusive attitudes toward others of different races, the average educational level, income, and occupational status of people in these congregations—especially for people belonging to traditionally marginalized groups—were higher than those of their counterparts who did not attend such congregations.

Again, we wondered, was this the case before they came to the congregation? We found that a great deal happened in these congregations that elevated the socioeconomic status of people after they joined. They made connections, found childcare, and often received funding that allowed them to get further schooling. People were hired for jobs that, if they had not been members, they might never have known about or have had a chance of obtaining, and they were hired because of their connections to others in the congregation who were well placed in the labor market. Multiracial congregations also seem to help people accrue resources that improve their access to good health care, neighborhoods, schools, and other social goods. Mixed-race congregations, then, seem to actually reduce the racial divide in inequality.

Bridge Organizations and Sixth Americans

Mixed-race congregations are bridge organizations. That is, they gather and facilitate social ties that cross racial boundaries, creating a "natural" setting where people of different racial groups meet and form relationships while they pursue a common purpose. (If you have ever studied contact theory, you'll know that these types of congregations easily meet the conditions that are necessary for forming friendships and reducing prejudice.) The average person in a mixed-race congregation is so different from the average American outside these congregations that Emerson calls them Sixth Americans, a reference to David Hollinger's description of the five melting pots in the United States. People in the United States come from hundreds if not thousands of ethnic backgrounds, but Hollinger (1995) writes that in this country, they are expected to meld into one of five racial melting pots: Indian/Native American, African American/Black, White/Caucasian, Hispanic/Latino/a, or Asian/Asian American.

But although people in mixed-race congregations often appear to belong phenotypically to one of these five melting pots, they seem to operate outside their particular melting pot in most of their social relations. Sixth Americans live in multiple melting pots simultaneously. To be sure, they are minorities among Americans, living in a world of primary relationships and associations that are racially diverse. Like other Americans, the Sixth American may work in a racially diverse setting, see racially different others at the grocery store, or perhaps have a friend of a different race. But unlike other Americans, the Sixth American's "world of racial diversity" does not stop here. It is not a racially homogenous world with some diversity sprinkled in, but a racially diverse world with some homogeneity sprinkled in. In his book *People of the Dream,* Emerson argues that these Sixth Americans are a different kind of American altogether. And the congregations where they gather to worship, serve, and support one another—despite the failures we described in Chapter 6—may be harbingers of the future (Emerson 2006).

BUT CAN WE CREATE AND MAINTAIN MULTIRACIAL CONGREGATIONS?

Religion in the United States is divided by a vast, thick, massive color wall. That color wall has had, and continues to have, severe implications for racial division and racial stratification. We have ignored the impact of religion on race for too long. By studying the small percentage of congregations that are racially mixed, we have found that, although there are some risks—such as cultural misunderstandings and the potential for greater racial strife due to conflicts—the overall trend is a reduction in racial division and inequality. These findings further highlight the deleterious effects that segregated congregations have on American race relations.

But it is easy to *say* that we ought to have more multiracial congregations. The fact is, there are plenty of barriers to creating them even if we all wanted to do so. One problem is the racial homogeneity of some areas in the United States. One of the authors lives and teaches in Bozeman, Montana, where over 90% of the residents are white. It is difficult in such a place to have racially mixed congregations. But most people in the United States live in more racially diverse communities. About 85% of Americans live in metropolitan areas, most of which are racially diverse, and they are becoming more diverse over time.

Another barrier to change is that it is difficult to alter congregations that already have a reputation as a single-race congregation. Remember Bishop Caldwell's offer to pay non-Blacks to attend services at his nearly all-Black congregation? With lightning speed, his offer became known not only all around Shreveport, but around the whole world. Newspapers, radio shows, television shows, and websites reported the story in different nations. Many, many people knew about his offer. What do you think happened? Here is what Bishop Caldwell told a newspaper reporter a year after his initial offer, as reported in an online blog (Rhoades 2004):

> "A year later, things are right back where they were. They [non-Blacks] came, they saw, they left and they didn't return."
>
> "And they came from as far away as London and Dallas–Fort Worth," he reminisced. "We had a great time. A lot of white people came, and they went back to their white holes. Because I'll say it again: 11 A.M. on Sunday morning is the most segregated hour in America."
>
> Bishop Caldwell withstood criticism from some, including a few members of his own church, that his cash offer was just a publicity stunt. The story made headlines around the world, and he's still getting calls about it.
>
> "It was never about the $5. It was about the need to come together," he said. "But after Aug. 31, it went back to where it was."
>
> "And God," he said, ratcheting up his voice like he does in the pulpit, "is angry with us."

Asked if differing styles of worship were keeping the churches segregated Bishop Caldwell said folks who use that excuse are "hypocrites."

"First of all, Madonna doesn't care who's in her audience, [and] neither does Usher," he said, referring to two pop culture icons whose music has crossover appeal. "We use 'style' as an excuse when it comes to what people don't want to do."

Changing the organization of American religion is not easy; apparently, even paying people doesn't work. But several scholars are now studying how multiracial congregations form, how to minimize costs and accentuate positives in the process of creating a multiracial congregation, and how people come to be in these congregations. If you are interested, we invite you to study books and other articles on this topic. As of this writing, the work of several scholars [see Suggested Readings at the end of this chapter for some specific books] are cutting-edge texts. But much of this work is limited to the Christian context, so future work must explore multiracial principles for other faiths and to discover the more general principles that are true across religions. Humans create their own social structures, so change is possible when humans decide that their current system will no longer do. Will enough people decide to make a change and put enough holes in the color wall to eventually collapse it? Time will tell.

SUGGESTED READING

Becker, Penny Edgell. 1998. "Making Inclusive Communities: Congregations and the 'Problem' of Race." *Social Problems* 45 (4): 451–72.

Christerson, Brad, Korie L. Edwards, and Michael O. Emerson. 2005. *Against All Odds: The Struggle for Racial Integration in Religious Organizations.* New York: New York University Press.

Edwards, Korie L. 2008. *The Elusive Dream: The Power of Race in Interracial Churches.* New York: Oxford University Press.

Emerson, Michael O. 2006. *People of the Dream: Multiracial Congregations in the United States.* Princeton, NJ: Princeton University Press.

Emerson, Michael O., and Christian Smith. 2000. *Divided by Faith: Evangelical Religion and the Problem of Race in America.* New York: Oxford University Press.

Garces-Foley, Kathleen. 2007. *Crossing the Ethnic Divide: The Multiethnic Church on a Mission.* New York: Oxford University Press.

Marti, Gerardo. 2005. *A Mosaic of Believers: Diversity and Innovation in a Multiethnic Church.* Bloomington: Indiana University Press.

Peart, Norman A. 2000. *Separate No More: Understanding and Developing Racial Reconciliation in Your Church.* Grand Rapids, MI: Baker Books.

U.S. Catholic Bishops. 2000. *Welcoming the Stranger Among Us: Unity in Diversity.* Washington, D.C.: United States Catholic Conference, Inc.

Yancey, George. 2003. *One Body, One Spirit: Principles of Successful Multiracial Churches.* Downers Grove, IL: InterVarsity Press.

11

Who Brought the Enchiladas to My Bar Mitzvah?

Immigration and Religious Change

1. What large-scale changes to U.S. religion have resulted from immigration?
2. What are the lessons of immigrants and religious change?
3. How does becoming religious help immigrants to become American?
4. Why do immigrants often become more religious after arriving in their new land?
5. How is religion transformed when it is transplanted from one place to another?

igration is a frequent behavior among humans. Except when political laws or other obstacles limit or prevent the crossing of international boundaries, groups of people commonly travel and come into contact with other groups that are new to them. The United States is often known as a nation of immigrants; about 99% of its citizens came from or have ancestors from other nations. Immigration law has long shaped who may legally enter and stay in the United States.

Back in 1965, U.S. immigration law fundamentally changed. And those changes have dramatically altered the United States. Before 1965, immigration laws were racially biased to freeze the racial and ethnic diversity of the United States at 1890 levels. The goal was to make sure that diversity in the United States did not increase.

In the wake of the Civil Rights movement, immigration laws were changed to overcome the biased immigration system. The modifications that occurred in 1965 and subsequently have been designed to allow into the country immigrants who (1) increase economic productivity (usually meaning highly educated, highly skilled, or well-to-do people), (2) need refuge from nations that do not support the United States, or (3) are joining members of their immediate family who already reside in the country. No nation may issue more than 20,000 visas per year, but visas are no longer distributed in accordance with quotas that are based on nationality and race. Because family reunification is deemed so important, most visas that are granted to reunite immediate family members do not count against the 20,000 upper limit.

How have these changes in immigration law affected religion in the United States? Whereas the vast majority of all voluntary immigrants prior to 1965 were from Europe and Canada (and nearly all were Christian or Jewish), the vast majority of immigrants since 1965 have been from Latin America, the Caribbean, Asia, Africa, and the Middle East. In 1900, the top countries of origin for immigrants were Italy, Russia, Hungary, Austria, and the United Kingdom—all European. From 2000 to 2010, the top countries of origin for immigrants were Mexico, India, China, Guatemala, Cuba, and Korea. Clearly, none of these countries is European. About 1 million immigrants per year legally enter the United States. They and their children are diversifying the racial and ethnic composition of the nation and now account for most of its population growth.

OVERARCHING CHANGES FOR RELIGION

This change in ethnic composition has led to important changes in the religious land-scape in the United States and, ultimately, the rest of the world. Currently, about two out of every three immigrants to the United States is Christian. But this fact masks important changes in the composition of the nation's religious people. First, the 65% of immigrants who are Christian are significantly fewer than the 82% of native-born Americans who claim a Christian identity. Within Christianity, immigrants—mainly Latino—are twice as likely to be Catholic as are native-born Americans (42%, compared with 22%). In fact, Latino immigrants are estimated to account for 40% of all Catholics in the United States and are responsible for about 90% of the nation's growth in Catholics (Levitt 2007, 14 and 205). Clearly, the ethnic composition of American Catholicism is changing dramatically.

What is more, most immigrant Christians who are not Latino end up in Evangelical Protestant churches. Usually these are ethnic-specific churches, but as we will see later, this pattern typically lasts only through the first generation, and later generations expand the ethnic composition of those with whom they worship. Tens of thousands of ethnic congregations exist across the United States. These multiracial, multiethnic congregations filled with immigrants appear to be increasing, and seminaries and divinity schools increasingly are populated by immigrants or their children. As with Catholicism, the immigrant effect on Evangelical Protestantism (and some mainline Protestant denominations) is profound and growing, so much so that the sociologist R. Stephen Warner (1998, 4) has said that the United States is witnessing a "de-Europeanization" of American Christianity.

Although the majority of immigrants to the United States are or become Christian, immigrants still are *four times* as likely as native-born Americans to claim a non-Judeo-Christian religion. As Helen Rose Ebaugh and Janet Saltman Chafetz (2000) and others have noted, these immigrants and their children worship in temples, mosques, gudwaras, meditation centers, and storefronts; they have fiestas and religious carnivals; and they meet in homes. Immigrants have been the driving force behind a fourfold increase in the number of adherents to non-Judeo-Christian religions in the United States since 1970. Although non-Judeo-Christian religions (such as Islam, Jainism, Buddhism, Hinduism, Sikhism, and Zoroastrianism) still account for only about 3% of Americans, this represents a substantial increase since 1970, when virtually no Americans belonged to these religions.

By sheer numbers, then, immigrants are simultaneously transforming American Christianity and increasing religious pluralism (Eck 2001, Warner 1998).

On the surface, Judaism has been changed the least by the arrival of the tens of millions of new immigrants, because few of them enter as Jews or convert to Judaism. But Judaism, too, confronts the influence of new immigrants even if they are not Jewish. Both Jews and new immigrants are heavily concentrated in the nation's large urban areas, so they frequently come into contact with one another.

RELIGIOUS CHANGES FOR IMMIGRANTS

The Story of Karen Chai Kim

Let's move beyond these large macrochanges to explore why religion is of vital importance to so many immigrants to the United States, how their religion changes when they enter the country, and how they change their religions after arrriving. Carolyn Chen (2008, 201) ends her supurb book about Taiwanese immigrants with the following words: "[I]mmigrants use religion to address problems of meaning, morality, identity, and belonging in the U.S. because Americans have given religion this sacred power. By becoming religious, immigrants become Americans." What does she mean?

We can understand what Chen means if we consider the story of Karen Chai Kim. Dr. Kim has a Ph.D. in sociology and has authored important works on immigration and religion (e.g., Chai 1998, 2001a, 2001b). She is also an immigrant herself. She has been kind enough to provide her religious autobiography for inclusion in this book. Her story, as well as that of her family, illustrates most of the lessons of immigration and religious change:

> I was born in Seoul, Korea, and moved to the United States with my family at the age of four. In Korea, religion had not played a major role in my parents' lives. My mother, Chae Hyun Chai, grew up with no religious education and has no memory of ever attending a religious service as a child. My father, Soo Hyuk Chai, only recalls attending Christian church services with his sister and her friend as a young elementary-school student in order to receive the "free notebooks, pencils, and candy" given out during Christmastime.
>
> My paternal grandmother, Young Sook Hong, actually converted to Christianity as a high-school student in Korea, even serving as a Sunday school teacher at her church. When she married Re Suk Chai, however, she adopted Buddhism, the religion of her husband's family. Her parents-in-law were very prominent members of their Buddhist temple, and, as their young daughter-in-law, Young Sook became very active herself. Despite her previous commitment to Christianity, Young Sook remained a devout Buddhist until the day that she died. She maintained an altar in her home and practiced daily devotions several times a day. It was well known among family members and friends that they were not to disturb or call upon Young Sook during certain hours of the day when she was saying her prayers. Both she and her husband Re Suk had Buddhist funerals in Korea. (For my family tree, see Figure 11.1.)
>
> My maternal grandmother, Sung Nam Chang, came from a prominent Buddhist family that helped establish several temples. According to family lore, Sung Nam's wealthy parents had been so delighted with her birth that they even established a temple in her honor, and they prayed that she would

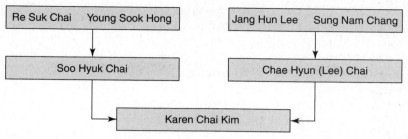

FIGURE 11.1 Karen Chai Kim's family tree.

live to be 100 years old. She has, in fact, reached the age of 100 and continues to reside in Seoul at this time. When Sung Nam married Jang Hun Lee, however, she also adopted the religious practices of her husband's family. The Lee family was not particularly religious, but they ascribed to Confucianism. Sung Nam did occasionally still visit Buddhist temples, especially after the passing of her husband, but she has never been a devout follower of any religion.

It was only after immigration to the United States that my parents began to practice religion regularly and with commitment. On one hand, it is not surprising that they eventually found themselves involved in a Korean ethnic Christian church, as the church has long been the most important social institution for Korean Americans. On the other hand, the experience of immigration is extremely difficult, and it is often during times of difficulty that people seek comfort and spiritual meaning.

As stated earlier, my mother, Chae Hyun Chai, grew up in a Confucian household and attended no religious services as a child. She was later introduced to Protestant Christianity when she attended Ewha Women's University, which had been founded by an American Methodist missionary. She remembers attending the mandatory courses on Christianity three times a week as a college student, but my mother had no interest in religion at the time. Similarly, my father, Soo Hyuk Chai, did not grow up attending regular religious services. Part of the reason that they were not particularly religious growing up was that religion was seen as ascribed by family association, and their family was considered Buddhist. The Buddhism that they subscribed to was not congregational (it was not expected that one regularly attend temple). It was just assumed that one was a Buddhist without having to attend regular services.

As a young child in New Jersey, I lived in a predominantly white neighborhood. Until my family moved to another neighborhood within the same town, my brother and I were two of the only three Asian children in school. It was quite a disorienting experience at first for my family and me, to not always be around Koreans.

After my family had been in the United States for about two years, my mother took my brother and me to a Korean Protestant church. We had been invited by a Korean acquaintance who attended the same college in Korea as my mother. A few weeks later, my father also attended the church with us. There we found many Koreans from back home. We made many new friends. This was a place for us.

But both of my parents were hesitant to convert to Christianity, because they had been warned by family members in Korea not to give into the temptation to convert to Christianity, as many Korean immigrants before them had done. My father even carried around a small piece of paper that had been given to him by a Buddhist monk in Korea prior to immigration. The paper was a talisman meant to protect the family. Converting to another religion was seen as dishonoring one's ancestors and a bad omen for the entire family lineage.

Because of his family heritage, my father seriously wrestled with converting to Christianity. He called his mother, Young Sook, in Korea and asked what she thought about his possible conversion to Christianity. She replied, "Whatever religion you practice, do it with all your strength, and become the salt and light of the earth." She still remembered Bible verses from her days as a Christian girl. About a year later, my family and I were baptized, and my father burned the Buddhist talisman that he had carried around so faithfully for protection.

I have not always been "Karen." My birth name is Jung Won, and that is what I was called all my life, that is until we started attending Korean church. At Korean church, my parents noticed right away that all of the children in the Korean church used American names. Not wanting their children to feel left out, my parents immediately went about finding American names for my brother and me. My parents chose names that they thought sounded very American. My brother went from being Sung Do to "Walter," and I from Jung Won to "Karen." Perhaps ironically, for quite a while we only used our American names in Korean church. So, during the week, my brother and I were Sung Do and Jung Won, but at Korean church we were Walter and Karen.

My parents continued their involvement at the church and eventually received lay leader positions. After the church experienced a schism (a common occurrence in immigrant churches), my family switched to a smaller Korean church that was very close to our home. By this time, I was bored with church and only reluctantly attended. There was little youth programming, so I kept myself busy by teaching Sunday school.

When it came time for me to go away to Wellesley College in the Boston area, my parents were anxious about sending their daughter so far away from home. They remembered hosting a pastor from Boston who was once a guest speaker at our church. When we got to Boston, my parents met that pastor for dinner and requested that he look after me. They then dragged me to a church Bible study on my second day of college orientation. So, in the mind of my parents, the Korean church would serve as a connection for me to the local Korean community, and its members would be there for me should I need help. Although I was a reluctant member at first, it was at this church that I gained a greater understanding of Christianity. I attended this church for over a decade, and my involvement even guided my career.

I eventually decided to pursue a Ph.D. in sociology at Harvard University. Although I entered the program with the intention of studying Japanese society, I stumbled upon an announcement of a fellowship program for sociologists who wanted to conduct research on ethnic religious organizations. I applied for the fellowship and was selected for the New Ethnic Immigrant

Congregations Project, headed by R. Stephen Warner. Through this fellowship, I began my study of the Korean Protestant Church in the United States.

While my family was very involved as Korean-American Protestants, other relatives either maintained their Buddhist traditions or practiced Catholicism. As I pondered the religious differences within my own extended family, I wondered how my life might have been different had my family chosen to join a Buddhist temple or a Catholic church. When it came time for my dissertation research, I decided to expand my studies to examine Korean-American Buddhists and Catholics. For over a year, I regularly attended services at a Boston-area Korean Catholic church and a Korean Buddhist temple, as well as my Korean Protestant church.

While I was growing up in the United States, the only time I saw a large group of Koreans was at church. The only context in which I saw Korean culture being celebrated was at church. Therefore, I realized that what I had come to consider as Korean culture was, in fact, *Protestant* Korean *American* culture. While I was doing my dissertation research, I saw that the celebrations of Korean holidays (such as New Year) were actually done quite differently across religions. Buddhists, for example, have no ban on traditional Korean traditions that are rooted in Shamanism. Korean Protestants, on the other hand, developed different ways of respecting elders while avoiding what they viewed as "idolatry" or "pagan" rituals. I even had to expand my Korean vocabulary, as I learned Buddhist and Catholic terms I had never heard before.

After I finished my dissertation, I met my husband Stanley Kim through church connections. Although we had never attended the same church or lived in the same city, we both knew the same pastor. Pastor Hoon Kyung Lee had been the pastor of my family's small Korean United Methodist Church in New Jersey. He then went on to become the senior pastor of one of the largest Korean churches in the country, located outside Detroit. Stanley's parents were active members of the church, and Reverend Lee decided to introduce Stanley and me to each other.

After we married, we attended Korean churches in Buffalo, New York, and Austin, Texas, for a number of years. Although we are both fluent in Korean, we are now much more proficient in English and prefer to worship in English. Therefore, we attended the English worship service at our Austin Korean church. However, when problems arose between the English ministry pastor and the senior pastor, the English ministry pastor was fired. This was done without consulting with or informing any of the English ministry lay leaders. The families in the English ministry were dismayed. They appreciated attending a Korean church and enjoyed fellowship with people from similar backgrounds while they maintained ties to the Korean ethnic community. I especially enjoyed being able to attend the same church as my parents (who had retired to Austin) for the first time since high school.

A common issue in Korean ethnic churches is the relationship between the Korean-speaking congregation and the English-speaking congregation. Differences in culture and lifestyle exist, as well in differences in beliefs about how churches should operate. Stanley and I enjoyed the Korean fellowship, but we also realized that the English ministry within a Korean ethnic church would always be treated as a branch of the "Sunday school," and the Korean ministry would always come first. Typically, the English ministry pastors in the Korean church are young—sometimes they are seminarians. We could live with this arrangement in our younger days, but we now had children of our own. How long could we remain in the ethnic church, relegated to the status of Sunday school students, even though we were grown adults?

The English ministry pastor who had been fired decided to start his own church in Austin, which a few families joined. Stanley and I did not feel a particular calling to establish a new church, but those few families wanted to support the pastor, whom they believed had served faithfully and had been wrongfully terminated. They worked hard in the new church for about 10 months, until the pastor realized that the church membership was dwindling and members were becoming burned out, and the church closed.

Stanley and I felt burned by our experience with Korean church in Austin, and we decided to take a break and attend a local church where I knew a few women from a community Bible study. The members are predominantly white, and there is a large Latino ministry. We had intended to "shop around" at different local churches, but our children love the Sunday school and insist on remaining at this church.

So, at the time of this writing, we are currently in limbo, hesitant to return to an ethnic church experience, enjoying more family time and the lack of required activities. On the other hand, we miss the fellowship that we had with other Korean-American families like ourselves, and we wonder if our children would be happier regularly meeting with fellow Korean Americans. As parents, our priorities have changed, and we now are considering what type of church environment might be best for our children's spiritual and social growth. Stay tuned . . .

Karen Chai Kim's story contains many of the lessons of immigration and religious change that have been revealed in thousands of studies. Let's examine an even dozen of the most important lessons!

LESSONS ABOUT IMMIGRATION AND RELIGIOUS CHANGE

Lesson 1: Religion is often more important to immigrants in their new nation than it was in their old nation. Karen Chai Kim noted that her parents were not particularly religious in Korea. They were Buddhist, but this was largely in name only; they were expected to follow Buddhism to honor living relatives and ancestors. Religion was largely taken for granted, rather than being a consciously chosen identity. Dr. Kim's parents gave little thought to it. After they moved to the United States, however, several factors contributed to changing the importance of religion in their lives.

If you spend your whole life in one social environment, you do not perceive your life as one possible life among many, but simply as life. Rights and wrongs, family obligations, and traditions seemingly have always been there. But if you are uprooted from your taken-for-granted world and placed in another—with different rules, languages, foods, laws, worldviews, and ways of doing things—you will be faced with questions that you never before needed to ask: What is right, what is wrong? Who am I, how should I act, what should I think, who are my people?

Immigration can open up new opportunities, but it is also unsettling. Immigrants often become more religious in their new countries than they were in their home countries because they are trying to figure out their place in the new world. Immigration is, in the words of Smith (1978) a "theologizing experience." Immigrants often react to the alienation, confusion, and uncertainty of their new land by seeking the reassurance that religion can bring. Migration and the experience of displacement draws religious questions to the forefront and opens people to change (e.g., see Chen 2008, 187). Religion can answer some of the questions that people have, and it can help them form connections with other people like themselves as they attempt to make sense of their new realities.

Lesson 2: The new religious groups that immigrants join tend to be organized into congregations. Some religions are organized around regular gatherings in congregations, where the faithful gather to worship, socialize, learn more about their religion, volunteer in the community, and so on. Congregations are important in Judaism and Christianity. But many other religions are not organized around congregational gatherings. Hinduism and Buddhism, for instance, are not congregationally based. Karen Chai Kim's parents did not regularly go to Buddhist temple in Korea not only because religion was not central to them, but because Buddhism is simply not congregationally based in Korea. You are not expected to regularly go to temple to be a good Buddhist. What is more, you do not go to temple to socialize, have lunch, or even learn about the Buddhist faith.

But something rather fascinating happens for immigrants who find religion in the United States. No matter what the religion is, the immigrants' religious life becomes congregationally based. In part, this is because U.S. law grants tax-exempt status to religious organizations. Thus, local houses of worship try to look something like congregations. But we also end up with *de facto* congregationalism because of religion's role in the United States. Local congregations serve multiple functions in this country: They are places to meet friends, find a mate, find community, make connections to get a job, and help the needy. Furthermore, they are run on the donations of those who attend, who also end up serving on committees and being appointed to positions to help run the congregations. So regardless of the religion, immigrants often find it advantagous to do as Americans do and to have their houses of worship serve these same functions. As Carolyn Chen noted earlier in the chapter, this is because "Americans have given religion this sacred power." As a result, people in the United States attend houses of worship "more frequently than any other nation at a comparable level of development . . ." (Levitt 2007, 17).

Lesson 3: Immigrants are usually drawn to congregations by invitations from coethnics. Why did Karen Chai Kim and her family start attending a Korean Protestant church when her family was, by tradition, Buddhist? In their case, Karen's mother was invited by a fellow Korean. Why did she accept? According to the literature on these processes, she accepted either because she was repeatedly asked (immigrant Protestants in the United States overwhelming are evangelical, meaning in part that they emphasize proselytizing) or because she was experiencing a sense of alienation in the new land and wanted to take temporary refuge with fellow coethnics. Regardless of which reason was actually the case for Karen Chai Kim's mother, the general lesson for us is that first coethnics draw immigrants to religious congregations, and as we will see, this is especially the case when the religion in question is a majority religion in the United States (Protestant and Roman Catholic forms of Christianity).

Lesson 4: Religious involvement offers nonreligious benefits. Once immigrants begin attending congregations, they find many benefits that keep them there. Dr. Kim's mother found fellow Koreans, Korean children to play with her children, Korean food and Korean culture, and much more. She likely shared the newfound benefits with her husband, who soon agreed to also attend. Research shows that immigrants often end up in such congregations not for religious reasons but for the other benefits they find there. These congregations quickly become the central social institutions for immigrants. Let's listen to their words:

Here's a Vietnamese immigrant who was originally nonreligious but is now Christian:

> When my family came here, everything came through the Catholics . . . even before we came. . . . How could I forget this? They helped us with the documents, they helped us find housing, they found jobs for my mother and father and they filled out the paperwork for us so that I and my two sisters could attend school. . . . At the very least, it was natural that their religion would make sense to me since I had no religion in Vietnam. (Ebaugh and Chafetz 2000, 38)

Here's a Sudanese immigrant, who is Muslim:

> The mosque helped us in the ghorba [the state of being away from home] and helped us get to know other Muslim people. (Abusharaf 1998, 98)

Here's a Korean immigrant who is Christian:

> When I came to Houston, I did not know a single person here. I had only about $200 in my pocket. As soon as I arrived, I went to a Korean church. . . . Soon, they found me a position in a restaurant that was operated by a church member. He allowed me to eat as much as I wanted and to sleep at the restaurant at night. . . . That's how I saved the money to start my . . . business. Later, when I opened my shop, many church members came . . . as customers. (Ebaugh and Chafetz 2000, 75)

Here's an Indian immigrant who is Hindu:

> OHM is like an extended family. It helps to alleviate problems—it helps in crisis management. There are many problems here—job related, domestic. Before OHM I had around 4 or 5 people to turn to, but now I have around 20 families that I can trust. I have several close friends, and we call each other one or two times a week for personal conversation. . . . OHM also helps us in practical matters. We have doctors with different specializations from psychiatrists to cardiologists, engineers, accountants, business people, scientists, and attorneys. So, whatever problem comes up, we have an expert who can help us. (Kurien 1998, 49)

Here's a Nigerian immigrant who is now Christian:

> I always go to the coffee and donuts after Mass to meet with any of the 20 families that are formally registered at St. Catherine's. . . . We try to get job opportunities available for our own group. Currently we have some working at [company X] and each time there are job openings they recommend each other for these positions. (Sullivan 2000, 219)

We can see from these examples that the benefits of involvement in congregations include partaking in fellowship; maintaining ethnic traditions and ties with one's original culture; receiving aid in learning the new culture, educational and economic assistance, and family support; finding a psychological and cultural refuge, as well as a social identity; receiving aid in navigating the immigration and naturalization system; and establishing and maintaining social connections. As this list suggests, the benefits are extensive. We could devote an entire book to what immigrants can gain through religious involvement (and several scholars have done so).

Lesson 5: Religious involvement offers religious benefits. Missing from the list of benefits in the previous lesson are the religious benefits that also accrue to immigrants. What makes a religious congregation different from other organizations is a transcendent locus of meaning (Christerson and Emerson 2003, 179; Kniss and Numrich 2007, 5; Wuthnow 2005, 162). That is, religion offers people ways to understanding the world that go beyond this world. Why do we suffer? What is the meaning of our journey in life? What are we on earth for? All these are questions that religion can answer. Religion provides immigrants with ways to interpret their experiences that go beyond themselves and give their lives direction.

Although it is common for social scientists to focus on what religion provides socially for immigrants, we must not overlook the religious benefits of religion. Carolyn Chen (2008, 186), like many other researchers, gathered data that revealed these benefits in her interviews of immigrants. For example, when she interviewed Taiwanese immigrant Mr. Hou, she asked him, "Was immigrating to the U.S. worth it?" His response was telling: "Life is harder for me here. I would be better off in Taiwan I think. But here I found God." Another interviewee, Mr. Tang, a Buddhist, agrees that he has gained religious benefits from his migration. Life was more full in Taiwan with his friends and family and the abundant social activities. But, he says, he would not have been "awakened" had he not come to the United States.

Lesson 6: Immigrants can become more American if they attend an ethnic congregation. Consider the following title of an article: "Becoming American by Becoming Hindu: Indian Americans Take Their Place at the Multicultural Table" (Kurien 1998). At first glance, the title of this article may puzzle you. How does one become American by becoming Hindu? For that matter, how does one become American by gathering with fellow immigrants in religious congregations? The answer has to do with the aid that fellow members of the congregation give to new members to help them integrate into American society by helping them find jobs and childcare, get access to information, learn English, and so on. Will Herberg (1955) wrote that while immigrants may be expected to eventually abandon their nationality and language, they were not expected to abandon their faith. Indeed, attending religious services is a way for immigrants to become more American and adapt to American society.

Karen Chai Kim was not "Karen" until she and her family began attending a Korean church. As she noted earlier, her birth name was Jung Won, but at the Korean church everyone gave their children American names. To help her fit into the new American context at the Korean church, Jung Won's parents gave her the American name Karen. Although at first she was called Karen only in the Korean church, she eventually adopted the new name as her identity and came to be called Karen by everyone. Ethnic religious congregations, then, actually faciliate the transformation of immigrants to Americans on multiple levels. In fact, Elaine Howard Ecklund (2006) found that American Koreans who were attending a

Korean church were in many ways more "Americanized" and concerned with being traditionally good Americans than were Koreans who attended multiracial congregations.

Lesson 7: Religious involvement helps immigrants process the differences between their internal selves and their outward roles in their new lives. Congregations may experience conflict and change from time to time. Two recurring issues are the role of women in the church and generational struggles.

The American emphasis on the individual and the nuclear family leads most immigrants to question roles that they have taken for granted and to search for their "authentic selves" in the new land. Religious language and conversion experiences "are ways for men and women to work out the contradictions between traditional gender expectations and the realities of their lives in the U.S." (Chen 2008, 145). Women often carve out an identity that is not solely shaped by family roles, and men often assert a true self that is independent of their career status.

Generational issues are particularly common among children of immigrants (e.g., Chai 1998, 2001a). Karen Chai Kim alludes to her struggles with Korean church over the course of her life. Her sense that she is "less Korean" than are immigrants who came to this country as adults has led to much frustration and conflict in her life; we often see this pattern repeated among the American-born children of immigrants. These second-generation children are more integrated into American society than are their parents, they are often more fluent in English than in their parents' native language, they have fully adopted American ways of living, and they struggle with what they often view as the backward ways of their parents. These conflicts are played out in congregations—what language will be spoken, what customs followed, what level of deference will be shown to elders, and what religious beliefs and practices will be emphasized.

Lesson 8: Immigrants often return to theological foundations. The changes that religion brings to the lives of immigrants—a *de facto* congregational form for worship, many benefits from joining a congregation, greater interest in religion, and changing gender roles and generational relationships—are accompanied by another process—what Fengang Yang and Helen Rose Ebaugh (2001) call "returning to the theological foundations of the religion." The many changes we have discussed thus far need theological justifications in order for people to accept them. So, too, does practicing a particular form of religion amidst the religious and cultural diversity of the United States. Many immigrant religious leaders and members perceive these changes not as straying from the true faith, but returning to it, resurrecting the way that their religion was originally meant to be practiced. For example, Yang and Ebaugh (2001, 278) write "For many Muslim immigrants in our study, the evolution of the mosque from simply a place to pray to a center of social activity and learning means a reversion to the dynamic role the mosque was given in the days of Prophet Muhammad." Yang and Ebaugh find this to be true for immigrants from a variety of religions and national origins. The vast religious changes they experience in their migration to the United States are perceived to be good, as they believe that they are returning to "true religion," their religion as it was intended to be.

Lesson 9: Religious majority/minority status matters. Examine Figure 11.2, which considers two variables: whether a particular religion is the majority or minority religion in immigrants' homeland and whether it is a minority or majority religion in the United States. For illustrative purposes, the figure also lists a few examples of each.

Immigrants experience religion and their immigrant status differently, depending on the cell they inhabit in this chart, what Ebaugh and Chafetz (2000, Chapter 3) describe as

Majority Religion in Homeland		Minority Religion in Homeland	
Majority Religion in the United States **A**	**Minority Religion in the United States** **B**	**Majority Religion in the United States** **C**	**Minority Religion in the United States** **D**
Mexican Catholic	Vietnamese Buddhist	Chinese Protestant	Indian Jain
Cuban Catholic	Pakistani Muslim	Argentine Brethren	Zoroastrian
	Indian Hindu	Mexican Protestant	Iranian Jew

FIGURE 11.2 Majority and minority religion status, by location.
Source: Adapted from Table 1 in Ebaugh and Chafetz (2000, 32).

environmental opportunities and constraints. Those who are in Cells B and D are double minorities—living in a foreign land and members of a foreign religion. Those in Cell B have the additional constraint of having lost what was once a majority religious status. But there are some advantages for those in Cell B—they are driven to learn more about their faith so that they can explain, defend, or present it to others. As one Muslim immigrant noted, "The Americans are always asking, 'Why do you Muslims do this or that?' I feel like I am a representative of Islam . . . so I read more so I can know how to answer them." (Ebaugh and Chafetz 2000, 35) And consider this priest of a Greek Orthodox Church:

> The average Greek is forced to . . . understand . . . his/her faith, because we have so many denominations around us . . . [B]ecause we are in America, we have to learn to back it up. . . . We do not have those [other faiths] in Greece; everyone is Orthodox. Here in Texas there are a lot of Baptists, so they say Orthodox? What is that? You have to be able to respond. (Ebaugh and Chafetz 2000, 34)

Immigrant congregations in Cells A and C find it difficult to recruit native-born Americans even if they wish to do so, because native-born individuals often have many congregational choices already. But immigrant congregations in Cells A and C do offer an attractive choice to fellow coethnics who are not specifically committed to a religion, because they can find fellowship in the context of joining the dominant religion of their new home. Conversely, immigrant congregations in Cells B and D often have more success in recruiting Americans, because Americans have limited choices of minority religion congregations. At the same time, they may struggle to recruit coethnics who are religiously unaffiliated, because for these people, joining them means adopting a double minority status.

Lesson 10: Religion shapes immigrants' civic engagement. In many ways, the United States runs on volunteers. Religious congregations, soup kitchens, ethnic organizations, neighborhood associations, voter registration drives, Habitat for Humanity, and many other organizations are operated largely by volunteers and directed by a few paid staff. Most volunteer opportunities in the United States come via religious congregations, which have the people, the social organization, and, importantly, appeals to transcendent authority and purpose that can both motivate volunteering *and* direct the type of volunteering. Studies find that different immigrant congregations volunteer in unique ways—some volunteer largely for the purpose of evangelism, while others volunteer largely to improve their communities. Some volunteer out of a personal feeling that volunteering is a good thing. Others volunteer because they believe that their religion requires it. Some focus their help only on coethnics, while others go beyond their own ethnic group. Why do these differences exist?

Two variables matter here—what we might think of as the means and the ends—and they shape religious orientations and engagement with the wider society. The first factor is the locus of moral authority. Moral authority "is concerned with the grounds for defining or evaluating ultimate ends" (Kniss and Numrich 2007, 38). How do we decide what is good, true, and worthy of pursuit? Moral authority provides such answers and direction. The locus of moral authority varies across religions. It ranges from the individual's reason or experience at one end to a collective tradition (a Holy Book or the teachings of a hierarchy, for example) at the other end.

The second factor of importance is the object of moral projects. Moral projects are the means by which we achieve the goals that moral authority has defined as good, true, and worth pursuing. Moral projects may attempt to maximize individual utility, or they may attempt to maximize the public good.

Figure 11.3 is a map of these two factors. For religious traditions in which the locus of authority is rooted in the individual, what is good, true, and worthy of pursuit varies across time, place, and person, and it must be determined by applying reasoning to the situation. With exceptions, of course, Buddhists, Hindus, Reformed Jews, and mainline Protestants tend to fall into the individual authority category. Conversely, for traditions in which the locus of authority is rooted in the collective, what is good, true, and worthy of pursuit is given by a transcendent absolute authority. Right and wrong are the same regardless of time, place, and person. Muslims, Conservative and Orthodox Jews, Catholics, and Evangelical Protestants tend to fall into the collectivist authority category.

The content of moral projects also varies by religious tradition. For traditions such as Hinduism, Buddhism, and Evangelical Protestantism, the individual is the moral project.

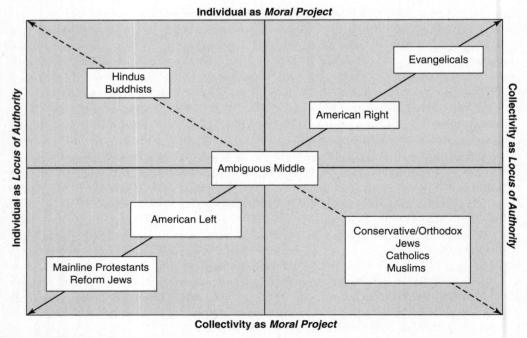

FIGURE 11.3 Moral order map.

Source: Adapted from Kniss (2003) and Kniss and Numrich (2007, 39).

That is, transformation of the individual is central to the purpose of the religion. For traditions such as Roman Catholicism, Islam, and Judaism, the collectivity or the community is the moral project. Transforming and ministering to the community of believers or of neighbors is the central purpose of the religion.

What does Figure 11.3 have to do with immigrants and volunteering? Studies repeatedly find that the combination of a person's faith tradition with respect to locus of moral authority and moral project, as well as whether the person is part of a majority or minority religion, shapes how much the person volunteers, what the focus and goals of that volunteering are, and to whom the volunteer work is directed (e.g., Chen 2008, Ebaugh and Chafetz 2000, Ecklund 2006, Foley and Hoge 2007, Kniss and Numrich 2007).

Immigrant Hindus and Buddhists tend to focus their volunteer activities on educating people about their faith. Because both these religions are minority faiths in the United States, immigrant followers are eager to spread the word and show that their religions need not be feared or seen as un-American. As a result, they take their message not just to members of their own ethnic community but to native-born Americans as well. Immigrants in Evangelical Protestant churches also tend to devote a great portion of their volunteering to evangelism. Even when they volunteer for a community organization—a soup kitchen, for example—they typically bring an evangelical message to the event. Elaine Howard Ecklund (2006) finds that immigrant Evangelical Protestant churches tend to focus their volunteering overwhelmingly on coethnics, especially immigrants from the same home nation. If immigrants or their children are members of racially mixed churches, though, they see their group as being broader than coethnics, and their volunteering efforts are often directed beyond their own ethnic group. Muslim and Catholic immigrants' volunteer work tends to focus on the community—for example, all other Muslims, regardless of ethnicity, or all people in the parish, including non-Catholics.

Thus, even if Muslim, Catholic, Evangelical Protestant, Jewish, Hindu, and Buddhist immigrants found themselves all working on building a Habitat for Humanity house (probably not likely for a variety of reasons), they would be there for very different reasons with different goals in mind. Religion, then, shapes the civic engagement of immigrants.

Lesson 11: Immigrants and their children become racialized (start to see themselves as members of a larger racial group). Immigrants come to the United States as Dominicans, Nigerians, Hmong, Mayans, Pakistanis, and so on. That is, they come as members of specific groups that share a common history and culture. The United States has a long tradition of turning ethnic peoples into racial peoples. For example, Chinese, Koreans, Japanese, Malaysians, Vietnamese, and so on become Asian; Nigerians, Bahamians, Sudanese, and Ethiopians become black; Mexicans, Puerto Ricans, Salvadorans, and Cubans become Latino. Of course, immigrants and their children often continue to consider themselves members of a specific ethnic or national group. But in addition to (or in some cases, in place of) an ethnic identity, they develop a racial identity (for all sorts of reasons too complex to cover here).

What this means for ethnic congregegations and immigrant religious identity is what Yang and Ebaugh (2001) label the "striving to include other peoples" principle. Immigrant churches, over time and across generations, often move from being ethnic-specific congregations to being race-specific congregations (Jeung 2005). And as we saw in the case of Karen Chai Kim and her husband and children, they may even move to multiracial congregations. This "striving to include other peoples" is a response on the part of immigrants to their new experience of religion and to the multicultural society they encounter in the United States. If they see their own religion as true and worthy, why should they keep it only for their own coethnics? The racialization process allows them to adopt a broader view of other people and to wish to include people of diverse ethnic backgrounds who are nonetheless considered by the general American public to be the same racial group. This openness and inclusiveness may move the church along its way to multiracial gatherings. (See Chapter 10 for more on race and religion.)

Lesson 12: Immigrants maintain contact with the religious culture in their countries of origin as they develop a new religious identity via transnationalism. When immigrants move to a new land, they do not lose all contact with their homeland. As Karen Chai Kim and her family were going through religious transformations, for example, they did so in dialogue with relatives who had remained in Korea. When they communicate with them, and particularly when they travel back to Korea for visits, they transmit new religious sensibilities back to their homeland, affecting people and organizations there. Transnationalism is the "the process by which immigrants forge and sustain multistranded relations that link together their societies of origin and settlement" (Basch, Schiller, and Blanc 1994, 7). Immigrants may be rooted a particular place, but they also transcend borders. As sociologist Peggy Levitt (2007, 23) writes, "In some cases, the ties between migrants and non-migrants are so strong and widespread that migration also radically transforms the lives of individuals who stay home. . . . In response, the religious, social, and political groups they belong to also begin to operate across borders."

Transnationalism means that the religious changes immigrants experience in the United States are communicated back to people and organizations in their homelands. One of the authors works with a Taiwanese immigrant who converted from atheism to Evangelical Protestantism in the United States. This man has taken several missionary trips back to Taiwan with his church (now pan-Asian), helping to establish congregations there, and his church helps fund the education of local pastors to lead these Taiwanese congregations. The influence is not just one way. Taiwanese ideas and practices, in turn, influence religious practice in the United States. Gauging the full impact of transnationalism on religion has thus far proved elusive, but it is clear that it has an effect. And the increasing ease of travel and the vastly improved and cheap forms of communication around the world mean that the impact of transnational influences may well increase.

LET'S CONCLUDE

Our exploration of a dozen lessons related to immigrants and religious change—as well as our earlier discussion of the significant changes that immigrants are having on religion in the United States—bring us to a few summary points. Religion is not transplanted unchanged from place to place. It is transformed in the process, just as are the people involved (Kwon, Kim, and Warner 2001). The lessons discussed in this chapter help us to understand the basic contours of this religious change. Immigrants use religion to address issues of morality, meaning, identity, and belonging. In the process, immigrants become Americans. As Ebaugh and Chafetz (2000, 148) conclude, as long as immigrants come to the United States, they will create "vibrant religious institutions that simultaneously recreate for their members feelings of the homeland while helping them to adapt to their new land." And in the process, religious change will continue.

SUGGESTED READING

Chen, Carolyn. 2008. *Getting Saved in America: Taiwanese Immigration and Religious Experience*. Princeton, NJ: Princeton University Press.

Ebaugh, Helen Rose, and Janet Saltman Chafetz. 2000. *Religion and the New Immigrants: Continuities and Adaptations in Immigrant Congregations*. Walnut Creek, CA: AltaMira Press.

Eck, Diana. 2001. *A New Religious America*. San Francisco: Harper San Francisco.

Kniss, Fred, and Paul D. Numrich. 2007. *Sacred Assemblies and Civic Engagement: How Religion Matters for America's Newest Immigrants*. New Brunswick, NJ: Rutgers University Press.

Levitt, Peggy. 2007. *God Needs No Passport: Immigrants and the Changing American Religious Landscape*. New York: The New Press.

Warner, R. Stephen, and Judith G. Wittner. 1998. *Gatherings in Diaspora: Religious Communities and the New Immigration*. Philadelphia: Temple University Press.

Yang, Fengang, and Helen Rose Ebaugh. 2001. "Transformation in New Immigrant Religions and Their Global Implications." *American Sociological Review* 2: 269–288.

12

Godless Science, Irrational Religion?

1. How do science and religion differ?
2. What do you make of the variety of creation stories? What do they tell us about ourselves?
3. Do you think that truth requires empirical support?
4. How and why do science and religion clash?
5. What role should religion play in our implementation of new technologies?

You may have heard people complain that science is mounting an attack on religion, or that "godless" scientists are undermining the sacred and divine by suggesting that fundamental questions about humans and their place in the world can be answered solely through reference to the natural world. There is no divine planner, these scientists claim, only a natural world whose workings science helps us to understand better every day. Many religious believers feel that science devalues faith or that scientists consider their field to provide more—or better—answers than religion. Many believers are also concerned that science as a worldview and scientific developments will supplant the moral codes and sense of divine order that faith brings.

You may also have heard that religion is attacking science, that "irrational" religion dismisses extensive empirical evidence that supports purely natural explanations for phenomena in favor of blind adherence to faith-based answers. In the United States, many religious people dismiss the evidence for evolution and believe instead that the earth was created in six days, less than 10,000 years ago. Part of religion's attack on science, you may have heard, is an attempt by religious groups to limit what science can achieve by blocking research on stem cells, protesting technologies such as nuclear power and genetically modified organisms, and objecting to various technologies that assist in human reproduction. Many scientists believe that, even as we add to our body of knowledge about how the world works and invent technologies to improve our lives, religious groups want to limit how we use our knowledge and technologies so that our actions fit their religious and moral codes—progress be damned.

The tension between science and religion is often framed as an either/or debate: You are either a scientist or a religious person. Certainly the most bitter and dramatic battles are fought between religious persons who mostly or wholly reject science, and scientists (and other rationalists) who mostly or wholly reject religion. The media tends to focus on these battles because they lay out the clearest issues and generate the best sound bites ("godless science!" "irrational religion!"). But this dichotomy is a gross oversimplification. Many people fall somewhere in the middle and constantly negotiate a balance between the extremes (Campbell and Curtis 1996; Tang and Mietus 2003). Indeed, many scientists are religious.

In this chapter, we will look at some of the issues that underlie the ongoing debate between religion and science. (See Box 12.1 for what we mean by "science.") We will examine how we know what we know and how the worldviews offered by science and religion differ. But we will also consider a broader question: How does the battle between religion and science—and its outcome—affect society-wide distributions of power, authority, and resources? This debate is often framed around differences in ideology (i.e., what people know or think). Such differences, however, also have profound implications for what and who counts in society and how knowledge of any sort is used. Thus, we will begin with an examination of ideological differences between science and religion, and we will conclude with a discussion of why this matters for the way that society functions. Let's start with the topic that has been a battleground for religion and science in the West for over 100 years: Darwinian evolution.

BOX 12.1

Science and Scientific Inquiry

According to the American Academy for the Advancement of Science, science presumes the following:

- The world is understandable because patterns in nature reflect general laws.
- Knowledge is durable because it is based on carefully collected evidence that accumulates over time.
- Ideas are modified as evidence accumulates and our knowledge base grows.
- Science cannot provide complete answers for all questions.

Scientific inquiry is a process:

- It demands empirical evidence.
- It blends logic and imagination as scientists formulate and test hypotheses and sort through observations.
- It explains data and predicts future outcomes.
- It tries to identify and avoid bias.

Adapted from AAAS 2006

FLASHPOINT: THE CURRENT DEBATE OVER EVOLUTION

In December 2005, Judge John E. Jones III, a Republican judge appointed by President George W. Bush, ruled that the teaching of intelligent design in public schools was impermissible because intelligent design was "nothing less than the progeny of creationism" (Easton 2005). (See Box 12.2 for a brief explanation of intelligent design.) The case arose after the Dover, Pennsylvania, school board adopted a policy requiring biology teachers to read a statement to all ninth graders at Dover High School. Here is an excerpt from the statement:

> Because Darwin's Theory is a theory, it continues to be tested as new evidence is discovered. The Theory is not a fact. Gaps in the Theory exist for which there is not evidence. A theory is defined as a well-tested explanation that unifies a broad range of observation. Intelligent design is an explanation of the origin of life that differs from Darwin's view. The reference book, *Of Pandas and People,* is available for students who might be interested in gaining an understanding of what Intelligent Design actually involves. (Jones 2005)

Evolutionary biologists were dismayed to hear intelligent design described as an "explanation of the origin of life that differs from Darwin's view." Why? First, Darwin did not publish a view of the origin of life. Instead, his theory explains the origins of diverse species, that is, how species are created through "modified descent from a common ancestor" via a combination of genetic mutation and natural selection (Darwin, 1857). And second, although intelligent design offers an explanation for the origins of life, it is not a falsifiable scientific theory, like Darwin's, which can be tested using methods accepted by the scientific community. Intelligent design is an explanation, but it is not science. Hence, scientists object to its presentation as if it were on par with a scientific explanation.

BOX 12.2

Intelligent Design and Science

Q: What is intelligent design?

A: Intelligent design consists of two hypothetical claims about the history of the universe and life: first, that some structures or processes in nature are "irreducibly complex" and could not have originated through small changes over long periods of time; and second, that some structures or processes in nature are expressions of "complex specified information" that can only be the product of an intelligent agent.

Q: Does intelligent design have a scientific basis?

A: . . . [Many] scientists have noted that the concept necessarily presupposes that there is an "intelligent designer" outside of nature who, from the beginning or from time to time, inserts design into the world around us. But whether there is an intelligent designer is a matter of religious faith. It is not a scientifically testable question.

AAAS 2008

The dispute over teaching evolution, creationism, and intelligent design plays out in our nation's classrooms every day. In May 2008, the *Chronicle of Higher Education* reported results from a number of national surveys:

- Twenty-five percent of biology teachers had discussed creationism or intelligent design in the science classroom.
- Of those, almost half had criticized creationism and intelligent design, while 40% had described it as a religious, but not scientific, explanation.
- In general, teachers who had completed more college-level biology credits or had taken at least one college-level class that focused on evolution were less likely to discuss creationism and intelligent design in the classroom. (Monastersky 2008)

Another survey found that 27% of college students reported learning about creationism in high school biology class and 15% of high school biology teachers admitted that they did not accept the scientific evidence for evolution (Monastersky 2008).

To continue our tour of U.S. schools, in the suburbs of Atlanta, the Cobb County School Board required that stickers be affixed to biology textbooks. The stickers read, "This textbook contains material on evolution. Evolution is a theory, not a fact, regarding the origin of living things. This material should be approached with an open mind, studied carefully and critically considered" (CNN 2005). But central to the practice of science is the opportunity for falsification (see Box 12.3). The scientific method is, by its very nature, open-minded—prepared to find, and even seeking, disconfirming evidence. Why, then, does a science textbook need a sticker telling its readers to remain open minded? Open to what? Ultimately, U.S. District Judge Clarence Cooper ruled that the stickers were unconstitutional:

> [T]he distinction of evolution as a theory rather than a fact is the distinction that religiously motivated individuals have specifically asked school boards to make in the most recent anti-evolution movement, and that was exactly what parents in Cobb County did in this case . . . By adopting this specific language . . . the Cobb County School Board appears to have sided with these religiously motivated individuals (Selman vs. Cobb County School District, 2005).

BOX 12.3

What Is Empirical Evidence?

Empirical evidence refers to observations that are obtained using the five senses—sight, hearing, touch, smell, and taste—or using technological extensions of those senses—microscopes, telescopes, X-ray machines, and other analogous instruments. Empirical observation is important because it allows claims to be confirmed or disconfirmed—falsified—using evidence that is shared among observers. It has "intersubjective" reality and is not unique to one person's experience.

We can observe the natural world empirically. The same cannot be said of the supernatural. Hence, science is limited to the realm of things that are empirically observable. That, which is not empirically observable, falls outside the bounds of science. It's not that it is uninteresting. It just isn't in the domain of science.

Meanwhile, the Kansas Board of Education has redefined science. The old definition was "science is the human activity of seeking natural explanations for what we observe in the world around us." The new definition describes science as "a systematic method of continuing investigation that uses observation, hypothesis testing, measurement, experimentation, logical argument and theory building to lead to more adequate explanations of natural phenomena" (Overbye 2005). Notice that a key phrase has been removed: "natural explanations." This act of redefinition made the supernatural an acceptable line of scientific explanation—in Kansas, that is.

These well-publicized instances of conflict between religious persons and evolutionists reflect a larger pattern of belief in U.S. society. That is, supernatural explanations for human origins and evolution are common among the general U.S. population. In June 2007, a Gallup poll asked 1007 American adults about their views of evolution and creationism. (PollingReport.com 2008). Eighteen percent thought that evolution—described as "the idea that human beings developed over millions of years from less advanced forms of life"—was "definitely true." Significantly more respondents, 39%, thought that creationism—described as "the idea that God created human beings pretty much in their present form at one time within the last 10,000 years"—was "definitely true." Among Americans, creationism is twice as popular an explanation for human origins than evolution!

What about intelligent design, the idea that life forms are so complex that they cannot have arisen by accident but instead must be a product of divine guidance? A 2008 Gallup poll, also reported on http://www.pollingreport.com, gave respondents a choice among three explanations for human evolution: (1) human evolution is "guided by God," (2) "God had no part" in human evolution, and (3) "God created human beings pretty much in their present form." Supernatural explanations were even more predominant in this formulation of the question. Fourteen percent chose "God had no part," but 36 percent chose "guided by God" and a whopping 44 percent chose "God created human beings pretty much in their present form."

RELIGIOUS AND SCIENTIFIC CREATION STORIES

So what are we and where did we come from? Human societies throughout history have wrestled with these questions. You may have heard the creation story that begins the Book of Genesis, which describes how God created the world in six days—first the light and the darkness; then the heavens and the earth; then land, sea, and plants; then the stars, sun, and moon; then the birds and the creatures of the sea; and finally the animals of the land and humans. But did you know that there is a second creation story in Genesis, one that differs in significant ways from this familiar one?

The story of Adam and Eve, found in the second chapter of Genesis, begins with a brief narrative about the origins of the world, but the events are in a different order. Heaven and earth are created, and then Yahweh creates man and a garden called Eden with fruit-bearing trees, including "the tree of life and the tree of knowledge." After that, to provide man with a helper, God creates animals and birds, but none of them is a fitting helper, so, finally, out of one of man's ribs, God creates a woman. Thus, within one sacred text there are two answers to the question of human origins, answers that vary substantially in the ordering of events. Despite their inconsistencies, however, both posit that God made man from scratch and placed him on the earth.

What about creation stories from other religious traditions? Here's one from the Menominee, a Native American group in northern Wisconsin. In their creation story, the Good Spirit, one of many spirits created by the Great Spirit, allows a bear to transform itself and the bear becomes human. Because it is lonely, the bear-turned-human invites an eagle, then a beaver, and then a sturgeon to join him, and all are also transformed into humans, each the founder of a different clan in Menominee society. In the Menominee tale, human origins are animal.

For the Maori, humans descended from heaven and earth, but their creation tale focuses on how darkness is defeated and light created. Here's the Maori creation tale, summarized in *Creation Stories Around the World* (2000), from Sir George Grey's 19th-century account:

> All humans are descended from one pair of ancestors, Rangi and Papa, who are also called Heaven and Earth. In those days, Heaven and Earth clung closely together, and all was darkness. Rangi and Papa had six sons: Tane-mahuta, the father of the forests and their inhabitants; Tawhiri-ma-tea, the father of winds and storms; Tangaroa, the father of fish and reptiles; Tu-matauenga, the father of fierce human beings; Haumia-tikitiki, the father of food that grows without cultivation; and Rongo-ma-tane, the father of cultivated food (p. 6).

In the Norse creation tale, also reported in *Creation Stories from Around the World,* humans arise from thawed ice:

> Where the sparks and warm winds of Muspell reached the south side of frigid Ginnungagap, the ice thawed and dripped, and from the drips thickened and formed the shape of a man. His name was Ymir, [and he was] the first of and ancestor of the frost-giants (p. 4).

Then there is the story told by the scientific theory of evolution, that human evolution, like that of other species, is a process of "modified descent from a common ancestor." (See Box 12.4 for some engaging books on evolution.) In some respects, evolution is yet another narrative about where humans come from: Belief in it is fairly widespread

BOX 12.4

More on Darwinian Evolution

A biology textbook will explain Darwin's theory of evolution and the empirical evidence that supports it. Here are some more good reads that do the same:

> Jones, Steve. 1999. *Almost Like A Whale: The Origin of Species Updated.* New York: Doubleday.

> Quammen, David. 1997. *Song of the Dodo: Island Biogeography in an Age of Extinction.* New York: Scribner.

> Weiner, Jonathan. 1995. *Beak of the Finch: A Story of Evolution in Our Time.* New York: Vintage.

in some circles and it has powerful implications for the meaning (or lack of meaning) of human existence. Specifically, Darwinian evolution posits that species evolve over time through random and contingent processes. Modification originates in gene mutations, which occur randomly and frequently. Not all gene mutations "stick," however. Instead, modification takes hold in a population of organisms through natural selection, in which survival and reproduction are contingent upon an organism's fit with its environment. Over time, certain characteristics become predominant when organisms with those features survive and reproduce more successfully than others. Other characteristics are lost when organisms with those features die or fail to reproduce. Darwinian evolution argues that change is constant and is driven by gene mutations, shifts in the environment, and natural selection. Organisms change in minor and major ways, sometimes to the extent that a whole new species arises from a series of modifications. In addition, change is explained via thoroughly natural processes—gene mutation, natural selection—and is not brought about by a supernatural guiding hand.

One may *believe* that there is an invisible guiding hand behind the appearance of species on earth—believe a supernatural explanation—but there is no empirical evidence for such a force. And this is an important way in which Darwinian evolution differs from the previously mentioned religious narratives: It is couched in the distinctive knowledge system of science and is supported by an impressive body of empirical evidence. You may wonder why the support of empirical evidence is so important. As fervently as you or others may believe *one* of these creation narratives—and a large proportion of Americans profess belief in the Judeo-Christian creation story, while the vast majority of scientists accept evolution's account—all of these tales cannot be *literally* true. That is, it is not possible for the Maori, Norse, Judeo-Christian, Menominee, and Darwinian tales to *each* accurately explain the empirical reality of what humans are and how we got here. First, the stories are inconsistent with each other. That is, they describe different and incommensurate mechanisms for the origin of humans. And second, the religious stories lack empirical support. Empirical evidence shows that the earth is more than 10,000 years old and suggests that humans descended from another primate rather than descending from melting ice, a bear, an eagle, a beaver, or a sturgeon or being placed on the earth in our present form. That does not mean the narratives are uninteresting or irrelevant. These narratives are powerful cultural stories that tell us about who we think we are and how we see ourselves fitting into the natural world. They are what religious historian Karen Armstrong (2000, *xv*) calls *mythos,* that which "[provided] people with a context that made sense of their day-to-day lives . . . [and] directed their attention to the eternal and the universal."

But the religious narratives do not explain the natural world in terms of evidence that is observable using our five senses or technological extensions of them. Darwin's theory of evolution, on the other hand, is a scientific theory that was always intended to explain an observable natural reality. For 150 years, biologists and other scientists have amassed empirical evidence that supports Darwin's theory of evolution, and it remains the only creation story for which there is significant empirical support.

This matters, however, only if empirical evidence is important to you. And this is one of the flashpoints in the disputes between science and religion: What if knowledge can be found in something other than observation and analysis of the material world? Scientists privilege knowledge that is backed by empirical observation; religionists allow for other sources of knowledge, including religious authority, doctrine, sacred texts and narratives, and even divine revelation.

RELIGION AND EVOLUTION: WHAT'S THE BIG DEAL?

Now we've done it: We have annoyed both scientists and religious believers, though probably not every scientist and every religious believer! The scientist is annoyed because we have referred to Darwin's theory of evolution as yet another "creation narrative," albeit one with significant empirical support that speaks to the likelihood of its accuracy. The scientist is bugged by the confounding of religious tales with scientific knowledge and the placement of the two on the same plane, as though they were equally valid or equally important. Many scientists argue that science represents something real and religion is only mythology—and thus they do not belong in the same space—or that religion is irrational and therefore outside the bounds of reasonable discourse. And, of course, the scientist worries about anyone who dismisses empirical evidence—what we can *see!*—in favor of other arguments or beliefs.

The religious believer is also annoyed with us, mostly because we have pointed out the absence of empirical support for religious creation stories. How dare we dismiss a religious creation tale as merely a *story*? Since when is empirical evidence such an important criterion for knowledge and truth? Religious persons argue that there exist other equally valid—if not more valid—kinds of truth, truths that are inaccessible to people who focus merely on what they can see, hear, smell, touch, and taste.

Darwinian evolution generates particularly strong resistance from many religious believers. What is so objectionable here? First, evolutionary theory does not require a God, a divine presence, or the supernatural as a driving force. The present shape of nature, as well as the way that natures changes over time, is understood using wholly natural explanations: random gene mutations, natural selection, and so on. Religious persons often read this explanation as a denial of the existence of God, and some scientists would agree. At the very least, most scientists see no evidence of God in the natural explanation for evolution and change in species. Nor do they see a "need" for God, given the power of the natural explanation. In addition to these obvious objections by religionists, evolutionary theory in particular and the model of scientific inquiry in general have implications for the basic nature of our world that many religious persons find disturbing.

Religion's Discontent with Scientific Inquiry

There are three qualities of science that may create discontent among religious persons:

1. Science is destabilizing.
2. Over time, science has picked up explanatory territory from religion.
3. Science's attitude is one of skepticism.

We will discuss each in turn.

SCIENCE IS DESTABILIZING   As a method of inquiry, science builds knowledge by asking questions and accumulating evidence. Scientists modify their ideas as evidence accumulates and sometimes alter them radically. Einstein (1936) certainly understood this when he argued, "We must always be ready to change these notions—that is to say, the axiomatic basis of physics—in order to do justice to perceived facts in the most perfect way logically." His special and general theories of relativity radically changed our understanding of Newtonian physics.

Scientific inquiry produces a knowledge base that is constantly changing and growing as we gather and interpret evidence. As a result, science is fundamentally destabilizing, always evolving, and never fully settled. Some people embrace this uncertainty, but it is profoundly unsettling for others. Consider the paradigm shift represented by Copernicus's contention that the earth revolved around the sun, and not the other way around. This theory, which was supported by observations and mathematical calculations, fundamentally changed how humans viewed the structure of the universe and, importantly, the place of human beings in it. Suddenly, human civilization was no longer the center of the natural world. This was a scientific reality that had profound implications for how humans thought about themselves and their significance in the natural world. Copernicus's theory was not warmly received by religious authorities.

The resistance was rooted in a larger concern: If the presumption of human centrality and dominance over the natural world could be so easily dismissed by science, what other timeless truths providing stability and constancy to our social and communal existence could be overturned by empirical observations, mathematical computations, and a new idea? We see other instances of this resistance today with the rejection of Darwin's theory of human evolution and of the accumulating scientific evidence that homosexuality is genetically determined. Scientific inquiry, by its very nature, has the power to challenge our taken-for-granted assumptions and disrupt the seeming inevitability of existing arrangements, including the assumptions that humans are at the center of the universe, that humans are by their very nature separate and distinct from other mammals, and that heterosexuality is the only "natural" option.

SCIENCE WINS TERRITORY FROM RELIGION OVER TIME   As scientific inquiry and discovery proceeds, the realm of the unknown shrinks over time and the terrain for which science provides explanation grows. Most scientists understand the limits of science—that science can provide answers to questions about the natural world but not answers to moral or ethical quandaries. But as our scientific knowledge accumulates, the successes of science mount, its legitimacy grows, and the authority of scientists is enhanced. Meanwhile, religious persons feel their influence waning and—with some justification— feel that these changes are at their expense.

Karen Armstrong (2000) argues persuasively in *The Battle for God: A History of Fundamentalism* that Western religions—Christianity, Judaism, and Islam—are not inherently resistant to science, scientific inquiry, or the knowledge generated by science. Each has a history and tradition, going back to the pre-Enlightenment era, of curiosity about and exploration of the natural world. But science has been remarkably effective at finding answers to particular questions, solving technological problems, and creating efficiencies. That success has led to an increase in the relative influence of science and scientists. In some cases, religion responds to its ebbing influence by digging in its heels on the central importance of religious tradition and belief (becoming more fundamentalist, as described in Chapter 6). In so doing, religion may reject what it sees as problematic in the modern world, especially science and its so-called advances, which often have troubling implications for the existing moral order. While we tend to think of fundamentalism as a return to the original way of doing things, Armstrong astutely points out that fundamentalism is itself a "new" way and is at heart a response to the rising tide of science and rationality in Western societies. For some groups, fundamentalism is a newly formulated answer to the challenges to the social order wrought by science, technology, and attention to the practical that so challenged traditional religious authority.

SCIENCE IS SKEPTICAL   Finally, science's "attitude" is troubling to many religious persons. Scientists are skeptical and doubtful. They constantly question what they know. And they try, though empirical testing, to prove themselves and others wrong—remember what we said earlier about "falsification" being the essential part of the scientific method. As scientists build confirming evidence, they become more certain that they are on the right track. But scientists are cautious about claiming that they or others are "right" or that they know the "truth." Scientists are comfortable with gaps in their knowledge but not complacent about them. They constantly seek ways to fill those gaps with new ideas, theories, and observations. Many religious traditions, including variants on Judaism, Christianity and Islam, have historically embraced questioning and skepticism. The modern bent towards religious fundamentalism, however, does not embrace these attitudes—as Karen Armstrong argues in *The Battle for God*. Fundamentalism claims that there are unchanging transcendental truths in nature and social order. These truths are challenged at the most basic level by the attitude and constant questioning of scientists.

Thus, how science is practiced and the consequences of the growth of scientific knowledge are destabilizing and disturbing to many religious persons. This response is especially true among religious fundamentalists, for whom the changes wrought by science threaten to upset an existing and taken-for-granted social, moral, and cosmic order.

Religion's Discontent with Darwinian Evolution

Darwinian evolution poses additional problems for some religious groups. To begin with, if Darwinian evolution is indeed true in the sense that empirical evidence supports the theory, then nature's categories (i.e., the boundaries around species) are flexible rather than fixed. Over the course of generations, sometimes many, many generations, cohorts of creatures change in their physical features, sometimes to the extent that they become whole new species. "This" becomes "that," calling into question the essential "this"-ness of a category that we might otherwise take for granted as fixed. In his book *The Beak of the Finch,* Jonathan Weiner (1995) describes the ebb and flow of change in species of finches, and analyzes how, over time and with shifts in fit with the natural environment, one kind of finch is transformed through natural selection into a new kind and sometimes later changed back again after further shifts occur in the natural environment. He makes it clear that species as natural categories are not fixed.

Thus, the theory of Darwinian evolution contradicts Judeo–Christian and other narratives in which all categories of creatures were fixed and established at the outset of creation. For religious persons, the larger implications of this claim can be disturbing: If the natural order is not fixed, what might that suggest about other forms of order, including the social and moral orders? Perhaps they, too, are tentative and shifting, a prospect that many people find upsetting.

In addition, evolutionary theory argues that humans evolved through the same basic process as all other living things. In this way, we are *like* other mammals, spiders, and even bacteria. What's the implication? Humans are not special or sacred in nature, and we are part of—but not central to—the natural world. Recall from Chapter 1 Peter Berger's definition of religion: "the audacious attempt to conceive of the entire universe as humanly significant." Western religion, in particular, typically privileges humans and assumes that they have a special place in the natural order. Darwinian evolution denies humans this place and says that we are no better and no worse than all other living creatures.

Finally, as we explore in more detail in the next chapter, the Judeo–Christian tradition also contends that the natural world was created for the use of humans. Humans are the *raison d'etre* of the natural world, which was—the story goes—created for the use of humans and placed under their dominion. But evolutionary theory suggests that humans came along only recently in the grand scheme of natural history. Perhaps more disturbingly, evolutionary theory also suggests that species come and go on the basis of their fit with the natural environment. Not only are humans not the pinnacle or center of the natural world, but quite possibly they are only a transient part of it. Species become extinct. We may not always be here.

In these ways, scientific inquiry picks away at religious explanations and authority, and Darwinian evolution challenges the basic assumptions of Judeo–Christian religion. But the effects of science on religion go even further than that. As we discuss in the next section, in its attempts to repel science and its discoveries, religion has ironically been pushed into appropriating scientific language and mimicking scientific ways of doing things.

RELIGION AND SCIENCE, *MYTHOS* AND *LOGOS*

In *The Battle for God,* former nun and religious historian Karen Armstrong (2000, *xvi*) distinguishes between *logos* and *mythos* as ways of approaching and knowing about the world. *Logos* refers to "rational, pragmatic, and scientific thought that enabled men and women to function well in the world." *Logos* is strategy and plans of action. It is useful in a practical sense as we try to get from here to there. *Mythos,* on the other hand, refers to that, which is

> . . . thought to be timeless and constant in our existence. Myth looked back to the origins of life, to the foundations of culture, and to the deepest levels of the human mind. Myth was not concerned with practical matters, but with meaning. (*xv*)

Mythos provides a vital function for human societies by connecting us to a larger narrative about our existence. It does not necessarily tell us how to live or what to do, but it helps us impose coherence on the world we see.

Mythos is, however, often overshadowed by *logos* in modern Western societies. Indeed, in order to defend against inroads made by science, religions find themselves pushed towards *logos* (doctrine that is arrived at by logical means and that can be shown to work in some practical way) at the expense of *mythos* (overarching narratives that provide meaning independent of plans of action).

We can see this trend clearly when we analyze the impact that science and scientific inquiry have had on religion. Darwinian evolution relies on empirical evidence for its legitimacy as an explanation. The empirical evidence provides consistent and far-ranging support for the theory, which suggests that the theory is robust. Meanwhile, religious explanations rely on the authority of religious leaders, sacred texts and narratives, and, more fundamentally, private faith and belief. The problem for religion is that empirical evidence has become the coin of the realm in rationalized modern societies. In a world shaped by advances in science and technology, empirical evidence often holds sway and seems more real, more persuasive, and more objective. We hear talk of evidence-based medicine (i.e., treatment decisions that are based on empirical evidence of what works), assessment of student learning outcomes (i.e., measurements of what kids learn in school), benchmarks for progress in war zones, and performance evaluations that are based on measurable criteria. Seeing is believing. And what works—*logos*—is what matters.

If you doubt the pervasiveness of this trend, just consider the ways in which even religious groups themselves increasingly use elements scientific thought to bolster their claims of truth. For example, some creationists and proponents of intelligent design have created the appearance of scientifically based, empirical support for their creation stories. An entire museum in Kentucky, just across the state line from Cincinnati, Ohio, purports to provide empirical evidence for the accuracy of the first Genesis creation story. The Creation Museum includes exhibits on the Seven Cs of history that claim to address "many of the common questions and erroneous notions that people have regarding creation and the book of Genesis [Creation, Corruption, Catastrophe, etc.] . . . The theme over and over again is how science—when rightly interpreted—affirms what the Bible teaches" (DeWitt 2007). For example, the Creation Museum presents what it considers to be scientific evidence supporting the Biblical flood. (See Box 12.5 for more on this.) Along the same line, nonprofit foundations like the Seattle-based Discovery Institute are devoted to advancing intelligent design as empirical science.

There is an important irony here. Although the evidence and conclusions accumulated by science are rejected by these vocal and active groups, the legitimacy of science and its method of working from objective facts are nonetheless used to bolster religion's claim to truth. This says quite a lot about the balance of power between religion and science and the vulnerable position in which religion presently finds itself. Faith and belief

---

BOX 12.5

The Creation Museum on Catastrophe

As the descendants of Adam and Eve married and filled the earth with offspring, their wickedness was great (Genesis 6:5). God judged their sin by sending a global Flood to destroy all men, animals, creatures that moved along the ground, and birds of the air (Genesis 6:7). Those God chose to enter the Ark—Noah, his family and land-dwelling representatives of the animal kingdom (including dinosaurs)—were saved from the watery *catastrophe*.

There was plenty of room in the huge vessel for tens of thousands of animals—even dinosaurs (the average dinosaur was only the size of a sheep, and Noah didn't have to take fully grown adults of the large dinosaurs). Noah actually needed only about 16,000 animals on the Ark to represent all the distinct kinds of land-dwelling animals.

This earth-covering event has left its mark even today. From the thousands of feet of sedimentary rock found around the world to the "billions of dead things buried in rock layers" (fossils), the Flood reminds us even today that our righteous God cannot—and will not—tolerate sin, while the Ark reminds us that He provides a way of salvation from sin's punishment. The rainbows we experience today remind us of God's promise never again to destroy the earth with water (Genesis 9:13–15). Incidentally, if the Flood were a local event (rather than global in extent), as some claim, then God has repeatedly broken His promise since we continue to experience local flooding even today.

McKeever n.d.

are not enough in the face of science's empirical evidence: To prevail, religion presents its own evidence and struggles to put forth evidence that matches in form, if not in substance, the model proffered by science.

Thus, increasingly, religion finds itself in the position of having to operate on science's terms rather than its own. The cost of ceding the science classroom to *scientists* is tremendous in terms of legitimacy—hence the attempts we discussed earlier to inject creationism and intelligent design into science education. Some people have suggested, by way of compromise, that creationism and intelligent design be taught in comparative religion classes. That compromise, however, does not appeal to many religious persons because it excludes religion from the domain of science and assigns it to the less powerful (and some might argue, less factual) humanities.

NONOVERLAPPING MAGISTERIA

You might conclude from our overview of these battles that science and religion fundamentally contradict each other. You might think that you can believe in one or the other, but not both. Not everyone, however, sees religion and science as inevitably clashing or fundamentally incompatible. The late Stephen J. Gould (1998, 271), a Harvard scientist, argued that religion and science occupy distinct domains:

> The lack of conflict between science and religion arises from a lack of overlap between their respective domains of professional expertise—science in the empirical constitution of the universe, and religion in the search for proper ethical values and the spiritual meaning of our lives. The attainment of wisdom in a full life requires extensive attention to both domains.

As long as science and religion remember their own places and remain within the bounds of their own competencies, there need be no conflict between the two. Gould refers to the domain of teaching authority of each subject as its magisterium. The separation of religion and science into nonoverlapping magisteria does not favor one realm over another:

> [It] cuts both ways. If religion can no longer dictate the nature of factual conclusions residing properly within the magisterium of science, then scientists cannot claim higher insight into moral truth from any superior knowledge of the world's empirical constitution. (Gould 1998, 282)

Gould makes it all seem so simple: If religion and science stay in their places, then all will be well. Dig deeper, however, and you find that there are no easy answers. In the real world where science and technology intersect with religion and morality, the notion of nonoverlapping magisteria becomes increasingly complex, at times even unworkable.

SCIENCE, TECHNOLOGY, AND RELIGION

If science is what we know—at least, what scientists know—then technology is what we do with what we know. And that opens a whole other can of worms. The conflict between science and religion is not limited to the debate over the origins of the earth and its various life forms. Science and religion butt heads in a number of areas where scientific discoveries lead to new technologies, including stem cell research, reproductive technologies, genetically modified organisms, nuclear power, population control, end-of-life care, and AIDS policy. Common to these issues is a clash between what science and technology *can* do and the moral boundaries posited by religion regarding what science and technology *should* do.

Stem cell research is a good example of this conflict. Research on embryonic stem cells holds promise for finding cures for diseases such as cancer, Parkinson's and Alzheimer's diseases, spinal cord injury, stroke, burns, heart disease, diabetes, osteoarthritis, and rheumatoid arthritis (National Institutes of Health 2008), so this research is of great interest to scientists. But in order to carry out experiments, scientists must use stem cells from human embryos, which are believed by some religious traditions, including the Catholic Church and many conservative Christian denominations, to be forms of human life and thus sacred. While we *can* conduct research using embryonic stem cells, and perhaps someday will be able to cure specific diseases using embryonic stem cells, many religious people question whether we *should* do this and whether this use of technology falls within acceptable moral boundaries.

These debates over science and technology extend far beyond objections by some prominent Christian groups to stem cell research. For example, assistive reproductive technologies generally are proscribed among Catholics and Muslims because such technologies challenge taken-for-granted assumptions about natural order in reproduction and what fundamentally constitutes "family" from the perspective of different religions. Traditionally liberal religious groups oppose technologies that may pose harm to our environment, including genetically modified organisms and nuclear power. In a number of arenas, religious groups have attempted to limit the uses of technology. Sometimes religion has been very successful at this.

Gould's "nonoverlapping magisteria" dramatically fails us at the nexus where technology meets religion. Science is knowledge, but so is religion, albeit a different sort of knowledge. We can argue, perhaps, that science knows one set of things, religion knows another, and never the two shall meet. As Christian theologian Frederick Beuchner (1973, 86) wrote in an early statement on the "nonoverlapping magisteria,"

> The conflict between science and religion . . . is like the conflict between a podiatrist and a poet. One says that Susie Smith has fallen arches. The other says she walks in beauty like the night. In his own way each is speaking the truth. What is at issue is the kind of truth you are after.

But the opportunities opened by technology force us to decide what we should do with what we know. Although a procedure may be scientifically and technologically possible, religion may deem it morally unacceptable. In the next section, we consider how various religious traditions have responded to the development of technologies for assistive reproduction (e.g., *in vitro* fertilization, egg and sperm donation, and surrogacy), focusing especially on how the use of technology can challenge taken-for-granted notions about family and also on how religions respond and adapt to new technologies.

RELIGIOUS UNDERSTANDING OF REPRODUCTIVE TECHNOLOGIES

In vitro fertilization (IVF) occurs when human embryos are conceived by the union of sperm and ova in a petri dish. The embryos develop over the course of up to seven days, after which some—but generally not all—are implanted in a woman's uterus. There are varieties of IVF and implantation. In the conventional form, ova are drawn from the woman who is expected to fill the child's mother role and sperm from the man who is expected to fill the child's father role, and the embryo is implanted in the woman's uterus. In this case, the biological parents are also the "intended parents." Sometimes, however, the sperm or ova are donated by other people, who are not the intended parents. And sometimes an embryo is implanted in the uterus of a woman called a surrogate who will bear the child but will not be the intended mother. IVF has the potential to blur otherwise taken-for-granted family roles and structures. What is a mother? Is she the woman from whose fertilized ovum the child developed, the one who gestated the fetus, or the one who raised the child to adulthood? Similarly, what is a father? Is he the man whose sperm contributed to making the child, or is he the person who raised the child? (Similar questions have also come up regarding adoption, but Christianity—the dominant religion in the United States—has little to say about this case. Some non-Christian traditions, including Islam, *do* have concerns about adoption, something we will consider later.) IVF makes reproduction more accessible to people who are not partnered in heterosexual relationships, including single people and gay and lesbian couples. This situation also challenges our notion of the traditional family, composed of a "father" and "mother" partnered for life and charged by society with childbearing and childrearing. Assistive reproductive technologies such as IVF make it easier for those outside such relationships to become parents and redefine the notion of family.

These questions matter, especially in religious traditions that posit the family unit as inherently sacred or a reflection of the divine order. To mess with the boundaries of the sacred, as some religions believe assistive reproductive technologies do, is dangerous not just for the people who are directly involved but for the larger society.

So how do different religious traditions understand these assistive technologies? You may know that the Catholic Church is opposed to IVF as a means of human reproduction and also as a source for embryos for stem cell research. The Vatican has stated unequivocally that "the Catholic Church condemns as gravely evil acts, both IVF in and of itself, and stem cell research performed on IVF embryos." That's a strong statement! What is so objectionable here? The Catholic Church holds that human life begins at conception. John Shea (2003) writes,

> IVF violates the rights of the child: it deprives him of his filial relationship with his parental origins and can hinder the maturing of his personality. It objectively deprives conjugal fruitfulness of its unity and integrity, it brings about and manifests a rupture between genetic parenthood, gestational parenthood, and responsibility for upbringing. This threat to the unity and stability of the family is a source of dissension, disorder, and injustice in the whole of social life.

For the Catholic Church, then, the use of IVF to produce embryos for implantation collides with religious understandings of the rights of children and the structure and functioning of the family. The *desire* to have children is not, in this tradition, the ultimate value, and individual wishes do not dictate whether a technology is appropriate. Instead, the religious tradition rules on whether the use of the technology fits within the bounds of the religion's morality. In short, religion wishes to constrain the use of this technology.

But that is only Catholic Church *policy.* As is often the case, things are not so clear cut in practice. For example, in ethnographic research on IVF clinics in Ecuador—a predominantly Catholic society—Elizabeth Roberts found that doctors and their clients not only defied the Catholic Church's prohibition against IVF but also redefined the fundamental meaning of the procedure (Roberts 2006). That is, rather than believing that assistive reproductive technologies were "threats" to the family, the clinics and their clients understood IVF as a sort of "miracle" that they could personally access without mediation from the church or its representatives. This use of technology at the local level thus undercut Catholic teachings and authority at two levels. First, the technology itself was reinterpreted in a way that was contradictory to the Church's position. Second, and perhaps more importantly, individuals benefiting from IVF bypassed the official structure and personnel of the church in realizing a miracle (albeit by technology).

In the United States, objections from the Catholic Church have not impeded the use of IVF. Indeed, cultural anthropologist Marcia Inhorn (2006a) goes so far as to describe the United States as having a relatively "free market" of assistive reproductive technologies, little regulated by the state or affected, in practice, by objections from religious groups. In other societies, however, religious traditions and authorities are more active in defining when such technologies are appropriate and when their use should be limited. Consider the examples of Islam and Orthodox Judaism.

Inhorn has studied assistive reproductive technologies in Islamic societies. In general, Islam places a very high value on marriage and parenting. Inhorn (2006a, 442) summarizes the Muslim view as follows:

> In the Middle Eastern Muslim world, marriage is highly valued, and nearly all adults marry if possible in most Middle Eastern countries . . . Middle Eastern societies are also pronatalist—they highly value children for numerous reasons and expect all marriages to produce them . . . Thus, the notion of a married couple living happily without children is unthinkable. Children are desired from the beginning of marriage in most cases, and are usually loved and cherished once they are born.

Despite the strong emphasis of this culture on family, especially on raising children, it also places strict legal and cultural limits on IVF. Among other limits, only the husband's semen may be used, the embryo must be implanted in the intended mother rather than in a surrogate, the parents must be married to each other, and they cannot donate embryos to other couples. Islamic law specifically prohibits sperm donation, egg donation, and surrogacy. Given the high value that is placed on family in Islamic societies, why is IVF so limited in its use? The answer to this question lies in the Islamic understanding of what constitutes "family." Inhorn reports on her research on adoption and egg donation:

> In the Muslim world, attitudes toward family formation are closely tied to religious teachings that stress the importance of "purity of lineage" . . . Indeed, Islam is a religion that privileges—even mandates—biological descent and inheritance.

Conception and birth are activities that take place within the marriage and third parties are not allowed to "intrude into the marital functions of sex and procreation" (Inhorn, 2006a: 433). Sperm donation, egg donation, and surrogacy all involve parties that are outside the marriage contract between husband and wife; they constitute adultery and thus disrupt the marital relationship. Additionally, a child who is conceived using sperm or egg donation is considered illegitimate and cannot be adopted by the husband. This understanding of family as a creation that occurs solely within the marital relationship and between blood relations extends also to adoption. Although Islam has a strong and honored tradition of fostering—caring for the needs of—orphaned children, formal adoption is not possible because the adoption of children who are not directly linked biologically to parents is not consistent with what constitutes family in this faith:

> The concept of social parenthood—of either an adopted or donor child—is considered untenable in most of the Muslim world. The kind of adoption practiced in the West—whereby an orphan takes the legal name of the adoptive parents (usu. the father's surname) and is treated as their own child through the mutually reinforcing mechanisms of residence, inheritance rights, and ongoing affective relations including unconditional love—is explicitly forbidden in Islam. (Inhorn 2006b, 95)

This understanding is not unique to Muslim societies. Many Americans prefer to give birth to their own biological children rather than adopting children even if they must undergo difficult, expensive, and time-consuming fertility treatments.

Remember that religion is a product of society. Religion is not static but constantly evolving, as is the society it emerges from. This fluid nature is apparent in recent developments in some Muslim societies—particularly predominantly Shi'a Muslim cultures such as Iran—where religious officials and the general population have become more open to the possibility of assistive reproductive technologies that incorporate donor ova. The shift is driven largely by a kind of *logos:* the potential for assistive reproductive technologies to be a practical solution to infertility problems in a population that values family very highly. IVF using donor eggs, in particular, is increasingly understood as a way to solidify marriage and bring happiness to it (Inhorn, 2006a).

In Israel, rabbinical law governs the use of assistive reproductive technologies. In this religious context, very different issues arise. Susan Martha Kahn (1998, 2006), an anthropologist at Brandeis University, has studied the use of reproductive technologies in ultraorthodox Judaism, with a particular focus on how the technologies are interpreted within a religious frame and how religious authorities develop guidelines for appropriate use of newly emerging technologies. We begin with the issue of sperm donation and adultery. Recall that in Islam no third party is permitted in the marriage, so sperm donation is not permitted. Adultery is also prohibited in Judaism. Specifically, rabbinical law prohibits sexual relations between a Jewish man and a Jewish woman unless they are married to each other. Fertilization, even technically assisted fertilization, is considered a type of sexual relation, and for that reason sperm donation is forbidden in ultraorthodox Jewish groups. But the law only prohibits sexual relations between a *Jewish* man and a Jewish woman outside of marriage; it does not explicitly prohibit such relations between a non-Jewish man and a Jewish woman. This quirk in the law has been used by ultraorthodox rabbis as a sort of escape clause with respect to sperm donation: Sperm donation is allowable as long as the sperm comes from a non-Jew.

You might wonder if having a non-Jewish biological father would compromise the ethnic identity of the child: Would he or she really be Jewish? The understanding in Judaism, however, is that "Jewishness" is passed from the mother to the child. Nonetheless, this seemingly simple principle becomes quite complex in practice, due to the rapid development of new assistive reproductive technologies like surrogacy and egg donation. If Jewishness is conferred by the mother, does that mean that the ovum should be from a Jewish woman? Or should the embryo be implanted only in the uterus of a Jewish woman? Should there be a genetic link, a gestational link, or both? These questions have not been resolved as quickly as the questions about sperm donation, which reflects the slow process by which Jewish rabbinical law works in the real world. But as the rabbis continue to debate this issue, Jews in Israel are nonetheless moving forward and using IVF technology.

In sum, depending on the religious context, assistive reproductive technologies are interpreted and implemented differently. Across religions, however, there is a clear theme in the tensions between religion and these technologies: "Family" is not just a chance creation. Instead, the family unit is part of a larger cosmic and transcendental order. The family looks different in different traditions—there are no universals or fundamentals—but across religions family, family relations, and family structure are infused with sacred meaning. When we introduce technologies that allow the family to be reconfigured, sacred meaning and order are challenged. Thus, it is not just what we know, but *what we do with what we know,* that matters. The bounds of acceptable behavior are, in many corners of the world, profoundly shaped by religious systems of meaning and conviction.

GODLESS SCIENCE? IRRATIONAL RELIGION?

As we noted at the beginning of this chapter, the disputes between science and religion are not just academic. They also have implications for the distribution of authority, power, and resources in society. The struggle over what to teach in science classrooms, the disputes over the use of embryos in scientific research, the debate about how and when to use new technologies that assist reproduction—each of these conflicts has ideological components as we collectively negotiate meanings and common knowledge (or, perhaps more accurately in the current context, fail to do so). But each is also a real dispute between social groups struggling to be heard and to exercise authority in particular arenas. Science and technology have had pretty good runs over the last few centuries. Scientists are, for the most part, respected professionals credited with making significant improvements in our quality of life: Thanks to science, we enjoy longer life spans, better overall health, clean water, fast cars, air travel, cell phones, and efficient food production. The list of achievements is endless. Some people dismiss science's findings, contending that evolution and global warming are fictions. But scientists continue to secure substantial research funding and are consulted about important policy issues. And few of us are true Luddites who really want to go backward in terms of scientific discovery and technological advancement (though some of us could do without the cell phone).

But science's victories have often come at the expense of religion. In the United States, scientists study cells taken from embryos, while religious persons worry about the morality of this line of research. This is one battle where religion, at least under the Bush administration, held its own as federally funded stem-cell research was limited to a constrained set of embryo lines. But even here, science made a comeback when some states (e.g., California) and private funding agencies stepped in to fill the void left by federal restrictions. Now, under the Obama presidential administration, an easing of restrictions is likely.

The debate over the teaching of creationism and evolution is also at something of a standstill. The Dover court decision quoted at the beginning of this chapter argued definitively and in great detail that intelligent design and creationism are not science and cannot be taught in science classrooms in public schools. It seems that science—and science teachers—have won this round against the deniers of evolution. While the debate quieted down after this court decision, proponents on either side have not changed their views, and we fully expect these issues to arise again in some other setting.

Finally, while assistive reproductive technologies have opened up parenthood to a wider range of persons, religious groups continue to express reservations about crossing these boundaries. At issue here, as well as in the ongoing debate about same-sex marriage, is what kind of unit will be defined as a "family" and what people will receive the privileges and benefits that go along with that designation.

Despite some scholars' calls to keep religion and science in their respective places, it turns out not to be so easy. Science and technology bring us knowledge and capabilities that were undreamed of in earlier eras. Religion sometimes embraces that knowledge and potential, but just as often it seems to resist it, especially when new knowledge and technology challenges or changes the taken-for-granted social order. The notion that humans shared a common ancestor with all other creatures on earth is profoundly threatening to people who prefer to believe that humans have a special place in the natural order.

For its part, technology can cure us of diseases, expand our food sources, and make parenthood available to more people. All of that, on the surface, seems desirable. But technology can also extend into activities that religions have prohibited. It can tinker with the fundamental beginnings of life—the creation of embryos—and it can reconstitute the family in new ways. The efficiency and effectiveness of technology can divert our attention from moral questions to mere technical questions, and in so doing, reshape the morality of a society. Religious persons worry about "godless science" just as scientists and their supporters worry about the limits that "irrational religion" may put on scientific and technological progress.

SUGGESTED READING

Armstrong, Karen. 2000. *The Battle for God: A History of Fundamentalism*. Random House.
Gould, Stephen Jay. 1998. "Nonoverlapping Magisteria." In *Leonardo's Mountain of Clams and the Diet of Worms*. New York: Three Rivers Press.

13

End of Days? Religion and the Environment

1. What is environmentalism, and what does religion have to do with it?
2. Are fundamentalist Christians antienvironmentalists? Why would we think that?
3. What are the alternatives to a worldview of man's mastery over nature?
4. Do environmentalists romanticize indigenous religions and their orientation to nature?

No living thing—no plant, microbe, or animal—exists on this earth without having an impact on the natural world around it. Humans are no exception, as historian Lynn White argued in his 1967 *Science* article "The Historical Roots of Our Ecologic Crisis":

> Ever since man became a numerous species he has affected his environment notably. The hypothesis that his fire-drive method of hunting created the world's great grasslands and helped to exterminate the monster mammals of the Pleistocene from much of the globe is plausible, if not proved. For 6 millennia at least, the banks of the lower Nile have been a human artifact rather than the swampy African jungle, which nature, apart from man, would have made it . . . In many regions terracing or irrigation, overgrazing, the cutting of forests by Romans to build ships to fight Carthaginians or by Crusaders to solve the logistics problems of their expeditions, have profoundly changed some ecologies . . . Quite unintentionally, changes in human ways often affect nonhuman nature. It has been noted, for example, that the advent of the automobile eliminated huge flocks of sparrow that once fed on the horse manure littering every street. (1203)

Human societies vary in how they understand their place in the natural world, their impact on it, and their responsibility to care for it. We will discuss in this chapter how those understandings are profoundly informed by religious belief and reinforced through religious rituals that are enacted in community.

ENVIRONMENTALISM AND ITS DISCONTENTS

Environmentalism is a social movement and worldview that prioritizes care and preservation of the earth's natural environment: water, air, forests and other natural landscapes, and wildlife and animals' habitats. It encompasses beliefs that our fate is intertwined with the fate of the environment and that we have a responsibility to care for the earth and minimize our impact on it. It also includes behaviors that many of you may practice: "reducing, reusing, and recycling," conserving energy, and living sustainably, among others.

The value of environmentalism is not obvious to everyone, and the term often sparks controversy. Environmentalists may believe strongly in their cause and actions, but others react just as strongly against a worldview that places such a high priority on the natural world. For example, one of us (Monahan) lives in Montana. The local paper's opinion columns and letters to the editor regularly refer to environmentalists as "ecoterrorists" and "ecowackos." Seriously, it is printed right there on the opinion page! The antipathy towards environmentalists has historical roots: Until recently, Montana's economy relied heavily on extractive industries like mining, an economic reality that shapes how residents view the natural environment. For the most part, Montanans (mostly those of European descent) have historically valued the natural world for what can be *extracted* from it for human use and for what is of immediate economic value: rangeland, wheat fields, metals such as copper and silver, coal, and natural gas. Fewer Montanans have prioritized the intrinsic value of the land or its value as a sustainable ecosystem that supports a variety of living creatures, from elk and wolves to human beings.

This regional culture exemplifies one of the fault lines in the way that humans understand the environment: Is the environment for human *use*, to be shaped to our purposes? Or it is our *context*, a place for us to fit in with other living things? In Montana, for example, both elk and wolves are indigenous to the state, and historically wolves held elk populations in check in a delicate balance between predator and prey. When wolves were eradicated in the early 20th century, the elk population exploded. This delighted Montana's hunters. In 1995, wolves were reintroduced to Yellowstone Park and have since spread outside park boundaries. As a result, the old balance has been restored and the elk population has leveled off. As elk have become scarcer, hunting has become more onerous.

Is this good or bad? On the one hand is the value of ecological balance. On the other is the value that many people place on elk and the enmity that they feel for wolves: Elk are game—useful to humans—and wolves are predators—disruptive to ranching. So we get a clash in worldviews between those who believe that elk, wolves, and humans are parts of a larger whole and those who view elk as, first and foremost, food, and wolves as separate from and the enemies of humans.

Much of the conflict between environmentalists and their objectors appears to be secular, rather than religious. Many so-called antienvironmentalists cite economic rather than religious principles to support their case: They worry that environmental preservation comes at the expense of economic growth or meeting human needs. For example, we often hear about how much it will cost a business or a landowner to protect a species that is at risk of extinction. "For what?" opponents of environmentalism ask. "So that we can save one kind of small bird or toad or fish? What's the point?" To these people, our priority should be human needs rather than those of obscure species. Others worry that protecting the environment will bring heavy-handed government intervention and restrictions on individual freedoms, including infringement of private property rights. People act in their own short-term interests; to get them to do otherwise, it is argued, requires significant government regulation that will ultimately do more harm than good.

RELIGIOUS DISCONTENTS

You might wonder what this has to do with religion. Though these objections appear to be differences in secular philosophy, they arise from differences in assumptions about the relationship between humans and nature. These assumptions are rooted in our foundational, often religious, understandings of how our world works.

Let's explore these questions in more depth: Are humans masters of nature, shaping nature for human purposes? Or are we part and parcel of nature, dependent for our survival on the health of the natural environment? To envision humans as "masters of nature" suggests dualism—the idea that humans exist separate from nature. Humans are "here" and nature is "out there," and the two domains do not overlap. It also implies a worldview of mastery over nature in which the natural world exists primarily to serve human needs. On the other hand, to view humans as part and parcel of nature, deeply connected to the larger ecology, suggests that humans and nature are integrated and that all creatures share a basic equality. None is more important than another. These contrasting worldviews are embedded to varying degrees in our religious traditions, and they play out not just as secular or political philosophies but as religious beliefs and practices that are maintained within religious communities.

Some Christian groups, including Evangelicals, also worry that worship of God the creator will be displaced by worship of the natural world (National Association of Evangelicals 2004, 11):

> As we embrace our responsibility to care for God's earth, we reaffirm the important truth that we worship only the Creator and not the creation.

In their view, worship of creation is a grave error. Many Christians feel that religions such as Wicca, which are oriented around the natural, rather than the supernatural, world, make this error. Fully aware of the negative connotations of environmentalism, some Evangelical Christians use the term "creation care" instead. In so doing, they join the environmental movement, as we describe in the next section, but they do so on terms aligned with their theology.

RELIGION FINDS ENVIRONMENTALISM . . .

In October 2004, the National Association of Evangelicals adopted the *Evangelical Call to Civic Responsibility*. It urged

> . . . Christians to shape their personal lives in creation-friendly ways: practicing effective recycling, conserving resources, and experiencing the joy of contact

with nature . . . [and] government to encourage fuel efficiency, reduce pollution, encourage sustainable use of natural resources, and provide for the proper care of wildlife and their natural habitats. (12)

In 2005, *The Washington Post* reported on the "greening of evangelicals," both nationally and at the local level:

> Evangelical churches are lowering the thermostat, unplugging the hot water heater at the baptismal font, recycling rainwater and switching over to fluorescent light bulbs. Among evangelical Christians in the US, environmental awareness is growing, as is the willingness to make significant lifestyle changes to address environment problems. For example, a survey conducted by John Green, a political scientist at the University of Akron, found that in 2000 45% of evangelicals were in favor of "strict environmental regulations." By 2005 support for such regulations had risen to 52%. (Harden 2005)

Most mainstream Protestant denominations have issued policy statements on environmental responsibility, and many local congregations engage in green activities including recycling and efforts to reduce carbon emissions. Among alternative religions, Wiccans place a high priority on environmentalism: They believe in a close and symbiotic relationship between humans and nature, their rituals frequently take place outside, and they emphasize the importance of protecting the earth (BBC 2008). Traditional Native American religions also emphasize the close ties between humans and nature, refer to the earth as "Mother," and view her as the source of human life and part of the human family, rather than separate from us and under our jurisdiction.

. . . BUT ENVIRONMENTALISM IS LEERY OF RELIGION

Environmentalists have begun to reach out to religious groups as they build broad-based coalitions to address environmental problems, including pollution, global warming, and habitat destruction. Nonetheless, as Carl Pope, the Executive Director of the Sierra Club noted, environmentalists are often suspicious of religious people. Those doubts have inhibited environmentalists' efforts to reach out to religion groups:

> . . . for almost 30 years most professional environmentalists stubbornly, almost proudly, denied the need to reach out to the religious community. Many of us have inherited and uncritically accepted the 19th-century idea that religion could be discarded because it had been superseded by science. We failed to realize—as some eminent scientists now tell us—that science and religion offer two distinct approaches to knowledge, and that neither has a monopoly on the truth. We sought to transform society, but ignored the fact that when Americans want to express something wiser and better than they are as individuals, by and large they gather to pray. We acted as if we could save life on Earth without the same institutions through which we save ourselves (1998).

Harvard entomologist E. O. Wilson, a prominent scientist and environmentalist, recently reached out to religious groups. His book *The Creation* is framed as a letter to a

Southern Baptist pastor. In it, Wilson (2006, 4) argues that scientists and religious leaders must work together to save the creation they both treasure:

> Pastor, we need your help. The Creation—living nature—is in deep trouble . . . Surely we can agree that each species, however inconspicuous and humble it may seem to us at this moment, is a masterpiece of biology and well worth saving . . . Prudence alone dictates that we act quickly to prevent the extinction of species and, with it, the pauperization of Earth's ecosystem—hence of the Creation.

Wilson's appeal raises an intriguing question: Of all the people to whom this appeal could be directed, why did he choose a *Southern Baptist pastor*? Why not Indy car fans? Why not hunters or fishermen? Why not college students? Wilson (2006, 5) explains,

> You may well ask at this point, Why me? Because religion and science are the two most powerful forces in the world today . . . If religion and science could be united on the common ground of biological conservation, the problem would soon be solved.

But why not a Catholic priest? Why not a Buddhist monk? Wilson's choice of audience, whether it is a rhetorical device or a sincere effort to speak to Southern Baptists, suggests that this group has a special responsibility for solving our environmental problems.

Wilson is not alone. As we mentioned, suspicions about fundamentalist Christians—of which Southern Baptists are the largest organized group—are common in the environmental movement. (Here, by "fundamentalist," we mean Christians who accept the Bible as the literal word of God.) For example, in 2004, PBS journalist Bill Moyers accepted the Global Environmental Award at Harvard's Medical School. In his acceptance speech, he said,

> When ideology and theology couple, their offspring are not always bad, but they are always blind . . . Remember James Watt, President Reagan's first Secretary of the Interior? The online environmental journal, *Grist,* reminded us recently of how Watt told the U.S. Congress that protecting natural resources was unimportant in light of the imminent return of Jesus Christ. He said, "after the last tree is felled, Christ will come back." Watt was serious. So were his compatriots across the country. They are the people who believe the Bible is literally true—one-third of the American electorate, if a recent Gallup poll is accurate. . . . Millions of Christian fundamentalists may believe that environmental destruction is to be welcomed—even hastened—as a sign of the coming apocalypse. (Moyers 2004)

Bill Moyers later conceded that James Watt did not actually say "after the last tree is felled, Christ will come back." Nonetheless his misstatement reflected a common fear on the part of environmentalists: that fundamentalists hold apocalyptic beliefs about the imminent arrival of the end times as reflected in religious literature like the *Left Behind* series, religious radio, and religious television. How did we get to this point? Why do environmentalists so strongly suspect that fundamentalist Christians are antienvironmentalists?

Social scientists have explored this question. In particular, researchers have homed in on a Judeo–Christian worldview that is focused on man's mastery over nature and explored how that worldview might cause some Christians to lack concern for the environment or to resist efforts to protect the environment. We now examine key findings that emerge from that research. As you will see, the relationship between Christian fundamentalism and antienvironmentalism is not as strong as many people believe. We then explore religious alternatives to a worldview of mastery over nature and the conundrums they create.

DO FUNDAMENTALIST CHRISTIANS CARE ABOUT THE ENVIRONMENT?

A Worldview of "Mastery of Nature"

We began with a quote from Lynn White's 1967 article, "The Historical Roots of Our Ecologic Crisis." White argued that elements of Christianity as a worldview profoundly affected the beliefs, norms, and values of the modernizing Western world and that Christianity bears much responsibility for the environmental crises of the 20th and 21st centuries. How is this so?

> Christianity inherited from Judaism . . . a striking story of creation. By gradual stages a loving and all-powerful God had created light and darkness, the heavenly bodies, the earth and all its plants, animals, birds, and fishes. Finally, God had created Adam and, as an afterthought, Eve to keep man from being lonely. Man named all the animals, thus establishing his dominance over them. God planned all of this explicitly for man's benefit and rule: no item in the physical creation had any purpose save to serve man's purposes . . . Especially in its Western form, Christianity is the most anthro-centric religion the world has seen. (1205)

In short, the Judeo–Christian creation story espouses a worldview of "mastery over nature." (See Box 13.1.) In this story, humans are set apart from and above the natural world, and the natural world exists for human use. In addition, humans are imbued with soul and consciousness, while nature is a lifeless set of resources to be taken and shaped as we wish. According to White, this worldview informed and drove technological development and scientific discovery from medieval Europe through the present and is thus implicated in the environmental problems that grow out of technology and science.

The creation story is a myth, a story we tell ourselves about our relationship with nature. Once it is internalized, the myth becomes a taken-for-granted reality that shapes how we relate to nature: It makes sense of our existence in the natural world and guides us. It is not necessary to *literally* believe the creation story in order to absorb its message

BOX 13.1

Mastery over Nature

Biblical Roots And God blessed them: and God said unto them, Be fruitful, and multiply, and replenish the earth, and subdue it; and have dominion over the fish of the sea, and over the birds of the heavens, and over every living thing that moveth upon the earth.

(The Bible, Genesis 1:28, American Standard Version)

about the relationship between dominant humans and the subordinated natural world. Certainly, if you believe the creation story to be the literal truth, then a belief in human mastery over nature might logically follow. But even if the creation story is only a *myth* to you, it may still embody larger truths for you, just like any other myth. You know the story about George Washington: When he was asked if he cut down the cherry tree, he responded, "I cannot tell a lie." As it turns out, there is no historical evidence that this event occurred, and many people know this. Nonetheless, it embodies a widely held belief about George Washington—about his essential goodness and honesty. The creation story has a similar effect: If the story resonates with you, then you have absorbed its message, whether or not you take it literally.

White provided a historical narrative to explain what he saw as the Western world's unique and harmful relationship between humans and nature. And although E. O. Wilson makes no reference to White or his article, his appeal to Southern Baptists jibes with a common reading of White's central argument: that the Judeo–Christian creation story in Genesis is taken literally by fundamentalist Christians and causes them, more so than others, to relate to the natural world as masters or rulers.

White's indictment of the Judeo–Christian creation story and the worldview that it informed drew both praise and criticism. The responses came in two waves. The first came in the years that immediately followed the publication of White's article, when scientists, historians, theologians, and social scientists variously accepted, refined, or rebutted his ideas. The second wave began almost 20 years after the article was published, when sociologists and political scientists began to test empirically the implications of White's argument.

THE FIRST WAVE: ACCEPTANCE AND CRITIQUE OF WHITE'S ARGUMENT

Lynn White's *Science* article was read widely after its publication. Over the last 40 years, it has been cited by over 500 articles in peer-reviewed journals in the sciences, social sciences, and humanities. It also spurred some mainline Christian denominations to rethink their theologies and practices with respect to the environment. Much of the early response was positive, in that theologians in a range of denominations and scholars in a variety of disciplines accepted White's argument and incorporated it into their own thinking and models about the relationship between humans and environment. (See, for example, Catton and Dunlap 1980, Goodman 1970, and Neel 1970.) Others, however, argued that White was partially or wholly wrong.

White's work generated a strong response among Christians. For example, at a 1970 national conference at the School of Theology in Claremont, California, 20 Christian theologians met to discuss environmental implications of Christianity. Edward Fiske (1970, 12) of *The New York Times* reported,

> [v]irtually all of the scholars agreed that the traditional Christian attitude toward nature had given sanction to exploitation of the environment by science and technology and thus contributed to air and water pollution, overpopulation and other ecological threats.

The group proposed a number of changes: smaller family sizes, slower economic growth, an end to the advertising that drives consumerism, more respect for simplicity of living, and the scaling back of conspicuous consumption. As we review their call to action, we are struck by how much the United States has moved since that time—in the *opposite* direction! In 1970, the world population was 3.7 billion. It now exceeds 6 billion. During the past 40 years we have seen significant economic growth and even bigger increases in consumption of goods and services—ask anyone who remembers the 1960s, and he or she will probably confirm this—along with a surge in the branding and advertising that accompanies a consumer society. There is even more pressure to "keep up with the Joneses," whether we can afford it or not. Although we talk a lot about being "green," our day-to-day lives have moved in the exact direction against which theologians warned 40 years ago!

Even today, theological discussions about environmentalism among Christians invoke Lynn White. For example, the evangelical magazine *Christianity Today* resurrected White's argument in a 2001 article on environmentalism and Christian responsibility. And his argument continues to inform mainline Christian denominations' work for environmental change. Other groups continue to refute White's argument, claiming either a "stewardship" relationship to the earth that sets humans above nature or dismissing the suggestion that humans and the rest of nature are on equal footing. For example, in a 2006 resolution the Southern Baptist Convention responded to calls for environmental responsibility by asserting,

> God created men and women in His image and likeness (Genesis 1:26–27), placing them in value above the rest of creation and commanding them to exercise caring stewardship and dominion over the earth and environment (Genesis 1:28; cf. Psalm 8) . . . [and] some in our culture have completely rejected God the Father in favor of deifying "Mother Earth," made environmentalism into a neopagan religion, and elevated animal and plant life to the place of equal—or greater—value with human life. (Southern Baptist Convention 2006)

While the Southern Baptist Convention embraced the stewardship of nature, the group countered that neither private property rights nor economic development should be compromised. In other words, man's needs and man's conventions (e.g., private property) come first.

White's argument drew both acclaim and criticism from secular scholars. Some of them questioned White's conclusions. In a 1970 *Science* article, Lewis Montcrief argued that White had oversimplified the causes of our environmental problems. What about other large-scale social changes? The mass movement of workers into cities and rapid population growth strained environmental resources. Capitalism, which emphasized private property and urged the accumulation of wealth, spurred consumption and waste. Democracy, along with dispersed property ownership, spread control of economic and political activity among the populace, creating a system in which individual behaviors—even when they cause long-term harm to the environment—are much harder to control or regulate.

William Coleman, a historian, disputes White, using arguments that overlap with those of Montcrief. Specifically, Coleman attributes environmental degradation to the rise and growing acceptance of "economic individualism" in late 17th-century Europe, a trend that was embodied by the capitalistic entrepreneur who accumulates material wealth and that was legitimated by Judeo–Christian theology. Coleman critiques White for missing the economic innovations of European society in his laser focus on innovation in science and technology.

Most importantly, Montcrief disagrees with White that these social trends can be directly or indirectly traced to back Judeo–Christian worldviews as embodied in the creation story. Specifically, he points out that non-Christian societies underwent these same social processes and experienced similar environmental consequences. Jared Diamond's 2004 book *Collapse: How Societies Choose to Fail or Succeed* narrates the story of a number of societies (generally ones in fragile natural environments). Groups of humans living on Easter Island and Greenland, as well as the Mayans and indigenous peoples in the American southwest, all depleted their environments. Of these, however, only the European immigrants to Greenland espoused Judeo–Christian religion.

For his part, British philosopher Robin Attfield doubts that a worldview of "mastery over nature" was universally accepted in medieval Europe or in the centuries that followed. Instead, he finds Biblical, theological, and historical evidence that supports a beneficent relationship between humans and nature. Calls to protect nature, care for the land, and act as responsible stewards of the earth recur throughout the historical period during which White sees an exploitative relationship developing between humans and nature. While Attfield concedes that there is much variety in how Christians relate to nature and that Christians do not always do well by nature, he concludes that

> . . . a despotic attitude to nature [is not] typical of Christians. The biblical position, which makes people responsible to God for the uses to which the natural environment is put, has never been entirely lost to view, and may be properly appealed to by the very people who rightly criticize the exploitative attitudes which prevail in many place throughout the contemporary world. (1980, 386)

Others have echoed Attfield's point and used Christian theology to justify a caretaking role for humans. Later, when we consider alternatives to the "mastery over nature" worldview, we will revisit this issue.

THE SECOND WAVE: TESTING "THE LYNN WHITE HYPOTHESIS"

The second wave of response to White's work began in 1984 with a series of empirical studies of the main researchable hypothesis that has been drawn from White's work: that Christians—of varying sorts—are less concerned about the environment than people who are not Christian. The earliest studies (Eckberg and Blocker 1989, Hand and Van Liere 1984) explored a wide range of aspects of religion and how they affected environmental beliefs and actions. Researchers found that people who had strong personal religious beliefs in God or a higher power were no more or less likely to espouse environmentalism in attitude or action than people who did not have these beliefs. The same was true of frequency of church attendance, the importance that people said they placed on their religion, their religious affiliation, and their frequency of prayer: None of these religious variables consistently predicted environmental attitudes or actions (Boyd 1999, Eckberg and Blocker 1996, Guth *et al.* 1993, Guth *et al.* 1995, Kanagy and Nelsen 1995).

In these early studies, only religious fundamentalism consistently predicted environmental attitudes and actions. Maybe E. O. Wilson *is* on to something here! Keep in mind, though, that fundamentalism has been operationalized in different ways. Some researchers even call it something else. For example, Guth *et al.* (1993) refer to "conservative eschatology," a combination of biblical literalism (self-reported belief that the words in the Bible are literally true) and "end times thinking" (self-reported belief in imminent catastrophe that will purify the world). Eckberg and Blocker (1989, 1996) refer to "sectarianism," an index that combines a slew of indicators including biblical literalism, a view of God as harsh and punishing, a belief in the value of obedience, affiliation with a conservative Protestant denomination, opposition to banning school prayer, rejection of Darwin's theory of evolution, belief in God's presence in everyday activities, and an appreciation for Gospel music. The index was constructed, one imagines, because these indicators were highly associated with one another and thus deemed to measure a larger dimension. Heather Hartwig Boyd (1999) looked at membership in a fundamentalist tradition. Andrew Greeley (1993) focused on biblical literalism. Each study got at a roughly similar aspect of religiosity: what is commonly called fundamentalist belief, identity, and/or denominational affiliation.

The relationship is what E. O. Wilson infers and researchers predict: In general, and all other variables being held equal, fundamentalist Christians are less likely to hold favorable views of environmentalists, less likely to support policies to protect the environment, and less likely to see the benefits of investing in environmental protection. In a sample drawn from Tulsa, Oklahoma, Eckberg and Blocker found that fundamentalists were less concerned than other people about the state of the environment. In national samples of clergy, religious activists, political activists, and the mass public, Guth *et al.* (1995) found that fundamentalists had more negative attitudes than others about environmental protections. Boyd (1999) found that fundamentalists were less likely to engage in environmentalist behaviors or to perceive danger in environmental risks. And, as we will discuss further in a moment, Greeley (1993) found that fundamentalists were less willing to spend money on protecting the environment. On the basis of this literature, we can better understand why E. O. Wilson makes a special appeal to Southern Baptists—America's largest fundamentalist denomination—to save the environment!

Some finer points of this research are worth noting. First, no researcher has found a *positive* relationship between fundamentalism and environmentalism. That is, no one has found that fundamentalist Christians care *more* about the environment than other people do. But some studies have found that, once they account for a variety of other factors, there is *no relationship* between fundamentalism and environmentalism. That is, they found that fundamentalist Christians were no more or less likely to espouse environmentalism than anyone else. For example, Greeley (1993) examined this question using data from the 1993 General Social Survey, a well-respected national survey. He found that the effects of fundamentalism dissipated once you accounted for political conservatism and a less gracious image of God (one that was more strongly associated with terms like "Father," "Master," "Judge," and "King" than with "Mother," "Spouse," "Lover," and "Friend"). Greeley concluded that it is not fundamentalism *per se* that drives antienvironmentalism among fundamentalist Christians. Instead, the predominantly conservative political leanings of such people and their predominant image of a judgmental God predict their opposition to environmentalism. Along similar lines, Conrad Kanagy and Hart Nelsen (1995) found that when other factors—education, age, gender, and region—are controlled, religious variables, including fundamentalism, personal religion, and attendance at religious services, are not statistically significant predictors of environmentalism. The research literature on this question is not unanimous.

We offer three additional caveats to the findings regarding the relationship between fundamentalist Christianity and environmentalism. First, although some studies found that there was a relationship between fundamentalist Christianity and antienvironmentalism, it was often not a strong relationship. For example, Guth *et al.* (1995) found that religious variables explain between 22% and 44% of the variation in environmental attitudes and beliefs among "elites" but less than 10% of the variation among the "masses" (ordinary, everyday believers). Thus, for the majority of believers, over 90% of the variation in environmentalism is explained by something *other than* the religion variables that Guth *et al.* tested. Similarly, Eckberg and Blocker (1995) found that very little of the variation in environmental attitudes was predicted by religious variables—generally less than 3%, which means that more than 97% of the variation in environmental variables is due to other factors. Thus, while there is a relationship between fundamentalism and antienvironmentalism, we should be cautious of making too much of that relationship or making fundamentalist Christians a scapegoat for our collective reluctance to address environmental concerns. We should be especially careful not to expect that addressing fundamentalist Christians directly with environmental appeals will have much of an impact on our collective level of environmentalism.

Some studies have shown that the relationship between fundamentalism and environmentalism is strongest among "elites." Guth *et al.* (1995, 1993) found that the groups of people for whom a fundamentalist identity and affiliation most helps to explain environmental views are clergy, religious activists, and political activists. Among the masses, fundamentalism explained less, if any, of the variation in environmental attitudes and behaviors. This might well justify E. O. Wilson's decision to appeal to Southern Baptist pastors, as their fundamentalism makes them more likely than other people to hold particular environmental attitudes and behaviors. They are also the most visible voices in those communities. But the research literature suggests that one should not assume that antienvironmentalist attitudes espoused by a relatively small group of fundamentalist clergy and religious activists are shared in the same force by their followers. According to studies by Guth *et al.*, everyday fundamentalist Christians are somewhat less likely to be antienvironmentalist than their leaders and in some cases their views may not differ appreciably from those of people who are not fundamentalist Christians.

Finally, environmental attitudes and behaviors are in rapid flux; recent survey data reveal that people's levels of concern about the environment are increasing across the board. Many studies of the relationship between environmental views and religion are, however, based on survey data from the 1980s and 1990s. Although the earlier data can help us understand some of the theoretical issues in play, they may not help us understand how people today—religious or not—understand and act toward the environment.

REVISTING WHITE: WHAT WAS HIS POINT?

The 1980s and 1990s saw the development of a veritable cottage industry of empirical research on the relationship between religiosity and environmentalism. Much of that research claimed White's 1967 argument as its starting point. This research addressed important questions, but along the way seemed to lose track of the heart of White's argument. Remember, White never claimed that Christians, in particular, were less likely to be environmentalists. Nor did he contend that those who believe in the literal truth of the Genesis creation story are less likely to be active environmentalists.

Though these hypotheses are suggested by White's argument and they address intriguing questions, White's argument was more general. He argued that the Judeo–Christian worldview of human mastery over nature, a worldview that shaped centuries of technological and scientific development, so pervades modern Western culture that even those who are not explicitly religious (in the Southern Baptist sense, for example) have adopted and enacted this belief. White (1967, 1205) points out that

> It has become fashionable today to say that, for better or worse, we live in the "post-Christian age." Certainly the forms of our thinking and language have largely ceased to be Christian, but to my eye the substance often remains amazingly akin to that of the past. Our daily habits of action, for example, are dominated by an implicit faith in the perpetual progress which was unknown either to Greco–Roman antiquity or to the Orient. It is rooted in, and is indefensible apart from, Judeo–Christian teleology . . . We continue today to live, as we have lived for about 1700 years, very largely in a context of Christian axioms.

White's point is deceptively simple: Scientists, engineers, entrepreneurs, and others—religiously motivated or not—adhere to the belief that humans can master the natural world, which has been infused with the Judeo–Christian worldview embodied in the creation story. This group includes, to at least some extent, you and almost everyone you know. Before you protest, answer these questions. Does your home have air conditioning? Does your water come from a reservoir formed by a human-made dam? Have you ever been cured by an antibiotic? Do you drive a car? Do you eat food other than wild berries gathered from the forest? If you answered "yes" to any of these questions, then you, like the rest of us in the United States and throughout much of the world, live a lifestyle that is made possible by our attempts to master nature. You have come to expect technology to tame the natural world and smooth it over for human habitation. You don't have to be religious to espouse this worldview. You just have to participate in a modern Western—and increasingly worldwide—culture whose historic roots lie in a Judeo–Christian tradition. That is Lynn White's point, one that has been overlooked by many scholars who were in a rush to interpret his work as a narrow claim that fundamentalist Christians, or Christians in general, are prone to be antienvironmentalists.

We point this out because it is exemplifies how an idea—even one that has compelling historical evidence to support it—can be transformed in the process of creating testable hypotheses. White did not argue that fundamentalists are less likely to be environmentalists than are nonfundamentalists. He argued that all of us live in a culture that is infused with the beliefs and practices of science and technology, and that science and technology itself were driven in part by a worldview that posits humans' separation from and superiority over nature. As a result, whether or not we are Christian, we all struggle with how to live in environmentally friendly ways. Whether or not we are religious, almost all of us adhere to some elements of this dualism, this ideology of mastery. White simply suggests its roots. In so doing, he argues for the power of religion to suffuse an entire culture: even when the religious belief itself dissipates, it remains deeply implicated in what we think and how we act.

OTHER RELIGIOUS APPROACHES TO HUMANS IN THE NATURAL WORLD

Assuming that humans can master nature is not the *only* way to conceive of our relationship with nature. Alternatives exist to the worldview that White attributes to the modern West. The notions of *stewardship, creation spirituality,* and *ecojustice* embody alternative ecotheologies.

In their research on environmentalism among Presbyterians, Laurel Holland and Scott Carter (2005) distinguish attitudes of "domination" from "stewardship." Domination "emphasizes our role as masters of the earth . . . God gives us dominion over the earth." In contrast, stewardship "emphasizes our role as caretakers of the earth . . . God expects us to care for the earth." Many Christians, liberal and conservative, use the language of stewardship to explain human relations with the earth. In a resolution in their 202nd convention, the Presbyterian Church (U.S.A.) (2002) declared that

> Earth-keeping today means insisting on sustainability—the ongoing capacity of natural and social systems to thrive together—which requires human beings to practice wise, humble, responsible stewardship, after the model of servant-hood that we have in Jesus.

As we noted earlier, the Southern Baptist Convention also used the language of stewardship, albeit in combination with that of "dominion," in their 2006 resolution on environmentalism:

> God created men and women in His image and likeness (Genesis 1:26–27), placing them in value above the rest of creation and commanding them to exercise caring stewardship and dominion over the earth and environment (Genesis 1:28, cf. Psalm 8) . . . (Southern Baptist Convention 2006)

In both cases, humans are understood to have a responsibility to preserve and conserve the earth. The notion of stewardship shares an important characteristic with that of domination: Both assume dualism, the idea that humans are distinct from nature. Stewardship goes a step beyond domination, however, in assigning humans a special responsibility for the preservation of nature. We will return to the idea of dualism when we discuss creation spirituality, another alternative theology of environmentalism.

Non-Christian traditions also draw on the language of stewardship. In the *Washington Report on Middle East Affairs,* Hasan Zillur Rahim (1991) describes the Qu'ran's perspective on human relations with the earth:

> The Islamic approach to the environment is holistic. Everything in creation is linked to everything else; whatever affects one thing ultimately affects everything. Man has been distilled from the essence of nature and so is inextricably bound to it . . . Because of its ability to reason and think, humanity has been made the trustee or steward of God on earth. Nature is created on the principle of balance, and as a steward of God it is the human's responsibility to ensure that his or her actions do not disrupt this balance. Stewardship does not imply superiority over other living beings: Because ownership belongs to God alone, stewardship invests humans with a moral responsibility in safeguarding God's creation.

In her study of different ecotheologies battling for ascendancy in the Christian tradition, Laurel Kearns (1996) notes that stewardship is a fairly *conservative* approach. It suggests that the answers to our environmental problems are to be found in our existing religious traditions, albeit with some adjustments in our understanding of the actions for which those traditions call. An ecotheology of stewardship does not, however, call for existing religion to be abolished or replaced by something else. It is thus not surprising that stewardship is embraced particularly by conservative Christian traditions, including Southern Baptists.

Stewardship is also an *individualistic* approach to environmentalism. It focuses on how each of us can do our part to care for creation by adjusting our behaviors. An alternative to stewardship, ecojustice, is a *structural* approach to environmentalism. As Kearns describes in her 1996 article, ecojustice has emerged from national bodies in a number of Christian denominations and focuses on how environmentalism is linked to broader questions of justice: poverty, inequality, and the suffering of disadvantaged and disenfranchised groups. This approach prevails in many mainline Christian denominations, including Catholicism, where environmentalism is framed around societal and governmental responses to issues including fair trade, globalization, climate change, and environmental racism. *The Natural World,* a publication of the United Methodist Church (2004, 160), puts it this way:

> Economic, political, social, and technological developments have increased our human numbers, and lengthened and enriched our lives. However, these developments have led to regional defoliation, dramatic extinction of species, massive human suffering, overpopulation, and misuse and overconsumption of natural and nonrenewable resources, particularly by industrialized societies. This continued course of action jeopardizes the natural heritage that God has entrusted to all generations. Therefore, let us recognize the responsibility of the church and its members to place a high priority on *changes in economic, political, social, and technological lifestyles* [emphasis added] to support a more ecologically equitable and sustainable world leading to a higher quality of life for all of God's creation.

Kearns argues that ecojustice is the most institutional of the approaches that religious groups take towards environmentalism. It is institutional in two ways. It emphasizes the transformation of society as a whole rather than one person at a time. And it emerges not from local congregations but from denominational headquarters. At the same time, it is also the most abstract ecotheology. It seems distant from our day-to-day lives because it focuses on changes at the level of society as a whole, changes that are slow to occur and distant from the immediate experiences of religious believers.

Creation spirituality is a third ecotheology. According to Kearns (1996, 61), creation spirituality understands humans as "just one part of a whole, different only in the potential for destruction which we have shown, and in our capacity for self-reflection." Creation spirituality envisions humans as neither separate from nor better than the rest of nature.

Think back to the beginning of this chapter, where we discussed a fundamental split in human attitudes toward the environment: Does nature exist for human use, to be shaped to our purposes? Or is it our context, a place where we fit in with all other living things? Worldviews of dominion or mastery over nature lean strongly toward the former attitude, and in many respects, even stewardship as a worldview assumes that humans have a special place in nature. Creation spirituality, however, leans strongly in the other direction. It understands humans as merely part of a larger whole. Indeed, creation spirituality argues that dualism—the notion that humans and nature are separate and distinct from each other—is a big part of the problem. Dualism blinds us to our integral but not privileged place in a broader natural world. It is, according to creation spirituality, the myth that drives environmental destruction.

Creation spirituality is particularly espoused by those who are ecumenical Christians—that is, not strongly tied to any denomination—and by those who do not belong to institutional churches. The religions of indigenous peoples are also often rooted in creation spirituality. In the novel *Ceremony,* Native American writer Leslie Marmon Silko (1977) described a ritual that followed the killing of a hunted deer. As the deer lay in the throes of its death, Tayo—a Pueblo Indian of Laguna in New Mexico— covered the deer's head with his jacket (to the consternation of his cousin, who had rejected Native religious practices). After the deer died, Tayo's grandfather and uncle

> . . . went to the deer and lifted the jacket. They knelt down and took pinches of cornmeal from Josiah's leather pouch. They sprinkled the cornmeal on the nose and fed the deer's spirit. They had to show their love and respect, their appreciation; otherwise, the deer would be offended, and they would not come to die for them the following year . . . Tayo wrapped the liver and heart in the clean cheesecloth [his grandfather] carried with him . . . Tayo held the bundle tighter. He felt humbled by the size of the full moon, by the chill wind that swept wide across the foothills of the mountain. They said the deer gave itself to them because it loved them, and he could feel the love as the fading heat of the deer's body warmed his hands.

Throughout *Ceremony,* Tayo seeks his proper place in nature, particularly in the landscape where he grew up, the southwest United States, after returning from serving as a soldier in World War II. Through the rituals and ceremonies of his people he seeks balance and harmony as a small and mostly insignificant part of nature. This view of humans' relationships to nature might seem strange to you: the notion that we need to love and respect our food sources, the idea that the animal chooses to die to supply us with food, and Tayo's emotional connection to the source of his food. Even his sense of humility and gratitude might seem unfamiliar. But this passage embodies an alternative approach to relating to nature, one that emphasizes the inclusion of all living things in a single circle.

Modern environmentalists who espouse creation spirituality have often aligned themselves with native or indigenous religions. In contrast to religions that embody dualism—the strict separation of the material from the spiritual world—native and indigenous religions see the divine in every element of the material world (pantheism) or throughout the material and unseen worlds (panentheism). Earth First!, a radical environmental group that espouses "deep ecology," is one example. Bron Taylor (1997) wrote about this group:

> Earth First! activists believe that the natural world has value apart from its usefulness to humans. This moral claim is often grounded in mystical experiences in the natural world that yield pantheistic and/or panentheistic worldviews, and is often combined with a sense that nature is full of animate, spiritual intelligences, including but not always limited to animals, who can communicate with humans. I have previously labeled Earth First!'s religious orientation "primal spirituality" because many within this subculture venerate and seek to learn from and emulate the world's remaining indigenous cultures, especially those cultures unassimilated into the global market economy. They generally consider such cultures to be spiritually and ecologically wise.

Indigenous groups have often found environmentalists to be sympathetic to their claims of land rights. Roy Parrett writes that environmentalists feel

> . . . admiration for what they have taken to be the environmental superiority of the traditional life styles of indigenous peoples. The assumption has been that supporting indigenous land rights is fully compatible with—even promotive of—environmental values.

ROMANTICIZED RELIGION: INDIGENOUS RELIGION AND CLASHES WITH ENVIRONMENTALISTS

Environmentalists, including those who espouse creation spirituality, have often found native or indigenous religions to be promising models of a healthy relationship between nature and humans. That said, the relationship between indigenous religions and environmentalism is not a simple one. Many environmentalists embrace indigenous beliefs and practices, particularly when these beliefs challenge the dualism that is inherent in Western culture and when they focus on the inherent value and importance of nature. At the same time, however, the interests of indigenous peoples and the beliefs and goals of environmentalists are not always perfectly aligned! Despite their apparent shared interest in environmental preservation, it is not uncommon for these groups to want different things. As a result, indigenous peoples and environmentalists can sometimes surprise and dismay each other.

Historically, indigenous societies shaped the environment to their needs, as detailed in Jared Diamond's book *Collapse* (2004). Before Europeans arrived in North America, the Anasazi used ditches and canals to capture and distribute the minimal rainfall in the desert Southwest of what became the United States. Meanwhile, the Mayans of Central America dug wells 75 feet deep to access water and created cisterns and reservoirs to store water. Both of these societies ultimately failed because the environment could not support their expanding populations, and the indigenous religions—whose leaders were typically concentrated in population centers that received rather than produced food—did not provide cultural tools that allowed the society to find a balance between human community and the environment. This pattern was especially apparent when the natural environment was harsh and unforgiving (e.g., little rainfall, poor soil, or unpredictable weather patterns).

Easter Island is perhaps the most dramatic example of an indigenous group destroying the natural environment it needed in order to survive. Early European visitors to Easter Island were struck by huge carved stone statues at Rano Raraku and elsewhere:

> Scattered [in the quarry] are 397 stone statues, representing in a stylized way a long-eared legless human male torso, mostly 15 to 20 feet tall but the largest of them 70 feet tall (taller than the average modern 5-story building), and weighing from 10 up to 270 tons . . . Scattered along the [islands'] roads are 97 more statues, as if abandoned in transport from the quarry. Along the coast and occasionally inland are about 300 stone platforms, a third of them formerly supporting or associated with 393 more statues, all of which until a few decades ago were not erect but thrown down, many of them toppled so as to break them deliberately at the neck. (Diamond 2004, 80)

More important, however, was the almost complete absence of *trees* on the island. Early on, scientists and explorers wondered how the huge statues had been moved and erected all over an island when the raw materials for the tools for this work (i.e., large trees) were completely absent. Baby boomers may even recall the sensationalized mystery of Easter Island: Did aliens from outer space populate the island and erect the statues?

Archaeological evidence points to a less spooky but more disturbing explanation: Over the course of several centuries, the residents of Easter Island cut down every single tree on the island. And, as Diamond (2004, 432) notes, "much of the deforestation on Easter Island had a religious motivation: to obtain logs to transport and erect the giant stone statues that were the object of veneration." But without trees, there was no raw material for building fishing canoes. The Easter Islanders lost access to an important food source. Without trees, soil erosion accelerated, which compromised farming. And the Easter Islanders permanently destroyed the source of other raw materials (e.g., wood, bark, feathers from birds) that would have increased their chances for survival. Diamond concedes that this conclusion is controversial:

> . . . there has been resistance among both islanders and scholars to acknowledging the reality of self-inflicted environmental damage . . . In essence, the islanders are saying, "our ancestors would never have done that," while visiting scientists are saying, "Those nice people whom we have come to love would never have done that."

Remember, too, that Easter Island was not a hospitable environment. It is never easy to survive on a small isolated island that has little rainfall and poor soil. But in the pursuit of cultural goals that had religious undertones—erecting huge statues—Easter Islanders accelerated the destruction of the very environment they needed in order to survive.

Today, two things drive conflicts between indigenous groups and environmentalists: differing interests and indigenous peoples' concerns that environmentalists borrow their religions in inappropriate ways. It may surprise you that indigenous persons have different interests than environmentalists. After all, many of the environmentalists consider indigenous persons to be models for a healthy connection to the earth and sustainable living. Of course, as we just noted, indigenous groups are as capable as anyone else of living in unsustainable ways. Setting that aside, however, romanticizing indigenous religion can lead us to overlook a second, and in many respects more important, interest of indigenous persons besides protecting their environment: an interest in independence, sovereignty, and cultural autonomy.

In his article on environmental ethics, Parrett (1998) is pessimistic that environmentalists and indigenous groups can consistently align and work together on environmental ethics, because in the end environmentalists demand environmentally friendly practices that indigenous peoples may reject because they compromise the economic well-being of the community or its autonomy. Remember, for example, the much-publicized case of the Makah of the Pacific Northwest, whose whale hunt was revived in 1998 after decades of no hunting. As a practice, the whale hunt has both economic and community-building purposes, and it is infused with religious meaning. But, despite the religious meaning that is attributed to the hunt by indigenous peoples, environmentalists vehemently opposed it. They argued that it threatened the already dwindling population of gray whales. As this conflict came to a head, it became clear that there was another agenda in play here, one that had little to do with environmentalism and in which environmentalists had little interest:

the sovereignty of tribal nationals and the principle of self-determination. Parrett identifies a number of such cases in which environmentalists are frustrated with or disappointed by indigenous groups, whom they had previously assumed would be allies.

In their research on alliances between environmentalists and indigenous persons in the Amazon basin, anthropologists Beth Conklin and Laura Graham (1995, 703) identify a similar dynamic: Environmentalists align with indigenous peoples, only to discover later that the central interest of Amazon natives is "self-determination to include control over their lands' natural resources and the right to use them as they see fit." In the view of environmentalists, these uses are sometimes destructive:

> The politically astute Kayapo [an indigenous group]—who probably have had more exposure to ecological arguments than any other Brazilian group—have rushed into the arms of the market economy. Several Kayapo leaders have granted timber companies concessions to log large tracts of virgin mahogany and other tropical hardwoods. The Brazilian news magazine *Veja* [April 28, 1993] reported that in February of 1993, Kayapo leaders met with Brazil's president, Itamar Franco, and "demanded the right to deforest sixteen areas that they occupy. If not permitted to cut down the trees, to sell the lumber, they [the Kayapo] would demand an indemnification of $800,000 per month.

Parrett's work, along with that of Conklin and Graham, suggests that we should not assume that indigenous persons are natural allies of environmentalists.

For their part, indigenous groups have often expressed dismay when environmentalists borrow their religious beliefs and practices. In his study of Earth First!, Bron Taylor (1997, 186) observed many ways in which the environmental group has adopted Native American religious practices:

> The sweat lodge, the burning of purifying sage, the passing of a talking stick during community meetings, ritual processes such as the Council of All Beings which involve a solitary seeking of nature spirits in a way that resembles vision quests, the taking (or discovery) of "earth names," group and solitary wilderness experiences undertaken under the influence of peyote or hallucinogenic mushrooms, "tribal unity" and war dances characterized by ecstatic dancing and prolonged drumming (which bear no resemblance, as far as I can discern, to Native American dancing); neopagan ritualizing that sometimes borrows elements from Native American religion such as prayers to the Great Spirit in the four directions; a variety of rhetoric such as "ho" to express agreement during "tribal" meetings, and "hoka-hey," an exclamation sometimes spoken to register approval of expressions of militant defiance against the oppressors of nature . . .

Native Americans do not always welcome such borrowing. They sometimes object to the adoption by another group of bits and pieces, rather than the larger, integrated whole, of their religion. They disapprove of attempts by environmentalists to reshape their religious beliefs and practices. And they worry that picking and choosing from Native American religion threatens the survival of the indigenous culture as a distinct and cohesive whole.

As we noted earlier, although indigenous religion is appealing to many environmentalists, relations between indigenous persons and environmentalists are not without dispute and conflict. We emphasize this because there is a real risk of romanticizing the relationship between environmentalists and indigenous persons and in so doing overlooking important social dynamics.

IS RELIGION THE ANSWER?

Lynn White (1967) concluded that religion, particularly Judeo–Christian, had gotten us into an environmental crisis, and some form of religion, probably one quite different from one that posited human dominance over nature, would likely be needed to get us out of it:

> Both our present science and our present technology are so tinctured with orthodox Christian arrogance toward nature that no solution for our ecologic crisis can be expected from them alone. Since the roots of our trouble are so largely religious, the remedy must also be essentially religious, whether we call it that or not. We must rethink and refeel our nature and destiny. (1207)

To the extent that religion informs our most basic worldviews, it can speak to and perhaps even redefine our relationship with nature. Creation spirituality, which has been adopted in one form or another by many environmentalists, may be that alternative. But our review of the literature on religion and environmentalism should also leave us cautious about the relationship between religion and environmentalism. Although many people believe that religion plays a central role in shaping environmentalism among believers, empirical evidence suggests that religion explains little of the variance in people's environmental beliefs and actions.

SUGGESTED READING

Conklin, B. A. and L. R. Graham. 1995. "The Shifting Middle Ground: Amazonian Indians and Eco-Politics." *American Anthropologist* 97 (4): 695–710.

Kanagy, Conrad L. and Hart M. Nelsen. 1995. "Religion and Environmental Concern: Challenging the Dominant Assumptions." *Review of Religious Research* 37 (1): 33–45.

Montcrief, Lewis W. 1970. "The Cultural Basis for our Environmental Crisis." *Science* 170 (3957): 508–512.

Silko, Leslie Marmon. 1977. *Ceremony.* New York: Penguin.

White, Jr., Lynn. 1967. "The Historical Roots of our Ecologic Crisis." *Science* 155 (3767): 1203–1207.

Wilson, E. O. 2006. *The Creation: An Appeal to Save Life on Earth.* New York: W. W. Norton.

14

Do We Need God to Do Good?

1. What is morality?
2. What are the roles of rules and community in morality and religion?
3. What is distinctive about religiously based moral systems?
4. Does religion ensure that we do good?
5. Are sociologists the spawn of Satan for acknowledging other moral systems?

In December 2008, *The Washington Post* reported on a gathering of secular humanists in Boston, Massachusetts (Shulman 2008):

> They are not religious, so they don't go to church. But they are searching for values and rituals with which to raise their children, as well as a community of like-minded people to offer support . . . Dozens of parents came together on a recent Saturday to participate in a seminar on humanist parenting and to meet others interested in organizing a kind of nonreligious congregation, complete with regular family activities and ceremonies for births and deaths.

Secular humanists like these parents espouse values including "reason, compassion and human dignity," according to Robin Shulman. But they do so without reference to religion, God, or other supernatural forces. Does that matter? Will the values and rituals that they seek work in the absence of religious belief? Or does religion provide something above and beyond what secular humanists find in "a positive philosophy of ethical living for the human good" (Shulman 2008)?

Wall Street Journal columnist Daniel Henninger argues that we do need religion, above and beyond secular kinds of morality. He discussed the root causes of the financial crisis that came to a head in late 2008:

> What really went missing through the subprime mortgage years were the three Rs: responsibility, restraint and remorse . . . Responsibility and restraint are moral sentiments. Remorse is a product of conscience. None of these grow on trees. Each must be learned, taught, passed down. And so we come back to the disappearance of "Merry Christmas." It has been my view that the steady secularizing and insistent effort at dereligioning America has been dangerous . . . Northerners and atheists who vilify Southern evangelicals are throwing out nurturers of useful virtue with the bathwater of obnoxious political opinions. The point for a healthy society of commerce and politics is not that religion saves, but that it keeps most of the players inside the chalk lines. We are erasing the chalk lines.

Is he right? Is religion a necessary foundation for morality?

DO WE NEED *GOD* TO DO GOOD?

This question matters because, while religion remains a vibrant force worldwide, it also faces pockets of challenge. We discussed these challenges in Chapter 5. In most of Europe, for example, secularization has proceeded largely as predicted: State and religion are distinct spheres, identification with religious groups has declined over time, and religion has been largely pushed out of the public sphere. In a number of societies, a national identity has developed independently of religion, and sometimes has explicitly pushed religion out of the way. The communist government in China and the mid-20th century secular government in Iran come to mind. And in the United States, religion remains a powerful force in politics and in the private lives of citizens but, as Henninger would most likely agree, it has been pushed out of public schools, and its role in government has become limited. We wonder what holds society together when religion is weakened or diminished, especially in the public sphere. Is morality integrally tied to religion? Can societies maintain a semblance of morality without religion?

Morality and Regulation

Though they are closely related, morality and religion are not the same thing. When we ask our students what "morality" is, they usually describe it as a way to regulate human behavior. To them, morality is about being able to tell right from wrong. It is about knowing how to behave. It is knowing rules, laws, folkways (patterns of conventional behavior in society), and all the stuff we take for granted. It is acting in predictable and acceptable ways. It is saying and doing the right thing and, just as important, not saying or doing things that are forbidden.

If you think about it, religion also acts as a regulatory system. It's the source of behavioral proscriptions and prescriptions: Do not, for example, kill, steal, lie, eat pork, dress immodestly, laugh at the misfortune of another, look an elder in the eye, or leave dog poop in a neighbor's yard. And do worship regularly, remember your ancestors, tithe, wash your hands carefully before a meal, remove your shoes to worship, and respect your parents. This is just the beginning—there are many more dos and don'ts that we won't list here. Of course, our list is drawn from several religions, and no single person is expected to adhere to all of them. The *what* of morality varies across societies. We tackle that later.

Sometimes the rules seem arbitrary. In the Bible, the book of Leviticus is full of rules that in a modern context seem picky and sometimes ridiculous. There are rules about clean and unclean animals, how to slaughter animals, how to shave, what you can and cannot eat and in what combinations, who can be a religious leader, and how religious celebrations should proceed. That's just the beginning! But seemingly arbitrary rules are not just limited to religion. Similarly odd rules, conventions, and patterns guide nonreligious life. Remind us again *why* we give the two-fingered wave to a passing car on a desolate rural road? (The two-fingered wave is *not* the same as flipping the bird! Instead, it is a simple acknowledgment of another driver—two fingers lifted off the steering wheel as you pass—that is the norm in rural areas.) Why does a man put the toilet seat down after, well, you know? Why do we address our elders more formally than we do our peers or juniors? This list, too, could be endless. Whether the rules are arbitrary or not, however, we generally adhere to most of them. The question is, why?

Morality and Community

Morality regulates our behavior. But sociologists understand that regulation is just a starting point for understanding morality. The rules are important. Equally important—maybe more important—is the community. By community, we mean the group from which morality emerges and to which moral behavior ties us. As we discussed in Chapter 4 on cohesion and conflict, engaging in collective religious rituals maintains and reinforces our religious communities by strengthening the ties among members and creating a sense of the larger group as an all-encompassing force. Similarly, adhering to moral rules integrally connects us to other people. Knowing and obeying these rules marks us as responsible members of society. Unfamiliarity with these rules—or worse, ignoring them—brands you as an outsider. Daniel Henninger (2008) gets this when he writes about "restraint" (i.e., adhering to rules, even when you would rather not) and "responsibility" to the larger group. We do not follow a vast array of rules just for ourselves. We do them for—and as members of—a community.

The sociological study of morality has its roots in the work of Emile Durkheim (1858–1917). Durkheim firmly believed that morality and religion are more than just what an individual person does. They are social facts that emerge out of and operate in the context of human community. Both draw their strength from transcending the individual and infusing the community as a whole.

Moral rules are shared within the group and become *building blocks* of community. You may recall from Chapter 1 that Durkheim used the term "moral community" to describe the collective that is formed when a group of people adhere to shared beliefs and practices regarding the sacred. As Chapter 4 described, this is what religion *does:* It takes individuals and out of them builds a cohesive whole. This fact points us to an important quality of religion that is also shared by morality: Before either can regulate human behavior, each must first construct the group, by forming ties among people and creating boundaries between the group and outsiders. We must be able to tell who is *in* the group and who is *out*, who is a *member* and who is an *alien* or *outsider*. A rich sociological understanding of morality thus encompasses "the rules" and also sees how those rules are tied to the cohesiveness of the group and the boundaries around communities. We have to see both aspects of morality: its obvious regulation of the behavior of members *and* its role in building and maintaining the social group itself.

How effective morality is at regulating behavior depends on how attached people are to the community. Durkheim explained this nicely when he wrote about moral education. Society regulates our behavior through moral codes, he wrote. On the surface, that seems to suggest that these moral codes are oppressive, weighty constraints on individual behavior under which people chafe and suffer. But that is not, as it turns out, how we generally experience morality. Instead, as it regulates, morality simultaneously brings us into society and provides a sense of belonging to the larger group. Morality pushes us to think of others first—our family, community, or nation—and to understand selflessness as a virtue. Again, recall that religion does something similar, providing a mechanism by which individualism is transcended and society itself becomes central.

This does not mean that morality always works to keep people's behavior in line! We see plenty of instances where the rules get broken. For these instances we have Henninger's third "R"—remorse. But, at its most effective, morality works often enough to produce predictable behavior in an integrated, coherent society.

Membership and belonging provide powerful motives for people to follow society's moral rules. As Peter Berger so eloquently discussed in his classic *Invitation to Sociology* (1963), breaking the rules brings sanctions or punishments: disapproval, condemnation, gossip, the silent treatment, and sometimes even criminal proceedings. Rule-breaking also calls into question the strength of one's ties to the society and the sincerity of one's attachments and sentiments. "Who do you think you are?" you may wonder when someone cuts in line, speaks disrespectfully, absconds with your garbage bin, or otherwise acts in ways that suggest he or she is following a different set of rules. That is not a question that begs for a person's name! It's a question about the person's identity and social location, elicited by the perception that he or she is out of line. When rule-breakers make serious breaches or repeated offenses, they come to be seen as problematic or harmful to the community: uncaring about others, unreliable, or selfish. They are pushed to the edges of the community, if not evicted from it altogether. (Think ex-communication, ostracism, expulsion, and prison.) Exclusion from the group is the ultimate punishment. Morality draws boundaries around groups, and generally those within groups willingly go along with the dos and don'ts of that group in order to support the group and maintain membership in it. This is what Daniel Henninger refers to as keeping "most of the players inside the chalk lines."

WHAT'S RELIGION GOT?

Although many communities are rooted in religious morality, religion is not the only possible basis for morality. Take, for example, a profession like medicine, where physicians adhere to ethical codes of conduct. Members follow principles for ethical decision-making (e.g., beneficence, autonomy), and the profession polices the boundaries around the community. At least in theory, miscreants who violate these principles are expelled from the community. Though it is not rooted in a religious tradition, the profession of medicine is nonetheless a moral community that regulates its members.

Another example is the military. Soldiers typically have a strong sense of community, bolstered by their mutual responsibilities to each other. The film *A Few Good Men,* which starred Tom Cruise and featured the now-famous line by Jack Nicholson's charac-ter ("You can't handle the truth!"), is a dramatic representation of the military as a moral community, with boundaries around the group and strict—if sometimes informal—codes of conduct. But though religious persons may serve in the military, and "God" is some-times invoked in military settings, the military is essentially a secular institution. Nonetheless, it constitutes a powerful moral community, as anyone who has served in the military can tell you.

Recall that at the beginning of this chapter you read about a group of secular hu-manists who wished to build a moral community for their children. Clearly, they believe that a nonreligious morality is possible and desirable for their families. Critics of reli-gion, including Sam Harris, who wrote *The End of Faith* (2004), would likely agree with them. Harris has himself proposed that religion be replaced by a rational approach to ethics akin to secular humanism. Is that really feasible? Can a morality that is not based in religion simply step in for religion, at no cost to the strength and effectiveness of the moral system?

Let's think about this. The rules that bind members of a secular moral community have significant force and legitimacy: It is widely accepted, for example, that doctors should "first, do no harm," and that members of the military should obey the legitimate commands of their superiors. But it is not hard to go back and find the human sources of these rules: the Hippocratic Oath and military doctrine. Religiously based moral systems are different because their human roots are obscured through beliefs and practices that, at least in our minds, link the moral system to a broader cosmic order.

In Chapter 1, we explored Peter Berger's claim that religion is our "audacious attempt to conceive of the entire universe as being humanly significant." By this, Berger means that religion is our way of making sense of our circumstances by linking them to a broader cosmic reality, a supposedly unchangeable and transcendent truth that exists out-side us but to which we are connected. This cosmic order transcends human culture: It is understood to simply *exist* as part of the natural order, the way things are meant to be. By invoking religion as a basis of our moral system, we obscure the very human roots of our community. We assert that not humans, but God or some other higher power or order, made our community and established its rules. As Berger (1967, 26) puts it,

> The cosmos posited by religion . . . both includes and transcends man. The sacred cosmos [confronts] man as an immensely powerful reality other than himself. Yet this reality addresses itself to him and locates his life in an ulti-mately meaningful order.

Once they have been connected in this way to the transcendent, human communities take on an air of inevitability, as if the structure and rules of human society were set from out-side that community and imposed on it by a higher power. This attitude, in turn, enhances the long-term stability of religiously based societies compared with secular ones.

It is not that such systems never change. Social change throughout recorded his-tory argues against that conclusion. But social stability is strengthened when the moral system appears to participants as if it encompasses, but is also beyond, human experi-ence. Let's return to the case of American civil religion, which we introduced in Chapter 4. American government is clearly a human creation, one that students in the United States learn about in grade-school history class. Human beings penned our founding docu-ments: the Declaration of Independence, the U.S. Constitution, and the like. But as

Robert Bellah (1967, 5) noted in his analysis of key presidential inaugural addresses, one theme in particular

> . . . lies very deep in the American tradition, namely the obligation, both collective and individual, to carry out God's will on earth. This was the motivating spirit of those who founded America, and it has been present in every generation since.

In specific historic eras, other themes emerge. The religious myth of exodus and escape from tyranny shapes our understanding of the Revolutionary War, with George Washington as the "messiah." The Civil War is often recounted using images of "death, sacrifice, and rebirth," with Abraham Lincoln serving as America's savior. The creation of Memorial Day, a commemoration of those who have died in war, "is a major event for the whole community involving a rededication to the martyred dead, the spirit of sacrifice, the American vision." (Bellah 1967, 11)

In the end, Bellah (1967, 12) concludes that American civil religion "is a genuine apprehension of universal and transcendent religious reality as seen in, or one could almost say, as revealed through, the experience of American people." But through that tradition, our understanding of our history, as well as our future, is infused with transcendent meaning. As a nation, we see ourselves as more than just a random collection of people thrown together willy-nilly. We see ourselves as having purpose and meaning, a collective self-conception that lends stability during treacherous historical times (e.g., revolution, civil war, other wars, presidential assassinations).

Although morality can and does exist in the absence of religion, religious foundations can significantly strengthen a moral system. Do we need God to do good? Probably not, but religion may help.

DOES RELIGION *ENSURE* THAT WE DO GOOD?

In the 1980s and 1990s, scandals surrounding clergy became public. Televangelists came under fire for cheating on their spouses, religious leaders lived in high style off the contributions of their followers, and scores of Catholic priests were found culpable of child sexual abuse. As these scandals developed, our students expressed shock and disappointment. They were, of course, outraged by the offenses themselves: They disapproved strongly of marital infidelities, financial shenanigans, and abuse of children. But what troubled them even more was that *religious* persons, especially religious *leaders,* would engage in immoral or illegal behavior. They would exclaim, "How could they? They are supposed to be *religious!*" Implicit in this common first response is an assumption that people who are religious are, by the very fact of their religiosity, inherently moral and law-abiding. These events challenged this assumption. Of course, critics of religion regularly cite the evils perpetrated in the name of religion. As Christopher Hitchens (2007, 13) put so succinctly: "Religion poisons everything." While we do not agree with that blanket statement, we acknowledge that it reflects religion's mixed record when it comes to "doing good."

Our students were coming face to face with something that sociologists and criminologists had been exploring empirically for quite a while: the relationship between individual religiosity and deviant behavior. To be sure, criminologists have accumulated empirical support for the notion that religious people are more moral or law-abiding than are nonreligious people (Glueck and Glueck 1950, Nye 1958). As recently as 2008, psychologists who reviewed eight decades of research on individual religiosity and self-control concluded that more pious people exercise higher levels of self-control (Tierney 2008).

But, beginning in the late 1960s, the presumption that religious people are less likely to engage in immoral or illegal behavior was challenged by criminologist Travis Hirschi and sociologist of religion Rodney Stark. While they were analyzing data on adolescent religiosity and delinquency that were gathered in Richmond, California, Hirschi and Stark (1969) were taken aback to find that regular church attendance did not make a teenager less likely to engage in a range of delinquent behaviors. And conversely, being unreligious did not make teenagers more likely to engage in delinquent behavior. More than 20 years later, Rodney Stark (1996) revisited these findings. He noted that subsequent research had at least occasionally confirmed the lack of a relationship between religiosity and delinquency (e.g., see Burkett and White 1974), and he pithily summarized that, at least in some communities, "Kids on their way home from Sunday school were as likely to strip your car as were kids on their way home from the pool hall." As these examples illustrate, being religious does not always, or even consistently, ensure that you will engage in moral and legal behavior. Something beyond individual religiosity is at work. To solve this puzzle, Stark stepped back from the question of whether going to church prevents a kid from engaging in deviant behavior. Instead, he focused on the broader social context—he is, after all, a *sociologist*! And he noted something intriguing. Studies that found a relationship between religiosity and good behavior at the individual level usually focused on communities where a lot of people are religious and attend church regularly (e.g., the South, the Northeast). Religion is infused throughout such communities. On the other hand, studies that found religious kids to be no more or no less deviant than nonreligious kids typically drew their samples from communities where the overall levels of religiosity, throughout the community, were much lower (e.g., the West). This led Stark to posit a truly *sociological* explanation for the relationship between religion and deviance: In communities where overall levels of religiosity are high, being religious protects against or prevents deviance. But in communities where overall levels of religiosity are low, individual religiosity has no effect on deviance one way or the other. Stark (1996) argues that, even if you are religious, whether you draw on religion to guide your behavior in your day-to-day life depends largely on how religious your friends are:

> Teenagers form and sustain their interpretations of norms in day-to-day interaction with their friends. If most of a young person's friends are not actively religious, then religious considerations will rarely enter into the process by which norms are accepted or justified. Even if the religious teenager does bring up religious considerations, these will not strike a responsive chord in most of the others. This is not to suggest that nonreligious teenagers don't believe in norms or discuss right and wrong, but they will do so without recourse to religious justifications. In such a situation, the effect of religiousness of some individuals will be smothered by group interference to religion, and religion will tend to become a very compartmentalized component of the individual's life—something that surfaces only in specific situations such as Sunday school and church. In contrast, when the majority of a teenager's friends are religious, then religion enters freely into everyday interactions and becomes a valid part of the normative system. (164)

In sum, for religion to be *activated* as a protection from deviance at the individual level, it must be a strong presence in the community as a whole, especially among those with whom you regularly interact. Individual religiosity alone is not enough.

And so we come back to the value of sociology as a discipline. Sociology focuses our attention beyond the individual. It asks questions that are bigger than "Is a religious person less likely to be deviant than a nonreligious person?" It asks questions instead about the social context within which we are embedded, what that context looks like, and how it affects both individuals and groups. We concede that it is far easier to study individuals and to measure their qualities and characteristics. But it is vitally important that we also find ways to "see" the social world that exists all around us and to discern its powerful effects on us.

What about the bad behavior by ministers, described by sociologist Anson Shupe as "clergy malfeasance?" How can religious leaders so egregiously violate the teachings and rules of their own religious groups? Evidence of clergy malfeasance has shaken the faith of many believers and their trust in their leaders. And, of course, they are justified in their concerns and doubts. But focusing only on individual misbehaving clergy may lead us to overlook important dimensions of clergy deviance.

In his 1995 monograph, *In the Name of All That's Holy: A Theory of Clergy Malfeasance,* Anson Shupe raises the broader question of how religious organizations respond to clergy malfeasance. He astutely points out that when cases of clergy malfeasance come to light they are usually not one-time occurrences. Instead, they are part of a larger pattern of deviance by the malfeasant, often extending over many years and sometimes across multiple congregations. Given this finding, Shupe argues that it is just as important to understand the organizational contexts within which clergy deviance occurs and where it is often absorbed and hidden for many years. In particular, he points to the authority structure of the group—is authority centralized outside the local congregation, or is it embedded within the local group?—as a key determinant of how religious organizations respond to the bad behavior of clergy. Do they put a stop to it? Do they neutralize it—that is, frame it as inconsequential or not so harmful? Do they normalize it—that is, frame it as typical and acceptable? The Catholic Church in the United States had a practice of removing from their churches clergy who had been accused of child sexual abuse. Sometimes priests were sent off for "treatment." Other times, they were immediately moved to other parishes. The new churches were not, as a general rule, informed about the priest's history. Such organizational practices provide a context that perpetuates bad behavior on the part of individuals. They also form the legal basis for large damage awards for victims.

The *response* is vitally important to long-term patterns of clergy deviance; it determines whether one bad act turns into a long string of such acts or whether malfeasant clergy are stopped in their tracks early on. As Shupe points out, the behavior that we find so objectionable on the part of clergy is a product of individual choices, but it happens within a larger social context that we would do well to understand.

Keep in mind too that social contexts are complicated. Thus far, our discussion of morality has suggested fairly black and white rule systems. Do this! Don't do that! But when it is embedded in real social worlds, morality is often not so clear. Yes, child sexual abuse or stealing money from a church is bad behavior. But when an authority figure— one who is considered to reflect or be connected to the sacred—engages in the behavior, complications arise. Can a victim challenge a sacred authority? Will people believe a victim or a leader? Are colleagues of the leader prepared to respond definitively to malfeasance? When religious organizations encounter deviance by religious professionals, extensive chains of command and complex bureaucratic rules may protect victims by rooting out and punishing perpetrators . . . or, rules and hierarchy may actually buffer the malfeasant clergy from the consequences of his or her actions. The religious *belief* system, the system of morality, is one part of this context. But the religious group and its structure and practices are also important parts of the equation. This is another instance where sociology—with its focus on structure, culture, and practice, along with the interactions among these things—enriches our understanding of perplexing situations.

A NOTE ON VIOLENCE AND MORAL COMMUNITIES

The role of community in forming and supporting moral codes helps explain another conundrum that often perplexes students and one that we explored in depth when we discussed religious violence in Chapter 6. That is, how can religions that espouse peace and love simultaneously elicit violence on the part of followers?

The boundaries around moral communities are key. Religious violence is almost always perpetrated against those who are viewed as existing *outside* the moral community—primitives, subhumans, nonbelievers, enemies, heretics, heathens, and infidels. Typically, outsiders are seen as untrustworthy with respect to the community's moral prescriptions and proscriptions: Because outsiders are not tied to the moral community in meaningful ways, members of the moral community are typically skeptical, at best, and downright disbelieving, at worst, that outsiders might be equally human or capable of living by the same rules that bind the community. It is not that outsiders are not expected to follow the rules—they are, because the moral community views the rules as applying to all. Instead, because they lack ties to the community, they are not trusted to follow the rules. More important, however, outsiders are not granted the same rights to be treated according to the code that applies to insiders. Different rules apply to outsiders to the community, rules that allow them to be targets for what we understand as religiously motivated violence, even when such acts would be impermissible against members of the community.

"Gook" is an ugly word. U.S. soldiers used it as derogatory slang for locals during the Vietnam War. A tragic low point of the war was the My Lai massacre, in which American soldiers killed 128 Vietnamese civilians—elderly people, women, and children. Psychologist Herbert Kelman and sociologist V. Lee Hamilton (1989) examined the massacre to identify its proximate and ultimate causes. They concluded that, among other factors, dehumanization was a significant contributor to the massacre. They wrote that

> . . . the inhibitions against murdering one's fellow human beings are generally so strong that the victims must also be stripped of their human status if they are to be subjected to systematic killing. Insofar as they are dehumanized, the usual principles of morality no longer apply to them. (1989, 19)

As we noted earlier, morality is integrally tied to membership in a community; moral standards that apply to insiders do not apply to outsiders because they lack that membership. Kelman and Hamilton identified two interrelated components of dehumanization:

> Victims are deprived in the perpetrators' eyes of the two qualities essential to being perceived as fully human and included in the moral compact that

governs human relationships: *identity*—standing as independent, distinctive individuals, capable of making choices and entitled to live their own lives—and *community*—fellow membership in an interconnected network of individuals who care for each other and respect each other's individuality and rights. Thus, when a group is defined entirely in terms of a category to which they belong, and when this category is excluded from the human family, moral restraints against killing them are more readily overcome. (19)

The process of dehumanization—which applies almost exclusively to *outsiders* to the group—goes far toward explaining why religious groups and their members may do to outsiders what they would never consider doing to their own members (e.g., murdering, torturing, kidnapping children).

MORAL RELATIVISM?!

Morality and religion are also complicated by their sheer variety, as we described in Chapter 2. Standards for behavior—prescriptions, proscriptions, laws, rules, taken-for-granted patterns—are not universal. Instead they vary, sometimes a lot, across settings. This is especially apparent when we step back and examine moral systems in societies other than our own. Some of what we see is familiar. But much of what we see seems strange: behavior that seems rude, odd ways of raising children, strange foods and eating rituals, unfamiliar notions about the roles of the elderly, teenagers, or women. The list seems endless.

We sometimes forget how strange our own moral system seems to outsiders. That is, we take for granted that our own moral system follows obvious, true rules. Of course it is wrong for men to marry men! Of course people should receive blood transfusions that are needed to save their lives! Of course an elderly parent must live with his children at the end of his life when he can no longer take care of himself! But in some other moral system, you will find the opposite statement to be the taken-for-granted truth: Men marrying men, fine with us! Accepting a blood transfusion leads to eternal damnation! My dad will be best off in a nursing home! How can that be if morality is *true*?

No matter how objectively true or universal a moral system may feel, moral systems do not precede human communities. Instead, they are products of human communities; they come from the community. As a result, what we think is "good" or "right" is largely determined by the community in which we are embedded. But it is hard for us to step back and critically examine our own moral system because it seems so true to us.

In a way, "Do you need God to do good?" is a trick question because it assumes that "good" is objectively knowable. You probably have some notion of what "good" *is,* but your notion is specific to your context. Someone else, in a different context, might well define "good" differently. For example, in the United States many people believe that it is good and right to provide extraordinary life-preserving care to people who are gravely ill, whether the ill person is a child or a 95-year-old man. What is the good of medical technologies if you don't use them to preserve human life? There is always hope! In other cultures, however, what we do in hospitals to gravely ill people is viewed as cruel: sticking needles in people, shoving tubes down their throats, isolating them in sterile hospital rooms, interfering with the natural course of their illnesses, pounding on their chests to restart their hearts. What is obviously right to some is not right to others. Moral systems both define what is good and guide our behavior, with more or less success depending on the strength of the moral system. But we should not take the definition of what is right and good for granted, because someone from a different social context may dispute it!

Sociologists are no different from anyone else. We hold strong and particular moral commitments although we may not all agree on what those commitments should be. We also know, at least intellectually, that "good" is defined and produced by the specific society of which we are a part. Thus, when we ask—"Do we need God to do good?"—we are not really asking whether we need religion to do the universally transcendent right thing. Instead we are asking whether we need religion to steer people toward what a given society has defined as good.

At this point, you might be hearing a ringing in your ears. It might sound something like moral relativism . . . moral relativism . . . moral relativism: the idea that there are a variety of equally valid moral systems out there. Sometimes moral relativism is invoked analytically. In these cases, it reflects the empirical reality that moral systems vary across settings and presumes that morality is less a fixed truth and more a product of specific human societies. Taking a moral-relativist stance allows an observer to see multiple moral systems on their own terms. Often, however, moral relativism is invoked pejoratively, as a criticism of anyone who acknowledges the reality or validity of alternative systems. Those who use the term moral relativism pejoratively typically view morality—specifically, their own—to be an absolute, transcendent, universal truth. They see other moralities as inferior, less developed, or simply wrong.

However strongly we may believe in our own understandings of right and wrong, rejecting other systems out of hand is problematic. Why? Because it interferes with dispassionate observation of the unfamiliar: Feeling disgust or distaste for that, which is unfamiliar, makes it very hard to understand others on their own terms. Does that mean that sociologists are moral relativists who believe that "anything goes," as some claim? Of course not: Even as sociologists recognize the variety of moral systems and their functions in a range of societies, we retain personal moral convictions. For many of us, that includes a belief in an ultimate good. Just because we recognize a range of moral systems and take them seriously as objects of study does not mean that we deny the precepts of our own morality.

CONCLUDING THOUGHTS

People do not need a "god" or a religion in order to do good. Nevertheless, religion most often strengthens human community, and does so because it lends stability by imbuing good behavior with transcendent meaning linked to a sacred cosmos. We don't just do something because a parent told us so, but because our religious community agrees and, ultimately, because the higher power in which we believe has ordained it as good and right. And, as we have discussed, neither individual religiosity nor religion collectively ensures that we do "good." Like other social institutions, religion is a human product. And like other institutions—politics, the military, education, family—it can work well or it can work poorly. It can do good or it can do harm.

The sociological lens provides tools to step back and examine religion's effects on our world today. And those effects are wide-ranging. There is a tremendous variety of religious belief and practice around the world. Religion forms our identity, not just our *religious* identity but how we understand race and ethnicity, nationality, social class, gender, and sexual identity. Religion molds our relations with other people—those in our religious group, those who believe something else, and those who reject religious belief altogether. It shapes how we view other nations and peoples and how we collectively interact with them. Religion is implicated in how we treat our natural world and whether we value scientific and technological advances. Some try to argue that religion is all good, and others that it is all bad. We merely argue that religion *is*.

Charles Darwin thought a lot about religion, especially as his developing theory of evolution began to challenge the religious beliefs with which he had been raised. He observed that "a belief in all-pervading spiritual agencies seems to be universal; and apparently follows from a considerable advance in man's reason, and from a still greater advance in his faculties of imagination, curiosity and wonder (1871, 513)." We concur. The varieties of religions, created by humans to connect themselves to a transcendent and sacred cosmos (which may or may not exist, but that is beyond the limits of science to know), are acts of creativity. Think about it. Rather than settling for what we can observe with our five senses, we seek the unseen. Rather than accepting life as mere random chance, we seek larger meaning. Rather than stumbling through each day, moment to moment, we search for order in what can appear a complex and chaotic world. And we do so through an endless variety of religions around the world. This variety and its impact on every corner of our lives is a testament to the richness of humanity.

SUGGESTED READING

Bellah, Robert. 1967. "Civil Religion in America." *Daedelus* 96 (1): 1–21.

Berger, Peter. 1967. *The Sacred Canopy*. Garden City, NY: Doubleday.

Durkheim, Emile. 1973. *Moral Education: A Study in the Theory and Application of Sociology of Education*. New York: Free Press.

BIBLIOGRAPHY

Abusharaf, Rogaia Mustafa. 1998. "Structural Adaptations in an Immigrant Muslim Congregation in New York." In *Gatherings in Diaspora Religious Communities and the New Immigration*, edited by R. Stephen Warner and Judith G. Wittner, 235–261. Philadelphia: Temple University Press.

Adherents.com. 2007. http://www.adherents.com al Ghazzali, Abu Hamid Muhammed. 1964. *Nasihat al-moluk (Counsel for Kings)*. Oxford: Oxford University Press.

Almond, Gabriel A., R. Scott Appleby, and Emmanuel Sivan. 2003. *Strong Religion: The Rise of Fundamentalisms Around the World*. Chicago: University of Chicago Press.

———. 2006. *Evolution on the Frontline: An Abbreviated Guide for Teaching Evolution, from Project 2061 at AAAS*. Washington, DC: Author.

———. 2008. "Questions and Answers on Evolution." http://www.aaas.org/news/press_room/evolution/pdf/QA_Evolution.pdf

Ammerman, Nancy T. 1987. *Bible Believers: Fundamentalists in the Modern World*. New Brunswick, NJ: Rutgers University Press.

Anonymous. 2000. *Creation Stories from Around the World*, (4th ed.). http://www.gly.uga.edu/railsback/CS/CSIndex.html, last accessed February 25, 2010.

Antoun, Richard T. 2001. *Understanding Fundamentalism: Christian, Islamic, and Jewish Movements*. Walnut Creek, CA: AltaMira.

Armstrong, Karen. 2000. *The Battle for God: A History of Fundamentalism*. New York: Ballantine.

———. 2005. *The Spiral Staircase: My Climb Out of Darkness*. New York: Anchor.

Association of Theological Schools. 2007. *Fact Book on Theological Education, 2006–2007*. Pittsburgh: The Association of Theological Schools.

Attfield, Robin. 1980. "Christian Attitudes to Nature." *Journal of the History of Ideas* 44 (3): 369–386.

Baker, Wayne E. 2005. *America's Crisis of Values: Reality and Perception*. Princeton, NJ: Princeton University Press.

Barrett, David B. 2001. *World Christian Encyclopedia*. New York: Oxford University Press.

Basch, Linda, Nina Glick Schiller, and Christina Szanton Blanc. 1994. *Nations Unbound: Transnational Projects, Postcolonial Predicaments, and Deterritorialized Nation–States*. Basel, Switzerland: Gordon and Breach.

BBC. 2002. "Buddhism: Theravada Buddhism," BBC Religion and Ethics. http://www.bbc.co.uk/religion/religions/buddhism/subdivisions/theravada_1.shtml———. 2004. "Hinduism: Texts," BBC Religion and Ethics. http://www.bbc.co.uk/religion/religions/hinduism/texts/texts.shtml

———. 2008. "Wicca." http://www.bbc.co.uk/religion/religions/paganism/subdivisions/wicca.shtml

Beaman, Lori. 1999. *Shared Beliefs, Different Lives: Women's Identities in Evangelical Context*. St. Louis: Chalice Press.

———. 2003. "The Myth of Pluralism, Diversity and Vigor: The Constitutional Privileging of Protestantism in the United States and Canada." *Journal for the Scientific Study of Religion* 42 (3): 311–325.

Bellah, Robert. 1967. "Civil Religion in America." *Daedelus* 96 (1): 1–21.

———, Richard Madsen, William M. Sullivan, Ann Swidler, and Steven M. Tipton. 1985. *Habits of the Heart: Individualism and Commitment in American Life*. New York: Harper and Row, Publishers.

Berger, Peter. 1963. *Invitation to Sociology*. Garden City, NY: Doubleday.

———. 1967. *The Sacred Canopy: Elements of a Sociological Theory of Religion*. Garden City, NY: Doubleday.

———. 1992. *A Far Glory: The Quest for Faith in the Age of Credulity*. New York: Free Press.

———. 1999. "The Desecularization of the World: A Global Overview." In *The Desecularization of the World: Resurgent Religion and World Politics*, edited by Peter Berger, 1–18. Washington, D.C.: Ethics and Policy Center.

Berryman, Phillip. 1984. *The Religious Roots of Rebellion: Christians in Central American Revolutions*. Eugene, OR: Wipf & Stock.

Beyer, Peter. 1997. "Religious Vitality in Canada: The Complementarity of Religious Market and Secularization Perspectives." *Journal for the Scientific Study of Religion* 36 (2): 272–288.

———. 2003. "Constitutional Privilege and Constituting Pluralism: Religious Freedom in National, Global and Legal Context." *Journal for the Scientific Study of Religion* 42 (3): 333–339.

Blau, Peter M., and Joseph E. Schwartz. 1984. *Crosscutting Social Circles: Testing a Macrostructural Theory of Intergroup Relations*. New York: Academic Press.

Bloom, Paul. 2005. "Is God an Accident?" *Atlantic Monthly*, 296 (5): 105–112.

Bock, Darrell, and Daniel B. Wallace. 2008. *Dethroning Jesus: Exposing Popular Culture's Quest to Unseat the Biblical Christ*. Nashville, TN: Thomas Nelson.

Boston, John. 2003. "At Long Last, Going to Church Finally Pays." Online. http://www.the=signal.com/News/ViewStory.asp?storyID=2906

Boswell, John. 1994. *Same-Sex Unions in Premodern Europe*. New York: Villard.

Boyd, H. H. 1999. "Religion and the Environment in the American Public." *Journal for the Scientific Study of Religion* 38 (1): 36–44.

Brasher, Brenda E. 2004. *Give Me That Online Religion*. New Brunswick, NJ: Rutgers University Press.

Brooks, Clem, and Jeff Manza. 1997. "Social Cleavages and Political Alignments: U.S. Presidential Elections, 1960–1992." *American Sociological Review* 62 (6): 937–946.

Bruce, Steve. 2000. *Fundamentalism*. Malden, MA: Blackwell.

———. 2001. "Christianity in Britain, R.I.P." *Sociology of Religion* 62 (2): 191–204.

Buechner, Frederick. 1973. *Wishful Thinking: A Theological ABC*. New York: Harper & Row.

———. 1993. *Wishful Thinking: A Seeker's ABC*. New York: Harper.

Bunkley, Nick. 2008. "Detroit Churches Pray for 'God's Bailout.'" *The New York Times*, December 8.

Bunt, Gary R. 2000. "Surfing Islam: Ayatollahs, Shayks, and Hajjis on the Superhighway." In *Religion on the Internet: Research Prospects and Promises*, edited by Jeffrey K. Hadden and Douglas E. Cowan, 127–151. New York: JAI-Elsevier Science, Inc.

Burkett, Steven R., and Mervin White. 1974. "Hellfire and delinquency: Another look." *Journal for the Scientific Study of Religion* 13 (4): 455–462.

Cadge, Wendy. 2005. "Lesbian, Gay and Bisexual Buddhist Practitioners." In *Gay Religion*, edited by Scott Thumma and Edward R. Gray, 139–153. New York: Altamira Press.

Campbell, Robert A., and James E. Curtis. 1996. "The Public's Views on the Future of Religion and Science: Cross-National Survey Results." *Review of Religious Research*. 37 (3): 260–267.

Carter, Stephen. 1993. *The Culture of Disbelief: How American Law and Politics Trivializes Religious Devotion*. New York: Anchor.

Casanova, Jose. 1994. *Public Religions in the Modern World*. Chicago: University of Chicago Press.

Catton, William R., and Riley E. Dunlap. 1980. "A New Ecological Paradigm for Post-Exuberant Sociology." *American Behavioral Scientist* 24 (1): 15–47.

Chai, Karen J. 1998. "Competing for the Second Generation: English-Language Ministry at a Korean Protestant Church." In *Gatherings in Diaspora Religious Communities and the New Immigration*, edited by R. Stephen Warner and Judith G. Wittner, 295–331. Philadelphia: Temple University Press.

———. 2001a. "Beyond 'Strictness' to Distinctiveness: Generational Transition in Korean Protestant Churches." In *Korean Americans and Their Religions: Pilgrims and*

Missionaries from a Different Shore, edited by Ho Youn Kwon, Kwang Chung Kim, and R. Stephen Warner, 157–180. University Park, PA: The Pennsylvania State University Press.

———. 2001b. "Intra-Ethnic Religious Diversity: Korean Buddhists and Protestants in Greater Boston." In *Korean Americans and Their Religions: Pilgrims and Missionaries from a Different* Shore, edited by Ho Youn Kwon, Kwang Chung Kim, and R. Stephen Warner, 273–294. University Park, PA: The Pennsylvania State University Press.Chaves, Mark. 1994. "Secularization as Declining Religious Authority." *Social Forces* 72 (3): 749–774.

———. 1997. *Ordaining Women: Culture and Conflict in Religious Organizations.* Cambridge, MA: Harvard University Press.—., Peter J. Schraeder, and Mario Sprindys. 1994. "State Regulation of Religion and Muslim Religious Vitality in the Industrialized West." *The Journal of Politics* 56 (4): 1087–1097.

Chen, Carolyn. 2008. *Getting Saved in America: Taiwanese Immigration and Religious Experience.* Princeton, NJ: Princeton University Press.

Christ, Carol P. 2007. "Why Women Need the Goddess." In *Women's Studies in Religion: A Multicultural Reader*, edited by Kate Bagley and Kathleen McIntosh, 163–174. Upper Saddle River, NJ: Prentice Hall Publishers.

Christerson, Brad, Korie L. Edwards, and Michael O. Emerson. 2005. *Against All Odds: The Struggle for Racial Integration in Religious Organizations.* New York: New York University Press.

Christerson, Brad, and Michael O. Emerson. 2003. "The Costs of Diversity in Religious Organizations: An In-Depth Case Study." *Sociology of Religion* 64:163–182.

Christianity Today. 2001. "Eco-myths." *Christianity Today*, June. http://www.christianitytoday.com/ct/2001/juneweb-only/6-25-32.0.html?start=1 CNN. 2005. "School board to appeal ruling to remove evolution stickers." January 18. http://www.cnn.com/2005/LAW/01/18/evolution.stickers/

Congregation for the Doctrine of the Faith. 2003. "Considerations Regarding Proposals to Give Legal Recognition to Unions between Homosexual Persons." http://www.vatican.va/roman_curia/congregations/cfaith/documents/rc_con_cfaith_doc_20030731_homosexual-unions_en.html

Conklin, B. A., and L. R. Graham. 1995. "The Shifting Middle Ground: Amazonian Indians and Eco-Politics." *American Anthropologist* 97 (4): 695–710.

Coser, Lewis A. 1956. *The Functions of Social Conflict.* Glencoe, IL: The Free Press.

Cousineau, Madeleine. 1998. "The Brazilian Catholic Church and Land Conflicts in the Amazon." In *Religion, Mobilization, and Social Action*, edited by Anson Shupe and Bronislaw Misztal, 85–99. Westport, CT: Praeger.

Craig, Robert H. 1992. *Religion and Radical Politics: An Alternative Christian Tradition in the United States.* Philadelphia: Temple University Press.

Cunningham, Lawrence S. 2002. "Murder in Palermo: Who Killed Father Puglisi?" *Commonweal*, Volume CXXIX, Number 17 (Oct. 11).

Curtis, Susan. 1991. *A Consuming Faith: The Social Gospel and Modern American Culture.* Baltimore, MD: The Johns Hopkins University Press.

Dallas Morning News. 2005. "10 Ideas on the Way Out." November 27: pp. 1P, 5P.

Darwin, Charles. 1859. *The Origin of Species.* London: John Murray.

———. 1871. *The Descent of Man.* New York: Penguin Classics.

Davie, Grace. 1994. *Religion in Britain Since 1945: Believing Without Belonging.* Oxford: Blackwell Publishers.

Davis, James Allan, and Tom W. Smith. 2006. General Social Survey (Machine-readable data file). Principal Investigator, James A. Davis; Director and Coprincipal Investigator, Tom W. Smith; Coprincipal Investigator, Peter V. Marsden, NORC ed. Chicago: National Opinion Research Center, producer, 2002; Storrs, CT: The Roper Center for Public Opinion Research, University of Connecticut, distributor.

Dawson, Lorne L. 2000. "Researching Religion in Cyberspace: Issues and Strategies." In *Religion on the Internet: Research Prospects and Promises*, edited by Jeffrey K. Hadden and Douglas E. Cowan, 25–54. New York: JAI-Elsevier Science, Inc.

Day, Katie. 2001. "Putting It Together in the African American Churches: Faith, Economic Development, and Civil Rights." In *Religion and Social Policy*, edited by Paula D. Nesbitt, 181–195. New York: Alta Mira Press.

Demerath, N. J., and Rhys H. Williams. 1992. "Secularization Assessed: The Abridging of Faith in a New England City. *Journal for the Scientific Study of Religion* 31 (2): 189–206.

DeWitt, David A. 2007. "A tale of two museums: A comparison between the Smithsonian National Museum of Natural History and the Creation Museum." September 10, 2007. http://www.answersingenesis.org/articles/2007/09/10/tale-of-two-museums

Diamond, Jared. 2004. *Collapse: How Societies Choose to Fail or Succeed*. New York: Viking.

Dobbelaere, Karel. 1999. "Toward an Integrated Perspective of the Processes Related to the Descriptive Concept of Secularization." *Sociology of Religion* 60 (3): 229–247.

Drumm, Rene. 2005. "No Longer an Oxymoron: Integrating Gay and Lesbian Seventh Day Adventist Identities." In *Gay Religion*, edited by Scott Thumma and Edward R. Gray, 47–66. New York: Altamira Press.

Durkheim, Emile. [1912] 1995 trans. *Elementary Forms of Religious Life*. Translated by J. W. Swain. New York: Free Press.

———. 1973. *Moral Education: A Study in the Theory and Application of Sociology of Education*. New York: Free Press.

———. [1895] 1982 trans. *The Rules of Sociological Method*. New York: Free Press.

Easton, Nina. 2005. "U.S. judge rejects intelligent design." *The Boston Globe*, December 21.

Ebaugh, Helen Rose, and Janet Saltman Chafetz. 2000. *Religion and the New Immigrants: Continuities and Adaptations in Immigrant Congregations*. Walnut Creek, CA: AltaMira Press.

Eck, Diana. 2001. *A New Religious America*. San Francisco: Harper San Francisco.

Eckberg, D. L., and T. J. Blocker. 1989. "Varieties of Religious Involvement and Environmental Concern." *Journal for the Scientific Study of Religion* 13 (4): 19–32.

———. 1996. "Christianity, Environmentalism, and the Theoretical Problem of Fundamentalism." *Journal for the Scientific Study of Religion* 35 (4): 343–355.

Ecklund, Elaine Howard. 2006. *Korean American Evangelicals: New Models for Civic Life*. New York: Oxford University Press.

Edgell, Penny. 1998. "Making Inclusive Communities: Congregations and the 'Problem' of Race." *Social Problems* 45 (4): 451–472.

Edwards, Korie L. 2008. *The Elusive Dream: The Power of Race in Interracial Churches*. New York: Oxford University Press.

Ehrman, Bart.. 2005. *Lost Christianities: The Battles for Scripture and the Faiths We Never Knew*. New York: Oxford University Press.

———. 2007. *Misquoting Jesus*. New York: HarperOne.

Einstein, Albert. 1936. *Physics and Reality*. London: World Scientific Publishing Company.

Ellingson, Stephen. 2007. *The Megachurch and the Mainline: Remaking Religious Tradition in the Twenty-First Century*. Chicago: University of Chicago Press.

Emerson, Michael O. 2006. *People of the Dream: Multiracial Congregations in the United States*. Princeton, NJ: Princeton University Press.

———, and Christian Smith. 2000. *Divided by Faith: Evangelical Religion and the Problem of Race in America*. New York: Oxford University Press.

Ethridge, Maurice F., and Joe R. Feagin. 1979. "Varieties of Fundamentalism." *Sociological Quarterly* 20: 37–48.

Fadiman, Anne. 1997. *The Spirit Catches You and You Fall Down*. New York: Noonday.

Fastnow, Chris, J. Tobin Grant, and Thomas J. Rudolph. 1999. "Holy Roll Calls: Religious Tradition and Voting Behavior in the U.S. House." *Social Science Quarterly* 80 (4): 687–701.

Feldman, Noah. 2008. "What Is It about Mormonism?" *New York Times Magazine*, January 6.

Field, Catherine. 2008. "Citizenship ban for burqa wife." *New Zealand Herald*, July 15. http://www.nzherald.co.nz/islam/news/article.cfm?c_id=500817&objectid=10521586

Finke, Roger. 1992. "An Unsecular America." In *Religion and Modernization: Sociologists and Historians Debate the Secularization Thesis*, edited by Steve Bruce. New York: Oxford University Press.

Finke, Roger, and Rodney Stark. 2000. "The New Holy Clubs: Testing Church-to-Sect Propositions." *Sociology of Religion* 62 (2): 175–190.

———. 2005. *The Churching of America, 1776–2005: Winners and Losers in Our Religious Economy* (2d ed.). New Brunswick, NJ: Rutgers University Press.

Fiske, Edward. 1970. "Christianity Linked to Pollution: Scholars Cite Call in Bible for Man to Dominate Life." *The New York Times*, May 1.

Foley, Michael W., and Dean R. Hoge. 2007. *Religion and the New Immigrants: How Faith Communities Form Our Newest Citizens.* New York: Oxford University Press.

Freeman, Curtis W. 2007. "'Never Had I Been So Blind': W.A. Criswell's 'Change' on Racial Segregation." *Journal of Southern Religion* 10: 1–12.

Gallup Poll. 2001. "Americans' Belief in Psychic and Paranormal Phenomena Is Up Over Last Decade." Online Report June 8, 2001. http://www.gallup.com/poll/4483/Americans-Belief-Psychic-Paranormal-Phenomena-Over-Last-Decade.aspx

Garces-Foley, Kathleen. 2007. *Crossing the Ethnic Divide: The Multiethnic Church on a Mission.* New York: Oxford University Press.

Geertz, Clifford. 1966. "Religion as a Cultural System." In *Anthropological Approaches to the Study of Religion*, edited by M. Banton, 1–45. London: Tavistock.

Gerth, Hans H., and C. Wright Mills (eds.). 1964. *From Max Weber: Essays in Sociology.* New York: Oxford University Press.

Glendinning, Tony, and Steve Bruce. 2006. "New Ways of Believing or Belonging: Is Religion Giving Way to Spirituality?" *The British Journal of Sociology* 57 (3): 399–414.

Glueck, Sheldon, and Eleanor Glueck. 1950. *Unraveling Juvenile Delinquency.* Cambridge, MA: Harvard University Press.

Goodman, Daniel. 1970. "Ideology and Ecological Irrationality." *BioScience* 20 (23): 1247–1252.

Goodstein, Laurie. 2005. "Evolution slate outpolls rivals." *The New York Times*, November 9.

Gould, Stephen Jay. 1998. "Nonoverlapping Magisteria." In *Leonardo's Mountain of Clams and the Diet of Worms.* New York: Three Rivers Press.

Greeley, Andrew. 1993. "Religion and Attitudes toward the Environment." *Journal for the Scientific Study of Religion* 32 (1): 19–28.

Griffin, Wendy. 1995. "The Embodied Goddess: Feminist Witchcraft and Female Divinity." *Sociology of Religion* 56 (1): 35–48.

Guth, James L., J. C. Green, L. A. Kellstedt, and C. E. Smidt. 1995. "Faith and the Environment: Religious Beliefs and Attitudes on Environmental Policy." *American Journal of Political Science* 39 (2): 364–382.

———, L. A. Kellstedt, C. E. Smidt, and J. C. Green. 1993. "Theological Perspectives and Environmentalism among Religious Activists" *Journal for the Scientific Study of Religion* 32 (4): 373–382.

———, Linda Beail, Greg Crow, Beverly Gaddy, Steve Montreal, Brent Nelson, James Penning, and Jeff Walz. 2003. "The Political Activity of Evangelical Clergy in the Election of 2000." *Journal for theScientific Study of Religion.* 42 (4): 501–514.

Gutman, Herbert G. 1966. "Protestantism and the American Labor Movement: The Christian Spirit in the Gilded Age." *American Historical Review* 72 (October): 74–101.

Gutterman, David S. 2005. *Prophetic Politics: Christian Social Movements and American Democracy*. Ithaca: Cornell University Press.

Hadden, Jeffrey K., and Douglas E. Cowan. 2000. "The Promised Land or Electronic Chaos? Toward Understanding Religion on the Internet." In *Religion on the Internet: Research Prospects and Promises*, edited by Jeffrey K. Hadden and Douglas E. Cowan, 3–21. New York: JAI-Elsevier Science, Inc.

Halker, Clark D. 1991. *For Democracy, Workers, and God: Labor Song Poems and Labor Protest, 1865–1895*. Urbana: University of Illinois Press.

Hamilton, David L., and Tina K. Trolier. 1986. "Stereotype and Stereotyping: An Overview of the Cognitive Approach." In *Prejudice, Discrimination, and Racism*, edited by John F. Davidio and Samuel L. Gaertner, 127–163. Orlando, FL: Academic Press.

Hammond, Philip E. 1974. "Religious Pluralism and Durkheim's Integration Thesis." In *Changing Perspectives in the Scientific Study of Religion*, edited by A. Eister, 115–142. New York: Wiley.

Hand, C., and K. Van Liere. 1984. "Religion, Mastery-Over-Nature and Environmental Concern. *Social Forces* 63: 255–270.

Hane, Mikiso. 1991. *Premodern Japan: A Historical Survey*. Boulder, CO: Westview Press.

Hanf, Theodor. 1994. "The Sacred Marker: Religion, Communalism, and Nationalism." *Social Compass* 41: 9–20.

Harakas, Stanley. 2005. "The Stand of the Orthodox Church on Controversial Issues." Greek Orthodox Archdiocese of America. http://www.goarch .org/ourfaith/ourfaith7101

Harden, Blaine. 2005. "The greening of evangelicals: Christian right turns, sometimes warily, to environmentalism." *The Washington Post*, February 6: A01.

Harris, Sam. 2004. *The End of Faith: Religion, Terror and the Future of Reason*. New York: Norton.

———. 2006. *Letter to a Christian Nation*. New York: Knopf.

Hart, Stephen. 1992. *What Does the Lord Require: How American Christians Think about Economic Justice*. New Brunswick: Rutgers University Press.

Hartman, Keith. 1996. *Congregations in Conflict: The Battle over Homosexuality*. New Brunswick, NJ: Rutgers University Press.

Hechter, Michael. 1987. *Principles of Social Solidarity*. Berkeley: University of California Press.

———. 2004. "From Class to Culture." *American Journal of Sociology* 110 (2): 400–445.

Henninger, Daniel. 2008. "Mad Max and the meltdown: How we went from Christmas to crisis." *The Wall Street Journal*, November 20: A19.

Herberg, Will. 1955. *Protestant, Catholic, Jew: An Essay in American Religious Sociology*. Garden City, NY: Doubleday.

Hewstone, Miles, Jos Jaspers, and Mansur Lalljee. 1992. "Social Representations, Social Attribution and Social Identity: The Intergroup Images of 'Public' and 'Comprehensive'." *European Journal of Social Psychology* 12: 241–269.

Higgins, Andrew. 2008. "Why Islam is unfunny for a cartoonist." *The Wall Street Journal*, July 12–13: W1.

Hirschi, Travis, and Rodney Stark. 1969. "Hellfire and Delinquency." *Social Problems* 17 (2): 202–213.

Hitchens, Christopher. 2007. *God Is Not Great: How Religion Poisons Everything*. New York: Twelve.

Hogg, Michael A., and Dominic Abrams. 1988. *Social Identifications: A Social Psychology of Intergroup Relations and Group Processes*. London: Routledge.

Holland, L., and J. S. Carter. 2005. "Words v. Deeds: A Comparison of Religious Belief and Environmental Action." *Sociological Spectrum* 25 (6): 739–753.

Hollinger, David. 1995. *Postethnic America: Beyond Multiculturalism*. New York: Basic Books.

Horsfall, Sara. 2000. "How Religious Organizations Use the Internet: A Preliminary Inquiry." In *Religion on the Internet: Research Prospects and Promises*, edited by Jeffrey K. Hadden and

Douglas E. Cowan, 153–182. New York: JAI-Elsevier Science, Inc.

Hout, Michael, and Claude S. Fischer. 2002. "Why More Americans Have No Religious Preference: Politics and Generations." *American Sociological Review* 67 (2): 165–190.

Houtman, Dick, and Stef Aupers. 2007. "The Spiritual Turn and the Decline of Tradition: The Spread of Post-Christian Spirituality in 14 Western Countries, 1981–2000." *Journal for the Scientific Study of Religion* 46 (3): 305–320.

Howard, John W., and Myron Rothbart. 1980. "Social Categorization and Memory for In-group and Out-group Behavior." *Journal of Personality and Social Psychology* 38: 301–310.

Hunter, James D. 1989. *Culture Wars: The Struggle to Define America*. New York: Basic Books.

Iannaccone, Larry R. 1997. "Toward an Economic Theory of 'Fundamentalism.'" *Journal of Institutional and Theoretical Economics*. 153: 100–116.

Inhorn, Marcia C. 2006a. "Making Muslim Babies: IVF and Gamete Donation in Sunni vs. Shi'a Islam." *Culture, Medicine and Psychiatry* 30: 427–450.

——. 2006b. "'He Won't Be My Son:' Middle Eastern Muslim Men's Discourses of Adoption and Gamete Donation." *Medical Anthropology Quarterly* 20 (1): 94–120.

Jenkins, Philip. 2002. *The Next Christendom: The Coming of Global Christianity*. New York: Oxford University Press.

——. 2004. *Dream Catchers: How Mainstream America Discovered Native Spirituality*. New York: Oxford University Press.

——. 2006. *The New Faces of Christianity: Believing the Bible in the Global South*. New York: Oxford University Press.

Johnson, Curtis. 1989. *Islands of Holiness: Rural Religion in Upstate New York, 1790–1860*. Ithaca: Cornell University Press.

Jones, John E. 2005. Kitzmiller vs. Dover School Board (Memorandum Opinion). http://www.pamd.uscourts.gov/kitzmiller/kitzmiller_342.pdf

Jones, Steve. 1999. *Almost Like A Whale: The Origin of Species Updated*. New York: Doubleday.

Juergensmeyer, Mark. 2003. *Terror in the Mind of God: The Global Rise of Religious Violence* (3rd ed.). Berkeley: University of California Press.

Kahn, Susan Martha. 1998. "Rabbis and Reproduction: The Uses of New Reproductive Technologies among Ultra-Orthodox Jews in Israel." Working paper #3. Hadassah International Research on Jewish Women at Brandeis University.

——. 2006. "Making Technology Familiar: Orthodox Jews and Infertility Support, Advice and Inspiration." *Culture, Medicine and Psychiatry* 30: 467–480.

Kanagy, Conrad L., and Hart M. Nelsen. 1995. "Religion and Environmental Concern: Challenging the Dominant Assumptions." *Review of Religious Research* 37 (1): 33–45.

Kanter, Rosebeth M. 1977. "Some Effects of Proportions on Group Life: Skewed Sex Ratios and Responses to Token Women." *American Journal of Sociology* 82: 965–991.

Kazemipur, Abdolmohammad, and Ali Rezaei. 2003. "Religious Life under Theocracy: The Case of Iran." *Journal for the Scientific Study of Religion*, 43 (3): 347–361.

Kearns, Laurel. 1996. "Saving the Creation: Christian Environmentalism in the United States." *Sociology of Religion* 57 (1): 55–70.

Kellstedt, Lyman A., and John C. Green. 2003. "The Politics of the Willow Creek Association Pastors." *Journal for the Scientific Study of Religion* 42 (4): 547–461.

——, John C. Green, James L. Guth, and Corwin E. Smidt. 1994. "Religious Voting Blocs in the 1992 Election: The Year of the Evangelical?" *Sociology of Religion*, 55 (3): 307–326.

Kelman, Herbert, and V. Lee Hamilton. 1989. "The My Lai Massacre: A Military Crime of Obedience." In *Crimes of Obedience*, 1–20. New Haven: Yale University Press.

Kniss, Fred. 2003. "Mapping the Moral Order: Depicting the Terrain of Religious Conflict and Change." In *Handbook of the Sociology of*

Religion, edited by Michelle Dillon, 331–347. New York: Cambridge University Press.

———, and Paul D. Numrich. 2007. *Sacred Assemblies and Civic Engagement: How Religion Matters for America's Newest Immigrants.* New Brunswick, NJ: Rutgers University Press.

Krakauer, Jon. 2003. *Under the Banner of Heaven: A Story of Violent Faith.* New York: Doubleday.

Kranish, Michael. 2006. "Democrats inspect faith-based initiative." *The Boston Globe*, December 4.

Krogh, Marilyn C., and Brooke A. Pillifant. 2004. "Kemetic Orthodoxy: Ancient Egyptian Religion on the Internet." *Sociology of Religion* 65 (2): 167–175.

Kurien, Prema. 1998. "Becoming American by Becoming Hindu: Indian Americans Take Their Place at the Multicultural Table." In *Gatherings in Diaspora: Religious Communities and the New Immigration*, edited by R. Stephen Warner and Judith G. Warner, 37–70. Philadelphia: Temple University Press.

Kurtz, Leslie. 1995. *Gods in the Global Village: The World's Religions in Sociological Perspective.* Thousand Oaks, CA: Pine Forge Press.

Kwon, Ho-Youn, Kwang Chung Kim, and R. Stephen Warner. 2001. *Korean Americans and Their Religions: Pilgrims and Missionaries from a Different Shore.* University Park, PA: The Pennsylvania State University Press.

Lawrence, Bruce B. 1989. *Defenders of God: The Fundamentalist Revolt Against the Modern Age.* San Francisco: Harper & Row.

Lechner, Frank J. 1991. "The Case Against Secularization: A Rebuttal." *Social Forces* 69 (4): 1103–1119.

Lee, Robert. 1964. "Introduction: Religion and Social Conflict." In *Religion and Social Conflict*, edited by Robert Lee and Martin E. Marty, 3–8. New York: Oxford University Press.

Leiken, Robert S. 2005. "Europe's Angry Muslims." *Foreign Affairs*, July/August.

Lernoux, Penny. 1982. *Cry of the People.* New York: Penguin Books.

Levitt, Peggy. 2007. *God Needs No Passport: Immigrants and the Changing American Religious Landscape.* New York: The New Press.

Linder, Eileen W. (ed.). 2000. *The Yearbook of American and Canadian Churches.* Nashville, TN: Abingdon Press.

Linville, Patricia W., Peter Salovey, and Gregory W. Fischer. 1986. "Stereotyping and Perceived Distributions of Social Characteristics: An Application to Ingroup–Outgroup Perception." In *Prejudice, Discrimination, and Racism*, edited by John F. Davidio and Samuel L. Gaertner, 165–208. Orlando, FL: Academic Press.

Lizardo, Omar A., and Albert J. Bergesen. 2003. "Types of Terrorism by World System Location." *Humboldt Journal of Social Relations* 27: 162–192.

Luckmann, Thomas. 1967. *The Invisible Religion.* New York: The MacMillan Company.

Luhman, Niklas. 1989. "Functional Differentiation." In *Social Theory: Roots and Branches, 2d Edition*, edited by Peter Kivisto, 194–199. Los Angeles: Roxbury Publishing Company.

Madan, T. N. 2006. "Thinking Globally about Hinduism." In *The Handbook of Global Religions*, edited by Mark Juergensmeyer, 15–24. New York: Oxford University Press.

Mahaffy, Kimberly A. 1996. "Cognitive Dissonance and its Resolution: A Study of Lesbian Christians." *Journal for the Scientific Study of Religion* 35: 392–402.

Marsden, George M. 1980. *Fundamentalism and American Culture: The Shaping of Twentieth-Century Evangelicalism 1870–1925.* New York: Oxford University Press.

Marti, Gerardo. 2005. *A Mosaic of Believers: Diversity and Innovation in a Multiethnic Church.* Bloomington: Indiana University Press.

Marty, Martin E. 1964. "Epilogue: The Nature and Consequences of Social Conflict for Religious Groups." In *Religion and Social Conflict*, edited by Robert Lee and Martin E. Marty, 173–193. New York: Oxford University Press.

Marx, Karl. 1843 (1970 trans.) *Contribution to the Critique of Hegel's* Philosophy of the Law. Cambridge: Cambridge University Press.

Maxwell, Bill. 2003. "A Capital Suggestion for Church Diversity." *St. Petersburg Times* online, http://www.sptimes.com/2003/08/03/Columns/A_capital_suggestion_.shtml

Mayer, Jean-Francois. 2000. "Religious Movements and the Internet: The New Frontier of Cult Controversies." Pp. 249-276 in Jeffrey K. Hadden and Douglas E. Cowan (eds.) *Religion on the Internet: Research Prospects and Promises.* New York: JAI-Elsevier Science, Inc.

McAllister, Ronald J. 1998. "The Mobilization of Prophecy: A Challenge to the Churches of Northern Ireland." In *Religion, Mobilization, and Social Action,* edited by Anson Shupe and Bronislaw Misztal, 160–173. Westport, CT: Praeger.

McCloud, Sean, and William A. Mirola. 2008. *Religion and Class in America: Culture, History, and Politics.* Brill Publishers.

McDaniel, Eric. 2003. "Black Clergy in the 2000 Election." *Journal for the Scientific Study of Religion.* 42 (4): 533–546.

McGreal, Chris. 2006. "McDonald's Changes its Brand to Suit Kosher Appetites." *Guardian International Pages,* March 13: 25.

McGuire, Meredith B. 1997. *Religion: The Social Context,* Fourth Edition. Belmont, CA: Wadsworth Publishing Company.

McKeever, Stacia. n.d. "War of Worldviews: What is a Biblical Worldview?" http://www.answersingenesis.org/articles/wow/what-is-biblical-worldview

McKinley, Jr., James C. 2001. "Church and State: Seeking Complicity in Genocide." *The New York Times,* June 10.

McRoberts, Omar M. 1999. "Understanding the 'New' Black Pentecostal Activism: Lessons from Ecumenical Urban Ministries in Boston." *Sociology of Religion* 60 (1): 47–70.

Mead, Frank S., and Samuel S. Hill. 2001. *Handbook of Denominations in the United States, 11th Edition.* Nashville, TN: Abingdon Press.

Mears, Daniel P., and Christopher G. Ellison. 2000. "Who Buys New Age Materials? Exploring Sociodemographic, Religious, Network, and Contextual Correlates of New Age Consumption." *Sociology of Religion* 61 (3): 289–313.

Mills, C. Wright. 1959. *The Sociological Imagination.* New York: Oxford University Press.

Mirola, William A. 2003a. "Asking for Bread, Receiving a Stone: The Rise and Fall of Religious Ideologies in Chicago's Eight-Hour Movement." *Social Problems* 50 (2): 273–293.

———. 2003b. "Religious Protest and Economic Conflict: Possibilities and Constraints on Religious Resource Mobilization and Coalitions in Detroit's Newspaper Strike." *Sociology of Religion* 64 (4): 443–462.

Monastersky, Richard. 2008. "Creationism persists in American science classrooms." *Chronicle of Higher Education,* May 20. http://chronicle.com/daily/2008/05/2902n.htm

Montanaro, Domenico. 2008. "Huck, the Constitution and God's standards." *FirstRead,* January 15. http://firstread.msnbc.msn.com/archive/2008/01/15/579265.aspx

Montcrief, Lewis W. 1970. "The Cultural Basis for our Environmental Crisis." *Science* 170 (3957): 508–512.

Moore, Laura M., and Reeve Vanneman. 2003. "Context Matters: Effects of the Proportion of Fundamentalists on Gender Attitudes." *Social Forces* 82: 115–39.

Moyers, Bill. 2004. "Acceptance Remarks by Bill Moyers for the Global Environment Award." Center for Health and Global Development, Harvard University.

National Association of Evangelicals. 2004. *For the Health of Nations: An Evangelical Call to Civic Responsibility..* http://www.nae.net/government-affairs

National Election Studies. 2004. "The 2004 National Election Study" [dataset]. Ann Arbor, MI: University of Michigan, Center for Political Studies. http://www.electionstudies.org

National Institutes of Health. 2008. "Stem Cell Basics." http://stemcells.nih.gov/info/basics/basics6.asp

Need, Ariana, and Geoffrey Evans. 2001. "Analyzing Patterns of Religious Participation in Post-Communist Eastern Europe." *British Journal of Sociology* 52 (2): 229–248.

Neel, James V. 1970. "Lessons from a 'Primitive' People." *Science* 170 (3960): 815–822.

Neitz, Mary Jo. 2005. "Queering the Dragonfest: Changing Sexualities in a Post-Patriarchal Religion." In *Gay Religion*, edited by Scott Thumma and Edward R. Gray, 259–280. New York: Altamira Press.

Nesbitt, Paula D. 1993. "Dual Ordination Tracks: Differential Benefits and Costs for Men and Women Clergy." *Sociology of Religion* 54 (1): 13–30.

Niebuhr, Reinhold. 1932. *Moral Man and Immoral Society: A Study in Ethics and Politics*. New York and London: C. Scribner's.

Nye, Ivan. 1958. *Family Relationships and Delinquent Behavior*. Westport, CT: Greenwood Publishing.

Obama, Barack. 2008. *Presidential Election Acceptance Speech*, November 4. Chicago, IL.

O'Leary, Stephen D. 1996. "Cyberspace as Sacred Space: Communicating Religion on Computer Networks." *Journal of the American Academy of Religion* 64: 781–808.

Olson, Daniel V. A. 1993. "Fellowship Ties and the Transformation of Religious Identity." In *Beyond Establishment: Protestant Identity in a Post-Protestant Age*, edited by Jackson Carroll and Wade Clark Roof, 32–53. Louisville: Westminster/John Knox Press.

Olson, Laura. 2000. *Filled With Spirit and Power: Protestant Clergy in Politics*. New York: SUNY Press.

Overbye, Dennis. 2005. "Philosophers notwithstanding, Kansas School Board redefines science." *The New York Times*, November 15.

Park, Jerry Z., and Joseph Baker. 2007. "What Would Jesus Buy: American Consumption and Spiritual Material Goods." *Journal for the Scientific Study of Religion*, 46 (4): 501–517.

Parrett, Roy W. 1998. "Indigenous Rights and Environmental Justice." *Environmental Ethics* 20 (2): 377–391.

Pavlik, Steve. 1992. "The U.S. Supreme Court Decision on Peyote in Employment Division vs. Smith: A Case Study in the Suppression of Native American Religious Freedom." *Wicazo Sa Review* 8 (2): 30–39.

Peart, Norman A. 2000. *Separate No More: Understanding and Developing Racial Reconciliation in Your Church*. Grand Rapids, MI: Baker Books.

Peterson, Richard A., and N. J. Demerath, III. 1942. "Introduction." In *Millhands and Preachers*, by Liston Pope, xvii–1. New Haven: Yale University Press.

Pettigrew, Thomas, and Joanne Martin. 1987. "Shaping the Organizational Context for Black American Inclusion." *Journal of Social Issues* 43: 41–78.

Pevey, Carolyn, Christine L. Williams, and Christopher G. Ellison. 1996. "Male God Imagery and Female Submission: Lessons from a Southern Baptist Ladies' Bible Class." *Qualitative Sociology* 19 (2): 173–193.

Pew Forum on Religion and Public Life. 2008a. "U.S. Religious Landscape Survey." Washington, D.C.: Pew Research Center. http://religions.pewforum. org/pdf/report-religious-landscape-study-full.pdf

———. 2008b. "Trends in Candidate Preferences among Religious Groups." November 3. http://pewforum.org/docs/?DocID=349

Pew Research Center. 2007. "Muslim Americans: Middle Class and Mostly Mainstream."

Pharr, Suzanne. 2001. "Homophobia as a Weapon of Sexism." In *Race, Class, and Gender in the United States (5th ed.)*, edited by Paula S. Rothenberg, 143–151. New York: Worth Publishers.

Phillips, Rick. 1999. "The 'Secularization' of Utah and Religious Competition." *Journal for the Scientific Study of Religion* 38 (1): 72–82.

———. 2004. "Can *Rising* Rates of Church Participation be a Consequence of Secularization?" *Sociology of Religion* 65 (2): 139–153.

PollingReport.com. 2008. "Science and Nature: Origin of Human Life." http://www .pollingreport.com/science.htm

Pope, Carl. 1998. "Way and means: Reaching beyond ourselves." *Sierra Magazine*, November. http://www.sierraclub.org/sierra/199811/ways. asp, last accessed February 27, 2010.

Pope, Liston. 1942. *Millhands and Preachers*. New Haven: Yale University Press.

Presbyterian Church, U.S.A. 2002. *Call to Restore the Creation*. http://www.pcusa.org/ environment/restore.htm

———. 2006. "Theological Task Force on Peace, Unity, and Purity of the Church, Final Report." http://www.pcusa.org/peaceunitypurity/

———. 2008. *Book of Order*. Louisville, KY: General Assembly of the Presbyterian Church, U.S.A.

Promise Keepers. 2008. "History of Promise Keepers." http://www.promisekeepers.org/ about/pkhistory Quammen, David. 1997. *Song of the Dodo: Island Biogeography in an Age of Extinction*. New York: Scribner.

Rahim, Hasan Zillur. 1991. "Ecology in Islam: Protection of the Web of Life a Duty for Muslims." *Washington Report on Middle East Affairs*, October: 65. http://www.wrmea.com/ backissues/1091/9110065.htm

Rhoades, Todd. 2004. "Paying people to attend church plan fails." September 23. http://www. mmiblog.com/monday_morning_insight_we/ 2004/09/index.html

Riesebrodt, Martin. [1990] 1993 trans. *Pious Passion: The Emergence of Modern Fundamentalism in the United States and Iran*. Translated by D. Reneau. Berkeley: University of California Press.

———. 2000. "Fundamentalism and the Resurgence of Religion." *Numen* 47: 266–87.

Roberts, Elizabeth F. S. 2006. "God's Laboratory: Religious Rationality and Modernity in Ecuadorian *In Vitro* Fertilization." *Culture, Medicine and Psychiatry* 30: 507–536.

Robinson, Leland W. 1987. "When Will Revolutionary Movements Use Religion?" In *Church–State Relations: Tensions and Transitions*, edited by Thomas Robbins and Roland Robertson, 53–63. New Brunswick, NJ: Transaction Books.

Rodriguez, Eric M., and Suzanne C. Ouellette. 2000. "Gay and Lesbian Christians: Homosexual and Religious Identity Integration in the Members of a Gay-Positive Church." *Journal for the Scientific Study of Religion* 39 (3): 333–347.

Roof, Wade Clark. 1998. "Modernity, the Religious, and the Spiritual." *The Annals of the American Academy of Political and Social Science* 558 (July): 211–224.

———. 1999. *Spiritual Marketplace: Baby Boomers and the Remaking of American Religion*. Princeton: Princeton University Press.

Rose, Fred. 2000. *Coalitions across the Class Divide: Lessons from the Labor, Peace, and Environmental Movements*. Ithaca, NY: Cornell University Press.

Rowell, Reverend Jeren. 2003. "The Law of Love." Sermon delivered at the Inaugural Chapel of the Wynkoop Center for Women in Ministry, Nazarene Theological Seminary. http://www .wynkoopcenter.org/index.php?option=com_ content&task=view&id=40&Itemid=69

Sacks, Jonathan. 1999. "Judaism and Politics in the Modern World." In *The Desecularization of the World: Resurgent Religion and World Politics*, edited by Peter Berger. Washington, D.C.: Ethics and Public Policy Center.

Savastano, Peter. 2005. "'Saint Gerard Teaches Him that Love Cancels that Out': Devotion to St. Gerard Maiella among Italian American Catholic Gay Men in Newark, New Jersey." In *Gay Religion*, edited by Scott Thumma and Edward R. Gray, 181–202. New York: Altamira Press.

Sawchuk, Dana. 1997. "The Catholic Church in the Nicaraguan Revolution: A Gramscian Analysis." *Sociology of Religion* 58 (1): 39–51.

Schnoor, Randal F. 2006. "Being Gay and Jewish: Negotiating Intersecting Identities." *Sociology of Religion* 67 (1): 43–60.

Schroeder, Ralph, Noel Heather, and Raymond M. Lee. 1998. "The Sacred and the Virtual: Religion in the Multi-User Virtual Reality." Journal of Computer-Mediated Communication [Online] 4 (2). http://jcmc.indian.edu/vol4/issue2/ Schroeder.html

Scully, Sean. 2005. "Breathtaking Inanity: How Intelligent Design Flunked its Test Case." *Time*, December 20.

Selman vs. Cobb County School District. 2005. "Decision of the Court Striking Down the Cobb County Evolution Disclaimer." U.S. District Court for the Northern District of George, Atlanta Division. Civil Action Number: 1:02-CV-2325-CC. January 13, 2005.

Sered, Susan Starr. 1994. *Priestess, Mother, Sacred Sister. Religions Dominated by Women.* New York: Oxford University Press.

Shea, John B. 2003. "The moral status of *in vitro* fertilization (IVF) biology and method." *Catholic Insight,* January/February. http://www .catholicinsight.com/online/church/vatican/ article_475.shtml

Shiskin, Philip. 2009. "Green revolution hits dead end in Georgia cemetery proposal." *The Wall Street Journal,* January 2, A1.

Shulman, Robin. 2008. "Humanist parents seek communion outside church." *The Washington Post,* December 21: A10.

Shupe, Anson. 1995. *In the Name of All That's Holy: A Theory of Clergy Malfeasance.* Westport, CT: Praeger Publishers.

Silko, Leslie Marmon. 1977. *Ceremony.* New York: Penguin.

Simmons, L. B. 1994. *Organizing in Hard Times: Labor and Neighborhoods in Hartford.* Philadelphia: Temple University Press.

Smidt, Corwin, Sue Crawford, Melissa Deckman, Donald Gray. Dan Hofrenning, Laura Olson, Sherrie Steiner, and Beau Weston. 2003. "Political Attitudes and Activities of Mainline Protestant Clergy in the Election of 2000: A Study of Six Denominations." *Journal for the Scientific Study of Religion* 42 (4): 515–532.

Smith, Adam. 1776 [1965]. *An Inquiry into the Nature and Causes of the Wealth of Nations.* New York: Modern Library.

Smith, Christian. 1996a. *Disruptive Religion: The Force of Faith in Social Movement Activism.* New Brunswick, NJ: Rutgers University Press.

———. 1996b. *Resisting Reagan: The U.S. Central American Peace Movement.* Chicago: University of Chicago Press.

———. 1998. *American Evangelicalism: Embattled and Thriving.* Chicago: University of Chicago Press.

———. 2003. *The Secular Revolution: Power, Interests, and Conflict in the Secularization of American Public Life.* Berkeley: University of California Press.

Smith, J. Harold. 1950. "God's Plan for the Races." University of Central Arkansas Archives and Special Collections. Fayetteville, AR: University of Arkansas Libraries.

Smith, Timothy L. 1978. "Religion and Ethnicity in America." *The American Historical Review* 83: 1155–1185.

Sointu, Eeva, and Linda Woodhead. 2008. "Spirituality, Gender, and Expressive Selfhood." *Journal for the Scientific Study of Religion* 47 (2): 259–276.

Southern Baptist Convention. 2006. "Resolution No. 8: On Environmentalism and Evangelicals." http://www.sbc.net/resolutions/amResolution. asp?ID=1159

Spiro, Melford. 1966. "Religion: Problems of Definition and Explanation." In *Anthropological Approaches to the Study of Religion,* edited by M. Banton, 85–126. London: Tavistock.

Stacey, William, and Anson Shupe. 1982. "Correlates of Support for the Electronic Church." *Journal for the Scientific Study of Religion* 21 (4): 291–303.

Stark, Rodney. 1996. "Religion as Context: Hellfire and Delinquency One More Time." *Sociology of Religion* 57 (2): 163–173.

———. 1999. "Secularization, R.I.P." *Sociology of Religion* 60 (3): 249–274.

Stokes, DaShanne. 2001. "Sage, Sweetgrass and the First Amendment." *Chronicle of Higher Education* 47 (36): B16.

Sullivan, Kathleen. 2000. "St. Catherine's Catholic Church: One Church, Parallel Congregations." In *Religion and the New Immigrants,* edited by Helen Rose Ebaugh and Janet Saltzman Chafetz, 210–233. Walnut Creek, CA: AltaMira Press.

Swarts, Heidi J. 2008. *Organizing Urban America: Secular and Faith-based Progressive Movements.* Minneapolis: University of Minnesota Press.

Tajfel, Henri. 1978. "Social Categorization, Social Identity and Social Comparison." In *Differentiation Between Social Groups: Studies in the Social Psychology of Intergroup Relations*, edited by Henri Tajfel, 61–76. London: Academic Press.

Tang, Shengming, and Kenneth Mietus. 2003. "Religious or Scientific Explanations: A Typology." *Social Science Journal* 40 (3): 471–477.

Taylor, Bron. 1997. "Earthen Spirituality or Cultural Genocide? Radical Environmentalism's Appropriation of Native American Spirituality." *Religion* 27: 183–215.

Taylor, S. E. 1981. "A Categorization Approach to Stereotyping." In *Cognitive Processes in Stereotyping and Intergroup Behavior*, edited by David L. Hamilton, 83–114. Hillsdale, NJ: Erlbaum.

Thomas, George M., and Douglas S. Jardine. 1994. "Jesus and Self in Everyday Life: Individual Spirituality through a Small Group in a Large Church." In Robert Wuthnow (ed.), *I Come Away Stronger: How Small Groups Are Shaping American Religion*. Grand Rapids, MI: William B. Eerdmans Publishing Co., 275–299.

Thumma, Scott. 1991. "Negotiating a Religious Identity: The Case of the Gay Evangelical." *Sociological Analysis* 52: 333–347.

———, and Dave Travis. 2007. *Beyond Megachurch Myths*. San Francisco: Josey-Bass Publishers.

———, Dave Travis, and Warren Bird. 2005. "Megachurches Today 2005." http://hirr.hartsem.edu/org/faith_megachurches.html

Tierney, John. 2008. "For good self-control, try getting religious about it." *New York Times*, December 30.

Tschannen, Oliver. 1991. "The Secularization Paradigm: A Systematization." *Journal for the Scientific Study of Religion* 30 (4): 395–415.

Turkle, Sherry. 1995. *Life on the Screen: Identity in the Age of the Internet*. New York: Simon and Schuster.

United Federation of Metropolitan Community Churches. 2005. http://www.mccchurch.org/AM/Template.cfm?Section=Home United Methodist Church. 2004. *Book of Discipline.*

Nashville, TN: United Methodist Publishing House.

United States Supreme Court. 1993. *Church of Lukumi Babulu Aye v. City of Hialeah*, 50 US 520. http://caselaw.lp.findlaw.com/scripts/getcase.pl?court=US&vol=508&invol=520

U.S. Catholic Bishops. 2000. *Welcoming the Stranger Among Us: Unity in Diversity*. Washington, D.C.: United States Catholic Conference, Inc.

Usman, Sushil K. 1998. "Islam and Social Movements in Asia: The Case of Malaysia." In *Religion, Mobilization, and Social Action*, edited by Anson Shupe and Bronislaw Misztal, 100–109. Westport, CT: Praeger.

Vaid, Urvashi. 1995. *Virtual Equality: The Mainstreaming of Gay and Lesbian Liberation*. New York: Anchor Books.

Van de Port, Mattijs. 2006. "Visualizing the Sacred: Video Technology, 'Televisual' Style, and the Religious Imagination in Bahian Candomble." *American Ethnologist* 33 (3): 444–461.

Viana, Francisco. 1993. "O Fim do Romantismo" [The end of romanticism]. *Veja*, April 28, 74–75.

Voas, David, Daniel V. A. Olson, and Alasdair Crockett. 2002. "Religious Pluralism and Participation: Why Previous Research Is Wrong." *American Sociological Review* 67 (2): 212–230.

Wallace, Ruth A. 1993. "The Social Construction of a New Leadership Role: Catholic Women Pastors." *Sociology of Religion* 54 (1): 31–42.

Warner, R. Stephen. 1993. "Work in Progress Toward a New Paradigm for the Sociological Study of Religion in the United States." *American Journal of Sociology* 98: 1044–1093.

———. 1998. "Immigration and Religious Communities in the United States." In *Gatherings in Diaspora: Religious Communities and the New Immigration*, edited by R. Stephen Warner and Judith G. Wittner, 3–34. Philadelphia: Temple University Press.

Weber, Max. 1947. *The Theory of Social and Economic Organization*. New York: Free Press.

———. 1967 [1922]. *The Sociology of Religion*. New York: Beacon Press.

Webster, Daniel. 1976. "On Theocracies." *American Anthropologist* 78 (4): 812–828.

Weiner, Jonathan. 1995. *The Beak of the Finch: A Story of Evolution in Our Time*. New York: Vintage.

White, Jr., Lynn. 1967. "The Historical Roots of our Ecologic Crisis." *Science* 155 (3767): 1203–1207.

Wikipedia. "Sicily," http://en.wikipedia.org/wiki/Sicily.

Wilcox, Melissa M. 2002. "When Sheila's a Lesbian: Religious Individualism among Lesbian, Gay, Bisexual, and Transgender Christians." *Sociology of Religion* 63 (4): 497–513.

———. 2003. *Coming Out in Christianity: Religion, Identity, and Community*. Bloomington, IN: Indiana University Press.

Wilder, D. A. 1981. "Perceiving Persons as a Group: Categorization and In-group Relations." In *Cognitive Processes in Stereotyping and Intergroup Behavior*, edited by David L. Hamilton, 213–257. Hillsdale, NJ: Erlbaum.

Wilson, Bryan. 1982. *Religion in Sociological Perspective*. New York: Oxford University Press.

Wilson, E. O. 2006. *The Creation: An Appeal to Save Life on Earth*. New York: W. W. Norton.

Wood, James R. 1970. "Authority and Controversy: The Churches and Civil Rights." *American Sociological Review* 35: 1057–1069.

Wood, Richard L. 2002. *Faith in Action: Religion, Race, and Democratic Organizing in America*. Chicago: University of Chicago Press.

Woodbury, Robert D., and Christian S. Smith. 1998. "Fundamentalism et al.: Conservative Protestants in America." *Annual Review of Sociology* 24: 25–56.

Woodhead, Linda. 2007. Gender Differences in Religious Practice and Significance. In *The Sage Handbook of the Sociology of Religion*, edited by James Beckford and N. J. Demerath, III, 550–570. Los Angeles: Sage.

———. 2008. "Gendering Secularization Theory." *Social Compass* 55 (2): 189–195.

Wuthnow, Robert. 1988. *The Restructuring of American Religion*. Princeton, NJ: Princeton University Press.

———. 1994. *"I Come Away Stronger": How Small Groups are Shaping American Religion*. Grand Rapids, MI: William B. Eerdmans Publishing Company.

———. 1998. *After Heaven: Spirituality in America Since the 1950s*. Los Angeles: University of California Press.

———. 2005. *America and the Challenges of Religious Diversity*. Princeton, NJ: Princeton University Press.

Yamane, David. 1997. "Secularization on Trial: In Defense of a Neosecularization Paradigm." *Journal for the Scientific Study of Religion* 36 (1): 109–122.

Yancey, George. 2001. "Racial Attitudes: Differences in Racial Attitudes of People Attending Multiracial and Uni-racial Congregations." *Research in the Social Scientific Study of Religion* 12: 185–206.

Yang, Fenggang. 1999. Chinese Christians in America: *Conversion, Assimilation, and Adhesive Identities*. University Park, PA: The Pennsylvania State University Press.

———, and Helen Rose Ebaugh. 2001. "Transformation in New Immigrant Religions and Their Global Implications." *American Sociological Review* 2: 269–288.

Yip, Andrew K. T. 1997. "Dare to Differ: Gay and Lesbian Catholics' Assessment of Official Catholic Positions on Sexuality." *Sociology of Religion* 58: 165–180.

INDEX

A

Abortion, 118–119
Abusharaf, Rogaia Mustafa, 180
Adoption, 202
African Methodist Episcopal
    Church of Zion (AMEZ), 22
Al-Ghazzali, Abu Hamid
    Muhammad, 121, 122
Allah, 100
Almond, Gabriel, 84–85, 87, 90, 91
Alternative spiritualities, 50–52
*America and the Challenges
    of Religious Diversity,* 127
American Academy for
    the Advancement of
    Science, 189
American Episcopal Church,
    134–135
AMEZ. *See* African Methodist
    Episcopal Church of Zion
    (AMEZ)
Ammerman, Nancy, 89
Animal sacrifice, 120–121
Animists, 4
Anthropologists, 45
Antiestablishment clause. *See*
    Disestablishment of religion
Antoun, Richard T., 87
Appleby, Scott, 84–85, 87, 90, 91
Armstrong, Karen, 12, 125,
    196, 198
Attfield, Robin, 215
Augustine, St., 99
Avatar, 40–41

B

Bainbridge, William, 70
Baker, Joseph, 2
Baker, Wayne, 96
Ban on state-sponsored
    religion, 128
Barrett, David B., 18
Basch, Linda, 186
The Battle for God, 125
*The Battle for God: A History
    of Fundamentalism,* 196,
    197, 198

The Beak of the Finch, 197
Beaman, Lori, 130, 143
Beliefs. *See also* Religious
    beliefs/practices
    defined, 6
Bellah, Robert, 33–34, 231
Berger, Peter, 8, 9, 10, 70, 86, 229
Berryman, Phillip, 122
Beuchner, Frederick, 201
Beyer, Peter, 70, 77, 129
Bhagavad Gita, 27, 28
Bible Believers, 89
Biblical flood, 199
"Big box" churches.
    See Megachurches
Biology textbooks, stickers on, 191
Bisexulas. *See* LGBT (Lesbian,
    Gay, Bisexual, or
    Transgender) groups
Black Protestantism, 22–23
Blanc, Christina Szanton, 186
Blau, Peter M., 65
Blocker, T. J., 215, 216, 217
Bock, Darrell, 12
Book of Common Prayer, 22
Book of Genesis, 192
The Book of Mormon, 11
Book of Order, 151
Bossuet, Jacques-Bénigne,
    99–100
Boston, John, 159
Boston Globe, 120
Boswell, John, 148
Boyd, Heather Hartwig, 215, 216
Brahmans, 28
Branches, 37
Brasher, Brenda, 43, 44, 45
Bridge organizations, 169
Brooks, Clem, 118
Bruce, Steve, 86, 88, 89, 95
Buddhism, 5, 28–29
Bureaucratic state, 69
Burkett, Steven R., 232

C

Cadge, Wendy, 156
Caldwell, Fred, 159–160

Campbell, Robert A., 189
Candomble, 45
Capitalism, 69
Carter, Jimmy, 117
Carter, Stephen, 14, 122, 124, 130
Casanova, José, 128
Catastrophe, 199
Catholic church, 54
Catholicism, 4, 19–20
    in Poland, 129–130
    in Sicily, 54–55
Catton, William R., 213
Ceremony, 221
Chafetz, Janet Saltman, 173
Charitable Choice initiative,
    119–120
Chaves, Mark, 70, 145
Chen, Carolyn, 174, 181
Chinese military conflicts, 100
Christ, Carol P., 145
Christerson, Brad, 181
Christian. *See also* Christianity
    exclusivists, 127
    immigrants, 173
    inclusivists, 127
Christianity, 2, 18–26
    Black Protestantism, 22–23
    Catholicism, 19–20
    and environmentalism,
        211–218
    Evangelical Protestants,
        23–24
    Protestantism, 20–22
Chronicle of Higher Education, 191
Church and state, 127–132
    freedom from religion,
        131–132
    implications of separation,
        127–131
Church of England, 21–22, 122
The City of God, 99
Civil religion, 60–62, 66, 230–231
    Obama's acceptance speech,
        61–62
Civil Rights
    law, 119
    movement, 119

Civil unions. *See* Same-sex unions
Civil War, 128, 231
Clergy malfeasance, 233–234
Cognitive psychologists, 163
Collapse, 222
Community, 7–8
Conklin, Beth, 224
Consumerism, 4
Cooper, Clarence, 191
Coser, Lewis, 64
Cosmos, 9
Cottage industry, 217
Cousineau, Madeleine, 114
The Creation, 210–211
Creation Museum, 199
Creation spirituality,
    220–222, 225
Creation stories, 192–194
    and nature, 212–213
*Creation Stories Around the
    World,* 193
Creed, Nicene, 22
Creeds, 19–20
Criminal justice system, 123
Crosstown, 165
Cultural clash, 2–3
The Culture of Disbelief,
    122, 124
Cunningham, Lawrence S., 56
Curtis, James E., 189

D

Darwin's theory, of evolution,
    193, 194
    Judeo–Christian tradition and,
        197, 198
    religious discontent with,
        197–198
Davie, Grace, 49
The Da Vinci Code ?, 2
Davis, James Allan, 75
Dawson, Lorne L., 41, 42
Day, Katie, 110
Death penalty, 123
*Defenders of God: The
    Fundamentalist Revolt
    Against the Modern
    Age,* 89
Dehumanization, 234–235
Demerath, N. J., 81, 82, 107,
    108, 109

Dethroning Jesus, 12
Dharma, 28
Diamond, Jared, 215, 222, 223
Dianetics, 2
Disagreements, 57–58
Disestablishment of religion,
    128–130
    costs of, 129
    Protestantism, 128–129
    from state, 128, 129
    U.S. Constitution, 128
"Disneyland Effect," 44–45
Disruptive Religion, 105
Diversity, 127
Division of labor, 135
Dobbelaere, Karel, 70
Dobson, James, 2
Drumm, Rene, 156
Dunlap, Riley E., 213
Durkheim, Emile, 6, 7, 8, 9, 13,
    14, 58, 228, 229

E

Earth First!, 224
Easter Island, 223
Eastern religious traditions, 37
Easton, Nina, 190
Ebaugh, Helen Rose, 173, 182
Eckberg, D. L., 215, 216, 217
Ecklund, Elaine Howard, 185
Ecojustice, 220
Eddy, Mary Baker, 24–25
Egyptian religion, 40
Ehrman, Bart, 12
Eightfold Path, Buddhism, 29
Einstein, Albert, 195
Ellingson, Stephen, 49
El Salvador, 117
Emerson, Michael O., 181
Empirical evidence, 191, 198–199
Employees, 131
The End of Faith, 230
Environment. *See*
    Environmentalism
Environmental crisis, 225
Environmental ethics, 223–224
Environmentalism, 207–225
    alternative ecotheologies,
        218–222
    Christianity and, 211–218
    concept, 208

creation sprituality, 220–222
and discontent, 208–209
ecojustice, 220
and Presbyterians, 219
religious discontents, 209
and religious groups, 210–212
stewardship, 219–220
theological discussions, 214
value of, 208
White's hypothesis. *See* White,
    Lynn, on worldview of
    human mastery
Environmentalists, 208
    and Amazon natives, 224
    and indigenous religions,
        222–225
    and Native American religious
        practices, 224
Eucharist, 20
European nations, and
    fundamentalism, 95–96
*Evangelical Call to Civic
    Responsibility,* 209–210
Evangelical pastors, 39
Evangelical Protestants, 23–24
Evolution
    Darwin's theory of, 193, 194
    debate over, 190–192
    empirical evidence of, 194
    gene mutations and, 194
    scientific theory of, 193–194
    supernatural explanations
        of, 192

F

Fadiman, Anne, 2
Faith-based organizations,
    119–120
Falwell, Jerry, 39
Feldman, Noah, 11–12
Fertilization, 204. *See also In vitro
    fertilization* (IVF)
Feudalism, 101
A Few Good Men, 229–230
Financial crisis, 227
Finke, Roger, 70, 129
First Amendment, of U.S.
    Constitution, 127, 128,
    130, 131
Fiske, Edward, 213
Flood, 199

Free exercise of religion, 130–131
The Functions of Social Conflict, 64
Functions of Social Conflict, The, 64
Fundamentalism
   characteristics of, 90, 91
   contextual effects of, 92
   defining, 85–86, 87–88
   European nations and, 95–96
   ideological, 91
   inception of, 88–89
   measuring, 94–95
   organizational, 91
   overview, 83–85
   Protestant, 88
   rise of, 89
   social life and, 91, 92
Fundamentalism Project, 87
Fundamentalist, defined, 85
"The Fundamentals: A Testimony of the Truth," 88

G

Gallup Poll, 51
Gautama, Siddhartha, 28. *See also* Buddhism
Gays, 156–157. *See also* Homosexuals; LGBT (Lesbian, Gay, Bisexual, or Transgender) groups
   as bishop, 134–135
   marriage, 117
   ordination of, 151–152
   social inclusion, 157–158
Gender. *See also* Women
   defined, 136
   distribution in major religious traditions, 137
   occupational segregation by, 146–147
   overview, 135–136
   and responses to religion and male power and privilege, 142–146
Gender differences, 137–141. *See also* Women
   in beliefs in a personal God, 137, 138, 140
   in frequency of prayer, 139
   in importance of religion, 138
   in worship service attendance, 139
Gender roles
   consolidation, 142–143
   countercultural religion and, 145–146
   defined, 136
   in patriarchy, 136
   questing and, 145
   tactical approach to, 143–145
Gene mutations, 194
Generational issues, among children of immigrants, 182
Goddess movements, 145–146
God's Politics, 2
Gould, Stephen J., 200
Governments, 119–121
   citizenship, 120
   faith-based organization, 119–120
   national priorities, 119
   rules and laws, 120–121
   taxes, 119
Graham, Laura, 224
Greek Orthodox Archdiocese of America, 40
Greenwood Acres Full Gospel Baptist Church, 159
Grey, George, 193

H

Habits of the Heart, 33
Hadden, Jeffrey, 70
Hajj, 26
Hamilton, David, 162
Hamilton, V. Lee, 234–235
Hanukah, 16, 30
Harris, Sam, 230
Heaven's Gate, 43
Henninger, Daniel, 227, 228, 229
Henry VIII, 122
Heterosexism, 136
Hindu God/Goddess, 27
Hinduism, 7, 27–28
Hindus. *See* Hinduism
Hirschi, Travis, 232
The Historical Roots of Our Ecologic Crisis, 207
Hitchens, Christopher, 231
Hmong, 2
Holy Days, in Sicily, 54
Homogenous congregations, 160
   attitudes, 168
   social ties, 165, 166
Homosexuals, 147–155. *See also* LGBT (Lesbian, Gay, Bisexual, or Transgender) groups
   differences in attitudes over social acceptance, 150
   Episcopal Church on, 151
   opposition to, 149, 150, 151, 152–153
   ordination of, 151–152
   religious belief/practices in public opposition to, 150
   Roman Catholic Church on, 149
Hubbard, L. Ron, 2
Huckabee, Mike, 123
Human burials, 121
Humans, and nature, 212–213
Hunter, James D., 81
Hurricane Katrina, 10

I

Iannaccone, Larry, 90, 93, 96, 97
Illegitimate child, 203
Imams, 26
Immigrants, 173
   Christian, 173
   civic engagement of, 183–186
   conflicts, 182
   congregations by invitations from coethnics, 179
   contact maintenance by, 186
   ethnic composition, 173
   ethnic congregation and, 181–182
   generational issues in children of, 182
   lessons about, 178–186
   majority/minority status of, 182–183
   moral authority, 184
   moral projects, 184–185
   non-Judeo-Christian religions, 173
   nonreligious benefits for, 180–181
   racialization of, 185–186

religions organized around congregational gatherings, 179
religious benefits, 181
religious changes for, 174–186
theological foundations and, 182
transnationalism for, 186
and volunteering, 185
Immigration
laws, 172–173
lessons about, 178–186
a theologizing experience, 179
Inanna, Sumerian goddess, 43
Indigenous religions, and environmentalists, 222–225
Individual religiosity, and deviant behavior, 231–234
Industrialization, 101
Inhorn, Marcia, 203
Institutional autonomy, of religion, 128–130
Intelligent design, 190, 192
Internet, 39–40. *See also* Online religion
In the Name of All That's Holy: A Theory of Clergy Malfeasance, 233
Invitation to Sociology, 229
In vitro fertilization (IVF), 201–205
Catholic Church on, 202–203
Iran, 116–117
theocracies and, 123–124
Islam, 26–27, 135
online presence, 40
Israel, rabbinical law in, 204

J

Jenkins, Philip, 26, 137, 143, 144
Jones, John E., III, 190
Judaism, 7, 29–30
online presence, 40
Judeo–Christian creation story, 212
Juergensmeyer, Mark, 92

K

Kahn, Susan Martha, 204
Karma, 28

Kelman, Herbert, 234–235
Khomeini, Ayatollah, 116
Kim, Karen Chai, story of, 174–178
King, Martin Luther, Jr., 22
Korean ethnic churches, 177–178
Krakauer, Jon, 11
Kshatriyas, 28

L

Labyrinth walking, 33
Lambeth Conference, 134
Larson, Sheila, 33
Latin language, 38
Lawrence, Bruce, 89
Lechner, Frank, 70
Lectionary, 32
Lee, Robert, 62
Left Behind, 2, 211
Lesbians. *See also* LGBT (Lesbian, Gay, Bisexual, or Transgender) groups
ordination of, 151
social inclusion, 157–158
LGBT (Lesbian, Gay, Bisexual, or Transgender) groups, 157–158
countercultural response of, 157
identity, 155–157
MCC and, 154
ordination of, 152
questing by, 156–157
recognition, 154
religious groups meeting spiritual needs of, 154–155
Roman Catholic policy, 152
sexual activity, 155, 156
tactical approach by, 156
Lincoln, Abraham, 231
Logos, 198
Lost Christianities, 12

M

Mafia, in Sicily, 54, 55–57
Mahayana Buddhism, 28–29
Maiella, Saint Gerard, 156–157
"Mandate of Heaven," 100
Manza, Jeff, 118
Maori, 193

Marriage. *See also* Same-sex unions
alternatives to, 154
as civil institution, 153–154
as religious institution, 154
Marsden, George, 88
Marty, Martin, 90
Marx, Karl, 5, 9, 122
"Mastery over nature," 212
MCC. *See* Universal Fellowship of Metropolitan Community Churches (MCC)
Megachurches, 36–37
adults in, 46–47
community in, 47–49
denominational affiliation of, 45
diversity, 46
praise bands in, 46
Memorial Day, 231
Menominee, 193
Migration, 172
Military, as moral community, 229–230
Minyan, 141
Misquoting Jesus, 12
Mission of St. Clare, 40
Modernization, 86–87
European nations and, 95–96
rationalization, 86
Moral authority, 184
Moral community, 228
medicine profession as, 229
military as, 229–230
violence and, 234–235
Morality
and behavior regulation, 227–228, 229
and community, 228–229
moral rules, 228–229
and rule-breaking, 229
Moral Man and Immoral Society, 164
Moral persons, 164
Moral projects, 184–185
Moral relativism, 235–236
Mormonism, 11–12
Mormons, 123
Moyers, Bill, 211
Multiracial congregations, 170–171

My Lai massacre, in Vietnam
War, 234
Mythos, 198

N

National Association of
Evangelicals, 209–210
Nation of Islam, 27
Native-born Americans, 173
Neckschot, Gregorious, 125
Neighborhood Partnerships,
120
New Age shops, 50
The New Faces of Christianity,
143
The Next Christendom, 26
Nicaragua, 117
Niebuhr, Reinhold, 164
Nomos, 9

O

Obama, Barack, 61–62
Old Testament law, 23
Online religion, 39
challenge to, 42, 44
diversity, 43
religious authority, 43–45
Online religious communities,
41–42
Online rituals, 37
Orthodox Churches, 19

P

Pahlavi, Muhammed Reza, 123
Park, Jerry, 2
Parrett, Roy, 222, 223, 224
The Passion of the Christ or
Veggie Tales, 2
Patriarchy, 136
Pentecostalism, 23–24
People of the Dream, 170
Pew Forum on Religion and
Public Life, 137
Peyote, use of, 131
Phillips, Rick, 123
Pluralism, 86
Poland, Catholicism in,
129–130
Political behavior, and religion,
118

Politics, and religion, 116–127
American political system,
117–119
faith-based organizations, 119–120
governments, 119–121
national priorities, 119
overview, 116–117
religion as a tool, 122–123
religious groups, 119
rules and laws, 120–121
tax system, 119
theocracies, 123–127
Polytheistic faiths, 4
Pope, Carl, 210
Powell, Colin, 119
Pre-Reformation Christianity, 38
Privileged status to the majority
religion, 130–131
Profane, *vs.* sacred, 6, 7
Promise Keepers, 135, 140,
142, 143
Protestant Christianity, 38
Protestant Episcopal Church, 22
Protestantism, 20–22. *See also*
Black Protestantism
Protestant Reformation, 38
Protestant reformers, 38
*Public Religions in the Modern
World,* 128
Public schools, intelligent design
in, 190
The Purpose-Driven Life, 2

Q

Questing, 145
QuickTime, 41
Qu'ran, 26

R

Rabbinical law, in Israel, 204
Racial inequality
in access to valued resources,
164–165
combating, 162
socioeconomic status and,
168–169
unselfishnes and, 163–164
Racially mixed congregations,
160, 161
bridge organizations, 169
social ties in, 165, 166–167

Racial separation
attitudes and, 167–168
categorization, 162–163
congregational segregation,
160–161
homogenous congregations, 160
mixed congregations. *See*
Racially mixed congregations
overview, 159–160
social ties and, 165–167
socioeconomic status and,
168–169
solution to, 165–170
Raraku, Rano, 222
"Real-time" community, 37
Religion
concept, 4–5
and cosmic order, 8, 9–10
free exercise of, 130–131
human product, 10–12
overview, 1–3
sociology, 12–14
Religion and Social Conflict, 62
Religious beliefs/practices
comparision, 17–18
contemporary practices,
30–35
overview, 16–17
role of, 35
worship style, 31–35
Religious conflict, 62–66
classification of, 63
internal, 65
social cohesion. *See* Social
cohesion
sociologically, 65
Religious freedom, 127–128
Religious goods/products, 2
Religious leaders, 38, 67–68
Religious texts, 38
Religious traditions, 2
Religious vitality, 74–78
concept of, 74
as religious market forces, 76–78
secularization and, 78–82
subcultural identity approach
to, 78
survey on, 74–76
Reproductive technologies,
201–205
rabbinical law and, 204

*The Restructuring of American
    Religion,* 118
Riesebrodt, M., 87, 89, 90
Righter, Walter, 151
Rituals, 7
    defined, 6
Robertson, Pat, 39
Robinson, Gene, 134–135, 151
Roman Catholic Church, 19–20,
    122, 123
Romero, Oscar, 117, 122
Rosh Hashanah, 29, 30
Rule-breaking, 229

S

Sacred
    defined, 6
    vs. profane, 6, 7
The Sacred Canopy, 10
Same-sex unions, 21. *See also*
    Homosexuals
Savastano, Peter, 156–157
Sawchuk, Dana, 122
Schiller, Nina Glick, 186
School board elections, 117–118
Schwartz, Joseph E., 65
Science
    American Academy for the
        Advancement of Science
        on, 189
    being skeptical, 197
    domain of, 200
    instability of, 195–196
    Kansas Board of Education
        on, 192
    overview, 188–189
    religious discontent of,
        195–197
    and technology, 201
    winning explanatory territory
        from religion, 196
Scientology, 2
Scopes Trial, 89
Scopes trial, 125
Second Life, 40–41
Sectarianism, 96, 97
Secular humanists, 226
Secularization, 68, 69–74, 95, 96
    debate over, 69–70
    at individual level, 73
    Iran, 123–124

at organizational level, 72–73
and religious vitality. *See*
    Religious vitality
at societal level, 71–72
Self-control, 232
Self-identification, for measuring
    fundamentalism, 94
Sered, Susan Starr, 142
Sexual identities, 135. *See also*
    Sexuality
    defined, 136
    diversity in, 147
Sexuality. *See also* Homosexuals;
    LGBT (Lesbian, Gay,
    Bisexual and Transgender)
    groups
    conflicts over, 147–148
    defined, 136
    overview, 135–136
Sexual orientation, 135,
    136, 151
Sexual revolution, 147
Shabuoth, 30
Shahada, 26
Shah of Iran, 116
Shang dynasty, 100
Sharia, 26
Shi'a, 26
Shudras, 28
Shulman, Robin, 226
Shupe, Anson, 39, 233
Sicily, 54
Siuda, Tamara, 40
Sivan, Emmanuel, 84–85, 87,
    90, 91
Sixth Americans, 169–170
Smith, Adam, 96
Smith, Christian, 105
Smith, Joseph, 25
Smith, Tom W., 75
Smoking/burning, candles
    and incense, 121
Social categories, 162
    biases and, 162–163
Social change, 101–105
    industrialization and, 101
    religion's influence on,
        112–114
Social cohesion, 58–62
Social conflict, 62–66
    and positive functions, 64

Social movements, 105–112
    activism, 105, 106–110
    activists, 110–112
    motivation for, 105
    religious resources for,
        105, 106
Social parenthood, 204
Social ties, 165–167
Society of Friends, 25
Sociological imagination, 63
Sociology, 12–14
The Spiral Staircase, 12
*The Spirit Catches You and You
    Fall Down,* 2
Spiritual quest, 49–50
Spiro, Melford, 4, 5, 9
St. Ann's Catholic Church, 40
Stacey, William, 39
Stark, Rodney, 70, 129, 232
State, church and, 127–132
State-sponsored religion, ban on,
    128
Stem cell research, 201
Stewardship, 219–220
Stickers, on biology textbooks,
    191
Sufism, 26–27
Sumerian goddess Inanna, 43
Sunni, 26

T

Taizé services, 32
Tax system, 119
Taylor, Bron, 224
Technology, 38–41. *See also*
    Online religion
Teen Mania Ministries, 83–84
Television, 38–39
Temple Israel of Greater Miami,
    40
Ten Commandments, 7
Terror in the Mind of God, 92
Theocracies, 123–127
    concept, 123–124
    defined, 123
    Iran as example of, 123–124
    religion in, 124
Theodicies
    concept, 103
    of dominance, 104
    of suffering, 103–104

Theravada Buddhism, 28
Torah, 140
Touched by an Angel ?, 2
Transgender. *See* LGBT (Lesbian,
    Gay, Bisexual, or
    Transgender) groups
Transnationalism, 186
Trolier, Tina, 162

U

Unitarian and Universalist
    churches, 25–26
United Methodist Church, 20
United Methodist General
    Conference, 151
United Methodists, 21
Universal Fellowship of
    Metropolitan Community
    Churches (MCC), 154, 157
U.S. Constitution, 127, 128,
    130, 131
U.S. Supreme Court, 131

V

Vaishyas, 28
Vatican, 43
Vedas, 27
Vietnam War, 234
Violence, and moral community,
    234–235
Virtual religious identities,
    42–43
Visas, 172–173

W

Wallace, Daniel, 12
Wallace, Ruth, 147

Wallis, Jim, 2
Wall Street Journal, 227
The Wall Street Journal, 125
Warren, Rick, 2
Washington, George, 231
The Washington Post, 210
Washington Post, The, 226
Watt, James, 211
Wealth of Nations, 96
Weber, Max, 68, 69
Websites, 40. *See also* Online
    religion
Weiner, Jonathan, 197
Wellness centers, 50
White, Lynn, on worldview of
    human mastery, 207,
    212–218
    acceptance/criticism,
    213–215
    creation story, 212, 213
    testing hypothesis, 215–217
White, Mervin, 232
Whole Foods, 37
Wicca, 209
Williams, Rhys H., 81, 82, 107,
    108, 109
Willow Creek Community
    Church, 37
Wilson, E. O., 210–211
Women
    as a bishop, 134
    in Buddhism, 141
    clergy, 146
    empowerment, 143–145
    identity, 142
    in Islam, 135
    in Judaism, 14, 140–141

mainstream, 142
marginal, 142
as ministers, 146
in New Testament, 141
occupational segregation of,
    146–147
in Old Testament, 140–141
ordination of, 146
power exercise by, 147
religious belief, 137, 140
segregation after giving
    birth, 140
spirituality of, 142
in Ten Commandments,
    140
in Torah, 140
Woodhead, Linda, 142
Worship style, 31–35
Worship wars, 31
Wuthnow, Robert, 65,
    118, 127

Y

Yamane, David, 70
Yang, Fengang, 182
Yom Kippur, 30
YouTube, 41
Yule, 16

Z

Zagat tax, 40
Zakat, 26
Zhou dynasty, 100